The Ruins of Experience

The Ruins of Experience

Scotland's "Romantick" Highlands and the Birth of the Modern Witness

MATTHEW WICKMAN

PENN

University of Pennsylvania Press

Philadelphia

Published by
University of Pennsylvania Press
Philadelphia, Pennsylvania 19104-4112

A Cataloging-in-Publication record is available from the Library of Congress

ISBN-13: 978-0-8122-3971-3
ISBN-10: 0-8122-3971-7

For Kerry, Hadley, and Elena,
the epitome of experience

Contents

Scottish Highland Romance
A Reappraisal

Phantoms pervade late modernity. Archival remnants, con-/hyper-/textual traces, and blinking technologies with their storehouses of undigested information represent but few of the spirits haunting our material world. This makes for a conflicted arrangement, to be sure. For one thing, specters do not reside easily amidst an ethos of skeptical disenchantment which remains our legacy—in some ways, our embattled ideal[1]—from the Enlightenment. For another, it seems inherently contradictory to accord spirit substance, or to acknowledge "[h]aunting [as] a *constituent* element of modern social life."[2] Nevertheless, a world of "post-"s (e.g., postmodernism, postindustrialism, poststructuralism) is a world of ghosts.

Can ghosts have ghosts of their own? Do some specters come into being only when we make ourselves critically self-conscious of others? This book contends that they do, and that experience is one such ghost. Like Poe's purloined letter, experience hides in plain sight, becoming more evanescent the longer we stare at it. Seemingly a universal category (doesn't everyone have experiences?), experience has been both requisite and inadequate to knowledge since the Enlightenment. In our world of modern objectivity—or, as I will engage it over the course of this book, our world of "evidence"—experience plays the part of the dubious witness, functioning as knowledge under erasure. Even to pretend to summon experience, to purport to "know" it, is to displace it all over again.

Experience, in short, is one of modernity's great phantoms, silently haunting models of being, doing, and knowing. But how do we undertake an investigation of experience—how do we come to understand experience objectively, as it were—without causing it to fade once again, phantasmatically, from view? In chasing this rainbow, I return to one of the quintessential sites of modern spectrality, the romantic Scottish Highlands. I do so somewhat anachronistically, for "romance" has been on the wane in scholarship on the Highlands for at least the past twenty years, during the era of the "return to history." Conjuring the spirit of such deromanticizing classics as James Kellas's *Modern Scotland* (1968) and T. C. Smout's *A History of the Scottish People* (1969), scholarship of the past two decades has drawn new attention to the traditionally mythic status of the Highlands, and to the uses and abuses of that myth. Peter Womack's landmark book *Improvement and Romance* (1989) highlighted the systemic relationship between the image of the primitive, picturesque Highlands and the false consciousness universally promoted by capitalism. Katie Trumpener's *Bardic Nationalism* (1997) revealed the impact of the eighteenth- and nineteenth-century Celtic peripheries on the widespread image of Highland romance, an image which permeated Britain and both magnified and distorted the influence of these local cultures. Leith Davis's *Acts of Union* (1998) divulged the instrumentality of the Ossianic Highlands in the formation of Scottish and British national identity during the eighteenth century. And Janet Sorensen's *The Grammar of Empire* (2000) reflected rigorously on the recurrent dynamics of core and periphery (e.g., "British" *versus* "Celtic") in the linguistic (and, by extension, cultural) mechanics of national and imperial identity.[3]

These books have built on each other in highly useful and interesting ways. More than that, they reflect (and reflect on) the core assumptions of modern historicism in a way which reveals the skeletons—or ghosts, rather—hiding in our scholarly closets. Womack's *Improvement and Romance* richly initiates the dialogue by arguing that Highland "ghosts are impotent . . . impalpable presence[s] of the past, into whose illusive whirlings everything is constantly slipping." For him, these ghosts are emblems of ideology, the negative reflection (and, hence, the ratification) of progress; the romantic Highlands are "*not* cultivated, *not* populous, *not* rational, *not* regulated—above all, *not* extant."[4] Trumpener concedes that "political and cultural imperialism" exerts a decisive influence on the Celtic peripheries of Scotland, Ireland, and Wales. However, she restores virility to the "impotent" Highland ghosts by portraying "the Highlands [as] one enormous echo chamber," a return of the repressed, whose traces in aesthetic forms like the historical novel uncannily inflect the Empire to which these peripheries are subject.[5] A similar dynamic informs Davis's *Acts of Union*, which self-consciously shifts the debate from Womack's "ideology critique" to new historicist "discourse analysis."[6] Invoking Benedict Anderson's "imagined communities" and Homi Bhabha's cultural hybrids, Davis imagines the British Union of 1707 as "a dialogue between heterogeneous elements," an Ossianic "forgery" in the dynamic sense of that term.[7] Sorensen, lastly, more closely examines the discursive economies enabling such dialogical feats of imagination, creating an interface between theories of language and cultural materialism (indeed, much like the generative and divergent nationalist traditions in Britain about which she writes). Perhaps of greatest interest here is the way in which Sorensen reconceives of the relationship between core and periphery on which the logic of romance is historically founded. Taking issue with Michael Hechter's pathbreaking *Internal Colonialism* (1975), specifically with Hechter's notions of an essential Celticism inhabiting the British peripheries, Sorensen traces the cultural modalities through which such identities historically emerged in Britain, preserving while revising Hechter's model of core and periphery as a way of addressing British hierarchies of power and uneven development.[8]

Experience assumes a shadowy, spectral existence in these postromantic studies. In one sense, it is the implicit axis on which they all turn in their mutual focus on identity as the consciousness of collective experience, whether of the hegemonic state (e.g., Womack's capitalist empire) or the dialogical nations within it. And yet, in another sense, and adopting Hechter's vocabulary ourselves, experience remains a peripheral concern in these texts, subordinate to the core issues of capital, empire, nation, culture, and even consciousness itself as the *knowledge* of identity, of experience. Davis and Sorensen in particular subject Highland romance (in its old and new varieties, propounded by Macpherson and Hechter among others) to "the touch of the real," even as they cannily redefine that reality in terms of signification, the "grammar" of nation and empire.[9]

Without necessarily renouncing the touch of the real, I seek to redirect it. In doing so, I implicitly shadow one of my favorite books of the late 1990s, Mary Poovey's *A History of the Modern Fact* (1998). While some scholars quibbled with certain aspects of Poovey's narrative—Barbara J. Shapiro's impressive study *A Culture of Fact* (2000) presented a different take on the "facts" in question—Poovey's book was certainly one of the most lucid commentaries on the culture of historicism. It focused on the emergence of systematic objectivity in a way which accounted reflexively for its own systematically objective study; as such, it highlighted the artifice of "evidence" which is the modern language of scholarship—indeed, of knowledge, including its (and our) own of the emergence of "fact." My project takes no issue with Poovey's, but instead poses a set of correlative questions, namely, what happened to those modes of knowing which were displaced by factuality? Did they simply disappear, or did they come to occupy alternative cultural forms? Hence, where Poovey makes the case for "evidence," I turn my attention to "witnesses"; where she investigates "facts," I examine "romance." I do so, moreover, in a similarly reflexive way—that is, through a romantic account of romance. In practical terms, this means that the connections which I establish between Highland romance and an array of cultural phenomena are as fanciful as they are factual, as suggestive as they are historical.

The fact is that romance has not disappeared from studies of Highland Scotland, as Sorensen's clever adaptation of core and periphery indicates. And, while recent scholarship of the Highlands has not exactly embraced romance, a few insightful studies touching on this region propose that we should. In his magisterial book *The Identity of the Scottish Nation* (1998), William Ferguson remarks that "no one of any sense today would wish to substitute ancient myth for present reality," or realism. But, he contends, those

> who would seek to understand the mental processes of past generations, and the residual substratum of those that are still embedded in our own consciousness, cannot afford to disregard the justifying myths and conveniently slanted pseudo-histories of the past. Besides, underlying all is a fundamental epistemological question—what is knowledge? Like us, our predecessors simply believed what was there to be believed; what, in short, could be grasped within the limits of their imagination.[10]

Murray Pittock has shed light on precisely these limits, historically and in our own era. For instance, his 1991 book *The Invention of Scotland* powerfully assailed the "fake Celtic Scotland which dominated the Victorian consciousness" and correspondingly vitiated a real politico-nationalist critique located in and around Highland Scotland.[11] However, in the book he published at the end of the decade, *Celtic Identity and the British Image*, Pittock underscored the historical power of romance in the formation of national identities, Celtic or other.[12] More self-consciously than most, Pittock's work divulges the fungibility of reality and romance—and the spectral presence of the one in the other—when imagined as a dialectical pair.

Hence, while acknowledging the scholarly gains of the recent historicist enterprise, I suggest with Pittock that it has caused us to overlook one of the most important historical features of Highland Scotland: quite simply, its persistent association with romance. Or rather, while we recognize this feature, we have restricted our purview of its scope in seeking rigorously to demystify it. Womack prepared the soil here by observing that the mythic Highlands "are not real; . . . not to be real is what they are for."[13] As he persuasively argued, the unreal Highlands provided an increasingly commercialized British public sphere with an image of its own primitive past even as the "unreal" region also presented the illusion of a sphere closed off from capital and therefore associated with strictly human (as opposed to profit-driven) "values." Womack argues that the Highlands accommodated the ideology of capitalism by harmonizing the potentially contradictory interests of progress and humanity. In essence, then, the Highlands distracted attention from the rising social conflicts—the inequalities, the slums, the urban unrest—associated with commercialism.

This is a powerful argument in the context of industrial history, and its impact has clearly registered with recent scholarship of the Highlands. But Jean Baudrillard reminds us that even the most compelling productivist theses like this one (i.e., Highland romance as "productive" of capitalist complacency, or of British national identity) do not escape the taint of ideology and self-misrecognition. As he put it in a famous pastiche of the opening lines of *The Communist Manifesto*, "A specter haunts the revolutionary imagination: the phantom of production. Everywhere it sustains an unbridled romanticism" in the service of a generalized humanism—the notion that one must not "be" as much as "produce" oneself.[14] Baudrillard's point is simple but beguiling, especially in a neo-"materialist" era like our own. By insisting on the "production" of identity, he argues, we neglect other ways of imagining "the human," or even thinking outside the latter's auspices. "Production" becomes compulsively repetitive, a hegemony unto itself.[15]

Baudrillard has found a powerful new ally in Alan Liu, whose recent book *The Laws of Cool* (2004) reduces our modern historicist ethos and its rage for context (e.g., the Highlands in the "context" of new archival materials, or discussions of national identity, or theories of signification, and so on) to a social compulsion. "Information work"—the production of knowledge—drives the business world *and* the inclusive world of the humanities which purports in some ways to oppose it (as do the romantic Highlands relative to Womack's portrait of the capitalist state). The difference, coarsely put, is that commerce generates capital and hence power whereas the humanities merely hemorrhage it. As Liu sees it, cultural studies of all stripes have thus become ciphers—ghosts—in a world of techno-logic that has assimilated, reshaped, and subsequently excreted them as so much refuse. His solution to digitized modernity is what he calls "ethical hacking," a Bhabha-like mimicry and "creative destruction" of information work which struggles valiantly to distinguish itself from mere cyber-terrorism.[16]

Baudrillard's solution is intrinsically milder, quainter, more romantic—literally. He invokes alternative, symbolic economies, and in doing so implicitly models his critique on Michel Foucault's discussion of romance in *The Order of Things* (1966). Like Baudrillard, Foucault attributes the productivist mentality and the invention of "man" (as a narrow definition of the human) to Enlightenment thought, and specifically to the historical emergence of the disciplines during the eighteenth century. These disciplines—notably natural history, philology, and political economics—instituted discourses which in turn mediated human understanding of the objects of its inquiry. They did so even while promoting the illusion of a direct contact with these objects. From thenceforth, however, knowledge implied less the direct engagement of objects than a negotiation of discourses. And, when these discourses acquired a comparative and thus historical quality in the nineteenth century (e.g., when the discourse of natural history encountered the discourse of evolution), knowledge became ever more implicated in language, and hence in the interpretation of texts. Foucault contends that this Enlightenment-discursive system, a veritable Borgesian maze, "still serves as the positive ground of our knowledge. . . ."[17]

In essence, Foucault attempts here a historical explanation of the issues to which scholars of Highland Scotland became so drawn in the late 1980s—the issues, specifically, of the "productive" ("forged") basis of Scottish and British national identities. Our contemporary rage for discourse derives from the model of knowledge which was born during the eighteenth century. This is why, for Foucault, these issues do *not* beg an elaboration on what discourses yield (e.g., nationalism) as much as what they repress. In effect, "discourse" displaces objects in the world (the ghosts of Kant and Freud haunt Foucault's narrative here), making specters of seemingly material things. If, as Bill Brown puts it, "things" appeal to us, it is "because they lie both at hand and somewhere outside the theoretical field, beyond a certain limit, as a recognizable yet illegible remainder . . . that is unspecifiable."[18] Things are spectral precisely because they defy reduction to discursive economies. In that respect, things are congealed experiences.

Conventional wisdom has it that experience in and of the world, experience conceived as the direct contact with objects, fuels scientific discourse; our experience with objects incites us to build models through which to interpret that experience. And yet, Foucault's point is that experience as "contact" is what science as "discourse" supplants. In essence, then, experience is to Foucault what the Highlands are to Womack: just as, for Womack, the Highlands presented a modernizing society with the illusion of human (as opposed to exchange) value, thus generating the impression that capitalism contributes to the progress of "humanity," so for Foucault does the image of "experience" in science perpetuate the "discourse" which sustains this illusion.

Discourse thus supplants "experience." But if science (i.e., knowledge-as-discourse) constitutionally converts experience into a specter, then what recourse is left to us if we wish to recover it? How is one to tell the truth about experience? If experience is implicitly opposed to discourse, or if discourse reanimates experience as a specter, then how is one to grasp experience when one is obliged to proceed by means of discourse? Isn't an examination of experience inherently contradictory? For Foucault in *The Order of Things*, the answer, surprisingly, is no. But to arrive at experience, one must tell a story which does not pretend to scientific "truth" per se. In other words, one must adopt a literary methodology: it is only through literature, conceived by Foucault as the discourse about discourse (and not

about things other than itself: natural history, philology, political economics, and so on), that we confront the "real" edges of our "symbolic," discursive being. "Literature" here is the same thing as Womack's "romance": it
designates discourse severed from the illusion of experience as the direct
contact with objects in the world.[19] However, unlike Womack, who casti-
gates romance for its patented unreality, Foucault turns this dynamic to
advantage. In romance, he argues, discourse reflects on itself as discourse,
removing itself from the supposed experience of objects; romance enables
the putative experience "of unthinkable thought," or of critical reflection
at the border where the symbolic meets the real.[20] As Foucault has it, *every*
discursive operation is inherently romantic in this way; that is, every "truthful" discourse struggles and fails to make contact with the world outside
itself. And yet, it is only in self-consciously "literary" places—e.g., the
Highlands—that we perceive how such romance "really" works.

Romantic self-reflexivity is a virtual cottage industry, and I have no
interest in entering it through either the front or back doors, especially
inasmuch as such discussions typically turn on questions of consciousness
rather than experience per se.[21] I rehearse Foucault's romantic model
only as an allegory of a problem which consciousness per se does little to
resolve, though one should add that we are also probably less conscious
of this problem (of experience) in our postphenomenological era of productivist humanism. Also, by identifying the eighteenth and nineteenth
centuries as the era of discursive self-reflexivity, the Foucaultian allegory
implicitly conjures the late-Enlightenment Highlands as an exemplary
site for reflecting on the spectral allure of experience in modernity. This
allure, and the romantic Highlands themselves, emerges, we will see,
from the rupture—institutional and epistemological—of experience
from knowledge. Highland romance of the latter half of the eighteenth
century partly functions as consolation for this rupture, but also as an
index of the strange new authority which, we will see, has accrued to
experience in its long, ghostly afterlife. These are the "ruins" to which
I refer in the book's title.

Getting hold of a topic as elusive as experience is a little like catching
lightning in a bottle. One cannot simply produce "evidence" for the
loss of experience, since it is evidence (the process of knowledge or, in
Foucault's words, discourse) which occludes experience in the first place.
Consequently, I do not envision this book as an examination of the experience of eighteenth-century Highlanders. That said, I engage Highland
romance in a variety of subjects, fields, and periods, and from the perspective of Highland and Hebridean Island natives as well as outsiders. In
doing so, I hope to bring into relief the contours of experience as the
vanishing point of knowledge. As I see it, this vanishing point, these
"ruins of experience," are among the farthest-reaching—and haunting—
legacies of "enlightenment."

Introduction

Experience and the Allure of the Improbable

In December 1749 or January 1750, roughly three and a half years after British forces extinguished the Jacobite Rebellion outside the Scottish Highland town of Inverness, the English poet William Collins penned his "Ode to a Friend on his Return &c," more famously canonized as "Ode on the Superstitions of the Highlanders of Scotland." Collins composed the poem for his recent acquaintance, the Lowland Scottish playwright John Home, who was returning from London to Scotland. Depicting the remote Highlands as "fancy's land," Collins urged Home to immerse himself in Highland folk traditions, assuring him he might find there "Themes of simple sure Effect/[To] add New conquests to [poetry's] boundless reign."[1] Home would partly make good on Collins's injunction with his play *Douglas* (1756), a sentimental tragedy about a noble Highland heir. Three years later, Home would also inspire young James Macpherson to share his translations of the legendary epic poet Ossian with Edinburgh literati, igniting a cultural event and controversy that would blaze well into the nineteenth century. Home, Macpherson, and others from their era embraced Collins's vision of the Highlands as a place where life and experience, "daring to depart/From sober truth, are still to nature true."

Though not addressing Collins's "Ode" per se, Hans-Georg Gadamer expounds on the phenomenon in which it was implicated. During the latter half of the eighteenth century, Gadamer observes, the romantic aura that Collins associates with the Highlands attained general currency as a new conception of experience, *Erlebnis*. Etymologically evocative of plural lives (from the German *Leben*, "life"), *Erlebnis* literally designates moments of heightened life experience cut out from the fabric of quotidian reality. While the word would not enter the German vernacular until the 1870s, Gadamer explains how its conceptual foundations were laid in the late eighteenth-century critique of Enlightenment rationalism in Rousseau, proceeding into modernity through Schiller, Hegel, Schleiermacher, Nietzsche, Bergson, and others.[2] Experience in this mode conforms, Gadamer argues, to a reflexive aesthetics, or to the reputed "power of the work of art [to tear] the person experiencing it out of the context of his life, and yet [relate] him back to the whole of his existence" (70). This was the power of the Highlands in Collins's mind, a power of romance which corresponded with such shifting aesthetic concepts as "genius" as creativity and "nature" as preserve: Collins imagines the Highlands as a sanctuary of poetic genius. For Gadamer, the problem with these romantic forays is that they recapitulate the rationalized norms they purport to evade: the rupture of aesthetic from everyday experience mirrors the industrial partitions of a divided labor force, and the association of meaningful experience with fancy merely inverts, and thus reinforces, the scientistic reduction of individual experience to fictive understanding. By this logic, the quixotic romances inspired by Collins's "Ode" in the late eighteenth century do little more than convert the romantic Highlands into an uncanny emblem of London or Edinburgh.[3]

The trajectory Gadamer describes of the problem of experience emerging in the eighteenth century, crystallizing in the nineteenth, and arriving at critical consciousness in the twentieth is one that had already gained wide currency by 1960, the year he published *Wahrheit und Methode* (*Truth and Method*). The pragmatism of William James, the *Lebensphilosophie* of Dilthey and Nietzsche, Heideggerian ontology, and other discourses had all been largely conceived to redeem the category of experience from the depths to which it had supposedly fallen. Consensus here was that Enlightenment thought had diminished experience by reducing it to a species of sensation (e.g., in Kant's *The Critique of Pure Reason* as the "experience" on which we predicate our knowledge of objects). A distinction became prevalent in these revisionist approaches between "inner, lived experience" and "outer, sensory experience," reflecting the German linguistic difference between *Erlebnis* and *Erfahrung*. Dilthey, for instance, interpreted *Erlebnis* and *Erfahrung* to mark a distinction between the human and natural sciences, and he attributed to *Erlebnis* and the human sciences a vitalistic "reality [that] is not resolvable into physical data."[4] In the work of Heidegger, Gadamer, and Walter Benjamin, the distinction between *Erlebnis* and *Erfahrung* underwent a further revision that restored to "outer, sensory experience," *Erfahrung*, a more encompassing quality that Martin Jay describes as one "of transmittable wisdom, of epic truth . . . a journey (*fahren*), a narratable exploration of parts hitherto unknown."[5] Hence, for Gadamer, "[w]hat we call experience" remains "a living historical process; and its paradigm is not the discovery of facts," as is the case with enlightened positivism, but rather "the peculiar fusion of memory and expectation into a whole" (221). Such French theorists as Roger Munier,

Gilles Deleuze, and Philippe Lacoue-Labarthe elaborate on Gadamer's point by enunciating a conception of experience that splits the difference between *Erfahrung* and *Erlebnis*, restoring to experience its etymological roots in the Latin *experiri*, meaning "to test, try, prove." According to this conception, "[t]he idea of experience . . . is etymologically and semantically difficult to separate from that of risk. . . . [I]n a fundamental sense, *experience* means to endanger."[6] Here, experience acquires the properties of a private condition—*Erlebnis*—that everyone passes through—*Erfahrung*. This formulation will prove to be central to my analysis.

Experience had been popularized in French thought by Jean-Paul Sartre through his notion of *expérience vécue*, "lived experience."[7] Raymond Williams describes *expérience vécue* as the vaguely "felt sense of [a] quality of life."[8] Jay, who has written authoritatively on the intellectual history of experience, observes that a "post-phenomenological generation" of such French intellectuals as Derrida, Althusser, and Lyotard "stigmatized" *expérience vécue* for its romantic inflections, proclaiming it "an ideologically suspect, discursively constructed, and woefully outmoded concept." The concept of experience already bordered on extinction long before the postphenomenological turn of the 1960s, "undermined" as it was "by capitalist techno-science, the mass life of the metropolis and the loss of any sense of temporal dialectic culminating in retrospective meaning," or in the feeling of something lived through.[9] And yet, as Jay notes, experience never really disappeared as a category of critical thought.[10] For instance, even after its denigration by Derrida, Althusser, et al., it remained a viable subject for Foucault: the "lightning-flash" of insight associated with Nietzsche, Nerval, and Artaud in *Madness and Civilization* and the *frisson* associated with transgression in his late work on sexuality speak to the anguishing allure which experience held for him as a critical category.[11] Even Derrida appeals to experience liberally and conscientiously in much of his later work.[12]

Today, one finds a renewed interest in experience on grounds that paradoxically reconfirm rather than deny the category's alleged deterioration. This interest takes many forms—ethical, aesthetic, consumerist, gendered, corporeal, postcolonial, and so on. "Local knowledge," as anthropology dubs the epistemology of experience, has compelled attention in recent years precisely because of the latter's perceived erosion. It figures significantly into such fields as trauma theory (in the interest in victims' testimonies), cultural studies of race, class, and gender (and their fascination with unique repositories of experience: the minority, the heteroclite, the subaltern, the cyborg, and so on), psychoanalysis (especially in the experiential shock Žižek describes when the Symbolic yields momentarily to flashes of the Real), poststructuralism (and its endless variations on themes of insight and irreducibility), postcolonial studies (and its disclosures of "native" cultural forms underwriting diasporic, globalized societies), and others. The diversity of these fields, and the degree to which they disagree with each other on a host of fundamental issues, calls attention to their structural coherence in accentuating variant forms of the unremitting strangeness of experience.[13] Even when the locality in their formulations tends—qua "theory"—toward the abstract and the universal (e.g., "the" gendered, differential, ideological, or what-have-you structure of "the" human subject), these universalisms, as Dipesh Chakrabarty has recently argued, can and should be read as deeply "provincial," that is, as local and experiential, despite or perhaps because of their generalizing claims.[14]

How are we to interpret this renewed interest in experience? There are countless potential explanations. For expository purposes, I refer here to one of modernity's most recognizable categories: that of "the" postmodern condition. In contemporary society, as well-worn theories of postmodernism assert (e.g., Jameson's, Lyotard's, Bauman's), the Enlightenment dream of rational knowledge transmogrifies into a morass of information; the traditional human subject shatters into fragments, aided by the schizoid forces of market capitalism, the constitutive and deconstructive threads of "discourse," and the technology of cybernetics; and even solid objects themselves appear to dissolve (e.g., in quantum physics). In this state, where there is precious little "real" knowledge that "real" subjects acquire of "real" objects, the cancellation and confirmation of reality become one and the same gesture: there are only Shelley's turtles—or Baudrillard's simulacra, or "local" experiences—all the way down.

This dilemma, wherein experience becomes alluring precisely to the extent that it becomes insuperable and no longer counts as knowledge, bears a long and provocative history. My aim is to recount a small but especially compelling chapter of this history. I focus particularly on the rupture between experience and knowledge that reputedly occurred during the Enlightenment, and to the haunting authority that accrued to experience precisely when that authority appeared to be waning. In exploring this issue, I neither attack nor defend the claims of experience: I reflect neither on what experience "truly" divulges to knowledge, nor on the inherent qualities of experience as such (e.g., in phenomenology). Rather, I undertake a critical history, a Foucaultian "genealogy," of the extinction and subsequent return of the epistemic authority of experience. I do so from an oblique angle that trains an eye on subsequent evaluations of this dilemma by way of its provocative cultural inscription in the late eighteenth-century Scottish Highlands—the "fancy's land" evoked by Collins.

The Epistemic Chiasmus of Enlightenment Experience

My decision to focus the discussion on Highland romance is born partly from the revitalized interest in experience; indeed, the current landscape of cultural theory suggests that we should revise the popular story
about the decline of experience by elucidating instead the course of its
uncanny return. Gadamer calls "the concept of experience . . . one of
the most obscure we have" (346), not least because it appears so ubiquitous and transparent. Everyone has experience or experiences, or so it
would seem, such that questions of the modality of experience typically
recede behind those concerning subjectivity and substance: *who* exactly
experiences *what*? When this happens, the result is often an implicit
ontologizing (e.g., of the "body," or of "identity," or of some notion of
collectivity) which disregards the modality of experience. But what does
it mean when we refer to "the experience" of a group of people—say,
eighteenth-century Highlanders? Indeed, it is because "experience" is
such a vague category in this context that theory—"science"—has traditionally compensated for unreflective reductions to experience by repu-
diating experience's epistemological authority. For example, Joan W. Scott
argues that "the evidence of experience" takes the question of identity
for granted; attestations of experiential "fact" beg the question of the
human subjects in which experience ramifies.[15] Her point is well taken,
but it is a point that has been made repeatedly, even compulsively, since
the inception of modern notions of factuality in the seventeenth century.
As Barbara J. Shapiro and Steven Shapin have both argued, the authority of experience has traditionally depended upon its sources (e.g., for
Shapin, the criteria of "the gentleman") for its credibility.[16] Meanwhile,
the more elusive questions concerning the status of experience go unreflected and unanswered.

Hence, rather than focusing on the human subjects in whom experience occurs, I turn my attention to the more obvious—but, oddly, more
overlooked, even today—modalities in which experience signifies, and
more particularly to the aporia obtaining between experience and
understanding. This is not an issue which has been entirely forgotten in
modern thought, as the interest in the subject by Gadamer, Jay, and others indicates. Nor is the subject of identity immaterial to my discussion:
gendered, racial, national, and other social dynamics are obviously
crucial to questions of experience and knowledge, and they factor
accordingly into my analysis. However, my inquiry is less philosophical or
sociological than genealogical; that is, I am less interested in engaging
phenomenology or in reiterating the critical tenets of cultural studies
than in tracing the contours of experience as the penumbral companion
of knowledge. To the extent that an enlightened, objective understanding

is ubiquitous if only as an affect—for instance, in the Socratic "knowledge" of the impossibility of the same—then experience is a shadow we cannot help but cast, again and again.

Two questions thus govern my discussion. First, *why is a genealogical analysis of experience necessary?* And second, *why pursue the problem of experience in modernity via an examination of late eighteenth-century Highland romance?* In response to the first question, I would justify a genealogy of experience by arguing that experience remains a highly mystified element in modernity, quietly informing a wide variety of epistemic configurations, including notions of identity and insight. At once blank canvas and perpetual supplement, experience helps us define who we are and how things happen. To the second, methodological question, I reply that Highland romance not only constitutes an important cultural exhibit from the era of experience's emergence as a problem but, when considered carefully, it also helps explain why the category of experience continues to elude critical reflection. Gadamer is right, I think, in claiming that aesthetic formations (e.g., Highland romance) idealize experience as *Erlebnis*. He is not the first to have made this observation, to be sure: Nietzsche argues toward similar ends in *The Birth of Tragedy*, his early critique of enlightened, scientistic realism. Gadamer reiterates Nietzsche's critique in his analysis of positivist "method," but he fails to duplicate the richness of Nietzsche's critical gesture, which launched its attack on modernity via a romance about ancient Greek tragedy. For Nietzsche, tragedy defamiliarized the problem of scientific reason, a problem which a "scientific" methodology alone would invariably misconstrue. Inasmuch as experience presents a similarly elusive conundrum, Highland romance functions for me as Greek tragedy does for Nietzsche: that is, Highland romance elucidates a central paradox in how we arrive at understanding, helping to explain why the category of experience remains so elusive.

What exactly is the Enlightenment paradox from which the problem of experience emerges? It may be stated most succinctly as the injunction to contextualize—to bracket off—direct perception. In other words, to know an object, one must experience it both directly and indirectly at the same time. This dynamic displays itself most vividly in modern evidentiary systems, which call witnesses to testify to facts on whose truthfulness disinterested juries decide. A strange but symmetrical relationship forms between Highland romance and theories and practices of legal evidence, a relationship which I pursue over the course of this book. During the eighteenth century, freshly constructed military roadways and a burgeoning tourist industry opened rugged Highland Scotland to new forms of commercial and tourist traffic at the same time as virtual blockades were being erected between the jurors' box and the witness stand, and between the witness stand and the judicial bench. Newly conceived schemes of probability in law, natural science, and economics supplemented the limitations of individual experience by extending experience into virtual realms, making it possible to determine likelihoods regarding, for instance, guilt in court, matter in space, and profitability in market ventures. For this reason, legal witnesses found themselves at increasingly remote distances from the epistemic centers of truth: direct experience was a necessary evil, but it was inadequate to meeting the high demands of knowledge. As a consequence, judges and jurors, traditionally conceived in English and Roman (including Scottish) law as witnesses, became more formally sequestered from those witnesses whom they summoned to testify, and whom they now prohibited from sitting in judgment. Meanwhile, however, the im- (or non-) probable remoteness of testimony was celebrated in effigy in the image of the Highland witness as a figure (whether native or tourist) venturing beyond the pale of modern society and experiencing phenomena of a sublime, supernatural, or otherwise strange nature. Such witnesses fulfilled Collins's fanciful reveries. Highland romance thus emerged in this context as a return of the repressed, an uncanny affirmation of direct experience at the historical moment of its supposed devaluation, underscoring the limits less of experience than of the technologies designed to extend it.[17]

The witness/juror distinction, and the attendant segregation of the "romantick" (or, as the spelling indicates, the eighteenth-century) Highlands from the cultural body of "modern" Britain, parallels the epistemic and disciplinary division of "fact" from "fiction" that informs so many eighteenth-century cultural formations, from scientific and economic practices to theories of literary fiction. In one sense, these shifts attest to a new emphasis on experience. After all, the ideology of "enlightenment" was born largely out of the insistent claims of experience against the orthodoxy of Scholastic tradition. Isaac Newton echoed the sentiments of Bacon, Boyle, Locke, and others by declaring that "the best and safest method of philosophizing seems to be, first, to inquire diligently into the properties of things and to establish those properties by experiments."[18] The word "experiment" was a direct corollary of "experience" during this period; William Wordsworth could still draw upon their mutual echoes a century later in his Preface to *Lyrical Ballads*, when he claimed the poems in the collection "were published as an experiment . . . to ascertain how far . . . that sort of pleasure and that quantity of pleasure may be imparted, which a poet may rationally endeavour to impart."[19]

And yet, however much Newton, Wordsworth, and legions of empiricists who lived and wrote in the century separating them may have insisted on direct contact with objects, it is not entirely accurate to characterize the Enlightenment conception of experience as *stricto sensu* "sensationist," as nineteenth- and twentieth-century revisionists like Dilthey and Gadamer imagined it to have been. As Newton and Wordsworth each in his way recognized, rather, the sensationist experience of things was "always already" mediated by a system of induction and interpretation—that is, for Newton and Wordsworth, by procedures and prefaces designed to produce and explain the truth of the "experiment." We may generally describe this system as an economy of probability.

Enlightenment conceptions of probability have received significant scholarly attention over the past two decades; monographs by Ian Hacking, Barbara Shapiro, Douglas Lane Patey, Lorraine Daston, and Mary Poovey, among others, divulge the abstractive nature of sensationist experiences during the seventeenth and the eighteenth centuries.[20] While making it possible to move beyond the limitations of experience by converting experience into projective calculation, probabilism also diminished the epistemological authority of experience by creating virtual, normative experiences that technically belonged to no one in particular.[21] In the laboratory, for instance, prescriptions of probability made the unique conditions of an experience reproducible, but these prescriptions also subordinated witness experience to the instruments and methods by which it was manipulated. A similar dynamic instilled itself in the courtroom as the roles of witness and juror became more rigorously divided from each other and as greater authority was arrogated to lawyers in the presentation of evidence.[22] The exigencies of evidence increasingly demanded objectivity of jurors, but jurors' experience was increasingly "virtual" given the mediating impact of lawyers with respect to the facts at issue. Probability thus became the impetus and end of empirical knowledge; it incited the need for concrete particulars as verification of its assumptions, but these particulars yielded only more likelihoods.

The blunting force exerted by probability on experience has become an axiom of modernity. The systemic features of probability conjure images of oppressive totalities, to wit: equations of probability subordinate experience to abstract calculations of means and ends; probabilism thus displaces authenticity with such bywords as instrumentality and efficiency. Or again, probability enables human agents to convert experience into capital by yoking contingency to a calculus of expectation; it thus permits these agents to rationalize their engagements of the world into occasions for profit.[23] These concerns attest to an epistemological and institutional innovation during the Enlightenment that has become for us a theoretical truism: models of virtuality, of probabilistic trueness-to-life, intrinsically frame perception; our experience is always already mediated.[24]

Today, the corrosion of systems of probability provides one explanation for the apocalyptic tone of much contemporary critical discourse (e.g., postmodernism, postcolonialism, postfeminism, post-Marxism, postindustrialism, etc.). The specter of direct experience does not "return" in postmodernity because it is either authentic or true, but rather because, quite simply, it is inevitable. Echoing Elie Wiesel, Shoshana Felman proclaims "our era . . . the age of testimony."[25] In a hyper-complex world in which theories of reality (e.g., in quantum physics) no longer bear more than trace resemblances to our perception of phenomena, simulacra effectively become real to the extent that they cease to divulge the substances they supposedly represent. Image becomes everything; we are thrown back on perception by default; and the "virtue" of experience in, say, cultural studies—the virtue of subversive difference—thus reveals itself to be a necessary (indeed, *the* postmodern) condition. Meanwhile, the probabilistic mechanization of the future begins to redound upon us in the unforeseeable form of environmental catastrophes, corporate failures, sub- and transnational terrorist activities, and so on, which means that our attempts at probabilistic mediation fail us.[26] In short, knowledge ironically finds itself hemmed in by experience rather than further sundered from it. This results in an uncanny, chiastic return of Enlightenment conceptions of experience: uncanny because it entails a revitalized focus on sensate particulars that never really obtained in the eighteenth century except as fodder—as "evidence"—for the period's probabilistic technologies of understanding (e.g., of science, law, commerce, etc.). With respect to the epistemological authority of experience, postmodernity is thus Enlightenment in drag: in the garish, Warholian form of simulacra, we "experience" Newtonian "things" for the first time.[27]

Collins, Scott, and the "Structures of Feeling"

In claiming that Highland romance lends us greater perspective on the history of this paradoxical chiasmus I by no means conflate Highland romance with Scotland *tout court*, or inflate such romance into a timeless essential. Rather, like Murray G. H. Pittock in his use of the term "Celtic," I appeal to Highland romance as a cultural form whose differences in the late eighteenth century and after nevertheless reproduce a consistent set of features, evocative of "a real substratum of shared experience" among those who invoke it.[28] The Scottish historian T. M. Devine justifies the term by referring to the Highlands as a "concept": "The concept of the 'Highlands' does not appear . . . before 1300 despite the geographical division between the north and south of Scotland."[29] During the medieval period, he observes, a tradition of anti-Highland

satire began to appear in Lowland Scottish poetry and song, and this tradition eventually spread into England after the Highland-led Jacobite
uprisings against the British Crown in 1715 and 1745-46.[30] A distinct
change becomes visible in representations of the Highlands in the latter
half of the eighteenth century. Up through the early part of the century,
writers typically described Highland topography as "gloomy" and characterized its inhabitants as impoverished savages. In the decades subsequent to the squelching of the Rebellion in the spring of 1746, however,
attitudes about the Highlands began to change. The region came to be
perceived as an epic seat of civilization, Highland scenery was upgraded
from gloomy to sublime, a tourist industry established itself, and such
fashions as the kilt became popular in Lowland Scotland as well as in
parts of England. This new spirit of Highlandism, this romanticization of
the region, "was quite literally the invention of a tradition." It contributed to Britain's sense of its own native cultural inheritance, laying
the foundation for Lowland Scottish identity in the nineteenth century
by cultivating nostalgic feelings of Scottish glory without stoking political fires. Highland romance thus "answered the emotional need for the
maintenance of a distinctive Scottish identity without in any way compromising the Union" with England which had formed Great Britain
in 1707.[31]

The critical trajectory linking Highland romance to experience is less
traveled than the one affixing it to, say, nationalism.[32] It is also less
causal: Highland romance is by no means at the seat of the dilemma of
modern experience. However, it is a powerful and ductile "language" of
this dilemma. One critical model indirectly preserves the experiential
élan of late eighteenth- and early nineteenth-century Highland
romance: Raymond Williams's "structures of feeling." Williams held
these structures to denote "a kind of feeling and thinking which is . . .
social and material, but . . . in an embryonic phase before it can become
fully articulate. . . ."[33] At once phenomenological and material, evoking
lived experience and its socioeconomic conditions, these structures
comprised for Williams a dialectical counterpart to Louis Althusser's
structuralist conception of ideology as "the 'representation' of an imaginary relationship of individuals to their real conditions of existence."[34]
Williams did not care for Althusser's model. Whereas the "structures"
evoked a gestative social consciousness, an "embryonic" universe perpetually unfolding, "ideology" presupposed a Platonic realm of higher
order reality, one which collective sentiment, casting shadows against
the walls of its own social consciousness, perpetually distorted.[35] Using
Heidegger's language, Williams's structures accentuated the "thrown-
ness," the existential fluctuation, of existence, whereas Althusser's ide-
ologemes presented the world as prepackaged and predetermined.

Williams made the "structures" appear especially relevant to the category of experience in an interview conducted with the *New Left Review*. His interlocutor reflected there on the difference between the conceptions of experience held by Williams and Althusser. "In Althusser's work, experience is simply a synonym for illusion," the interviewer observed. "It is ideology in its pure state—the opposite of science, or truth." In his reply, Williams conceded that experience "is a limited word, for there are many kinds of knowledge it will never give us, in any of its ordinary senses." But despite these limitations, Williams felt compelled to preserve experience as a tool of cultural critique if only because he found "appalling . . . the claim that all experience is ideology, that the subject is wholly an ideological illusion. . . ." This admission, he declared, "is the last stage of formalism," the reduction of the world to a rebus legible to all but amenable to none—a world of caves and shadows.[36] According to William V. Spanos, a similar dynamic inheres in "the discourses of textuality, of psychoanalysis, of ontology, of feminism, of critical genealogy, [and] of neo-Marxism," among others. "[E]ach of these interpretive strategies tends to assume a base/superstructure model. Each, that is, assumes that the site at which it situates its own inquiry constitutes the determining ground of all the other (superstructural) regions of knowledge. . . ."[37] Williams's structures of feeling differed from these "theoretical" divisions of (a truthful) base from (a merely experiential) superstructure by concerning themselves "with meanings and values that are actively lived and felt. . . . An alternative definition would be structures of *experience*: in one sense the better and wider word. . . ."[38] He thus flouted convention by rendering experience integral rather than subordinate to the task of knowledge.

If anything, Williams's reflections have acquired greater pertinence (if not wider circulation) since the 1970s, as "culture" has become an increasingly popular and vexed category. To underscore the relevance of these "structures" to Highland romance and to the epistemic chiasmus of Enlightenment, we might briefly consider two vivid examples of Highlandism from the eighteenth and the early nineteenth centuries.[39] Collins's posthumous "Ode" provides one such example. When the poem was finally published in 1788, the poet's qualitative distinctions between "sober" and "fanciful" (or rational and imaginative) truth and experience had become customary in representations of the Highlands. As I mentioned above, the normative status of "sober" truth throughout Britain had continued its enlightened drift during the eighteenth century toward new models of probability in the form of scientific induction, legal evidence, and commercial investment. The fanciful Highlands thus came to seem anachronistic and, literally, im-probable (or comparatively unenlightened) within the context of Britain's institutions and modern identity. And yet, it was the region's affective difference which was the source of their appeal.

Walter Scott would capitalize on these images of Highland difference in his inaugural historical novel *Waverley; or, 'Tis Sixty Years Since* (1814). Scott's protagonist, Edward Waverley, journeys into the "primitive" Highlands in 1745, where he is overcome by "wild feeling[s] of romantic delight" and temporarily secedes to the rebellious Jacobite army. Eventually, however, he awakens to the powers of "sober" reason, reaffirms an ethos of rational progress, and returns to his English estate. Most recent scholarly discussions of *Waverley* typically and persuasively turn on the novel's ideological self-reflexivity. In the frame which narratologists define as "story" (*histoire*), Scott creates a protagonist who represents a unified Britain cognizant of its past but devoted to progress; and, in the frame of "narrative" (*récit*), or the process by which the story develops, Edward's journey from England into the Highlands and back reifies progress through a spatialized historicism that configures the difference between "Britain" (principally England, Wales, and Lowland Scotland) and the Highlands as the difference between enlightened and primitive states. This historicist sensibility, this ability to map the passage of time, serves for Scott as the hallmark of modernity, distinguishing progressive Britain from the barbaric Highlands. It is the affinity—shared by the narrator, Edward and, presumably, the reader—for chronotopic abstraction that characterizes this modernity. "Enlightenment" effectively turns here on the issue of literacy as the power to perceive, and hence to legislate, a constitutive difference between the present and the past.[40]

This attitude of modernity in *Waverley* has come to inflect criticism of Scott as much as it has Scott's novel. Interpretations which focus on this attitude perceive in Scott's Highland romance such discourses as historicism, imperialism, and capitalism; and in harboring these discourses, Scott's work becomes a virtual Highland line dividing ancient and modern.[41] While generally ratifying this view, Ina Ferris opens another window onto Scott's novel. Compared with such national tales as Maria Edgeworth's *Castle Rackrent* and Sydney Morgan's *The Wild Irish Girl*, in which an idealized past appears truncated from the present, Scott's *Waverley* transforms the folklore from which it was partly cobbled "into the national-historical time that was central to the development of the historical sense in the nineteenth century."[42] Scott's novel does not fetishize the past as much as hitch it to the wagon of progress. Katie Trumpener and Clifford Siskin address this motif in Scott's fiction and criticism as a tool (in Siskin's rubric, a technology) for repressing Celtic and feminine influences in the British state.[43] For Ferris, however, Scott thematizes modernity for the purpose of accentuating its break from the past, and specifically from "the valuable code of conduct" which he identifies with "the displaced social order."[44] She thus reads *Waverley* as an elegy of a lost past rather than as propaganda for a glorious future.

Ferris's emphasis on the self-differentiating narrative of *Waverley* powerfully concurs with the model Williams suggests through his "structures of feeling." Here, Edward's indulgence of Highland exoticism belies Scott's purported ideological agenda of enlightenment. In this other, experiential reading, primitive Highland society serves in *Waverley* as a relic against which British progress measures itself; but this progressive attitude must therefore preserve Highland Scotland as a site of irreducible alterity. Highlandism, from this view, represents the perpetual possibility of the experience of difference in a way that magnifies the contingency of the "real." Or rather, as Žižek would have it, Highlandism provides fuller access to the Real precisely by unmasking as contingent the Symbolic social forces—the probabilistic discourses of history, science, and economics, and the division of "primitive" Highlands from progressive Britain—that were naturalizing themselves in British society.[45] Rather than an ideological instrument of progress, Scott's novel reflexively examines the categories through which "we moderns" interpret it. (This seems especially to be the case in the trial scene near the end of *Waverley*, when Evan Dhu's loyalty to Fergus, his condemned clan chief, highlights the incidental basis of his—and, as the narrator persuasively suggests, the "modern" reader's—notion of justice.) Scott's Highlands are thus less the reservoirs of pastness than structures of feeling, less consumable commodities than sites of gestative, critical self-consciousness, enabling reflection on the contingency of historical progress and the Enlightenment rationality upholding it.

By this reading, Scott elicits the Highlands for the purpose or with the effect of commenting on divergent levels of experience. Without essentializing "Highland" or "British" experience, the affective difference between the two may be taken to reflect the shifting and increasingly complex nature of modernizing British society. This recognition of a spectral underside to progress then complicates (as redundant or, in Freud's terms, compulsively repetitive) any subsequent "enlightened" claims (e.g., by modern critics) that would pretend to a demystified understanding of *Waverley* as an ideological instrument. That is, to demystify Edward's Highland excursion is to remain within the purview of the rationalized "progress" that Scott's narrative implicitly complicates. Hence, it seems more satisfying to perceive in Scott's novel an appeal to the Highlands as a problematic place of (witness) experience that defies reduction to the scientific or cognitive model of normative truth on which ideological interpretations rely.

Collins's "Ode" presents an especially compelling testimony in this regard. In projecting in 1749 or 1750 an image of the Highlands that Scott would virtually take for granted, Collins thus effectively predicts how the region was to become a quintessential land of enigmatic experience. Deborah Elise White makes a strong case for this ambiguous improbability in her rich reading of Collins's poem. As White sees it, the "Ode" shares with other poems of the late eighteenth century a vision of imagination as a mediatory agent between the poles of enlightenment and romance. She shows how Collins situates imagination along the border separating "superstition and enlightenment, mapped by the 'Ode' as the difference between the Scottish highlands and England."[46] Ultimately, however, this border does not accommodate a simplistic ideological division of past and progress, romance and history, as much as ground a new "subject" of poetry, with *subject* denoting the topic of poetry as imaginative foray and also a human identity composing itself through a complex array of evanescent representations.[47] Hence, Collins's "Ode" does not merely concern itself with the new aura accruing to poetry in the decades following Pope (e.g., in Joseph Warton's dismissive *Essay on the Genius and Writings of Pope* [1756 and 1782]), but also with the shifting status of individuals during this era of the emergent liberal humanist subject.[48] As such, "Collins's preoccupation with . . . the *effects* of poetry" rather than simply its composition also amounts to a tacit exploration of experience (56, White's emphasis).

Considered schematically, Collins's "Ode" thus encrypts the historical quandary of experience into its enthusiastic lines about the Highlands. On the one hand, the poem appears to celebrate the dizzying contingency—the witness-like experience—associated with the Highlands; on the other hand, however, and in its belated publication, the "Ode" effectively calculates the presumable im-probability of Highlandism's allure in the eighteenth century, thus apparently converting witness experience into jury-like abstraction. Collins's poem, in short, presents a paradox: it is probable, the poet argues, that that which is improbable will become increasingly attractive to a progressive society and, as White helps us see, begin to appear integral to the task of subject formation. And yet, at the same time, the category of experience which resides at the seat of this progressive history (as the crux of the emergent liberal humanist subject) will come to occupy an increasingly vexed position as the origin of the knowledge which eventually transcends it—the experience which gives way to knowledge—and also as the idealized object of that knowledge (as the odyssey of the human subject in its accumulation of experience). In this way, Collins's "Ode" articulates a prophecy not only *for* Highland romance as a fad, but also *of* Highland romance as a palimpsest of modernity. Highland romance crystallizes the perpetual allure of the improbable, the alluring ruins of experience, in an ever-more enlightened age.

Highland Diasporas

Experience is an elusive category whose study presents an obvious methodological problem. Fredric Jameson historicizes this difficulty at the conclusion of his opus *Postmodernism*. While discussing the gradual transition from ideological processes "long generally associated with the Enlightenment" (e.g., "the desacralization of the world, the . . . secularization of the . . . sacred, [and] the standardization of both subject and object") to the hegemonic regime of global capital, Jameson observes how, in western society, "the phenomenological experience of the individual subject," which is "limited to a tiny corner of the social world, a fixed-camera view of a certain section of London or the countryside" or wherever, began during the eighteenth and the nineteenth centuries no longer to coincide "with the place in which it takes place. The truth of that limited daily experience of London [now] lies, rather, in India or Jamaica or Hong Kong: it is bound up with the whole colonial system of the British empire that determines the very quality of the individual's subjective life. Yet those structural coordinates are no longer accessible to immediate lived experience and are often not even conceptualizable for most people." The world has grown too complex and integrated to reveal its secrets to the inherently limited organon of lived experience. Hence, "[t]here comes into being . . . a situation in which we can say that if individual experience is authentic, then it cannot be true; and that if a scientific or cognitive model of the same content is true, then it escapes individual experience."[49] Divorced from scientifically legitimated (e.g., a juror's) knowledge, experience (i.e., of witnesses) begins to register the truth only of its own bewildered homelessness.

I analyze Jameson's remarks at greater length in Chapter 4, for in this same section of his book he elicits the Scottish Highlands in proposing a solution to this problematic rupture of experience from knowledge. He argues that the kind of stark difference which Collins asserts between life and experience in the romantic Highlands when compared with enlightened Edinburgh impresses upon consciousness a critical recognition of the artifices of its own media, its own bases of knowledge. Essentially, Jameson elicits Highland romance less for the purpose of reconciling experience to knowledge than of imparting to experience a heightened awareness of the factitiousness of the construct—"knowledge," especially knowledge in the postmodern age—that devalues it. The Highlands thus configure a critical poetics that Jameson had extolled twenty years earlier as "defamiliarization, a making strange (*ostranenie*) of objects . . .

restoring conscious experience . . . [by] breaking through deadening and mechanical habits of conduct . . . and allowing us to be reborn to the world in its existential freshness and horror."[50]

The methodological problem which Jameson highlights follows from the rupture of experience and truth. How is one to make a credible case for experience without perpetuating this rupture? Can there be a truthful examination of experience, or does such an investigation already preclude the category—experience—which it places under the microscope? In his *Dictionary of the English Language*, Samuel Johnson describes the word "romantick" through such terms as "wild," "fanciful" and, most significantly, "improbable." Can there be anything other than a "romantick," "improbable" approach when probability itself is the problem under investigation? But, if one takes this approach, does one not risk compromising the validity of one's claims? My way of dealing with this problem is to undertake a genealogy of experience whose viability turns less on the marshaling of irrefutable evidence (a conceit I overtly unsettle by attending to the historical displacement of witness testimony by "objective" forms of evidence) than on the conjuring of suggestive associations. This is why I approach the problem of experience through the lens of Highland romance rather than more directly, "in itself"; without renouncing claims to truth, I light upon the topic of experience from an oblique angle which apprehends the category in the process of its dissolution under the glare of objectivity.

But if my approach to experience makes for a different book than, say, Martin Jay's excellent *Songs of Experience* (which focuses less on the paradox of experience than on the latter's historical development and conceptual variations), then my account of Highland romance also differs fundamentally from landmark studies of Highland Scotland by Peter Womack, Katie Trumpener, and others which I discuss in the Preface. Highland romance here is less the object of my analysis than its lens, its medium. Descriptively, I undertake something of a Kantian shift in my examination of the Highlands, attending less to *what* Highland romance "really was" (*pace* Womack) or to *who* local Highlanders "actually were" (which Trumpener and others partly explore) than to *how* Highland romance's alluring improbability sheds a fortuitous light onto a wider and more elusive problem. To be sure, I discuss a number of texts and phenomena pertaining to the "actual" Highlands and its inhabitants, from trials and treatises to forgeries and works of fiction. Additionally, I address figures both canonical and noncanonical. But the end of my analysis is not to be found in these items or figures themselves, but rather in the broad dilemma of experience that is refracted through them—a dilemma which, we will see, impacted local Highlanders as much as outsiders, like Collins, who romanticized them. These refractions of the problem of experience are the "Highland diasporas" to which I refer in this section heading, and not (or not simply) the emigration of Highlanders as a result of the notorious clearances.

My analysis of this problem of experience proceeds in a series of imbricated tableaux. I have divided the body of my analysis into two sections, "Structure" and "Feeling," echoing Williams. In the first of these complementary sections, I underscore the integral relevance of the problem of experience to shifting theories and practices of legal evidence and to the socioeconomic transformation of the Highlands, while emphasizing the significance of both evidence and improvement (as it was called) to Highlandism. In the second section, I show how the evidential dynamics of Highland romance inflect longstanding ideas concerning the purported decline of experience in the eighteenth century and after.

While the chapters differ in their specific topics, they resemble each other in their methodology. I ground my wide-ranging survey of Highland romance by charting two parallel courses with consistent points of contact. One course follows the logic of Highlandism in more or less chronological fashion, beginning with a famous 1752 murder trial and proceeding through schemes of Highland "improvement" (or capitalist rationalization) from the 1760s and '70s, James Macpherson's *Ossian* translations of the 1760s, travel narratives and local descriptive poetry from the 1760s and '70s, and, as a kind of epilogue, inflections of Highland romance in two pairs of novels from the modern and postmodern periods. The other course is less chronological than topographical, less temporal than spatial, reflecting the conceptual parameters and palimpsests of Highlandism's (chrono)logic in nineteenth- and twentieth-century thought. Here, I follow influential Frankfurt School evocations of the relationship between experience and literature through Marxist critiques of political economy, the evidential parameters of trauma theory, the aura surrounding technology, and the nostalgia for experience intrinsic to the modern conceptual space of literature. My aim in employing this time-space methodology is to uncover in suggestive fashion the common ground—the Highland terrain, as it were—between the cultural inscription of experience during the Enlightenment and the legacy of that inscription in contemporary theory and culture. The logic here is critical and genealogical rather than taxonomic: while I have tried to be as representative as possible in my inclusion of texts (*Ossian* and Scott's *Rob Roy* are predictable choices; the criticism of Adorno, Benjamin, and Jameson and the high modernist fiction of Virginia Woolf are less so), my aim is not to turn a wide lens onto the Highlands, but rather to discern the shadow of experience as it stretches beside it.

Because legal witnessing is a crucial and recurrent dynamic in my discussion (in both literal and figurative ways) I devote two chapters to it.
Evidence functions here in both a literal and a figurative register. As I
see it, the modern dilemma of experience emerges gradually over the
course of the eighteenth century, and the best way to signal this dilemma is to highlight another gradual but more concrete development: the
elaboration of modern customs and practices of evidence. The "literal"
emergence of evidence thus serves as a "figure" of the more elusive
problem of experience. I should add that it is legal rather than religious
witnessing which is my object. I do this fully aware that there is a strong
tradition of religious witnessing in Presbyterian Scotland. But again, my
aim in this project is neither taxonomic nor positivistic; I try less to document varieties of witnessing in the Highlands, or to martial texts as witnesses for or against "The Man" (e.g., Empire or Enlightenment), than
to unpack the structure which most vividly displays the problematic status of the modern category of experience. As I understand it, we best
capture that status by lighting on the division between witnesses and
jurors—those who see *versus* those who know, without imputations of
heresy on the part of those who deny the faith. Indeed, in religious
terms, jurors were functionally *required* to "deny the faith" of the witness.
Or rather, they were to have no more than faith, or belief, in things they
were not permitted to know.

I open in Chapter 1 by discussing the origins of the modern legal concept of evidence, its repercussions for the reception of witnesses, and
various ways in which these legal shifts informed eighteenth-century
Highlandism and the Enlightenment category (and legacy) of experience. I outline this dynamic by way of a 1752 murder mystery, its trial,
and the affective border which they delineate separating two regions
and two types of experience. The Highlands figure here as a recalcitrant
place of witness testimony, with England and Lowland Scotland coming
to signify a modern region of juridical probability, and hence of mediated rather than direct experience.[51] Chapter 2 further explores this
dynamic by tracing this particular trial's legacy in Scott's *Rob Roy*, in
Robert Louis Stevenson's companion novels *Kidnapped* and *Catriona*,
and, implicitly, in Walter Benjamin's essay "The Storyteller." My aim
here is to show how the allure of witness experience began to haunt the
processes of enlightened, evidential understanding which had consigned it to the margins, the affective Highlands, of knowledge.

The next two chapters address Highland "improvement," the eighteenth-
century strategy of capitalist rationalization. I devote two chapters to this
topic because Womack and others rightly perceive improvement as the
complementary pair to "romance" and, implicitly, experience. Chapter 3
extends the discussion of legal evidence by unpacking the latter's logic in

programs of improvement which pervaded the Highlands in the latter half of the eighteenth century. After showing how the dynamics of witness and juror inform these programs, especially in the case of Adam Smith, I examine in Chapter 4 their residual presence in the critique of capitalist modernization by Smith, Marx, and Jameson.

Part II moves from law and political economics to subtler cultural configurations. I reflect in Chapter 5 on the problems and allure associated with the idea of immediacy. Taking trauma theory in and after Freud as my vehicle, I explore notions of direct experience in Macpherson's *Ossian* translations, Adorno's criticism (including the racialized formulation of Judaism in his and Max Horkheimer's *Dialectic of Enlightenment*), and Binjamin Wilkomirski's *Fragments: Memories of a Wartime Childhood* (1995). This last text is a scandalous (indeed, Ossianic) and unwonted parody of Adorno's Enlightenment critique in an imagined set of memoirs of the Nazi death camps. Together, these texts illustrate how the dream of immediacy, born during the Enlightenment, transmogrifies into the mediated (and manipulatable) forms of experience evocative of jury deliberation and, horrifically, a Fascistic insistence on sensation. However, the logic occasionally leads to other outcomes, as I discuss in Chapter 6. Here, I review traditional and more recent conceptions of how the Byzantine complexities of technology end up reproducing the immediacy they purportedly disable. I focus here on a provocative dialectic between mediatory and immediate qualities of experience which instills itself between Samuel Johnson's account of Highland second sight and the bardic poetry of native Highland poet Donnchadh Bàn Mac-an-t-Saoir (Duncan Bàn Macintyre), a dialectic which in turn finds a compelling echo in the technological criticism of Heidegger, Derrida, and Paul Virilio.

Given the frequency with which my analysis moves from the Enlightenment into later modernity, Chapter 7 functions as an epilogue and capstone by uncovering residual traces of "romantick" Highlandism. I focus here on two sets of Highlandist narratives—Neil Gunn's *Morning Tide* and Virginia Woolf's *To the Lighthouse*, and Alan Warner's *Morvern Callar* and Sophie Cooke's *The Glass House*—which negotiate the complex dialectical stand-off between experience and knowledge. I discuss these novels in particular because they cast varying shades of light, high- and postmodern, on the legacy of Highland romance as a repository of human experience in the era of its reputed devaluation.[52]

Taken together, I hope these chapters demonstrate that the Highlands and the fascination they once aroused remain an integral part of the cultural memory of the West. Current social, cultural, and academic trends bring Highland romance back into focus, even if impressionistically, because of renewed interest in lived experience and local knowledge.

Indeed, as Benjamin, Heidegger, Jameson, and others recognize in ruing its decay, experience remains with us: this is our legacy from the Enlightenment. While the "romantick" Highlands themselves seemingly reside today as ruins at the edges of cultural consciousness, their alluring improbability increasingly delimits the structure and concerns of everyday life.

Part One
Structure

Chapter 1

A Musket Shot and Its Echoes
The Romantick Origins of the Modern Witness

Four men, strung out in a lengthy line, picked their way along the narrow, rocky track through the wood of Lettermore. Below them and to their right, the blue waters of Loch Linnhe gleamed through occasional gaps in birch and conifer. Flanking the old bridleway on the other side, the hill rose steeply in a tumble of mossy boulders, bushes and stunted trees. The leading wayfarer was on foot, the others on horseback. The middle rider, Colin Campbell of Glenure, held the post of Crown factor, or land-agent, for the estate through which he was travelling. A red-haired man in his mid forties, he was on his way to evict several tenants on the morrow, 15 May 1752. The time was around half-past five in the afternoon.

A single shot cracked the silence. Two musket-balls pierced Glenure's back. He shouted: "Oh, I am dead. He's going to shoot you. Take care of yourself. . . ."[1]

So begins a recent account of the event now remembered as the Appin Murder. The delectation with which the narrator paints the scene (e.g., the "gaps in birch and conifer") testifies to the seductive material on which he reports. The murder and ensuing Trial of James Stewart were sensations in their era and continue to arouse interest for reasons ranging from the mysterious identity of the assassin and the odor of injustice clinging to the court proceedings to the benchmark the trial represents in the social transformation of the Highlands. The murder both resulted from and eventually motivated schemes of Highland "improvement" which included "the introduction of trades and manufactures, the encouragement of fisheries, the building of roads and bridges, the establishment of towns and villages and . . . the modernisation of agricultural practices."[2] These schemes mostly failed to generate the degree of reform their proponents envisioned, but the specter of radical change haunted certain Highland and Hebridean Island communities in the 1750s and '60s. The murder of Glenure in Argyll and the subsequent vengeance exacted in the trial were, by all accounts, reactions to the phantoms which harrowed local residents and government officials.

As we will see, other ghosts of a more generally "enlightened" nature also inhabited the scene. The Trial of James Stewart brings into compelling relief the parallel logic of evidence, experience, and Highland romance which emerged during the eighteenth century. Advocates on both sides debated the case by delineating a virtual geography of evidence, situating witness testimony (and, with it, the claims of experience) in a romantick hinterland at the far side of knowledge. Indeed, we might say that the trial marks the birthplace of the modern witness, not because such witnesses were literally invented there, but rather because it was there that witness testimony acquired the vivid hallmarks of difference and anachronism which would define it ever after, even down to the present day. It was with this trial that testimony and experience most clearly attained the place they hold in modern consciousness.

But before we arrive at that vantage point, we have stories to tell about the Appin Murder and the emergence of modern evidential codes and practices. Let us begin, briefly, with the former. Colin Campbell of Glenure was dead, and James Stewart's guilt, whether actual or merely symbolic, was preordained. Stewart, after all, was the brother of a rebellious clan chief who had fled the country after the Jacobite defeat on Culloden Moor, outside the Highland town of Inverness, in April 1746. Subsequently, the Crown annexed the Stewart estate and appointed Glenure its factor, or agent. True to his appointment, Glenure infuriated James by clearing peasants from small fief holds on it.

Glenure would prove to be the least of James's problems. Archibald Campbell, the Third Duke of Argyll and Lord Justice General of Scotland, presided over the trial as judge. Moreover, Argyll was Glenure's kinsman, leader of the Campbell clan, an enthusiastic Highland supporter of Britain's Hanover dynasty during the Jacobite Rebellion, and a landlord avidly dedicated to improvement. William Grant, the Lord Advocate of Scotland, was an equally imposing foe. Anxiously desiring justice, Grant also seized the political symbolism of the moment in heading the prosecution (or, in Scottish legal terminology, the "pursuers"). He would exclaim in court that Glenure's murder threatened "to make the world or the public believe, that the civilising of the Highlands of Scotland was . . . vain and impracticable. . . ." He had therefore determined "to attend the trial where-ever it should be, and to do all that in [him] lay, consistently with law and justice, to convince the disaffected part of the Highlands of Scotland, that they must submit to this government, which they have several times in vain endeavoured to subvert."[3] Hence, from the beginning of the legal process, the deck seemed hopelessly stacked against James Stewart.

However, the pursuers faced two chief obstacles in making their case. The first was that Stewart was indicted as an accessory to the crime, and

Scottish law dictated that accessories not be tried prior to principals. This was deemed a technicality, which the law might easily sidestep in a case of such magnitude.[4] But the second hurdle was more imposing. The pursuers lacked evidence; that is, according to the prevailing customs of Scottish law, they lacked witnesses. Members of Glenure's party had spotted a man in a dun coat running up the hill after the shot was fired, but they were not close enough to see his face. True, they might summon witnesses to testify to other, potentially incriminating details: Stewart had been heard cursing Glenure in the weeks prior to the murder, even exclaiming that he would never help Glenure "or any of his name, unless it were to the gallows"[5]; he had sent money to his nephew, Alan Breck Stewart (believed to be the trigger man), immediately after the murder so that Alan could flee to France; and he was known to harbor weapons on his estate, contrary to the Disarming Act of 1747. Unfortunately for the pursuers, or so it initially appeared, such facts were merely circumstantial. But as it turned out, the epistemological and legal-evidential climate in Britain during this period would enable the pursuers to convert this handicap into an insurmountable advantage.

Enlightenment "Evidence": An Overview

In order to see how the pursuers obtained this advantage, we should survey the context of legal "proof" during the eighteenth century. This was a transitional epoch in English and Scottish legal history, especially pertaining to the prevailing customs of evidence. And yet, it has long been considered a staple of legal history that "even into the middle of the eighteenth century the modern law of evidence was not yet in operation," and would not emerge until the early nineteenth century with the publication of Jeremy Bentham's compendious *Rationale of Judicial Evidence* (1827).[6] Even as late as 1913, the American jurist John H. Wigmore could invoke the spirit of Francis Bacon and pronounce his *Principles of Judicial Proof* an innovative "*novum organum* for the study of Judicial Evidence."[7] At the 1794 trial of Warren Hastings, Edmund Burke sarcastically alluded to the inchoate status of eighteenth-century evidential law when he commented that "something had been written on the law of Evidence, but very general, very abstract, and comprised in so small a compass that a parrot . . . might get them by rote in one-half hour and repeat them in five minutes."[8]

Burke's quip obscures the history of legal evidence, which was not quite as primitive during the eighteenth century as the legal tradition leads us to imagine. In step with developments in natural philosophy relating to the reception of empirical data, treatises on evidence began appearing in England early in the century, and what John H. Langbein

refers to as the "relatively sudden" proliferation of evidential codes during this period attests to the fact that theories of evidence were already
very much in the air.[9] One important factor in the emergence of these
codes was the advent of the modern adversarial trial. Langbein remarks
that the traditional process of marshaling witnesses, especially those who
were offered special protection for testifying against fellow transgressors,
incited concerns that "the system encouraged false witnesses, who found
it all too easy to bring about the condemnation of innocent men. . . .
[T]he relatively sudden rise of the law of evidence and of adversary trial
procedure was, at least in part, a response."[10] According to legal historian Stephan Landsman, such procedures emerged in three phases. "In
the first phase, up until the 1730s, there was little adversarial action of any
sort." Accused persons usually spoke for themselves before the court. In
the second phase, from the 1730s through the mid-1770s, "litigant and
lawyer participation at trial intensified and a variety of evidentiary restric-
tions were recognized. . . . The third phase of development occurred in
the last quarter of the eighteenth century when adversary procedure was
extended to a substantial portion of all cases. . . . By 1800, adversary procedure predominated."[11]

Together, these transformations placed judges and juries at an ever-
greater remove from the conflicts over which they presided. Since their
inception in the thirteenth century, juries had been regarded as fact-finding bodies called from the neighborhoods of persons accused of crimes,
and jury members were expected to possess an intimate knowledge of the
facts in question. Even through much of the eighteenth century, courts
"did not require decisions by tribunals that had no first-hand knowledge
of the alleged facts."[12] However, in the latter half of the century, courts
began enforcing rigorous distinctions between witnesses and jurors,
attesting implicitly to a widening fissure between witness experience and
legal knowledge, and to a will to construct a more systematic process for
weighing evidence. English courts of law, especially, instilled the principle that evidential knowledge should predicate itself on "estimates of
probabilities . . . based on [normative] experience" rather than on pro-
fessions of certainty associated with witness testimony, that is, particular
experiences.[13] Evidence, in other words, should measure up to the standards of plausibility, or probability, rather than absolute certainty.

Probability in estimations of factual truth had already long been a part
of trial procedure in English courts.[14] It is important to recognize, however, that the very concept of probability was evolving throughout Europe
during the seventeenth and the eighteenth centuries, and that this shift
had a massive impact on conceptions of evidence and on attendant trial
procedures. Since the nineteenth century, determinations of probability
have generally implied a matrix of mathematical equations and statistics.

However, in its earlier forms, probability was less a numerical than a rhetorical device. The concept traces its roots back to Aristotle, who regarded probability as a "generally approved proposition," whether by everyone, the majority, or simply those in authority (e.g., the most trustworthy philosophers). Robert Newsom elaborates that "[i]n English, the concept of the probable bears the stamp of its Latin derivation from *probabilis*, meaning the provable and the *ap*provable, which in turn derives from the verb *probare*, meaning to test . . . or approve. That in turn comes from *probus*, meaning simply virtuous or good (and giving us the modern *probity*)."[15] Philosophers associated Aristotelian probability, Barbara J. Shapiro contends, with "the fluctuating realm of sense impression, common experience, and opinion," and with rhetoric as opposed to logic and demonstrative certitude.[16] In practical terms, this means that probability in the Aristotelian sense shaped general attitudes as well as perceptions of everyday life. Shapiro remarks that probability functioned in this manner into the seventeenth century. At this point, however, the hard and fast distinctions drawn between probability in matters of opinion and science began to erode, primarily due to the empiricist ideology of the new science. A heightened attention to natural phenomena shifted the emphasis in knowledge away from received opinions of the physical world to the logical apparatus of inductive proofs derived through experimentation. Robert Boyle's air pump, for instance, authorized members of the Royal Society to draw likely inferences about the nature of vacuums and combustion. Determinations of probability thus began to mediate between knowledge and supposition, the high and low sciences (e.g., physics and medicine), philosophical propositions and material objects, and facts and fictions.

By the eighteenth century, these new schemes of probabilistic calculation (by such British philosophers as Locke and Hume, and by French thinkers like Pascal, Laplace, and Condorcet) underwrote momentous transformations in economics, history, law, and other disciplines, as thinkers developed innovative methods for projecting future markets, interpreting past events, authenticating circumstantial evidence, and so on. David Hume recognized the implicit role of narrative in equations such as these, which sought to collapse the distance between present and future, forge resemblances between particular phenomena and abstract principles, and transmute virtual into actual realities. He described such ratiocinative processes as "fictions of the imagination" that create illusions of identity and duration.[17] These fictions promoted an enlightened mastery over contingencies of space and time by converting expanses of seemingly boundless possibility (e.g., the behavior of savages, weather patterns in the Atlantic, and the imminent value of silver) into legible plots of likelihood.

The first treatises on evidence in Britain—William Nelson's *The Law of Evidence* (1717), Geoffrey Gilbert's *The Law of Evidence* (written in the 1720s, but not published until 1754), and John Morgan's *Essays upon the Law of Evidence* (1789)—testified to the probabilistic sea change in the theories of evidence. For the most part, these treatises sought to formalize such technical issues as the summoning of juries, the objection to witnesses on grounds of interest or hearsay, and the acceptable forms and uses of written evidence. But these treatises also promulgated an epistemology of probability by translating Lockean empiricism into the terms of law. John Locke's chief contribution to jurisprudence lay in his articulation of the "degrees of assent" we supposedly feel when deciding upon propositions of which we have no certain knowledge. These "degrees" coincided with Locke's reflections concerning probability, which "is nothing," he says, "but the appearance of [truth] by the intervention of Proofs, whose connexion is not constant and immutable. . . . Probability . . . suppl[ies] the defect of our Knowledge, and . . . guide[s] us where that fails. . . ."[18] Gilbert's treatise confirmed these premises by opening with a reference to Locke's scale of assent, which runs "from full Assurance and Confidence, quite down to Conjecture, Doubt, Distrust, and Disbelief. Now what is to be done in all Trials of Right is to range all Matters in the Scale of Probability, so as to lay most Weight where the Cause ought to preponderate, and thereby to make the most exact Discernment that can be, in Relation to the Right."[19]

The significance of this privilege accorded to the "Scale of Probability" is that we begin to perceive the rudiments of an open confederacy between "fact" and "system" rather than the dichotomy purportedly subsisting between the two in the empirical doctrines espoused by Bacon and the Royal Society in the seventeenth century. Superficially, of course, the opposite appeared to be the case. The Royal Society apologist Thomas Sprat insisted on the discrepancy between facts and systems, the latter of which bore the taint of scholasticism. Sprat went so far as to lobby for the expurgation of eloquence; language should instead aspire, he argued, to "Mathematical plainness." The "purpose" of factual science, he argued, is "to heap up a mixt Mass of Experiments, without digesting them into any perfect model," replacing "compleat Schemes of opinions," or scholastic systems, with "bare, unfinish'd Histories."[20] Lorraine Daston expands on Sprat's point, asserting that "[t]he facts so prized by seventeenth-century natural philosophers," like Bacon, such as "monstrous births, rains of blood and wheat, giants and dwarfs, earthquakes, prodigious sleepers," and so on, "were particulars that stubbornly resisted assimilation to . . . universal[s]." They were "events so strange as to defy induction, much less deduction."[21]

However, the reputed "stubbornness" of facts lent itself to an Aristotelian systematicity of a whole new stripe. If for Bacon and Sprat facts represented natural phenomena irreducible to the schemes laid out for them by scholastic conceptions of authoritative probability, then facts in the new sense of that term, the term set forth by the new science, designated truths arrived at through processes of induction. Here, conclusions remained *merely* probable to the extent that they did not pretend to arrive at the teleological ends of the objects under examination. That is, and referring again to the example of Boyle's air pump, we might infer the nature of respiration through experimentation, but not the end for which air was created, nor the uses to which it might be put.[22] Knowledge of such things thus became "probable" and "systematic" to the extent that subjects might harness it toward certain ends (e.g., steam engines), but they could never fully comprehend objects in the infinite variety of their forms and uses.

This confederacy between fact and system bears important repercussions for the concept of experience inasmuch as particular, sensate experiences were already being inducted into this new system of interpretation even as former (e.g., scholastic) systems were revised according to the exigencies of empirical observation. Reflecting the general systematicity already informing the interpretation of natural phenomena, courts in the mid-eighteenth century began to shift the emphasis away from the uniquely "Singular" and "Deviating Instances" of nature that redounded upon the credibility of the source—that is, the witness. In its stead, courts instituted a subtler, qualitative difference between positive testimony on the one hand and the fact-system, or the forensic production of probabilities (e.g., the circumstantial evidence utilized in the Stewart Trial), on the other.[23]

In part, the evidential shift toward probability was itself motivated by changes in commercial law and the economic climate to which this law responded. Daston shows how the need to guarantee fair returns on commercial ventures overseas led to a reappraisal of speculative investments according to standards of reasonable expectation rather than the hit-or-miss logic associated with gambling. "Aleatory contracts," as she calls these arrangements, "included any formal agreement in which chance might figure, including not only insurance and games of chance, but also inheritance expectations and even risky investments . . . assur[ing] all parties of maximum 'reciprocity' or equality of terms."[24] The significance of this incipient commercialism to the formation of modern evidentiary codes lies in shifting the focus onto hidden factors which interpreters—a jury, for instance—might not (or, by custom or statute, *could* not) directly see, but about which it might safely (and indeed, *must*) speculate. Placing evidence in economic terms, we might

say that the probabilistic standard of judgment began to shape conviction into the product of a system in which proof acquired "value"
according to its degree of believability—its rate of currency—on the
market of justice.

The speculative nature of probabilistic thinking was not without its
critics. At the turn of the nineteenth century, Jeremy Bentham, often
regarded as the father of modern evidentiary theory, reacted caustically
toward decisions derived principally from estimations of probability. He
complained that such decisions reek of "the pestilential breath of
Fiction, [which] poisons the sense of every instrument it comes near."
Probabilities, he claimed, are artificial constructs which exist in mathe-
matics rather than nature: facts either have "existence, or [have] it not:
there is no medium." However, he realized that without these fictions,
which are "feigned for the purpose of discourse . . . [such] discourse
could not be carried on"; without such fictions, in other words, there
could be no *sentencing*.[25] And indeed, the fictions promoted by schemes
of probability were perceived to strengthen belief; that is, they tended to
foster conviction.[26]

Such fictions bolstered the "reasonable doubt" rule which came to
play such a pivotal role in English jurisprudence during the eighteenth
century. The legal historian Anthony A. Morano remarks that this rule
would eventually come to place a higher burden of proof upon the prosecution—that is, eventually the prosecution would need to prove its case
beyond a reasonable doubt. At its inception during the eighteenth century, however, "the reasonable doubt rule was actually a prosecutorial
innovation that had the effect of *decreasing* the burden of proof in criminal cases. . . . Prior to the rule's adoption, juries were expected to acquit
if they had *any* doubts—reasonable or unreasonable—of the accused's
guilt."[27] By increasing the likelihood of conviction and affixing a new
standard of judgment, this rule thus tended to tighten the enforcement
of law.

Besides liberally revising the basis of conviction, jurists also believed
that the growing evidential preference for probability and reasonable
doubt over a witness's alleged certainty (or a fact-finding jury member's
prior knowledge) ensured against the corruption of judges and jurors:
if each party had equal access to the same facts, then verdicts and sentences might hypothetically be rendered more equitable and uni-
form.[28] One consequence of this process of normalization, however,
was that in time witness testimony became all the more incidental to evidential truth for occupying a position all the more immediate with
respect to the facts at issue. During the famous English parricide trial
of Mary Blandy in 1752, an apothecary who testified against the defen-
dant was asked whether "the horrors and agonies, which Miss Blandy

was in" after the death of her father "were not, in [his] opinion, owing solely to an hearty concern for her father?" The apothecary replied, "It is not easy, you know, to form a true judgment of the heart; and I hope a witness need not deliver his opinion of it."[29] Indeed, jurists considered it axiomatic that "Witnesses are sworn to tell the Truth, not what they believe; for they are to swear to nothing but what they have heard or seen."[30] Inasmuch as such "judgment[s] of the heart" *were* required of the jury, however, percipient testimony increasingly acted as the mediating surface through which the penetrating gaze of the jury might ascertain the secret truth of a case, "the Pauline evidence of things not seen."[31]

Evidence thus fell under a province of reasonability that now intrinsically separated jurors from witnesses, thereby streamlining and narrowing the purview of judgment and disqualifying glimpses which either party might construe as intransigently private or irreducible to consensus.[32] A concurring and ubiquitous platitude contended that "circumstances cannot lie," whereas witnesses might prevaricate, misremember incidents, or be deceived by what they claim to have seen or heard.[33] A popular late seventeenth-century pamphlet reprinted several times during the eighteenth century declared that testimonies "delivered to induce a Jury to believe, or not to believe . . . [are] called in Law EVIDENCE, because thereby the Jury may out of Matters of Fact, *Evidere veritatum*; that is, *See clearly the truth*, of which they are the proper Judges."[34]

This endowment of insight effectively displaced the authority of witness testimony over the events at issue on trial, leading, if anything, to greater liberality in the reception of witnesses inasmuch as their testimonies might figure as sites of multiple and contested interpretation, thereby reaffirming the position of disinterested jurors as the ultimate arbiters of evidence. For instance, while women were traditionally considered less reliable sources of testimony, lawyers began calling them to the stand with greater frequency. The renowned jurist William Blackstone articulated a common sentiment during this period of increasing witness participation and lawyer influence in the courtroom when he attested that "as much may be frequently collected from the manner in which the evidence [of witnesses] is delivered, as from the matter of it."[35] One might learn as much from how a witness speaks as from what she says. So, while the fear of witness imposture continued to inform the legal process, such concerns became increasingly superfluous as the specter of deceit justified a more rigorous definition of deliberative responsibilities and corresponding division of judicial labor.

Changes in evidential theory and practice accentuate correlative shifts in the conceptions of experience. The extensive nature of eighteenth-century probabilism placed new burdens on the role of experience in constructions of knowledge. As Peter Dear explains, "[a]n 'experience' in the Aristotelian sense was a statement of *how things happen* in nature, rather than a statement of *how something had happened* on a particular occasion." This is why Aristotle argues that poetry is philosophically superior to history: poetry deals in universals or in experience at a general level, rather than with particular details and, hence, with aberrations from perfect form. "But," Dear continues, "the experimental performance, the kind of experience upheld as the norm in modern scientific practice, is unlike its Aristotelian counterpart; it is usually sanctioned by reports of historically specific events."[36] This is to say, experience in the later seventeenth century began to devolve more directly on witness testimony as an attestation of particular events under particular conditions at particular moments.[37]

However, and despite the increasing formal reliance on witness testimony, a constitutional distrust of testimony accompanied the new, probabilistic allegiance between experience and experiment. While most obvious in the courtroom, as I detail above, it would oversimplify matters to assert that jurists simply devalued testimony even if we recognize that the reputed reliance of the new science on witnesses was in some respects a smokescreen. (Dear helps us contextualize this last point: witness testimony became more prominent in attestations of "fact" in part because legal practice diminished the authority of "experience" in line with the new epistemological privilege accorded to evidential probability.) Indeed, as I argue over the course of this book, it would be more accurate to say that the former authority associated with witness testimony did not disappear as much as transmogrify. Steven Shapin and Simon Schaffer imply as much in showing how in the new science "witnessing was to be a *collective act*. In natural philosophy, as in criminal law, the reliability of testimony depended upon its multiplicity."[38] They call this phenomenon "virtual witnessing," a dynamic which derives from the reproducibility of supposedly unique experiences in the laboratory. Expanding on this point in his examination of late seventeenth-century experiments on electricity, Schaffer shows how (literally hair-raising) experimental results were considered to be credible only to the extent that they could be measured on an examiner's body. In other words, such experiments appeared viable only to the extent that they might be made universally (or self-) evident to the public. Schaffer further argues that over the course of the eighteenth century the belief generated by these public displays accommodated, on the one hand, a rational gaze personified by the now-disembodied observer as one who perceives rather than displays the truth, and, on the other, a transference of credibility from personal experience onto the *instruments* (and by extension the *system*) of experimentation.[39] A parallel shift occurred with legal-evidentiary codes. The authority that had once been attached to witnesses' perception and testimonial oath-taking metamorphosed into, in one sense, an objective gaze of judge and jury, and, in another, a redirected faith onto the forensic system and its methods of factual inquiry. Testimonial authority thus came to reside with the system rather than its witnesses per se.

Hence, from a model in which certainty was the criterion for conviction, legal evidence entered its modern phase by formally excluding declarations of positive (i.e., testimonial) certainty from the privilege of judgment. So, whereas traditional juries presumably had personal knowledge of the events in question, the exigencies of impartiality and objectivity separated eighteenth-century juries from such knowledge. And, whereas traditional juries swore that they knew the truth of the issues in question, eighteenth-century juries essentially took the Socratic position of knowing that they knew nothing—at least, not in the "positive" manner of witnesses. Their judgments were to derive, rather, from convictions of "moral certainty," that is, from attestations of likelihood based on the facts mediated by lawyers and presented in court.

We should recognize here an ironic circumstance which stemmed from the implicit splitting of private experience from reliable knowledge. As the instruments and methods of knowledge became more sophisticated, and as they increasingly required degrees of specialization in order to interpret (degrees of specialization unavailable to most laypersons), those who wielded these instruments as a means of circumventing testimonial contingency actually reproduced the effects of testimony in reporting their findings to the public. In my introduction I have referred to this paradox as the chiastic structure of enlightenment—the ultimate devolution of rational understanding to the discrete experience it purports to transcend. On this subject, Shapin quotes William James remarking how "truth lives 'on a credit system': 'Our thoughts and beliefs "pass," so long as nothing challenges them, just as bank-notes pass so long as nobody refuses them.'" Shapin adds that the mechanized and technocratic world that emerged after the Industrial Revolution amplified this condition of trust: "Modernity produces a highly complex array of social information while reducing the familiarity with people [including, we might add, the familiarity of jurors with those accused of crimes] that was the basis of traditional trust. In the past, we made judgments of other people; now we are obliged to trust in impersonal systems . . . ."[40] Not coincidentally, it was during the late seventeenth and the eighteenth centuries when courts began calling expert witnesses and when jurists thus found themselves troubled by testimony that neither judges nor jurors were fully capable of evaluating. Expert testimony provided a textbook case of the "credit system" of which James would speak.[41] In effect, the morphology of testimony thus outlived its own probabilistic demise. And indeed, it is a central argument of this book that the cultural disavowal of witness experience at one level merely served to empower it at another—the level of what I am calling Highland romance.

Event and Signification: A Murder and Its Meaning(s)

As we have seen, the historical origins of the modern legal fact involve the disavowal and partial sublimation of witness experience. Witnesses were called with greater frequency, in part, because of their diminished authority; meanwhile, the epistemological privilege of witness experience largely migrated from individual persons to forensic procedures. This contradictory dynamic would figure prominently in the Stewart Trial. Indeed, the case assumed many forms contradictory to those it purported to take. Designing to put an end to lawlessness in the Highlands, the pursuers nonetheless circumvented the law at several turns; feigning to abrogate clan society, they drew heavily upon clan spirit in attaining their ends.

It may be helpful at the outset to review a few of these discrepancies. For starters, and contrary to law, officers detained Stewart in solitary confinement for several months prior to his trial, where he was at first allowed no visitors at all and later permitted to visit only with those friends and family whom the pursuers deemed unable to help him rally his defense. In like fashion, officers unlawfully imprisoned Stewart's two sons, two of his servants, and other associates so that they could not act on his behalf. Next, they denied Stewart counsel for several months. Enough time transpired, arguably, to prevent the preparation of an adequate defense. More blatantly, however, Stewart's unlawful imprisonment allowed an important deadline to lapse—a deadline that would have permitted him to petition to have the case tried in the relatively neutral environs of Edinburgh rather than in Inveraray, which was the stronghold of the murdered Colin Campbell's relatives.[42] What is more, while the case was tried by three judges, the presiding judge—the Duke of Argyll—was leader of the Campbell clan. (Argyll's statements after the verdict revealed for him the axiomatic connection between the murder and the Jacobite Rebellion which his family had opposed.) Furthermore, although the court called a standard Scottish jury of fifteen, eleven of them were Campbells (an important number since the law required only a two-thirds vote, or ten jurors, for conviction), and members of the Campbell clan were also assigned as translators for Stewart's Gaelic-speaking witnesses. Additionally, pursuers called James's wife and children unwittingly and, by many counts, illegally, to testify against him, or at least to verify specific facts that constituted key links in the pursuers' case.[43] Finally, and according to Scottish custom, jurors heard the trial straight through without recess, commencing the morning of September 21, 1752, and not adjourning until two days had passed. During the defense's closing argument, "one of the jurors interrupted [Stewart's] counsel, and cried, 'Pray, Sir, cut it short; we have enough of it, and are quite tired, the trial having lasted long'" (Mackay 275n).

The defense (or "defenders," in Scots legal parlance) objected to the specific practices of their opponents, but, significantly, they approved of the spirit in which these actions were taken. For instance, they praised the new political and legal climate in the Highlands as "the days which our fathers wished to see" (Mackay 65). The unwitting—though telling—ideological complicity between the two sides manifested itself most portentously in their nominal arguments over the validity of circumstantial evidence. It was in debating this issue that the parties elicited a nascent cultural trend by symbolically marginalizing and romanticizing the Highlands, linking the Highlands to witness testimony in the process.

On the surface, the appeal to circumstantial evidence was not without controversy in Scotland, especially given the particularities of Stewart's case. Defending the viability of such evidence, William Grant, the Lord Advocate and chief pursuer, cited trials in 1718 and 1750 as precedents for its use in Scotland (114–16).[44] Later commentators, however, were less sanguine about its applicability in the Stewart Trial. One, writing later in the eighteenth century, objected that "[t]he circumstances from which the prosecutors inferred the prisoner's accession to this murder, may perhaps be fit enough to excite a suspicion of guilt in the speculations of the closet, but I apprehend them to be in the highest degree improper and dangerous, to be produced as evidence to affect the life or fortune of a prisoner in the tribunal of justice."[45]

Crucially, though, as I discuss below, the pursuers, the defenders, and later commentators all seemed to recognize that "probability"—the sine qua non of circumstantial evidence—served here to furnish proof for this particular trial as well as for Scotland's disavowal of retrogressive (i.e., Highland) social customs and of primitive evidential standards. Indeed, the parties' recourse to probability represented not only a circumvention of witness testimony, but also Highland Scotland's social progress into a more enlightened, ideologically "British" age. For instance, Stewart's defenders marshaled perfunctory and largely passé arguments against the reliability of circumstances, but acknowledged its viability at a deeper level by insisting with the pursuers on the supremacy of facts and the attendant unreliability of witness testimony. The pursuers' distrust of testimony revealed itself in their heuristic of circumstantial "facts which speak for themselves," whereas the defenders divulged a similar inclination in their attempt to sully the prosecution's evidence by intrinsically associating such animated facts with witness experience and an im-probable Highland mystique.

Grant was the primary exponent of the circumstantial case against Stewart. He strung together a story about how Stewart and Colin Campbell of Glenure feuded in the months prior to the crime, how locals heard Stewart hurling invectives against Glenure, and how they saw Stewart conspiring with his nephew Alan Breck shortly before the murder. Grant maintained that there was sufficient evidence to show that Stewart had illegally harbored firearms, that he allowed the flamboyant Alan to wear his clothes during the murder, and that he arranged for the fugitive to receive money to flee safely to France. In all of these points, and in anticipation of Bentham's evidential doctrines of the late eighteenth and early nineteenth centuries, Grant's insistence upon objective standards of evidence conjured a speculative process in which reasonable reconstruction of the facts displaced firsthand experience of the events.[46] Hence, by means of certain undisputed claims—that witnesses saw Stewart quarreling with Glenure, that Stewart possessed weapons, and that Alan Breck had recently been seen in the neighborhood conversing with his uncle—Grant wove together a compelling chain of associations which sequentially bound discrete fragments of information to the corporate body of evidence. This narrative strategy intrinsically based itself on the inductive reasoning employed by juries rather than the putatively direct experience associated with witnesses.

One of the more symptomatic indications of the axiomatic split between jury and witness perspectives in this trial was to be found in the testimony of a local peasant, John Breck Maccoll. Consistent with the principle that witnesses report on what they had seen or heard, John Breck testified that Alan Breck had appeared to him a couple of times in the days following the murder, and that Alan had responded evasively to John's questions on that subject. However, John also placed himself in a superior adjudicative position with respect to the facts to which he testified by revealing that he had been speculating about Alan's culpability with other members of the community. His de facto assumption of judicial robes became apparent in his account of an exchange with a female peasant and kinswoman from his neighborhood:

Upon the evening of the . . . 16th day of May last, Katharine Maccoll, spouse to Hugh Maccoll . . . told [John Breck] that she had seen a man in the heugh [or deep, hollow place] of Corrynakeigh that day, at some distance, and was greatly frighted: . . . [John] told her, there used to be bogles [or specters] seen in that place, but she must take no notice of what she had seen, for fear of frighting the women of the town, and prevent them from attending their cattle in that part; and . . . the reason of telling her so, was for fear it would be known it was Allan Breck she saw. (186)

The images and impressions that Katharine Maccoll related to John Breck—that she saw a man whom she did not presume to identify, and that she felt frightened by what she saw—agree more with the legal prescriptions of witnessing that were outlined in the eighteenth century than does John's penchant for speculating on the implications of his conversations with Alan.[47] And, consistent with the juristic reaction to such testimony during this period, John exploits Katharine's vision for its indispensable confirmation of his own case, while reducing her experience to something as immaterial as the superstitious vision of "bogles." He was able to do this less because his kinswoman spoke falsely than because, as a witness, she legally lacked either the perspective or the authority fully to comprehend what she had seen, or at least to draw conclusions from it. To be a judge or juror, John implied, is to transcend the contingency of the senses and to set one's information to work in the service of a more encompassing narrative, as illustrated by Grant and the other pursuers. Comparatively speaking, witnessing was for girls.[48]

As one of Stewart's attorneys, George Brown, tried to show, however, the facts used to condemn Stewart might also be manipulated in his defense. Brown rebutted Grant's circumstantial case by replicating Grant's narrative economy while presenting a contrary chain of events. With Grant, and in conformity with the probabilistic prejudices that were rapidly coming to assume the status of common sense (thus effacing their own historical origins), Brown agreed that facts should take precedence over fictions, and that witness testimony is suspect by its very nature. And yet, as we will see, Brown sought to convert the pursuers' finely reasoned conclusions into a form of the testimony against which they implicitly reacted. His divergence from Grant was therefore a matter of perspective rather than principle: the pursuers, he asserted, resorted to the visionary, Highland-tainted, witness-like tactics against which they reviled in endeavoring to implicate his client.

Brown imitated and implicitly parodied Grant's forensic methodology by presenting a counternarrative whose effect was to call the pursuers' circumstantial case into question. First, he averred that Stewart's character "goes far to protect him from any suspicion" of murder, since

in private life [he] was never stained by any dishonourable action. . . . Secondly, [Stewart's] guilt is still the more improbable, as he could not possibly propose any benefit by it. He was a man of too good understanding not to see that Glenure's place as factor would soon be supplied; that the strictest search would be made for the authors of this enormous crime; and that his family, as being nearly connected with the forfeited person, would be first suspected. (266–67)

If the first argument spoke to Stewart's integrity, the second spoke to his intelligence, which, crucially, was made to seem less exceptional than average, and hence (as with the evidential assumptions shaping new conceptions of the jury) normative: *anybody* in Stewart's position, Brown implied, would have known that such a crime could not escape punishment. Third, Brown showed through "written evidence, which cannot lie" (267), that at the time of the murder Stewart was in the process of taking legal action against Glenure, who had been attempting to remove the local peasantry from the lands of the forfeited estate. Brown produced letters written by Stewart to other members of the community attesting to the battle his client waged in the courts. Brown reasoned that at the time of the murder the courts had yet to rule; therefore, there was as yet, at least, no reason for physical violence, which could only have adversely affected Stewart's plaint.

By showing that the facts conscripted to testify against Stewart might also be marshaled in his defense, Brown implied that the very ductility of circumstances to competing interpretations should inspire an enlightened skepticism on the part of the jury toward the pursuers' case. In effect, Brown spun his narrative for the purpose of inciting an interpretive crisis in which the conclusions reached by *any* circumstantial inquiry appeared peripheral with respect to the received borders of solid evidence. Circumstantial narrative, he implied, intrinsically reproduced the marginality and contingency associated with the Highlands, through whose dark lens, as Samuel Johnson would later lament, "the inquirer is kept in continual suspense, and by a kind of intellectual retrogradation, knows less as he hears more."[49] Brown thus turned the logic of circumstantial evidence against itself. Grant, by contrast, implicitly maintained that circumstantial evidence promoted an economy of "improvement"—a system of narrative progress—whose appropriation of facts in the service of evidence overwhelmed any (i.e., a comparatively "Highland") state resisting it.

The circumstantial narratives proffered by the two sides intrinsically promoted two views of Highland Scotland. If Grant argued for Highland improvement, then Brown argued for Highland romance: in the Highlands, he implied, many things might be true; it is difficult there to distinguish fact from fancy. In taking up this torch for Highland romance, Brown was not only prescient but also highly astute. As he observed, the implication of Grant's "improvement" paradigm was that Stewart's guilt, circumstantially derived and socially motivated, would result less from his actual involvement with a crime whose facts, after all, remained open to dispute, than from a vested interest in expanding the domain of British justice. That is, Brown implicitly contended that evidential improvement could not be kept distinct from political motives. Indeed, Brown seemed to argue that the very form and social determinants of the evidence presented in the case had already condemned

Stewart and Highland "types" like him. The state would never exonerate Stewart as a Highlander, since the Highlands themselves were under condemnation in the wake of the Jacobite Rebellion; only as a British citizen could Stewart hope for an impartial verdict. And yet, Brown contended, the state denied such citizenship to Stewart in every phase of the trial process, from his arrest and imprisonment to the stacking of the jury with Campbells and the nature of the prosecuting evidence. In effect, Brown argued, Stewart was a victim of Britain's romance of anti-romance—the romance of progress. And "factual" evidence, he implied, was the vehicle of this (anti-) romantic economy.

Brown's insistence on the relative nature of facts thus aimed to destabilize circumstantial evidence by warping it into the image of its opposite—that is, the image of witness testimony. By conjuring a chain of circumstances that nobody could verify with certainty, Brown implied, Grant and his team transmuted themselves into the visionary agents of superstition whose remnants in the Highlands they so claimed to despise. At best, they converted themselves into secondary witnesses of animated circumstances "speaking for themselves," thus rendering their own vision as myopic as that of the direct witnesses they could not call (given the unobserved nature of the crime) and whom they therefore affected to supersede. To be sure, Brown's defense team presented a counternarrative portraying Stewart's circumstantial innocence. But even were this account tarnished by imputations of untruth (and, by Brown's argument's own standards, nothing would prevent this conclusion given that Brown arrived at his inferences in the same probative manner as the pursuers), the defense would presumably make its case simply by raising a reasonable doubt in the minds of the jurors. Indeed, after the advent of adversarial procedures in the eighteenth-century criminal trial, the defense would typically find itself less concerned with the truth of its own case than with the falsehood of the prosecution's. In this respect, Brown's rebuttal in one of the early landmark cases regarding the legality of circumstantial evidence was prototypical of the kind of arguments jurists would henceforth marshal against it as a matter of course.

And yet, two issues Brown implicitly raised in elaborating his argument implicate him in the modernizing attitudes held by the pursuers, attitudes which demonized James and the Stewart clan. First, and most simply, the circumstantial case Brown made in order to refute his opponents only further legitimated circumstantial evidence as grounds of proof. So, by making a probabilistic argument against a judicial overreliance on probabilism, Brown only extended its scope. In effect, he seemed to acknowledge the sway of probabilistic techniques in court—the kinds of techniques which, in economic and political circles, were being used to transform Highland society and alarm natives like James. (I discuss these techniques more fully in Chapter 3.) And, by using them himself, he seemed to confirm the inexorable course of progress.

The second and subtler issue surrounding the Stewart Trial with respect to the logic of modernization is that it effectively delimited the line beyond which probability passes into doubt—indeed, the line demarcating the terrain stretching "beyond reasonable doubt"—as the border separating the civility of disinterested judgment from the nether vagaries of direct, testimonial experience. This line of demarcation evoked a structure of feeling that separated Enlightenment schemes of progress from damning associations of Highland retrogression. This last point, which was crucial in every way to Brown's argument, actually reveals a powerful affinity between Stewart's defenders and the arguments which Grant and his team of pursuers marshaled against Stewart. In defending a Highlander through a probabilistic argument that painted the pursuers in the renegade plaids which the pursuers in turn attributed to the Highlands, Brown implicitly condemned the Highlands by connecting them with the unruliness of unreflected, unimproved, im-probable (i.e., witness) experience. Hence, despite their differences, and despite their varying positions on romance (i.e., the romance of progress *versus* the romance of the critique of progress), the pursuers and defenders each condemned the Highlands. Grant and other British citizens with a vivid memory of the '45 identified the region with the irrational assault on the government and with images of violence, clanship, and feudalism. For Brown, however, the Highland tactics of feudal power adopted by the pursuers and the bench represented, if anything, a more insidious and pervasive propensity toward the type of witness authority which threatened the very structure of factual evidence and, as a consequence, truth itself.[50] To this extent, Brown effectively yoked the shadowy Highlands to the Enlightenment conception of evidence as the experiential component that advocates on both sides of the Stewart case and, in a sense, advocates forever after, would need to deny in order to substantiate their own claims to truth. The Highlands, for Grant, represented a place of the recalcitrant past; for Brown, however, they seemed to represent an infectious spirit of romance which haunted the institutional present and consequently threatened the future.

Both sides in this trial, then, deemed direct experience suspect, whether transmitted by witnesses, observers, advocates, or circumstances; "facts" preserved their supremacy over "fictions"; and "improvement" represented a worthy ambition provided it put an end to the prejudice, mysticism, and superstition associated with the Highlands. The defenders and their apologists suggested that the pursuers' case was flawed, primarily because it reverted into the primitive Highland forms—the animistic volubility of circumstances (or their power to "speak for themselves") and the demagoguery of folksy narrative—which it affected to transcend. The point I wish to underline is that a consistent myth emerged out of the differences of opinion and perspective expressed in this trial: both parties linked and transported the Highlands and witness experience to the far regions of an enlightened empire in which objectivity and progress mutually confirmed each other. Moreover, this myth arose in conjunction with another great eighteenth-century article of faith: the presumption of evidence as determined through disinterested judgment. This conception united the Scottish and English legal systems (and, indeed, legal systems throughout Europe and the American colonies) despite their historical and institutional differences. The hydra of Highland romance and witness testimony conjured in the Stewart Trial formed the direct obverse of the evidential, progressive ideology emerging in law. And, as we will see in subsequent chapters, the category of direct experience would acquire an uncanny force, an alluring improbability, as it began to haunt knowledge from this remote, "Highland" corner of the evidential (and institutional) imaginary.

Ironically, even though Stewart was convicted and hanged, the defense enjoyed the partial fulfillment of its wish for evidential transparency in the manner in which local authorities displayed James's body. One of the trial's historians relates that after James's execution, his "dead body was hung in chains . . . till it began to fall in pieces," at which point it was reattached "with wire for tendons. Years passed, and the skeleton still rattled on the gibbet. In 1755 it fell, and the officers of State thought it necessary not only to replace it on the gibbet, but to institute inquiries as to the circumstances of its fall; and then it vanished mysteriously," supposedly repossessed by members of the family (Mackay 40). The gibbet was thrown into a river and washed ashore several miles downstream. The alleged murderer, Alan Breck, seems to have stayed in France for the most part, reappearing as a historical personage in Walter Scott's preface to *Rob Roy* (1817) and as a dashing figure in Stevenson's *Kidnapped* and *Catriona* (as I discuss in Chapter 2). As far as the case itself is concerned, it would pass into local legend: Mackay relates that 150 years later the trial was "still a common conversational topic" even though "very few of the inhabitants of Appin . . . ha[d] ever seen any printed account of [it]" (365).[51]

From the standpoint of a burgeoning Highland cultural mystique, the most compelling aspect of the case concerns the manner in which both the pursuers and the defenders delimited the Highlands as a mystified place of witness experience. While the legacy of this experiential geography in the cultural phenomenon of Highlandism would eventually overshadow the trial altogether, the circumstantially derived verdict against James Stewart tells us an important story. It recounts the emergence of modern evidentiary codes throughout Europe (despite the different legal systems and traditions), and it crystallizes the cultural evolution of the Scottish Highlands as a place associated with experience and romance. It also foretells the broader, if more diffusive, decay and "romantick" revival of experience in modernity.

The Stewart Trial thus presents what Walter Benjamin would call a "dialectical image" of the story of experience during and after the Enlightenment; that is, the trial distills the historical process whereby experience fell into ruin and acquired a commensurately heightened allure.[52] While this dynamic far exceeds the unique instance of the Appin Murder, we will see in the next chapter how the fragmented residues of the case in local and international memory attest to its symbolic significance in shaping this complex image.

Chapter 2

Aftershocks of the Appin Murder
Scott, Stevenson, and "Storytell[ing]"

"Experience has fallen in value," Walter Benjamin lamented in his 1936 essay "The Storyteller," perhaps modernity's most famous jeremiad on the decay of experience.

> And it looks as if it may fall into bottomlessness. . . . Wasn't it noticeable at the end of the [First World W]ar that men who returned from the battlefield had grown silent—not richer but poorer in communicable experience?. . . And there was nothing remarkable about that. For never has experience been more thoroughly belied than strategic experience was belied by tactical warfare, economic experience by inflation, bodily experience by mechanical warfare, moral experience by those in power. A generation that had gone to school on horse-drawn streetcars now stood under the open sky in a landscape where nothing remained unchanged but the clouds and, beneath those clouds, in a field of force of destructive torrents and explosions, the tiny, fragile human body.[1]

In this passage, the nature of experience is complex and elusive. It designates both a phenomenological immersion in the world—the experience of the "fragile body" beneath "destructive torrents"—and an epistemological mastery of that world, providing a knowledgeable perspective onto the chaos of experience. As such, the passage implicitly plays up the dissociation of sensibility between perception (e.g., of "explosions") and knowledge. And in doing so, it conjures the institutional status of evidence which, during the eighteenth century, precipitated this dissociation by widening the gap between witnesses and jurors, or between those who experience and those who know.

As we have seen, this institutional division bears a history; so does Benjamin's essay. These histories intersect, compellingly, in the Stewart Trial. Granted, they do not do so in any obvious or self-evident way, and to that extent they might be said to perpetuate the rupture of experience from knowledge: the "experience" of reading Benjamin's essay does not necessarily conduce to "knowledge" of the sources in which it is implicated. Rather, this intersection of evidence and "The Storyteller" in the Stewart Trial occurs through an exploration of fragments.

Benjamin felt drawn toward fragments. He orchestrated a poetics of the fragment in his magnum opus *The Arcades Project*, which cobbled together thousands of historical, aesthetic, and architectural excerpts pertaining to nineteenth-century Paris. From these, Benjamin crafted a mosaic of voices and perspectives from which he hoped to instill in his readers an appreciation of the fragmentary nature of experience in modernity—of the heterogeneous composite of sensations to which experience had been reduced due to commodity capitalism, the hegemony of scientistic thought, and so on. At the same time, however, he wished to impart an understanding of these modern forces, and to inspire an epiphany regarding the experience of fragmentation which, ironically, alienated human subjects increasingly shared.[2] Reading *The Arcades Project*, and "getting it," presumably would instill such an epiphany.

Though conceived on a much smaller scale, "The Storyteller" (which Benjamin wrote and revised while assembling *The Arcades Project*) works toward a similar end. The decline of experience, he postulated, "has been going on for a long time." Taking as his vehicle the purported decay of oral narrative tradition, Benjamin characterizes this experiential anomie as "a concomitant of the secular productive forces of history" which divide laborers from capitalists, specialists in one field from those in another, and "narrative from the realm of living speech" (146). This is why, he argues, the novel emerges in its modern form in the eighteenth and nineteenth centuries: its subject matter, mass production, profitability to authors, and consumption by solitary readers all reflect the divisive, fragment-producing forces of industrial society and the latter's relations of private property. However, he observes, the situation is not entirely bleak: the disappearance of traditional storytelling and, with it, a conception of collective experience is "making it possible to find a new beauty in what is vanishing" (146). The collective consciousness of decay generates the type of communal sentiment reputedly under siege. As a sign of this redemptive possibility, Benjamin points to the vestiges of storytelling (and hence of collectivity) in modernity "in Leskov [and] in Hauff, in Poe [and] in Stevenson" (162). He concludes his essay on this note of hope.

It is in this irenic conclusion where we may discern the lineaments of the Stewart Trial, specifically in the reference to Stevenson. Though he was a fine storyteller, Stevenson's is the one name that seems out of place in this context. After all, Benjamin's essay directly addresses the work of Nikolai Leskov, and Wilhelm Hauff was well known for his early nineteenth-century fairy stories. Poe's inclusion seems logical if only because of his powerful influence on Charles Baudelaire, who, in Benjamin's mind, was the quintessential figure of burgeoning Parisian modernism during the era of the arcades.[3] But Stevenson? True, Stevenson stories like "Thrawn Janet" possess a strong, demotic flavor reminiscent of Leskov or Hauff, but Benjamin never speaks of these stories, here or elsewhere. He seems to have appreciated Stevenson more for his other work, notably the essay "A Plea for Gas Lamps," which addresses nineteenth-century Paris, and *The Master of Ballantrae*, Stevenson's most complex novel. Still, it is in the context of storytelling that Benjamin elicits Stevenson, converting him into a metonym of a quality of experience which is richer than what modernity typically affords, but immanent to those cultural critics who know how to perceive it. In this respect, Stevenson's elliptical inclusion also functions metonymically as a key to Benjamin's essay: just as the massive *Arcades Project* requires its readers to intuit the design of modernity from the fragments of nineteenth-century Paris, so here readers must reconcile Stevenson's place beside Leskov, Hauff, and Poe.

So, where does Stevenson most resemble a storyteller implicitly engaged with the problem of experience? The answer probably lies less in Stevenson's stories per se than in the companion novels which delve into the Appin Murder and the accompanying Stewart Trial. *Kidnapped* and *Catriona* are not "stories" in the traditional sense of short (and perhaps orally transmitted) narratives, but they possess traits which Benjamin most centrally identifies with storytelling. For one thing, their first-person narrative resists the clinical objectivity associated with the *Bildungsroman*: unlike Walter Scott's titular protagonist Edward Waverley, Stevenson's David Balfour does not distill the "real, historical relationships" of his age in a way which Georg Lukács triumphantly identifies with the characters of literary realism.[4] Instead, David resembles Benjamin's itinerant *raconteur*, "the man who finds his way around the world without getting too deeply involved with it" (144–45). For Benjamin, storytellers were those individuals who, deeply integrated in communities, embarked on adventures and then returned bearing the tales of their travels. The growing complexity of modernity (Benjamin vividly refers, we recall, to the heavy artillery explosions of World War I) made it more difficult for these individuals to communicate the substance of their experience in any meaningful or accessible way, leading to the decline of storytelling. Stevenson's David Balfour does not venture into war, but he does present to us the augmenting complexity (and corruption) of his increasingly "evidential" and modernizing society. In this respect, he closely models Scott's Highland traveler Frank Osbaldistone of *Rob Roy* (1817), who too, as I discuss below, presents us with a first-person narrative defying the sweeping objectivity which purportedly typifies *Waverley*.

The second important feature of storytelling found in Stevenson's novels concerns their professed devotion to wisdom. Benjamin observes that the storyteller, unlike the novelist, is someone "who has counsel for his readers" (145). At the conclusion of *Catriona*, when David begins speaking in the second person, we learn that he has related these narratives for the purpose of transmitting them to his posterity, in whose places we have vicariously been sitting. The message he conveys ultimately amounts to little more than a sales pitch for the value of experience: "For the life of man upon this world of ours is a funny business. They talk of the angels weeping; but I think they must more often be holding their sides, as they look on; and there was one thing I determined to do when I began this long story, and that was to tell out everything as it befell."[5] If this moral fails to bring angels to tears, then it only strengthens the link to Scott's *Rob Roy*, in which the protagonist gestures flaccidly toward a lesson of obedience which the narrative barely sustains.

I underscore the connection between Stevenson's companion novels and *Rob Roy* because they bear features of Benjaminian storytelling, and because they occupy themselves with the Appin Murder and accompanying Stewart Trial. In *Rob Roy*, this motif is understated, but key references to Alan Breck in Scott's Introduction play out in the novel's themes, episodes, and characters. To this extent, these novels attest to the legacy of the Stewart Trial while also foregrounding with Benjamin the problematic rupture of experience from knowledge. They do so, moreover, from the perspective of storytelling. However, this is not to say that Scott, Stevenson, and Benjamin frame the Stewart Trial, experience, or storytelling in the same way. We will see, in fact, how the three writers present something of a Scottish stagist history when read alongside each other. In *Rob Roy*, the "first stage" of this history, the remnants of the Stewart Trial exert an uncanny power which unsettles the complacency of the disinterested judgment associated with juries. In *Kidnapped* and (especially) *Catriona*, Stevenson takes pains not only to present uncanny fragments, but to identify his narrator (and narratives) with them, suggesting not only the failure of knowledge but also the persistence of alternative modes of understanding. Benjamin, finally, reads modernity as an elaborate fragment made whole; for him, Stevenson's alternative modality already (and somewhat mystically) informs the everyday. Hence, from Scott's disturbing reminder of the limits of progressive ideology, we arrive with Benjamin at a radical image of progress turned from the divisive exigencies of production to the collective pulsations of experience.

Of Evidence and Fragments

Like Benjamin, Walter Scott felt drawn toward fragments. Of course, for him these fragments took the form of Scottish cultural remnants rather than Parisian artifacts. As Scott's critics have observed, his presentation of "local color" often reflected the sheen, what James Buzard calls the "finish," of the commodity, presenting Scottish history (most famously of the Highlands, e.g., in *Waverley*) as picturesque and antiquated.[6] In this respect, Scott's novels anticipated Benjamin's characterization of commodities as fossils—that is, as husks bearing the imprint of the social activity which produced them, and which they then outlived.[7]

And yet, critics have also remarked that *Rob Roy* unsettles the tidy fossilization of culture. There, in Scott's reprisal of the Highland motif, clan society is not embalmed, but rather migrates from the north into the bustle of modern society, where it alters the meaning of "local color."[8] No longer evoking the vestiges of history, cultural fragments in *Rob Roy* instead bespeak an uncanny relation to a present whose forces we perceive only in snatches. As a result, as Jane Millgate provocatively notes, "[t]he reading of *Rob Roy* is not a comfortable experience. Although the narrative design appears conventional, there is a persistent sense of disturbance at deeper levels, and the satisfactions of a romance story ending in marriage are modified by the presence of much that is dark, violent, and unredeemed."[9]

What in this novel produces such discomfort, and why? As Millgate mentions, it is not the "narrative design" per se, which appears "conventional" enough. Here, as in *Waverley*, a callow protagonist ventures into the northern wilds, confronts Highland savagery with a mixture of fascination and disgust, and eventually returns to more civilized territory where he marries and settles, having become "a sadder and wiser man" in the mode of Coleridge's mariner.[10] In executing this design, Scott seems almost to have regressed: Donald Davie famously proclaimed in 1961 that "*Rob Roy*, written four years after the appearance of *Waverley*, challenges comparison with that masterpiece and comes badly out of the comparison."[11] Others, citing the later novel's gerrymandered design, have widely agreed.[12] Here one is tempted to propose the mock equation that *Rob Roy* equals *Waverley* plus gallstones (from which Scott suffered as he composed the narrative).

Scott actually concocts a similar calculus in *Rob Roy* in the person of Owen, the clerk of the protagonist's father: "Mr. Francis seems to understand the fundamental principle of all moral accounting, the great ethic rule of three. Let A do to B, as he would have B do to him; the product will give the rule of conduct required."[13] Scott makes fun of such arithmetical moralizing, which actually took serious form in the moral philosophy of Francis Hutcheson.[14] Scott departs from this philosophy much as he does from *Waverly*, venting (in Millgate's words) "much that is dark, violent, and unredeemed" in the earlier novel. For instance, Ian Duncan suggests that Scott's narrative imports clan spirit into the progressive ideology of commerce, with the novel's title character serving as the ultimate emblem of this contagion. Scott's Rob, he says, seems "not

entirely [to] belong in the book that bears his name. Far from occupying the foreground or centre of the narrative he seems to be at once
nowhere and everywhere in it . . ." ("Introduction" to *Rob Roy*, xii–xiii).
And, while Rob is the novel's iconic figure of Highland romance and
primitive society, he also functions as its shrewdest trader, "the archetype
of economic man" (xxvi). As the Glasgow merchant (and, fittingly, Rob's
kinsman) Nicol Jarvie tells Scott's protagonist Frank, Scottish Lowland
and Highland societies are indeed historically quite distinct. And yet,
the harshness of the Highland climate and the immunity of the region
to "honest" improvements of agriculture breed in men like Rob an
opportunistic spirit which blurs the line between freebooting and stock-
jobbing. So, while Rob had once worked as "a weel-doing, pains-taking
drover" who was "civil and just in his dealings," when "the times cam[e]
hard . . . Rob was venturesome" (302). His property seized by Lowland
creditors, Rob "looked east, west, south, north, and saw neither hauld
nor hope" and thus "became a levier of black-mail," selling himself and
his "band o' blue-bonnets" to any party willing to pay for his services
(303). With George I having withdrawn the Highland chiefs' pensions,
the blackmailing spirit prevailing in the Highlands rapidly turned
against the British government, selling itself to the Lowland Scottish and
English Jacobite sponsors of the 1715 rebellion (304–8). Not that this
would involve Rob directly. In true Highland spirit, "Rob is for his ain
hand . . . [and will] take the side that suits him best" (307). Ultimately,
this would prove to be the side of the king: for Scott's Rob, Jacobitism
was smart business.

Rob's actions collapse the reputed distance between Highland habi-
tudes and modern (in this case, commercial) norms.[15] In contrast with
the more historically minded *Waverley*, the universality of self-interest in
Rob Roy brings the Highlands into propinquity not only with Glasgow,
but also with London. In Franco Moretti's words, "the 'Before-and-After'
[of *Waverley*] is transformed into an 'Alongside.'"[16]

And commerce is not the only way in which this uncanny approximation occurs. Bruce Beiderwell analyzes a similar phenomenon with
respect to questions of legality in Scott's novel. He argues that while
Scott in *Rob Roy* "never calls into question the rightful power of king and
parliament in early post-union Scotland," he does highlight the competing models of justice which any "union" involves as well as the tendency
of civilized jurisprudence to function according to principles of revenge
and sacrifice.[17] Drawing implicitly on expansive critiques of legal violence by Jean-François Lyotard, René Girard, and Benjamin, Beiderwell
makes his case by turning his attention to perhaps the most violent and
disturbing episode in the novel—the murder of Morris.[18] Craven agent
of the villainous Rashleigh (who is scheming to ruin Frank's father and

incite the bankrupt Highland chiefs to rebellion), Morris has been taken hostage by Helen Macgregor, Rob's "Amazon" of a wife (*Rob Roy* 349), as security for her captured husband. There will be no such exchange, however. Decrying the British government which has seized her property and left her "neither name nor fame" (the Macgregor name being blacklisted and replaced by the more tepid "Campbell"), and "neither house nor hold, blanket nor bedding, cattle to feed us, or flocks to clothe us" (349), Helen has Morris bound, weighted, and tossed from a cliff into a loch, where he drowns. Scott punctuates the ferocity of the deed by providing detailed descriptions of Morris's desperation and Frank's horror. Still, as savage as this deed may appear to Frank and to Scott's readers, Beiderwell remarks that Morris represents for Helen "a history of treachery against her people, a representative of laws 'from which they had often experienced severity, but never protection'" (Beiderwell 50–51). What Helen does to Morris has already been done to her through legal channels. In this respect, and mirroring the "venturesome" Rob, Helen's barbarous act reflects the progressive hegemony it means to oppose.

Scott's disclosure of the Highland aura accruing to commerce and law is linked to a third area of contagion. This area concerns the discursive division—or, in this case, the collapsed distinction—of enlightenment and romance. Lukács famously set the tone for this issue when he argued that Scott's novels achieve "a renunciation of Romanticism" in the name of "a higher development of the realist literary traditions of the Enlightenment."[19] Contemporary critics often preserve this distinction while overturning Lukács's conclusion. It has become fashionable, Andrew Lincoln observes, to portray Scott as complicit with a larger romantic project of British imperialism in the nineteenth century. "Katie Trumpener's wide-ranging account of the Romantic novel, for example, and Saree Makdisi's ambitious survey of Romantic imperialism" have powerfully demonstrated the complicity of romanticism with the forces of empire and capital. In doing so, and in making Scott one of their central exhibits, these scholars energize "the traditional view of Scott as combining nostalgia for lost traditions with a satisfied acceptance of progress."[20] Far from renouncing romanticism, as Lukács suggests, Scott embraces and extends it.

However, as Lincoln shows, what is often argued of *Waverley* is far more tenuous when applied to *Rob Roy*. This later novel depicts the anxieties rather than the complacencies associated with empire: it "seems at least as concerned with the uneven economic and social development within the new Union, with the prospects for commercial expansion, and with the effects of British power on its periphery" (Lincoln 43). The Highlands thus symbolically represent the plight of colonized communities elsewhere, notably in India, in the south Pacific, in military "clashes with American Indians," and even in industrializing British cities like London, Manchester, and Glasgow and the oppression there of an emergent "urban proletariat" (46). This is more in keeping with Lukács's contention that "Scott ranks among those honest Tories in the England of his time who exonerate nothing in the development of capitalism, who not only see clearly, but also deeply sympathise with the unending misery of the people which the collapse of the old England brings in its wake" (Lukács 95). In this way, the novel restores the former view of Scott, all while preserving the conventional associations of "enlightenment" and "romance": Scott's residually romantic discourse in *Rob Roy* actually contemns the logic of colonization even as the demystifying arguments proffered by Trumpener, Makdisi, et al. become (by their own terms) "romantic" in their "colonizing" image of Scott as an imperial apologist.

Hence, as with the cases of commerce and law, and as personified by Rob himself in Scott's novel, "imperial romance" migrates back and forth across the border separating the Highlands from modernity. If *Waverley* sets up seemingly convenient categories through which to interpret all of Scott's fiction *in toto*, then *Rob Roy* takes them apart. In doing so, this later novel accentuates the point which I suggest in my brief and schematic reading of *Waverley* in the Introduction: Scott's work conduces less to "knowledge" of the type associated with juries than to an "experience" in the mode of witnesses. That is, for all the mobility of their protagonists, Scott's novels do not map out the clear dimensions of modernity as much as dramatize the insufficiency of our attempts at doing so. And so it is that in matters of commerce, law, and enlightenment, civil society comes out appearing as clannish as the primitive Highland tribes which it historically supersedes. Those who purport to know are themselves witnesses to something they cannot fully grasp.

In *Rob Roy*, these dynamics operate according to a logic of the uncanny: objects and categories which are familiar to us (e.g., primitive *versus* modern, Highland *versus* Lowland) appear increasingly alien the longer we reflect on them. However, while customary items become strange, a recognizable pattern also emerges from out of the maze. Scott's disclosure of clannish features of modern commerce, justice, and pretensions to enlightenment (or the romance of antiromance) reiterates the key motifs of the Stewart Trial, especially as it was characterized by Stewart's defenders. And, as it turns out, this is far from an incidental similarity. In his 1829 Introduction to *Rob Roy*, Scott reveals that his narrative is a composite of fragments: he professes to have selected the material for his story "from many anecdotes of Rob Roy, which were, and may still be, current among the mountains where he flourished" (53). One of these fragments is the "remarkable Highland story" of the Appin Murder and the subsequent trial. Scott briefly relates how James Stewart "was tried as being accessory to the murder, and condemned and executed upon very doubtful evidence" (49). From here, he tells of how one of Rob's descendants, James Mohr Drummond, who fled to France after being found guilty of abducting a Lowland heiress, conspired with the relatives of the murdered Colin Campbell to capture the fugitive Alan Breck Stewart, who had also escaped to France. After receiving a tip from "two country-men," Alan escaped James Mohr's clutches and thereafter "threatened to put [Mohr] to death in revenge . . ." (50).

This story bears an overdetermined significance in Scott's account. On the one hand, Scott recounts it for the purpose, seemingly, of describing the diminished persistence of internecine conflict between the clans. Once, he suggests, such strife mobilized large groups of gallant heroes; in the past century, it even implicated an entire nation (e.g., in the Jacobite conflicts of 1715 and 1745). Now, however, it has degenerated into a spitting match between shriveled expatriate cons. In a footnote to his Introduction, Scott punctuates this impression with a picturesque description of the vitiated Alan Breck: "a friend" of Scott's "found, sitting by the fire" of a residence in Paris "a tall, thin, raw-boned, grim-looking old man. . . . His visage was strongly marked by the irregular projections of the cheek-bones and chin. His eyes were grey. His grizzled hair exhibited marks of having been red, and his complexion was weather-beaten, and remarkably freckled." The friend struck up a conversation with Alan Breck about "the streets and squares of Paris," to which "the old soldier" replied, "Deil ane o' them is worth the Hie street of Edinburgh!" Scott adds here that the enervated warrior "lived decently on his little pension, and had, in no subsequent period of his life, shown anything of the savage mood, in which he is generally believed to have assassinated the enemy and oppressor, as he supposed him, of his family and clan" (460n). This picture conforms with the image which Scott allegedly propagates of petrified Highland society in *Waverley*.

However, there is a far more radical dimension of the Stewart Trial which winds its way through *Rob Roy*. While Scott's Introduction, for instance, mostly recounts the history of Rob and his clan, its opening description of "clan MacGregor" strikes a far more general chord which draws provocatively from popular motifs of the Stewart Trial. Way back in 787, Scott tells us, Rob's descendants went by the name of "Clan Alpine," or family of the mountains, metonymically representing all Highlanders. In a later period, and in anticipation of Colin Campbell's murder in the fateful spring of 1752, the Earl of Argyle and a fellow neighbor managed legally to usurp the MacGregor lands—thus symbolically precipitating the course of Highland improvement. Spited clan members "defended themselves by force, and occasionally gained advantages, which they used cruelly enough" (7). However, also foreshadowing the events of 1752, the clan's conduct "was studiously represented at the capital [*sic*] as arising from an untamable and innate ferocity, which nothing, it was said, could remedy, save cutting off the tribe of MacGregor root and branch" (7). The MacGregors even murdered one John Drummond, "a forester of the royal forest of Glenartney," which incited "an act of the Privy Council, directing another crusade against the 'wicked clan Gregor, so long continuing in blood, slaughter, theft, and robbery'" (7). Reprising the argument of George Brown, Stewart's defender, Scott remarks that "[o]ther occasions frequently occurred, in which the MacGregors testified contempt for the laws, from which they had often experienced severity, but never protection" (7).

In the Introduction alone, Scott thus lights on the themes of improvement, aggression, and official denunciation which were the central elements of the Stewart Trial. He does so, moreover, by mentioning the trial's key players by name (including William Grant, though with respect to a different case).[21] While not commenting on the trial per se in his analysis of justice in *Rob Roy*, Beiderwell shows how the themes we identify with the trial permeate the entire novel. Accused of high treason (like other Scott protagonists Edward Waverley and, from *Old Mortality*, Henry Morton) early in the story, Frank declares that "it is the most provoking thing on earth, that every person will take it for granted that I am accessory to a crime," much like Alan Breck (*Rob Roy* 164; Beiderwell 47). Later, when Helen MacGregor wastes Morris, Beiderwell comments that she "aggressively invokes an 'old' time 'day of revenge' as a model of her present authority" (50), much as James Stewart allegedly did in executing Glenure. Furthermore, as Brown vehemently argued in Stewart's defense, Beiderwell comments on the injustice implicit to the enforcement as well as the infraction of law: in Helen's mind, "civilized laws" condemn rather than immure Morris from his association with the powers that have left her and her clan "neither name nor fame," "for legal authorities sanction Morris's 'crime.'. . . [I]n killing Morris, [she thus] passes judgment on the justice she has been subject to" (Beiderwell 52). The ambivalent reaction which this episode seems to generate in its readers—horror coupled with voyeuristic fascination; feelings of condemnation for an action with which one sympathizes at some level—mirrors the dynamic as it played out in the Stewart Trial. Stewart's appropriation of justice in conspiring against Glenure was not only decried by the court, but it incited the court to a reflexive gesture as its symbolic verdict punished the Highland conception of justice to which "British" citizens had been subjected, most recently with the '45.[22]

Ultimately, and perhaps most significantly, these matters of uncanny approximation and (in)justice in Scott's novel devolve on questions of evidence. And, as with the Stewart Trial, "evidence" here possesses a symbolic as well as a literal significance. In the trial, we recall, circumstantial evidence (of "doubtful" validity, Scott claims) determined Stewart's guilt. More importantly, William Grant and his team of pursuers portrayed the recourse to circumstantial evidence as proof of modern Britain's supersession of primitive evidential codes. For Grant, as we discussed, circumstantial evidence accommodated a romantic history of British improvement, whereas for George Brown and his team of defenders such evidence bore a discomfiting similarity to the testimony on which it purportedly "improved." Even so, Brown appealed to favorable "circumstances" of his own, thus reaffirming the ideological value of evidence. Such ideological currency was practically sufficient of itself to send James Stewart and, vicariously, his primitive society to the gallows.

Scott's novel reopens this wound by telling its tale through the medium of a myopic, first-person narrator—in effect, through the faulty lens of an unimproved witness. Duncan calls this narrative device a "pioneering" achievement of Scott's, presenting as it does a historically situated character "whose modes of feeling and telling (including his failures of telling) are themselves part of the story" ("Introduction," xiii).[23] However, in Alexander Welsh's estimation, Scott's move from third-person narration in *Waverley* to first-person in *Rob Roy* was rather more regressive in character. Adopting the attitude of emergent Enlightenment evidentiary codes, Welsh reasons that while any narrator "may lie or be mistaken . . . verbal representations can be made in such a way as to prove a certain case." The strongest narratives are thus those which emulate the position of attorneys arguing before a jury of readers, and which therefore "openly distrust direct testimony."[24] He makes his own case on this score by conducting an extended reading of *Waverley*. Such a case would be harder to make in *Rob Roy*; or rather, it would be made in negative, by showing the novel's patented failures.[25] Lincoln takes this tactic one step further, arguing that Scott conscientiously warps the narrative perspective as a means of underscoring how the novel's "polite English narrator . . . is shaped by the values of a system of [commercial and imperial] power" which works over everything under its auspices. And, by enabling this narrator to prattle on, Scott plays the part of an advocate cross-examining his witness: the narrative essentially damns itself ("Scott and Empire," 44).

While these critics make strong arguments for the literal problem of evidence in *Rob Roy*, there is an additional, symbolic aspect of the problem which supersedes questions of truth and falsehood, and which operates far more subtly than through the exercise of imperial power. This aspect concerns the rupture of experience from knowledge—a split which frustrates the possession of truth, and which affects colonizers and colonized alike. Jane Millgate points to this rupture by highlighting an apparent paradox in the figure of Scott's narrator: "The hero, though young, courageous, and quick to take the offensive, is repeatedly involved in scenes of conflict and bloodshed not as actor but as powerless witness. . . ." By taking the perspective of the disenfranchised witness, "the private action" of the narrative, "though played out against important historical events, remains stubbornly separate from them." Hence, while the text is "marvelous in its eyewitness fidelity," it remains "resolutely resistant to . . . opportunities for commentary, analysis, and moralization."[26] All of this lends the narrative an unsettling quality which implies that knowledge, truth, and power are perpetually elsewhere, inaccessible to narrator and reader alike except in the form of occasional fragments.

One telling instance of this fragmentary perspective occurs when Frank, the narrator, having heard that he is suspected of conspiring in the Jacobite Plot, appears before Justice Inglewood to set the matter straight. The evidence against Frank is largely circumstantial, consisting mostly of Frank's father's business dealings with Highland chiefs, coupled with wry innuendos Frank drops to Morris. Now, before Inglewood, Frank understands that "the tricks [he] had played to this man, Morris, had made a strong impression on his imagination; for [he] found they had been arrayed against [him] as evidence . . ." (135).[27] Frank does what he can to overturn these presumptions: "Having heard the extraordinary accusation, I replied to it, that the circumstances on which it was founded were such as could warrant no justice, or magistrate, in any attempt on my personal liberty" (136). Jobson, the attorney, contradicts Frank on this point, citing statutes which verify not only Inglewood's authority, but also the presumption of guilt. A "strange gentleman," Mr. Campbell (a.k.a. Rob Roy), comes to Frank's rescue, however, testifying on his behalf. While this testimony is sufficient to procure Frank's release, his perspective onto Campbell's presence and the events to which Rob speaks indicate just how little he truly understands:

I looked at Campbell as he uttered these words [in Frank's defense], and never recollect to have seen a more singular contrast than that between the strong daring sternness expressed in his harsh features, and the air of composed meekness and simplicity which his language assumed. There was even a slight ironical smile lurking about the corners of his mouth, which seemed, involuntarily as it were, to intimate his disdain of the quiet and peaceful character which he thought proper to assume, and which led me to entertain strange suspicions that his concern in the violence done to Morris had been something very different from that of a fellow-sufferer, or even of a mere spectator. (142)

Though Rob is technically the witness during this proceeding, Frank's position most fully reflects the Enlightenment conception of witnessing. Trapped in webs of complexity which exceed his understanding, Frank is relegated to what he sees and hears as well as to what he intuits (in this case, of "Campbell's" implication in the plot which Morris ascribes to Frank). Frank thus experiences things which he professedly cannot comprehend; and, while the reader may not be quite as obtuse, we are not given enough information fully to compensate for Frank's limitations. Hence, we, like Frank, are forced to extrapolate from the fragments of his/our experience, even as the narrative leaves Rob (with whom its secrets reside) and follows Frank on his meandering journey. The whole novel thus embraces the strategy of a detour, ultimately making its silences more powerful and disturbing than its remarkable polyphony of voices.[28]

Rob Roy presents "evidence" as Frank's "circumstantial" enemy and as a source of privileged understanding to which neither he nor we are entitled. Which is to say, especially when we recall Scott's evocative Introduction, that the novel places us in the position of James and Alan Breck Stewart, or at least on the side of James's defender, George Brown, who realized that testimony alone determined the outcome of the trial, however much it may have been disavowed by the pursuers. Indeed, as we discussed in the Introduction, the reversion of objective knowledge to contingent testimony is one of the most persistent themes of modernity. But to the extent that this theme inflects *Rob Roy*, it in turn alters the meaning of the myriad cultural remnants from which Scott cobbles together his narrative.[29] For Lukács, such remnants combine to create the "local color" of the Waverley novels, "color" through which we purportedly arrive at a greater visceral comprehension of the forces and directions of history. But if there is one thing virtually every critic agrees on, it is that *Rob Roy* is not *Waverley*; and, if in that earlier novel Scott presents a contrast between Highland and British, primitive and modern, then Scott's later narrative transforms the Highlands from a region and a chapter in history into the normative condition of modernity. That is, *Rob Roy* purveys the impression that progress and its institutional and epistemological hallmark, "evidence," are less removed from associations of clannish self-interest and myopia than productive of them. If his novel depicts the Highlands as more modern than we might typically imagine (especially in the portrait of Rob as stockjobber), then it also illustrates modernity as more benighted than an ideology of "enlightenment" comfortably admits.

Extending the Witness

Robert Louis Stevenson loved *Rob Roy*. At least, he loved it compared to *Waverley*. David Daiches tells of how Stevenson "once wrote to his father that *Guy Mannering, Rob Roy* and *The Antiquary* are 'all worth three *Waverleys.*'"[30] However, he felt baffled that Scott could have passed over the Appin Murder and subsequent Stewart Trial with such apparent brevity. As William Gray informs us, "Stevenson had been planning to write something on the murder of 'Red' Colin Campbell of Glenure . . . at least since early November 1881," almost five years prior to the publication of *Kidnapped*. That is when he wrote to his father from his temporary home in Davos, Switzerland, "asking for records of the trial . . . ." Of Scott's Introduction to *Rob Roy* and its cursory reference to the Stewart Trial, "Stevenson later commented: 'Why Scott let it escape him I do not know.'"[31] Of course, as I discuss above, it may well be that Scott did not let the trial "escape him" at all; nevertheless, it is true that Stevenson addresses the trial at far greater length than Scott, and that he interprets its legacy of witness testimony vis-à-vis Highland romance in a slightly different way. If for Scott the Stewart Trial presents one of many provocative Highland fragments which uncannily unsettle our "enlightened" consciousness, Stevenson inflates the fragment into a polemical position, enlisting the trial as a sustained testimonial against the corruptions of modernity. If the effect is no longer uncanny per se, it nevertheless amounts to a powerful complaint which attests to the problematic legacy of the Enlightenment conception of experience. It was this facet of Stevenson's work which eventually attracted Benjamin.

Kidnapped and *Catriona*, the pair of novels in which Stevenson depicts the murder and trial, seem conscientiously to engage Scott's narrative. Like *Rob Roy*'s Frank Osbaldistone, Stevenson's protagonist effectively ventures on a tour of Scotland; and, like Scott, Stevenson underscores the rapid social transformation of the Highlands in the latter half of the eighteenth century. In fact, Stevenson reportedly wrote these two novels in the place of a history of the eighteenth-century Highlands.[32] Like Scott, Stevenson integrates Rob Roy into his story, though here in the person of James More Drummond, Rob's contemptible son. Most importantly, Stevenson emulates Scott in building his tale around a comparatively unenlightened first-person narrator—or, in effect, around a witness's testimony.

Here, Stevenson goes further than Scott. Critics have long referred to *Kidnapped* and *Catriona* as the David Balfour novels, after their protagonist; these critics take their cue from Stevenson himself, who initially entitled the second novel *David Balfour*.[33] The narrator-witness plays an important symbolic role in Stevenson's tale: he personifies a "natural" perspective (in the Enlightenment tradition of natural law) against which Stevenson measures and criticizes "the corrupt legal system [and] the ubiquitous expediency and social hypocrisy [of] a debased modern Scotland."[34]

The Appin Murder and Stewart Trial are central to this portrait of "debase[ment]." Stevenson's friend and enthusiastic reader Henry James even suggested that Stevenson conclude the story with James Stewart's hanging. Stevenson did not oblige, tacking on a more conventionally "romantic" element in the love story of David and Catriona. He did, however, make the famous murder and trial the unmistakable centerpiece of the novels. Fittingly, we initially come upon them in the way a witness would—that is, by accident. *Kidnapped* opens not with the murder, but with David venturing out on his own after the death of his parents to meet his uncle. The uncle, miserly and paranoid, tries to kill David, then contracts with an avowedly trustworthy but deeply mercenary ship's captain, Hoseason, to have David transported to the New World. As the ship passes through the Hebrides, it runs over a small boat carrying Alan Breck. When Hoseason learns that Alan is carrying gold, he conspires with his crew to kill him. But David learns of Hoseason's plans and enters into a defensive and successful league with Alan. Separated from Alan after their ship runs aground off the Isle of Mull, David goes seeking his friend (symbolic of Scotland seeking its "authentic" history) in Alan's native country of Appin. This is where the story takes a dramatic turn. David comes across a small company led by Colin Campbell of Glenure, asks Glenure for directions to James Stewart's estate at Aucharn, and fields Glenure's suspicious questions regarding his interest in the local inhabitants. An instant later, David watches Glenure fall after hearing a shot. "'Oh, I am dead!' [Glenure] cried, several times over" (*Kidnapped* 108). David looks up and spies "the murderer" fleeing the scene, and begins running after him when he is diverted by Alan, who helps David escape from those in Glenure's company who are chasing him, and who believe David to be a conspirator in the crime. The remainder of the novel recounts the fugitives' journey across the West Highlands to Edinburgh, where David seeks to clear his name and legally claim his inheritance.[35]

Legal rights, however, prove to be of little emotional succor to David, and so *Catriona* picks up where *Kidnapped* leaves off: Stevenson's protagonist must clear himself of suspicion, but he also intends to testify on behalf of the fugitive Alan and the imprisoned James. He takes up his suit with William Grant, a.k.a. Lord Prestongrange, the Lord Advocate in the Stewart Trial. Grant quickly perceives David's innocence, but he wishes at all costs to prevent David from testifying and subverting his case against Alan and James. Grant goes so far as to have David captured and temporarily confined on an island off the eastern coast of Scotland. David somehow manages to escape and to make it to the trial a day before it concludes, but he never gives his testimony. Instead, he sees how ineffectual his testimony is likely to be and the corrupt ends to which it might be applied by Stewart's defenders, whom Stevenson portrays as unrepentant (and petty-minded) Jacobites. And so, coming of age, David learns sobering lessons about the bureaucratic nature of justice, its sway in Scottish society, and its instrumentalizing power over the private needs of human subjects.

The Appin Murder and Stewart Trial not only serve as the pretext of Stevenson's tale; they also ratify the epistemic, Highland geography dividing juror from witness which was delimited in the Stewart Trial. To a large extent, this geography had inscribed itself into the generic structure of the novel as a literary form. Since the eighteenth century, one of the distinguishing features of the novel's structure had been its assimilation of probabilistic techniques of representation. These techniques manifested themselves in a variety of ways, from attempts at verisimilitude to the adjudicative distancing of the narrator from his or her subject matter. In his landmark study, Ian Watt summarized what he deemed the novel's key aspect, "formal realism," "in terms of . . . the jury in a court of law. Their expectations and those of the novel reader coincide in many ways," he argues: both want to know all the circumstantial particulars, both react skeptically to the testimony of dubious characters, both "expect the witnesses to tell the story 'in his own words,'" and so on.[36] John Bender expands on the significance of this insight, commenting on these legalistic techniques in the novel and novel criticism in figures running from Henry Fielding and Samuel Richardson to Hans Vaihinger and Catherine Gallagher. The novel, he argues, "shares the impulse toward formal proof so strongly voiced in the embrace of induction by scientific theorists" of the late seventeenth century. "In point of both thematic exposition and narrative strategy . . . novels force readers into the position of neutral observers," or jurors, "arriving, probabilistically, at judgments based upon the weight of available facts and reasonable inferences."[37] This is essentially Watt's argument, but Bender reflects further on the implications of this juridical attitude. Even as novelists later in the eighteenth century attempted to bridge this divide between witness and juror, the relation of novelistic discourse to scientific factuality consigned the novel to the representation of supposedly "higher truths" that were more but, hence, less than fact on account of their patented un- (or sur-) reality. In essence, then, "factual" discourses like natural philosophy codified matters of truth, whereas the "fictive" discourse of the novel spoke to flights of imagination and, crucially, the pulsations of experience. Hence, the novel was paradoxically "higher" than factual truth (since it exceeded the limits of fact) and "lower" than it because of its irreducibility to fact.[38]

This tension became endemic to literary realism which, Fredric Jameson observes, purported to unite "the experience of daily life with a . . . well-nigh 'scientific' perspective" of the same.[39] Michael McKeon elaborates on these dynamics in his revision of Watt's thesis, remarking that realism "validates literary creation for being not history but history-like, 'true' to the only external reality" that is empirically verifiable, "but also sufficiently apart from it (hence 'probable' and 'universal') to be true to itself as well." Anticipating Bender, McKeon refers to literary truth—"poetic faith"—"as a demystified species of spirituality."[40] According to Ian Duncan, this "spiritual" dynamic sits at the very heart of late eighteenth-century romance: "Romance is the essential principle of fiction: its *difference* from a record of 'reality,' of 'everyday life.'" Because of this extrinsic quality, romance fails to measure up to a reality which it nevertheless unsettles: "The old commonplace of an antithetical relation between romance and reality, invoked by the novel in its own apologies of origin, produces a new, dialectical figure of romance as the fulcrum against which—positioned on its edge, between inside and out—reality can be turned around."[41]

This double logic—more and less than truth, higher and lower than reality—is what eventually drew Benjamin to the novel, and more expressly to Stevenson. As Benjamin recognized, novels historically came to occupy the discursive and epistemological place of the legal witness—the place at (or just beyond) the limits of the real. Of course, one problem for Benjamin of conceiving of experience in this way was that it essentially preserved the compartmentalizing, alienating structures of science and capital: in claiming a position removed from normative reality, romance perpetuated the divisive logic of property, labor, scientific methodology, and so forth. It devalued experience by consigning it to the margins—the Highland regions, so to speak—of knowledge.

For Stevenson, however, the association of literature and witnessing with "higher truth" was more palatable, even desirable. And, like his protagonist David Balfour, Stevenson embraced this quality of witness experience in *Kidnapped* and *Catriona* with a willful naïveté.[42] He attested to this purposeful gullibility in noting that the techniques of factual judgment had also been assimilated by biography. In that genre, "something like a true [hence, a true-to-life], general [and hence, probabilistic, normative] impression of the subject may at last be struck." And yet, while appreciative of such techniques, Stevenson seemed to prefer those associated with fiction, and with its biographical equivalent, "the short study," in which "the writer, having seized his [witness-like] 'point of view,' must keep his eye steadily to that. He seeks, perhaps, rather to differentiate than truly to characterise," or to achieve a critical (in Bender's words, a "higher") perspective rather than a normative one.[43]

This problematic, testimonial element (i.e., "higher," and yet subdivided, alienated, and hence, for Benjamin, normative on precisely that basis) worked its way into Stevenson's narratives about the Appin Murder and Stewart Trial. As we have seen, both the pursuers and the defenders in the Stewart Trial employed what Bender would describe as novelistic techniques of circumstantial probability. However, Stevenson calls frequent attention to the conflict between David's (and, by extension, the narrative's) witness-like naïveté and the disillusioning complexity of the world around him. In *Kidnapped*, he delineates this testimonial position at a crucial point in the novel, right before David comes across Glenure and his party. Contemplating a return to his own country rather than seeking out Alan at Stewart's estate, David catches sight of Glenure's "imperious and flushed face" and makes a monumental (and, by his own account, un-self-reflective) decision: "I had no sooner seen [Glenure and his] people coming than I made up my mind (for no reason that I can tell) to go through with my adventure" (107). He stops Glenure and asks him the way to James's farm. As Glenure stops to speak with him in bemused consternation, David hears "the shot of a firelock . . .; and with the very sound of it Glenure fell upon the road" (108). David's decision to prolong his Highland adventure is thus bound up in his witnessing of the Appin Murder; and, having stopped Glenure long enough for the shooter to aim his weapon, David also unwittingly becomes an accomplice in the crime. Seen from this perspective, *Kidnapped* is about the interventions—conscious and unconscious—of the witness. David has not conspired in the plot against Glenure, but in stopping Glenure and making him a stationary target he is complicit in it nonetheless. To this extent, the testimony of the witness (indeed, of "romance," of the novel) is brought under condemnation in the tribunal of (factual) truth.

In the later novel, *Catriona*, Stevenson underscores these "outlawed" (literally extra-legal, extra-evidential) dynamics of testimony. Still technically a fugitive, but harrowed by the vision of James Stewart's imminent and unjust execution, David determines to seek out Grant and announce his intention to testify for Stewart's defenders. Aware of the boldness of this decision, David no sooner sets his plan in motion than he catches sight of "a gibbet and two men hanged in chains. They were dipped in tar, as the manner is; the wind span them, the chains clattered, and the birds hung about the uncanny jumping-jacks and cried" (234). The scene unsettles David because it portends his own possible destiny should Grant seize on him like the fugitive he is; but it also identifies David with James (and testimony with unlawfulness), and hence motivates him to follow through with his design even as it incites the narrative.

David's meeting with Grant comprises the moral and meta-discursive center of the novel. There, Grant tries vainly to reason with David not to "plunge [his] country in war, to jeopardise the faith of [his] fathers, and to expose the lives and fortunes of how many thousand innocent persons" by muddying the case against Stewart and, more generally, the barbaric Highlands. "[I]f this man James escape[s]" judgment, Grant warns, "there will be trouble with the Campbells," Glenure's kinsmen. "That means disturbance in the Highlands, which are uneasy and very far from being disarmed" (246–47). David replies that he believes Grant's "policy to be sound. . . . But for me, who am just a plain man . . . the plain duties must suffice. I can think but of two things, of a poor soul [i.e., Stewart's] in the immediate and unjust danger of a shameful death, and of the cries and tears of his wife that still tingle in my head." Like a witness confined by the substance of what he perceives, David professes that he "cannot see beyond, my lord" (247). In coming to the supposed rescue of someone found guilty for utilitarian purposes, David's testimony thus condemns the system which fabricates truths to meet its needs. "Romance" here is truer, less fictive, than "fact."

Stevenson goes to great lengths in pounding this point home. Grant, touched by David's integrity though wary of the potentially deleterious effects of David's testimony, brings David back to his office two days later. There he has Simon Fraser, Lord Lovat, recite the circumstantial case against David in an effort to convince him not to testify. "My dear sir," Lovat sneers, "the facts declare you guilty. . . . The evidence of Mungo Campbell," who was standing beside Glenure when the shot was fired, "your flight after the completion of the murder; your long course of secrecy— my good young man . . . here is enough evidence to hang a bullock, let be a David Balfour!" (257) Though shaken, David sticks to his story, only admitting that when he "left [Grant] that afternoon [he] was for the first time angry." So, he "counted [his] enemies: Prestongrange [i.e., Grant] with all the King's authority behind him; and the Duke [of Argyll] with the power of the West Highlands; and the Lovat interest by their side to help them with so great a force in the north," where Lovat's father had been a notorious clan chief executed after the '45; "and the whole clan of old Jacobite spies and traffickers" (280). Basically, all of Scotland seems to be conspiring against David, Hanoverians as well as Jacobites (much as the pursuers and defenders had unwittingly joined forces to ratify the viability of circumstantial evidence and, with it, the image of Highland retrogression in the Stewart Trial). Growing ever more disillusioned with the entire process, David later has "forced home upon [his] mind" a point which Scott conveys in *Rob Roy*, namely that the Stewart Trial and the entire furor surrounding it, all of which "had the externals of a sober process of law, was in its essence a . . . battle between savage clans" (346).

Never called to testify in the trial itself (since even Stewart's defenders realize that David's testimony puts Alan at the scene and thus strengthens the circumstantial case against both Alan and James), David instead bears witness in and through his narrative, which inflates itself into a testimonial against the corruptions of modernity. And so it is that, "in course of time, on November 8th, and in the midst of a prodigious storm of wind and rain, poor James of the Glens was duly hanged . . ." (382). And David's plaint after the fact takes on the wise if disconsolate perspective of the Benjaminian storyteller:

So there was the final upshot of my politics! Innocent men have perished before James, and are like to keep on perishing (in spite of all our wisdom) till the end of time. And till the end of time young folk (who are not yet used with the duplicity of life and men) will struggle as I did, and make heroical resolves, and take long risks; and the course of events will push them upon the one side and go on like a marching army. James was hanged; and here was I dwelling in the house of Prestongrange, and grateful to him for his fatherly attention. He was hanged; and behold! when I met Mr. Simon [Lovat] in the causeway [in Edinburgh], I was fain to pull off my beaver to him like a good little boy before his dominie. He had been hanged by fraud and violence, and the world wagged along, and there was not a pennyweight of difference; and the villains of that horrid plot were decent, kind, respectable fathers of families, who went to the kirk and took the sacrament! (382–83)

The morbid refrain ("James was hanged . . . He was hanged . . . He had been hanged") underlines the injustice soiling the "decent, kind, [and] respectable" appearance of modern society.[44] Here, witness testimony, the perspective and word from the consummate outsider, becomes the ideal (and, putatively, the only) vehicle of meaningful social critique. And yet, testimony functions in this context to bewail events it cannot change, thus highlighting the incongruity between perception and power, experience and actuality. This is the thread Benjamin would seize and respool, making like Stevenson in weaving experience into the texture of literary genre.

The Messianic Witness: Experience and/as Redemption

Though critics have been mixed in their reception of *Catriona*, Stevenson was most pleased with it: he remarked in an 1894 letter that he would "never do a better book than *Catriona*," calling it his "highwater mark."[45] He wrote it when he was living in Samoa, having left Scotland for reasons of physical and emotional health. There, he took up the pseudonym Tusitala, a Samoan word for storyteller.[46]

Despite—indeed, because of—its inherent complexity, Benjamin was drawn to this experiential quality of Stevenson's work. His esteem for Stevenson's power as *raconteur* was only heightened when in 1938 (two years after the publication of "The Storyteller") he read one of Stevenson's short essays, "A Plea for Gas Lamps." Here, Stevenson writes in mythical terms about the progress made in the lighting of large cities. In a manner anticipatory of Benjamin's cabbalistic social criticism, Stevenson idealizes the ante-modern (though not exactly primitive) device of the gas lamp: "When gas first spread along a city . . . a new age had begun for sociality and corporate pleasure-seeking." These lights brought people together outside the confines of the workplace: "The city folk [now] had stars of their own; biddable, domesticated stars." At the time at which he is writing, however, these lamps have regrettably been replaced by electricity, which causes Stevenson to pine for the lamplighter: "not much longer shall we watch him speeding up the street and, at measured intervals, knocking another luminous hole into the dusk. The Greeks would have made a noble myth out of such an one; how he distributed starlight" in the manner of Prometheus. Now, however, "like all heroic tasks, his labors draw toward apotheosis, and in the light of victory himself shall disappear. For another advance has been effected. Our tame stars are to come out in future, not one by one, but all in a body and at once. . . . *Fiat Lux*, says the sedate electrician. . . . Starrise by electricity, the most romantic flight of civilization; the compensatory benefit for an innumerable array of factories and bankers' clerks." The new lighting seems indicative of a new age: bureaucratic, technocratic, and consumptive in the instrumentalizing sense. "In Paris" especially, Stevenson argues, "a new sort of urban star [i.e., an electric lamp] now shines out nightly, horrible, unearthly, obnoxious to the human eye; a lamp for a nightmare . . . . To look at it only once is to fall in love with gas, which gives a warm domestic radiance fit to eat by."[47] Benjamin referred to this essay in "The Paris of the Second Empire in Baudelaire" (1938), likening it to Poe's short story "The Man of the Crowd," in which Poe "lets it grow dark. He lingers over the city by gaslight" in a manner evocative of Baudelaire's idyllic *flâneur*.[48] Benjamin also mentioned Stevenson's essay in similarly glowing terms in a 1938 letter written to Theodor and Greta Adorno.[49]

It is easy to see why Benjamin would have been so attracted to this essay: in both its ironic lyricism and its romantic survey of nineteenth-century Paris, Stevenson's "A Plea for Gas Lamps" anticipates Benjamin's monumental *Arcades Project*. And Stevenson's aims in this piece, if not so massive as Benjamin's, nevertheless seem consistent with those which Benjamin expresses in "The Storyteller." In Benjamin's words, the displacement of gas light by electricity might be seen as "a concomitant symptom of the secular productive forces of history, a concomitant that . . . at the same time is making it possible to see a new beauty in what is vanishing" (146). For Benjamin, as for Stevenson, it is a complex case of something lost, something gained.

In "The Storyteller," as in *Kidnapped* and *Catriona*, the apparent loss of traditional social bonds accords a new aura to the category of (witness)

experience. For Stevenson in particular, the verdict of death pronounced upon James Stewart metonymically signifies the "enlightened" attenuation of witness experience in modernity even as it hails
the redemptive return of experience in literature. But, for Benjamin,
what exactly is this redemption worth? Seemingly, very little: epipha-
nies inspired by literature may be privately meaningful, but they correspond more to the solipsistic quality of experience as *Erlebnis* than to
the holistic *Erfahrung* which he idealized. And yet, even something as
mundane as literary experience always portended something greater in
Benjamin's mind. This was his way of underscoring the immanent possibility of meaningful social reform. He adopted this optimism from Marx
and Engels, who, in *The German Ideology*, insisted that the dynamics of
alienation inspired rather than suppressed the likelihood of revolution.
Marx and Engels argued there that industrialization etiolates social
bonds, fragmenting collective units into composites of discrete individuals. However, Marx and Engels claim, "only by this fact" of alienation
are these modern subjects "put into a position to enter into relation with
one another *as individuals.*"[50] The effect is one of dialectical reversal:
once alienation becomes "universalized," collectivity begins once again
to prevail. But this time, predicated on the mutual experience of alienation, it attends the heightened self-consciousness of its subjects. This
consciousness—this "enlightenment"—putatively differentiates solidarity in an advanced egalitarian society from mere self-sameness in a
primitive one.

Fragmented experience—the experience of the witness, experience
as *Erlebnis*—is thus the condition of genuine social reform. Hence, it
remained eminently provocative for Benjamin. He called images of immediacy, of witness testimony, "wish images . . . deflect[ing] the imagination
. . . back upon the primal past . . . to elements of a classless society . . . .
[T]he experiences of such a society—as stored in the unconscious of the
collective—engender, through interpenetration with what is new, the
utopia that has left its trace in a thousand configurations of life, from
enduring edifices to passing fashions."[51] These images enabled
Benjamin to address his own historical moment, and its isolation of consciousness from shared traditions and objective social conditions, from
an Archimedean point outside it. Essentially playing the roles of witness
and juror simultaneously, Benjamin was thus able to document, to witness, the inhuman state of modernity while also creating a reasonable
model explaining how alienation (the hallmark of this state) might be
converted into an unforeseen ground of solidarity.

Benjamin makes this point emphatically in his 1933 essay
"Experience and Poverty." This essay would function as a palimpsest for
"The Storyteller," which was published three years later. In it, Benjamin

first composes key sentences and phrases which he later reprises in "The Storyteller"—for instance, that "experience has fallen in value . . . ; [that a] generation that had gone to school in horse-drawn streetcars now stood [after World War One] . . . in a force field of destructive torrents and explosions" in which everything seemed to have changed except "the tiny, fragile human body."[52] Benjamin had argued these points before, if not quite in this language. In a 1932 essay entitled "The Handkerchief," he mused that one "reason for the decline of story-telling is that people have ceased to weave and spin, tinker and scrape, while listening to stories."[53] Elsewhere, in an unpublished fragment written sometime between 1928 and 1933, he reflected that "we are poor in remarkable stories. Why is that? It is because no events reach us without being permeated by explanations," or by the kind of "informa-tion" privileged in Enlightenment conceptions of experience and understanding.[54]

In "Experience and Poverty," the essay that most closely parallels his reflections in "The Storyteller," Benjamin converts the decay of experi-ence into a potential basis of solidarity and critique. He expounds first on the "poverty [which] has descended on mankind," a "poverty of human experience" which results from the "tremendous development of technology." This poverty, in turn, has produced "a new kind of bar-barism." However, Benjamin puts a happy spin on this degenerate con-dition: "what does poverty of experience do for the barbarian? It forces him to start from scratch" (732). Appealing to the spirit of the avant-garde, he cites Descartes, Einstein, Paul Klee, and others (including Mickey Mouse) as exemplars of a new kind of immediate experience which draws from the example of modernist aesthetics. In the miasma of modern life, "[n]ature and technology, primitiveness and comfort, have completely merged" (735). Fascism arises from the desire for inte-grated experience (*Erfahrung*), producing a bastardized version of Marx's vision of equality. As Benjamin saw it, fascism reinforced class dis-tinctions, substituting a myth of national (and racial) destiny in the place of real social reform. True experience, true collectivity, required a different type of vision—one personified for Benjamin by Einstein and others who have managed to "step back and keep [their] distance" from the ruse of fascistic totality by insisting on "starting from the very begin-ning," or by refusing to accept authoritarian pronouncements of things as they are (735, 733). In essence, they have rejected the corrupt medi-ations of modern society (which Benjamin calls "the dirty diapers of the present" [733]), and have insisted instead on seeing the world—directly, as witnesses—through fresh eyes.

This is an ideal which is far easier to imagine than to achieve, of course, and for Benjamin's friend Theodor Adorno it seemed that

Benjamin succumbed in such moments of fancy to the lure, the short-cut, of the fascist vision.[55] But in "The Storyteller," as we have already seen, Benjamin would take up these issues in a subtler way, applying Marxian dialectics to the question of literary form (specifically, the form of the novel) in the promotion of cultural materialism. In doing so, he echoed Georg Lukács's *Theory of the Novel* (1920) by associating the novel with a modern thirst for information rather than epic wisdom, and with alienated experience rather than its integrative counterpart. For Benjamin, our contemporary passion for information attests to the growing diversity and general uselessness of knowledge. In his mind, information differs from wisdom in laying claim "to prompt verifiability. The prime requirement is that it 'appear understandable in itself'" or, in the parlance of Enlightenment conceptions of legal evidence, that it "speak for itself" in a way that converts it to some end—usually, to profit or to purposes of administration. In modern society, Benjamin argues, the novel emerges as a kind of poor compensation for instrumentalized social relations, which explains why characters *in* novels and readers *of* novels reflect each other as alienated subjects defined by lack and driven by desires for plenitude. Again, Benjamin follows Lukács's lead here: for Lukács, the novel's traditional focus on individual human subjects (especially in the nineteenth-century *Bildungsroman*) bespeaks the hegemony of consumerist dynamics, the economy of lack and desire whose governing trope is irony.[56]

For Benjamin, it is this ironic condition, a condition of desire and alienation, rather than any "real" resemblance between character and reader, which defines the novel: "The novel is significant . . . not because it presents someone else's fate to us . . . but because this stranger's fate by virtue of the flame which consumes it yields us the warmth which we never draw from our own fate" (156). The chill of "fate," of formative and insuperable material conditions, emanates as a dim glow from the lives of characters about whom we read; that is, in novels we see through a glass, darkly, the social conditions which "produce" and "consume" us. The cultural ascendancy of the novel thus disseminates this experience of alienation, "making it possible to see a new beauty in [the social solidarity, the epic wisdom, the *Erfahrung*, that] is vanishing" (146). For Benjamin, novel criticism thus doubles as social criticism.

In conventional literary terms, what is "vanishing" for Benjamin is the art of the storyteller, which figuratively illustrates the integrated experience which he idealized. The "*new* beauty" that he hopes to recapture through criticism is an attendant quality of experience which storytelling illuminates in negative. In stories, the process of consumption occurs differently than it does in novels, reflecting an immersion in communities rather than an instrumentalization of consumer desire. "The storyteller: he is the man who could let the wick of his life be consumed completely by the gentle flame of his story" (108–9); he is the one whose narratives adumbrate the integrated lifeworlds out of which they emerge. "This is the basis of the incomparable aura about the storyteller" (109), an "aura" that had become most insidiously apparent to Benjamin in the counterfeit form of fascism, which "introduc[ed] aesthetics into political life" and "pressed [it] into the production of ritual values."[57] However, the remnants of a desirable dialectical counterpart to fascism endure, he insists, in the stories of "Leskov [and] Hauff, in Poe [and] in Stevenson" (109). As I noted above, Benjamin concludes his essay on this note of hope.

But in what register does this note resound? In light of Stevenson's "stories" about the Stewart Trial, what are we to make of Benjamin's experiential ideal? As we have seen, Stevenson's protracted telling of this story across two novels (and through the eyes of a self-styled witness, the callow David Balfour) attests not only to its author's ostensible desire to expand the scope (or at least the duration) of his witness's authority, but also to the provocative legacy from which this desire was born. The Stewart Trial laid the foundations for this desire by delineating the difference between witness and juror along the lines of Highland periphery *versus* progressive "British" core, presenting Stevenson with a rich cultural and epistemological metaphor for his trademark appeal to the "dissociation of sensibility." In Scott's *Rob Roy*, as we saw, the Stewart Trial's epistemic geography of witness experience takes a slightly different form, inscribing itself into cultural fragments which haunt us on account of their uncanny testimonial quality and their disclosure of the residually "clannish" features of modernity. Stevenson took these fragments and fashioned something almost systemic from them—a working theory of literature as compensation for the ills of progress.

Benjamin goes further still. His evocation of storytelling draws implicitly upon both Scott and Stevenson. Like Scott, Benjamin detects uncanny traces of primitive culture in the interstices of modernity, though he is less unsettled by their appearance than inspired by them: clannish irrationality in Scott becomes latent proletarian energy in Benjamin. In this respect, "The Storyteller" reiterates Stevenson's bias for the primacy of David's testimony and of "literature"—not merely as compensation, but also as the portent of messianic, revolutionary force. The literal arrival of this force is at once debatable and disturbing, to be sure: in the 1930s, it loomed as the specter of fascism. However, the roots which Benjamin's messianic concept of experience uncovered were less national or racial than epistemological in nature, implicitly recalling the Stewart Trial, albeit in transmogrified form. This trial, demarcating a marginal but alluring space of witness experience, directly (in Stevenson) and obliquely (in Benjamin) inspired visions of experience as the dialectical corollary of literary narrative's "romantick" geography. This geography transports us across the "Highland line" of evidence, considerably complicating evidence as a notion with unsettling historical implications.

Chapter 3

Evidence and Equivalence
The Parallel Logics of Proof and Progress

One of the more compelling ironies associated with the Stewart Trial is that ultimately the greatest denunciation of feudal Highland society was articulated in the feudal Highlander's own defense. In the closing hours of a trial which ran for over two consecutive days without recess, George Brown, Stewart's defense counsel, argued cunningly that the pursuers' circumstantial narrative actually extended the domain of clan fealty, bringing it uncomfortably within the realm of law and the intimacy of the everyday in "civilized" Britain. Evidence of this nature, reducible to witness testimony in contrast to the enlightened ideal of probability, leveled the accusers with the accused, Brown insisted. As such, it threatened to reinstate those barbaric Highland customs which nominally progressive leadership had vainly affected to transcend.

It would not be the last time the Highlands and its inhabitants were scorched by friendly fire, nor was the evidential logic to which Brown referred confined to the legal sphere. As we will see, there was a strongly legal-evidential flavor to the schemes of "improvement," or commercial rationalization, which made over Highland Scotland—or rather, which continued to transform an already evolving region, and often for the worse—in the eighteenth century. And, as was the case in the Stewart Trial, the logic of progress conformed to the strictures of evidence, even as the Highlands themselves became associated with the residue of witness experience.

Commensurate with one of the effects of Highland improvement, I might describe the story I am telling here as one of emigration—in this case, of legal-evidential codes from the "law" proper into other domains of British society, like the discourse of political economics. In doing so, and in keeping an eye to the impact of "progress" on the category of experience, I follow in the spirit of recent scholarship concerning Highland improvement, which over the past fifteen years has presented this phenomenon in relation to many things other than capitalist progress per se (for instance, literature, culture, nationalism, and modernity).[1]

Experience is a more elusive category than these, but it is also in many ways more fundamental. In relation to these other topics, the ruins of experience—the aura accruing to experience as a function of its rupture from knowledge—help explain the emergence of a modern concept of literature as imaginative (as opposed to factual) discourse. These ruins also delineate the contours of theories of culture and nationalism (in the "experience" of social groups), while adumbrating the plight of the human subject amid the complexities of the modern world. We will see how the dilemma of experience which we discussed in the first two chapters—a dilemma illustrated most vividly in Chapter 1 by the split between witnesses and jurors—became an essential component of both Highland improvement and, just as importantly, the latter's partial failure. Indeed, by the nineteenth century the appeal to Highland experience served as a powerful tool in the critique of capitalism.

This critique found a powerful and surprising voice in the eighteenth century in the seminal work of one of the most renowned apologists for improvement, Adam Smith. Today, we best remember Smith for delineating rigorous systems of equivalence—for instance, the sameness of feeling which constitutes sympathy, or the equation of labor and value. Crucially, these systems reflect the logic of legal evidence; Smith even works them out in the context of a discussion of law in his *Lectures on Jurisprudence* (1762–63). Consistent with the pragmatics of arriving at a jury conviction, this logic sublimates the contingent experience of individual subjects—in *The Theory of Moral Sentiments* (1759), the experience of those who seek sympathy; in *The Wealth of Nations* (1776), the experience of individual laborers—into a generalized, true-to-life, probabilistic simulacrum of that experience. In the earlier book, this simulacrum takes the form of "impartial spectatorship"; in the later one, it re-emerges as "value." But because Smith's work evinces the logic of evidence, witness testimony also appears there in uncanny form. That is, whereas juries convert witness testimony into evidence, the category of labor reflects the status of testimony in *The Wealth of Nations*: commodities in the marketplace and evidence in court each results from a process of refinement, of improvement. For this reason, we may consider Smith's work as exemplary not only because of its landmark treatment of eighteenth-century concepts such as sympathy and commerce, but also because of its elevation of legal evidence to paradigmatic status with respect to the probabilistic reasoning on which these and so many other Enlightenment notions were grounded.

Witness experience provided raw material for the refinement of evidence, but we have seen how it also formed an inassimilable residue haunting probabilistic claims to knowledge. The formal exclusion of witnesses from jury deliberation potentially rendered jury verdicts flawed (since witnesses might have seen something more or other than that to which they eventually testified) or specious (since, as in the Stewart Trial, lawyers and juries might end up resembling the witnesses against which they defined themselves). What is more, the marginalization of testimony on grounds of its contingency also implicitly contributed to the idealization of witnesses as the emblems of a direct contact with objects: testimony's literal im-probability only heightened its allure. And so it is in *The Wealth of Nations*: when Smith departs from the general purport of his probabilistic treatise in order to express reservations about certain aspects of it, his demurrers take the form of testimony. But that is a story for Chapter 4.

Highland Improvement: An Overview

The tale of Highland improvement has been told often and well.[2] At its simplest level, it thematizes the social transformations which accompanied changing practices of land use. As historians like R. A. Dodgshon and Eric Richards have recently shown, the traditional view that Highland improvement was principally an eighteenth- and nineteenth-century phenomenon is inaccurate: the erosion of clan relationships and the corresponding modernization in agricultural practices (e.g., the consolidation of lands, the introduction of cattle and sheep, and so on) had been occurring since at least the late sixteenth century, and were merely accelerated in the latter half of the eighteenth. And yet, the accelerated pace of improvement during the late eighteenth century is crucial: the relative belatedness of large-scale clearances in the Highlands and Hebridean Islands, especially those that occurred in the early part of the nineteenth century, became key exhibits in the popular condemnation of Western (and especially British) industrialization.

It is this relatively late phase of Highland improvement that most concerns me in this chapter. My aim in briefly rehearsing this portion of its history is less to present new information than to underline less recognized aspects of its structure and legacy, for it was during this period that evidential epistemology and capitalist ideology became strongly allied in promoting programs of economic development. Hence, this is also the period when the relative failure of these programs began to correspond with the popular appeal to the Highlands not only as a land of romance, but also as a place of witness testimony, and therefore as the geographical and cultural repository of a decaying quality of experience.

I open with an anecdote. Three years prior to his journey into the Highlands and Hebridean Islands, Samuel Johnson expounded a commonly held view of the region that firsthand experience would later cause him to recant. Through an Irish reverend who had been privy to this conversation, James Boswell relates that "[s]omebody [once] observing that the Scotch Highlanders, in the year 1745, had made surprising efforts, considering their numerous wants and disadvantages: 'Yes, Sir (said [Johnson],) their wants were numerous; but you have not mentioned the greatest of them all,—the want of law.'"[3]

The British government held similar ideas after the Jacobite defeat on Culloden Moor in April 1746. One modern commentator observes that

[f]ollowing the battle of Culloden, the Government's plan for the Highlands was "pacification"—the rooting out, by violent means, of the danger posed by Jacobitism to the established order. . . . With the Act of Attainder of June 1746 (19 George II c. 46) heads rolled; the Disarming Act (20 George II c. 52) of the same year forbade the Gaels to possess arms; the wearing of Highland dress was outlawed in 1747; and heritable jurisdictions were abolished (20 George II c. 53). In 1747 the Vesting Act (20 George II c. 41) was passed, in which everything that belonged to those attainted in the rebellion was turned over to the Crown. . . .[4]

These laws effectively revolutionized Highland society, though not always in the manner in which they were intended. When Johnson ventured into the Highlands some twenty-five years after the passage of these acts, he remarked that the rule of law there remained uneven at best, leaving a disturbing impression on the visitor. At the strictly local and practical level, the abolition or suspension of the baronial courts was not sufficiently compensated for, Johnson argued, by the installation of new magistrates. Consequently, the frequent "complaint is, that litigation is grown too troublesome, and that the magistrates are too few, and therefore often too remote for general convenience."[5] At a more basic level, however, Johnson lamented that the influx of imperial law had wrought deleterious changes to Highland society: Highlanders' "pride has been crushed by the heavy hand of a vindictive conqueror, whose severities have been followed by laws, which, though they cannot be called cruel, have produced much discontent, because they operate upon the surface of life, and make every eye bear witness to subjection" (97). To some degree, these changes were general throughout Scotland and most of the British kingdom.[6] Unique to the Highlands, though, is the depth and the extent of the pathos that accompanied improvement, particularly in popular associations between change and "subjection." In the Highlands, that is, the economics of improvement amplified the heightened experience of its observers.

In evaluating Highland improvement, there are thus two issues to consider. First, we must note the nature of the changes improvement wrought; and second, we should recognize the effects of these changes on the category of experience, specifically the individual experience of native and itinerant observers, and the collective experience invoked by the region's inhabitants and sympathizers (e.g., in the reports circulating in travelogues like Johnson's).

With respect to the first issue, it is important to acknowledge that improvement was general throughout Scotland. The historian Bruce Lenman observes that "[b]etween 1745 and 1770," or shortly before Johnson's tour, "the pace of rationalization, specialization and change in the Scottish countryside accelerated in response to urban demand for food and raw materials."[7] The effects of these transformations were most striking in the Highlands and Islands, where the revaluation of traditional values and the infusion of new economic ideals accelerated the metamorphosis of Highland society from a clan- to a class-based system. This radical transformation not only undermined traditional social customs, but also inaugurated a host of economic innovations that altered the face of the countryside and the profile of its population. T. M. Devine remarks that during this period there "was a decisive change of pace" in the Highlands "which was brought about by an enormous expansion in the rest of Britain for such Highland produce as cattle, kelp, whisky, wool, mutton, timber, slate and a host of other commodities."[8] Highland land and resources became coveted sources of capital, which led to enclosures and a corresponding displacement of peasantry from arable tracts. Despite this devastation to local Highland communities, though, the population in many Highland regions continued to grow, or at least hold steady, until around the turn of the nineteenth century, when even the introduction of new crops (such as the potato) and increasing agricultural efficiency could no longer sustain an indigent class of disenfranchised subsistence farmers. Emigration reached its peak during this period, and would continue to drain the Highlands of its population for the next several decades.[9]

In reviewing the course of Highland improvement after 1746 (i.e., after Culloden), we should remember that the incentives for improvement at mid-century differed slightly from those expressed in the later eighteenth or early nineteenth centuries, and that, as Scott and Stevenson underlined with respect to the Stewart Trial, the ideology of improvement—"the days which our fathers wished to see"—often preceded the effects of actual progress. A. J. Youngson contends that the real aims of the imperial laws prohibiting tartan attire, abolishing heritable jurisdictions, and so forth were political rather than economic, aiming to destroy "the political separateness of the Highlands."[10] Youngson cites an earlier Scottish historian, Ramsay of Ochtertyre, who claims that the "whole weight of government was employed to dissolve every tie between the chief and the clan, and to abolish all distinctions between the Highland and Lowland Scots." These views are supported by the British government's conception of the Annexing Act of 1752 "for the Purposes of civilizing the Inhabitants upon the [seized] Estates, and other Parts of the Highlands and Islands of Scotland, and promoting amongst them the Protestant Religion, good Government Industry and Manufactures, and the Principles of Duty and Loyalty to his Majesty."[11]

The government, its factors, and anxious clan lords effectively communicated this political message to many Highland farmers long before any concrete developments actually affected their food supply, means of subsistence, wages, or other material facets of life. Peasants like those whom Colin Campbell of Glenure removed from the Ardshiel estate, an action which led to the Appin murder, initially experienced improvement less as enlightened progress than as political punishment. In other words, at mid-century, improvement was less a social program than a culture war. Hence, even late in the eighteenth century, when the political motives for improvement had mostly evolved into economic incentives, the ideological aura of change as a social value often continued to precede actual material transformations. Eric Richards remarks that the "gale of improvement did not reach some parts [of the Highlands] until the nineteenth century, but it is perfectly clear that the change of attitudes preceded" visible changes of policy. Hence, despite the relative stasis of Highland life in some quarters, the specter of improvement "nevertheless invested the movement with dramatic urgency."[12]

These spectral-ideological improvements, where there were any, usually proceeded either at the behest of factors appointed to manage forfeited properties or at the command of the official Commissioners for the Annexed Estates. These Commissioners, of whom there were usually between two and three dozen at one time, held possession of the estates from 1752 until the government returned those lands to the families of their original proprietors in the 1780s. Commissioners were generally respected gentlemen of Edinburgh—judges, lairds, noblemen, and the like—who disapproved of the sparse productivity of the estates (taken as it was to be a sign of indolence) and the underfed appearance of their tenants. Youngson writes that "the Commissioners' attention" in monitoring improvements "was directed chiefly to agriculture, concerning which they formulated general rules. . . . Tenants were to 'house and inclose' at night in winter 'their Horse, Black Cattle, Sheep and all other Bestial,' and there were detailed rules about rotations—tenants were 'bound to follow annually in a regular Course not under five Aikers of ground for each Plow . . . ' and were to have at least two acres each year in red clover, as well as two fifths of their enclosed arable land sown to grass. Tree planting was encouraged . . . [etc.]."[13] The Commissioners also introduced the spade and hoe into rocky or mountainous areas where plowing was deemed to be inefficient. For all these modest innovations, however, the enduring legacy of the Commissioners may consist mostly of their having further sown progressive economic ideals and tastes for luxuries in the Highlands, cultivating a strong spirit of emulation in the descendants of clan patriarchs and heightening their desires for improvement. This partly explains, then, how the political genesis of improvement gradually evolved into an economic program, and why the ideology of progress—the atmosphere of commercial interest—often preceded the material manifestations of change.

These post-Culloden efforts at improvement would intensify later in the century. Several things contributed to this dynamic, including the steady erosion of clan loyalties (and their replacement by landlord/tenant relationships), industrializing progress in England and Lowland Scotland, the renewed domestic focus of the British government after the loss of its American colonies, and pressures of internal colonialism exerted on the region by Highlanders as well as Lowlanders. From the 1770s through the middle of the nineteenth century, numerous philosophers, economists, moralists, and politicians from England and Scotland, and from the Highlands as well as Lowlands, devised programs to galvanize Highland industry and morally redeem the region's inhabitants. Educational reform, for instance, undertaken mainly by the Scottish Society for the Propagation of Christian Knowledge (SSPCK), took on the creation or refurbishment of hundreds of local schools. Religious reform would consist in purging Catholic priests and establishing Episcopalian and Presbyterian churches.[14] Still other schemes were hatched to reconcile economic and moral aims by fostering greater civility among Highlanders, thus improving relations between the British nation and its Gaelic peripheries. John Sinclair, a noted improver who produced the first detailed statistical account of the Highlands and Islands in the late 1790s, praised the SSPCK, claiming that its schools "are of great benefit in dispelling ignorance, and giving to the lower orders of the people, a degree of cultivation and improvement, that may . . . dispos[e] a greater number of them . . . to part with their prejudices, and may, in the end, prove very important to agriculture."[15] Other improvers, such as John Knox and James Anderson, believed that government aid in sponsoring the fishing industry would lead to the creation of new towns and villages in the Highlands' thousands of natural harbors, and that these newly self-sustaining communities would then be better able to enter into commercial relations with the rest of Britain.[16] Still others, such as Thomas Telford, believed that "the construction of roads, bridges, and canals . . . would provide the short-term benefit of employment with the long-term benefit of an infrastructure upon which further improvements could be made."[17] For its part, the British government maintained that the establishment of urban communities and the improved communication resulting from a network of roads and canals would create centers of order, "effectually . . . Reclaim[ing] the Inhabitants . . .

from their long habits of Sloth and inactivity and reconcil[ing] them to the love of Labour, Industry and Good order."[18]

For all the bromides extolling the moral and economic effects of improvement, the deeper ambivalence expressed by Johnson and others took an institutional form in the Highland Societies of London (organized in 1778) and Edinburgh (1784). More formally known in Edinburgh as "The Highland and Agricultural Improvement Society," this coterie of intellectuals and bureaucrats declared its formal mission to consist of the following:

1. An inquiry into the present state of the Highlands and Islands of Scotland, and the condition of their Inhabitants.
2. An inquiry into the MEANS OF THEIR IMPROVEMENT, by establishing Towns and Villages—by facilitating Communication through different parts of the Highlands of Scotland, by Roads and Bridges—advancing Agriculture, and extending Fisheries—introducing useful Trades and Manufactures—and, by exertion to unite the efforts of the Proprietors, and call the attention of Government, towards the encouragement and prosecution of these beneficial purposes.
3. The Society shall also pay proper attention to the preservation of the Language, Poetry, and Music of the Highlands.[19]

The clearest indication of the Society's ambivalence lay in the inherent tension between the professed objectives of the second and third statements, or in the aspiration at once to improve and preserve Highland society and culture. The Highland Society's resolution to "preserve" the "Language, Poetry, and Music of the Highlands" (unwittingly echoing a pun spoken by Swift's cannibalistic philanthropist in "A Modern Proposal," who aspires to "*preserve* the [Irish] nation" by consuming its infants as delicacies) expressed a desire to embalm Highland culture, not only by protecting its artifacts but also by sustaining the social conditions which had produced such art and had attracted such interest in the Highlands in the first place.[20] Robert Clyde states that the Highland Society at London overtly embraced this latter aim, seeking "to preserve the dress, music and 'martial spirit' of the Gaels. [This Society] was composed of chiefs, clan gentry and other interested parties resident in London, and among its immediate priorities was the encouragement of piping and the composition of Gaelic poetry."[21] The sheer novelty of primitive Highland culture and the fascination it aroused served to place ideas of economic and cultural vitality in opposition to one another, inciting a stand-off between, on the one hand, support for innovative economic policies and, on the other, an expanding taste for antiquity and primitivism. By the end of the eighteenth century,

Highland Scots would begin more fully to embrace this opposition in articulating what Katie Trumpener calls a "bardic nationalism" that was "constituted, in many ways, as a critique of modernization and of the uneven regional development it perpetuate[d]."[22]

With this ideological bifurcation of culture and economics, we may begin to perceive the valorization of traditional Highland culture throughout Great Britain as the rudiments of an emergent cultural capitalism, which Pierre Bourdieu describes as "the representation of culture as a kind of superior reality, irreducible to the vulgar demands of economics."[23] Hugh Blair, one of James Macpherson's fiercest public advocates, associated the Ossianic poems and Highland life generally with this sort of cultural superiority: "many circumstances of those times we call barbarous, are favourable to the poetical spirit. That state, in which human nature shoots wild and free, *though unfit for other improvements*, certainly encourages the high exertions of fancy and passion."[24] As Bourdieu would persistently maintain, however, any specifically "literary (or artistic, or philosophical, etc.) capital functions within an 'economy' whose logic is an inversion of the logic of the larger economy of the society."[25] From Bourdieu's perspective, and in the context of late eighteenth-century Highland improvement, this means that generative distinctions between the moral value of Highland poetry, music, and dress on the one hand and the commercial value of improvement on the other necessarily obscured the economic basis of measurement (i.e., "value") through which such difference—such cultural superiority—might be asserted in the first place. Adopting Bourdieu's rhetoric, we might say that the circulation of cultural capital in Highland nostalgia tended to "invert"—that is, to reverse and reflect, and hence, to confirm and preserve—the dominant economic climate.

Crucially, however, the Highlands did not always simply reflect and hence legitimate the prevailing economy. Indeed, to many observers, the Highlands became a dark spot in Britain's mirror of production, which is why they identified the region with the phenomenon of *witnessing* and the problematics of experience. The radical disjunction between the probabilistic calculations of improvement and the actuality of Highland industrial output became apparent as travelers and political economists increasingly described the region as economically depressed instead of quaintly primitive. One after the other, commercial ventures in the Highlands either failed outright or produced such devastating effects on the local population that even the government expressed alarm. And yet, neither government intervention (in the form of bounties on trade or acts designed to prevent mass emigration) nor private ingenuity met with much success: the fishing and kelp industries failed to develop; linen manufacture, always a cottage industry in the

Highlands, was undermined by the cheaper material produced in Scotland's Central Belt; and, most dramatically, the conversion of tenant farms into pasture for sheep-grazing displaced thousands of peasants and initiated a floodtide of emigration into industrial centers such as Glasgow, and into Scottish settlements in the American colonies, Nova Scotia, and Australia. Eric Richards observes that the "most obvious difference between the Highland clearances and similar events in other parts of upland Britain was the rapidity and lateness of the changes in the extreme north. The clearances required the shifting of large numbers of peasants off the land in short periods of time in an age in which the public conscience was more responsive to allegations of inequity and cruelty. There w[as] undoubtedly more drama and more concentrated human suffering than in most other forms of enclosure."[26] Still other projects, such as the construction of canals, cost the government dearly, and produced sparse benefits to the Highland economy. Few people used these canals "due partly to insufficient depth of water . . . partly to problems of navigation and the dilapidated state of the works, but largely, no doubt, to the collapse of the west-coast fishing trade." All told, the Caledonian Canal, the largest of the projects, "secured the employment of 50 people with a total annual income, between them, of about 1,800 pounds per annum, as a result of a capital expenditure of close [to] a million pounds!"[27]

These failures were not those which inspired efforts at improvement; rather, these were the failures *of* improvement, of those schemes which had been devised to galvanize Highland economies and societies. Naturally, the reasons for such failure are numerous and, depending on which facet of Highland industry we examine, may be ascribed either to poor planning, contradictory goals, culture clash, or an eighteenth-century favorite, indolence.[28] The point that I wish to underscore here, especially in light of the implicit connection I am pursuing between Highlandism and experience, is not so much any particular reason *why* improvement failed than simply *that* it failed, and failed so spectacularly. For, whatever the cause, the effect was that the Highlands posed a direct affront to British pretensions of economic calculability and speculative induction. Instead of consistently acting "as a spur to the inventive faculties, [and] bond of union between different communities,"[29] improvement served in many instances as a scourge that depressed cottage industries, widened the gap between rich and poor, and further magnified the difference between progressive Britain and the remote, retrograde Highlands.

IMPROVEMENT AND THE EVIDENTIAL LOGIC OF EQUIVALENCE

There are many ways to describe the failure of Highland improvement. From the standpoint of the symbolic significance of this failure and the subsequent romanticization of the Highlands—that is, from the standpoint of Highland*ism*—we might best describe this failure as an inability of the improvers successfully to ensure an economic and legal *equivalence* between commercial Britain and the feudal Highlands. In other words, Highlandism might be said to have emerged as a "romantick" index of the discrepancy between the Highlands and other "improved" regions in Britain. Highlandism originated, in short, as difference. And this difference, we will see, reproduced the dynamics of witness testimony.

The equivalence which Highland improvement was designed to promote essentially modeled itself on the logic of evidence, and especially on the perspective of juries. In the opening letter of his epistolary *Observations on the Means of Exciting a Spirit of National Industry* (1777), James Anderson rhetorically configures this ideology of judicial equivalence in his analysis of a friend's journey into Scotland. "You say," he says to this friend, who has recently returned to England from a visit to Edinburgh, that

> you could not help remarking, that there was a very manifest difference between the look and appearance of the ordinary people in that part of Scotland through which you passed, and those of the same rank in England. Their countenances were not so open,—their gait and manner less hardy and unconcerned; you perceived more marks of politeness and complaisance, but, along with that, you thought you saw more care and anxiety of mind; so that you could not help feeling a kind of uneasiness at drawing the parallel between them that constantly obtruded itself upon your imagination.
>
> Had you proceeded farther in your intended tour, you would have had much greater room for making this remark. For in many parts of Scotland, the lower class of people are so abject in their behaviour, so mean in their apparel, so dejected and melancholy in appearance, and so thin and emaciated in their looks, as cannot fail to excite very uneasy sensations in the mind of any one who has not been accustomed from his infancy to see them. This is the only disagreeable circumstance that you would probably have met with, had you proceeded in your intended circuit: but it would probably have made such an impression on you, as would have greatly diminished the pleasure you might have received from other objects.[30]

I cite this passage at length less out of a desire to ruminate over Anderson's vivid portrayal of the "abject" condition of the Scots than in the interest of dramatizing, with Anderson, the complex status of the "ordinary" (e.g., "the ordinary people" of Edinburgh) in the late eighteenth century. Anderson's friend, it seems, has been struck by the defective "strangeness" of Scotland's lower-middle classes, and specifically by their extra-ordinary "difference" when compared with "those of the same rank in England." In the Highlands—the "farther" point in the "intended tour"—Anderson informs his friend that he would have found this "uneasy" difference to be even more extreme (though perhaps, for that reason, less uncannily discomfiting).

From the standpoint of my argument, one of the most significant aspects of the passage is Anderson's partial nullification of the disturbing "strangeness" of his friend's report through a confirmation of their mutual (and hence, jury- as opposed to witness-like) perspective—a perspective that unites them with each other and their English readers. Anderson reasons that the unsettling encounter with the abnormal Scottish "ordinar[ies]" "is the only disagreeable circumstance that [Anderson's friend] would *probably* have met with . . . but it would *probably* have made such an impression" on him as to erode the pleasure he took from other aspects of his tour. Comfortable recourse to the "probable"—to the likely, the normal, the average, the "ordinary"—protects the correspondents from "deject[ion] and melancholy" by sheltering them as objective observers from unseemly contact with the Scottish squalid sublime.[31] Mutually horrified by the spectacle of poverty, the correspondents reaffirm their own social connection in a civil society whose distinguishing features differentiate them, as spectators, from the object of their reports. By implication, therefore, the Scottish subjects described in the report, and especially those Highland subjects dwelling in the outer (and purely imaginary) reaches of abjection, presumably suffer a *menial* condition because they are prevented economically from enjoying a *medial* or "ordinary" (i.e., a "British") one.

The "improving" rationale of equivalence to which Anderson appeals here is essentially tautological: the image of prosperity serves to justify a universalizing ideal of economic practice, which he then marshals as evidence of the possibility of Highland revitalization. This logic is typical of Highland improvement, which justified itself on two points it had yet to prove, namely that a commercial economy would breed equality and that Highland Scotland was destined to prosper in a free market similar to ones developing elsewhere in England and the Scottish Lowlands. This tautology based itself on a transference between economic and legal notions of equivalence—an idea of equality under the law, tendering the promise of universal prosperity—that strengthened both sides of the equation.

As scholars have long noted, this mutual reinforcement of economics and law would become especially pronounced with the onset of heavy industry in the early nineteenth century, and with the proliferation during that period of statutes designed to protect private enterprise and the interests of capital.[32] In eighteenth-century Britain, neither commerce nor law had yet reached this later stage of systematic rationalization; however, intersections of economy and law were coming increasingly to characterize the foundational precepts of improvement. In analyzing

Adam Smith's vision of a free market economy, Ronald L. Meek claims that Smith's aim was to reduce "[t]he role of the State . . . from . . . actually guiding economic affairs to . . . providing a suitable legal and political framework within which economic affairs might safely be left to guide themselves."[33] In such a system, the forces of law and economics would function transparently with respect to one another, invoking a hypostatized "invisible hand" in their defense, much like exponents of circumstantial evidence demanded that facts "speak for themselves." The trend toward the legal homogenization of evidence—the leveling of testimonial differences to create a "universal" perspective for the jury— thus also informed policies of improvement and economic governance. Suppositions of a free market enabled improvers to imagine a qualitative (if not quantitative) reconciliation between disparate Highland Scottish, Lowland Scottish, and English economies through the establishment of normative systems of measurement for charting, interpreting, and modifying Highland economic and social phenomena.

Smith is probably the most renowned, influential, and representative of the philosophers of wealth and virtue. As we will see, his recourse to a logic of equivalence reflects both the structure of Highland improvement and the failure of the region to develop according to expectations. Numerous commentators have observed that Smith's economic program was fundamentally, in Mary Poovey's words, "a philosophical enterprise that subordinated description to systematic analysis." That is, while Smith apparently devoted himself to an empirical survey of economic conditions in the British kingdom, especially England, he "was more self-consciously interested in the interpretive act by which abstractions [such as 'value'] are generated. . . . Smith believed that creating abstractions was essential to the production of general knowledge, not simply because a single eye could not see all the workmen at the same time, but because what one needed to analyze," namely, the workings of the free market at large, "was nowhere visible as such."[34] Smith's aim, Poovey argues, was less to document existing economic conditions than to establish a system of economic practice and interpretation whereby empirical data—things as they *are*—might eventually be brought into conformity with the presuppositions of the improvement-minded observer—things as they *should (hereafter) be*. Smith's *Wealth of Nations* thus became a "bible to the Highland improvers"[35] because, in rigorously explicating the principles of economic productivity, it also enacted a program of improvement. It brought empirical knowledge into compliance with desire, or the virtuous strength of the British will. Improvers saw what they wanted, or felt they needed, to see.

It is ironic, as we will see below, that "abstraction" should have acted as such a formidable tool in Smith's "production of general knowledge" because, as certain contemporaries and later critics would remark (and as we will see in Chapter 4), Smith himself failed to account fully for the abstract and systematic implications of his own theory. His aim was to explain how every sector of society, rich and poor, would necessarily prosper from an economy of unfettered trade. He reasoned that British commercial society had created conditions wherein "the accommodation of an European prince does not always so much exceed that of an industrious and frugal peasant, as the accommodation of the latter exceeds that of many an African king, the absolute master of the lives and liberties of ten thousand naked savages."[36] As scholars have often recognized, Smith attributed the universal enjoyment of wealth in Britain to the division of labor: "The greatest improvement in the productive powers of labour, and the greater part of the skill, dexterity, and judgment with which it is any where directed, or applied, seem to have been the effects of the division of labour. . . . It is the great multiplication of the productions of all the different arts, in consequence of the division of labour, which occasions, in a well-governed society, that universal opulence which extends itself to the lowest ranks of the people" (9, 16). This labor theory of value was one of Smith's true innovations.

However, James Anderson and Karl Marx—two critics with radically different outlooks and objectives—each identified contradictions in Smith's theory, particularly in its bifurcation of value into categories of the "real" and the "nominal." The problem for both Anderson and Marx lay in the relationship between labor and capital, and in the respective difference between wages and profit. This was a relationship which the distinction between "real" and "nominal" value obscured and mystified. Meek remarks that "[t]o Smith's predecessors, generally speaking, profit had appeared as 'profit upon alienation'—i.e., as the gain from buying cheap and selling dear. To Smith, on the other hand, profit began to appear as an income uniquely associated with the use of capital in the employment of wage labour."[37] Marx, of course, would later theorize how the deployment of capital for the purpose of producing "surplus value" involved the appropriation and exploitation of labor as the means of increasing either the quantity or quality of commodities. Indeed, Marx's opus *Capital* (1867) might be considered a thoroughgoing reply to Smith's capitalist manifesto *The Wealth of Nations*. In Smith's system, despite the fact that labor comprises the material base of value, ownership plays a still more crucial role in that it both directs labor and disperses the effects of wealth throughout society. Reprising a famous trope from his *Theory of Moral Sentiments* (1759), Smith claimed that "by directing that industry in such a manner as its produce may be of the greatest value, [an owner] intends only his own gain, and he is [therefore] in this, as in many other cases, led by an *invisible hand* to promote an end which was no part of his intention" (*Wealth of Nations* 351–52, my emphasis).[38]

Much to Marx's chagrin, it was thus self-interested ownership which maintained the upper (invisible) hand in Smith's system. Labor seemingly existed to ensure substantial gains for proprietors. The propitious effects of the commercial economy to the residue of commercial society consisted, then, in trickle-down benefits to wage laborers.

Anderson's grievance—the Highland "improver's" grievance—with Smith is subtler, but it turns on essentially the same issue. He found it odd that Smith seemed to fetishize the role of labor. Smith famously claimed that "a measure of quantity, such as the natural foot, fathom, or handful, which is continually varying in its own quantity, can never be an accurate measure of the value of other things; so a commodity which is itself continually varying in its own value, can never be an accurate measure of the value of other commodities. . . . Labour alone . . . never varying in its own value, is . . . the ultimate and real standard by which the value of all commodities can at all times and places be estimated and compared. It is their real price; money is the nominal price only" (39). With this evocation of the "real" as a quality that "never var[ies] in its own value," Smith accorded to labor the quality of a mathematical constant. For improvers like Anderson, however, such a formula only obscured the nature of the system in which such "reality" possessed any actual purchase. Anderson argued that to define value by labor, as Smith did, was still to devolve at some level upon the goods a given unit of labor might purchase; and this quantifiable unit, without which labor would be meaningless (or, literally, *worthless*), necessarily implied a system of abstract equivalencies—that is, the "unit" as such—upon which the concept of labor was predicated. In essence, Anderson collapsed the difference between Smith's partitioning of "real" and "nominal" value: "The real value of any commodity," Anderson wrote, "when speaking in a commercial style . . . [is] the quantity of subsistence which that particular commodity is able to procure to the person who possesses it. [And] in commercial countries, where all commodities are readily exchanged for money, the quantity of that universal medium . . . will indicate exactly its real value to the possessor."[39]

The notion of equivalence which informed the concept of money—"the best equivalent," according to the eighteenth-century political economist James Steuart[40]—not only grounded Enlightenment economic theories, but it also served as a signifier for the nationalistic ideology of British progress. Money, the unit of equivalence *par excellence*, betokened civilization. Invoking a scheme of stagist progress that Scottish philosophers like Smith would soon make famous, Steuart divulged that he "deduce[d] the origin of the great subordination under the feudal government," the popular perception of the Highland form of government prior to the age of improvement, "from the necessary dependence of the lower classes for their subsistence. They consumed the produce of the land, as the price of their subordination, not as the reward of their industry in making it produce" (208). To Steuart, feudal peasants did not earn wages, or tradable commodities, as a third term mediating between themselves and their benefactors (for purchasing shelter, food, clothing, and the like); instead, these peasants dwelled in a more immediate relation to their benefactors, without the asset of an objective mediator.[41] In this way, Steuart "deduce[d] modern liberty from the independence of the [lower] classes, by the introduction of industry, and circulation of an adequate equivalent for every service" (209), or by the introduction of a mediating third term. For Steuart, money, the unit of equivalence, was the sign of civilization.

Anderson's criticism of Smith becomes clearer in light of Steuart's theory: labor must necessarily denote a price, an equivalent, or a quantity of subsistence on the market in which it functions. A mediating third term is essential because without it labor risks regressing to a stage of barbarism that civilization has surpassed. For Anderson, any argument for the "real" (e.g., for labor as "real" value) was thus implicitly a reversion to comparative savagery.

Hence, despite their different viewpoints, Anderson and Marx identified problems with Smith's labor theory and its abstractions of value. For Anderson, Smith's fascination with labor pushed his theory regressively to a feudal condition that commercial society had superseded. For Marx, by contrast, Smith's definition of labor as "real value" improperly extracted value from an activity—labor—that, technically, precedes the possibility of value since it is the basis from which value is manufactured.

The disjunction of labor and value contradicts the popular perception of the Marxian "labour-theory of value," so it bears closer examination. Marx breaks value into the categories of use and exchange, but claims that in modern commercial society only "exchange-value [functions] as the necessary mode of expression . . . of value."[42] Exchange value appears in the form of commodities, which are "quantities of congealed labour-time" (130, emphases deleted). This does not mean, however, that commodities bear the imprint of "real" labor; they are, rather, manifestations of *abstract* labor which, in turn, devolves on systems of equivalence. For this reason, Marx argues, "Human labour-power . . . creates value, but is not itself value" (142); that is, raw labor is the material from which abstract, equivalent labor becomes evident in commodities as exchange value.

Thus far, Marx reiterates Anderson's argument against Smith. For Marx, Smith never ceased to do the very thing which Anderson claimed he should do more explicitly: that is, Smith never ceased to mediate labor through a system of equivalencies, a notion of "value." And this, Marx believed, led Smith to mystify the "real" conditions of his own ideological system. In his reliance upon the unit of equivalence, Smith and other "classical" economists like him obscured the evolving stages of labor, the increasing exploitation of the laborer, and the bad faith of the capitalist.[43] Smith (and Anderson) thus fetishized commodities by failing to recognize in them the apparatus of equivalencies which "transforms every product of labour into a social hieroglyphic. . . . It is precisely [the] finished form of the world of commodities—the money form [preferred by Steuart and Anderson]—which conceals the social character of private labour and the social relations between the individual workers" (167, 168–69). As Fredric Jameson remarks, Marx's aim in *Capital* was to demystify the "mysterious phenomenon of equivalence" on which the entire capitalist program was predicated. For this reason, Jameson argues, Marx's theory "should . . . be distinguished from . . . the so-called labor theory of value" propounded by Smith. Unlike Smith, "Marx seeks to defamiliarize . . . the seemingly natural set whereby we weigh distinct kinds of objects against each other and even occasionally exchange them as though they were somehow the same."[44] Reprising the famous example invoked by Smith and Marx, a coat is *not* simply equivalent to its price or to a corresponding set of commodities possessing similar value.

In this respect, Marx, like Anderson, took Smith to task for his evocation of the "real." Both critics recognized that societies derive commodities from a process of labor, but that, whether for good or ill, a "universal medium" determines their value. Commodities thus necessarily reflect not only the sweat of the worker, but also the "invisible hand" of the commercial system that codifies, quantifies, and directs that work. The question these divergent critics implicitly raised thus concerned the epistemology of equivalence on which commercial economics turned. And this question returns us once again to the issue of legal evidence.

SMITH'S EVIDENTIAL SPECTATOR

Reading against the exceptionalist case for *The Wealth of Nations*—the conventional view that Smith's capitalist credo differs from his earlier work—scholars in recent years have noted that Smith's opus actually serves as a culmination rather than a departure. While I reset a version of the exceptionalist argument in Chapter 4 (albeit in an unconventional way), we should first recognize the merits of the revisionist position. For instance, Smith first employs the trope of the "invisible hand" (albeit disparagingly, in reference to primitive beliefs in the supernatural) in his "History of Astronomy," an essay he mostly composed sometime in the mid-1740s.[45] And it was in the *Lectures on Jurisprudence* where Smith most rigorously outlines the stagist theory of social progress, the passage from savagery to commercial prosperity, which codifies improvement. However, it is *The Theory of Moral Sentiments*, published in 1759, on which most critics have focused. They tend to perceive there less a self-enclosed moral program than a model of mutual sympathy which would anchor Smith's later theory of the inherently virtuous nature of commercial exchange. Noel Parker, for instance, argues that "*The Theory of Moral Sentiments* constructs the theoretical framework for . . . processes of enculturation . . . [in] the society which [Smith] sees emerging." And John Dwyer has recently labeled Smith's concept of sympathy "the ethical foundation of [his] economics."[46]

It is to *The Theory of Moral Sentiments* that I now turn as well, with the intent of illustrating the formative, evidential transference between legal and economic concepts of equivalence that would so deeply inform *The Wealth of Nations*. It has become something of a commonplace to interpret Smith's philosophy as a response to general anxieties which permeated Britain in the mid-eighteenth century. The breakdown of monarchical absolutism and mercantilism, and the corresponding efflorescence of a commercial economy and consumer society, made questions of collective governance and the regulation of desire in individuals seem especially urgent.[47] Sympathy provided Smith with a model through which to sort out these issues. In *The Theory of Moral Sentiments*, sympathy appears as a primordial social phenomenon that exerts a powerful shaping force on individuals. Smith's argument describes this force; it also exemplifies it within the fabric of its own prose by harnessing the entropic energy of observation (and the sheer accumulation of social facts) into a probabilistic abstraction of social mores: the impartial spectator. This spectator governs not only the expression of an individual subject's feelings, but also, to a certain degree, the provenance of those feelings. For this reason, the impartial spectator serves as the anchor of Smith's moral argument.

How does this spectatorial system function? The desire for sympathy, which Smith imagines as a primal urge, mandates that individuals "lower the pitch" of their passions "in order to reduce [them] to a harmony and concord with the emotions" of others. This dilution of feeling alters the very nature of the original sentiment. "What [spectators] feel, will, indeed, always be, in some respects, different from what [the individual subject] feels," and this palliation of feeling "not only lowers [that feeling] in degree, but, in some measure, varies it in kind. . . . These two sentiments, however," both the original one and its modified representation, may "have such a correspondence with one another, as is sufficient for the harmony of society. Though they will never be unisons, they may be concords, and that is all that is wanted or required."[48] In essence, Smith constructs a model of investment and return: individuals who seek sympathy must intuit the social acceptability of their feelings and calculate the probable effect of their own subsequent gestures so as to reap the reward of sympathy which they desire.

In one sense, we appear to arrive with Smith at a socialization of private sentiments: one becomes that which one observes in others. In another sense, though, one already is that which the others have observed; that is, private sentiments are always already social to the extent that the desire for sympathy conditions the initial impulses of feeling. This follows from the logic of Smith's model, in which he makes explicit the fact of mediation, the system of equivalencies. For Smith, the face-to-face encounter with others is mediated by the impartial spectator: one "applauds [one]self by sympathy with the approbation of this supposed impartial judge" (85). But to win sympathy from the impartial spectator, one must first have assimilated the ideals that this spectator personifies, including the ideal that it is *sympathy*, say, and not protection (the Hobbesian premise), property (Locke's preference), or respect-in-difference (a more modern cultural value) that individuals "naturally" seek. Hence, the passions that one sculpts in order to achieve "concord with the emotions" of others are already fashioned from the inside by the initiation of a sympathetic exchange.

Hence, in order to posit this concord, Smith argues in something of a circle, presuming the universality that his model of spectatorship sets out to prove. Smith wants to show that individual subjects achieve sympathy by bringing themselves into conformity with a pre-existing set of social criteria, thus replacing solipsism with sociability. However, the impartial spectator, whose presence serves as the impetus for the transformation of the individual subject, and whose union with that subject stands as the prototype of social harmony, is already the abstract representative and implied product of the type of social process that he or she inspires. This circularity first becomes evident in the opening of Smith's moral treatise, when he proclaims that "[h]ow selfish soever man may be supposed, there are evidently some principles in his nature, which interest him in the fortune of others, and render their happiness necessary to him, though he derives nothing from it except the pleasure of seeing it. . . . As we have no immediate experience of what other men feel, we can form no idea of the manner in which they are affected, but by conceiving what we ourselves should feel in the like situation" (9). This supposition serves as the axiom which grounds Smith's argument: the individual subject will win sympathy from others, and thus become more civilized, because he or she internalizes the principles of sociability and molds his or her behavior accordingly. This already appears to be the case with the impartial spectator, who is the abstract embodiment of propriety, and who thus personifies the process that Smith subsequently tries to demonstrate by way of argument. In Smith's closed system, sympathy is assured for the individual subject because it a priori informs the spectator, who is the exemplar of proper, sympathy-garnering behavior. Smith is thus able to make his point about the universality of moral sentiment if for no other reason than that he first enlists it as a premise.

This move is emblematic of the deductive turn in Smith's political economy, or its tendency to ground supposedly empirical observations and "real" phenomena in philosophical systems that lend the empirical data context and meaning. (Indeed, Anderson and Marx imply as much in their critique of Smith's category of "real" labor.) This deductive turn was not uncommon to the empirical methods that dominated eighteenth-century British science and philosophy, even given their supposed basis in experience. As we saw with burgeoning eighteenth-century legal-evidential codes, jury experience was qualitatively and even statutorily different from witness experience, and yet, in the laboratory, such judicial experience—the mediated experience of procedures, signs, and equivalencies—often passed as firsthand, with Bacon and Boyle functioning as "witnesses" in their presentation of data. Legal evidence is thus a crucial epistemological category in that it vividly highlights a fissure between positions—witness and juror—that otherwise were all too easily conflated during the long eighteenth century.

On this score, it seems fitting ultimately to characterize Smith's moral economy as an *evidential* one. Modeling the perspective of a judge or juror removed from the site of the event in question, Smith's "impartial spectator" putatively has no comprehension of experiences whose "pitch" or "tone" has not yet been calibrated to an abstract and universal level. Possessing access only to such experience as meets the norm, the "moral" spectator thus becomes the "morally [or evidentially] certain" spectator as well in that this spectator sublimates particular experiences (i.e., those of the individual subject with which he as a mere spectator cannot sympathize) into *probable* experiences (i.e., those that fall under the purview of abstract likelihood). Smith's individual subject, or the figure appearing before the tribunal of moral reflection, thus exemplifies the historical transformation of the juror-as-witness into the juror-as-disinterested-judge: originally cast in the mold of a witness—the mold, that is, of a sensorium or agent of "strange" particularities—the individual subject eventually becomes an emblem of the probable, normative experience of the impartial spectator.[49] Hence, the "moral sentiment" of which Smith writes seems finally to denote an evidential domain of likelihood. And, while such sentiment would appear to promote feelings of social unity, it also systematically elides the contingency of individual experience. Smith, in short, replaces convictions of testimony with those of probability such that unmediated experience acquires the properties of a return of the repressed.

Witness experience does return in Smith, specifically in *The Wealth of Nations* in the form of Highland romance. As we will see in Chapter 4, Smith may be the most provocative witness of improvement's failure, even though—or, perhaps, precisely because—we usually remember him as its poet laureate of progress.

Chapter 4
Improvement and Apocalypse
Afterimages of the "Promised Land" of Modern Romance

Like so many other treatises on improvement, *The Wealth of Nations* registered the peculiarity of Highland society and geography as a problem. Combined with the relative aridity of the soil, these points of difference made it difficult to blanket the region in a system of rational equivalencies. Hence, Smith argued,

> [t]here are some sorts of industry, even of the lowest kind, which can be carried on no where but in a great town . . . . In the lone houses and very small villages which are scattered about in so desert a country as the Highlands of Scotland, every farmer must be butcher, baker, and brewer for his own family. In such situations we can scarce expect to find even a smith, a carpenter, or a mason, within less than twenty miles of another of the same trade.[1]

In explaining why the Highlands defy improvement, Smith spatializes progress—a motif which we have already seen at work in the Stewart Trial. In *The Wealth of Nations*, Smith converts this motif into a theory. Some places, he reasons (e.g., England and Lowland Scotland), lend themselves to the division of labor and are thus capable of sustaining improvement; others (e.g., the Highlands) are characterized by conditions that are unfavorable to progress. Such places are thus comparatively primitive. However, these places also evoke a quality of unified experience; there, in a trope which Marx and Engels would later convert into an ideal, one lives simultaneously as a "butcher, baker, and brewer."[2] The Highlands thus emit an aura of residual primitivism that is at once alienating and enticing: though perennially impoverished, the region attracts the enlightened observer with a prospect of integrated, undifferentiated existence.

This dialectical reversal comprises the subject of this chapter. Having discussed the parallel logic between evidential and economic equivalence in eighteenth-century schemes of Highland improvement, I turn now to a consideration of the grist and detritus of those systems—that is, to the specter there of witness testimony. What renders Smith's "testimony" in particular so compelling in *The Wealth of Nations* is that the subject which prompts it—namely, the problematic status of labor—takes the form of Highland romance. Smith refers to the Highlands as a region whose sparse population renders it incapable of meaningful improvement; but the Highlands thus come to symbolize other facets of British society which also resist improvement, most unsettlingly the position of wage labor. Laborers benefit from the trickle-down expenditures of capitalists, but inasmuch as "improvement" literally denotes the surplus value accruing to an initial investment, laborers generate the wealth—the improvement— which others enjoy. The system which generates wealth thus also produces a kind of primitivism of the lower class.

This does not mean that the natives are restless: Smith's laborers/ virtual Highlanders do not present the image of insurrection—Jacobite-rebels-*cum*-proletariat—as much as incite melancholic reflection in the improver. The romantick Highlands retain this function in Marx's opus *Capital*, resurfacing still later in Fredric Jameson's *Postmodernism*. As such, these texts undertake as well as criticize the logic of improvement. They denounce progress, yes, but they also "improve" upon the latter's evidential logic. This may explain why Highland testimony functions in all three cases as the modality of revision: it provides a figure through which Smith, Marx, and Jameson invite their readers to see as they have seen, and thus to experience improvement in an alternative register. But this in turn foregrounds experience itself as the element which commercial improvement has perennially undersold; Highland testimony of the eighteenth, nineteenth, and twentieth centuries thus adumbrates experience as the allure not only of the improbable, but also of the unimprovable.

Highland Testimonies: Labor and the Ballad of the "Half-Starved Highland Woman"

"Women did not figure in Smith's philosophy."[3] Deborah A. Symonds pronounces this verdict against Smith in reviewing Smith's moral philosophy and, mostly, she is right. But there are powerful exceptions to this rule. Most strikingly, Smith punctuates the ambivalent allure of the Highlands by way of a reference to the hardiness and virtue of the region's "fair sex." A "half-starved Highland woman frequently bears more than twenty children, while a pampered fine lady is often incapable of bearing any, and is generally exhausted by two or three. Barrenness, so frequent among women of fashion, is very rare among those of inferior station" (83). Here, Smith rehearses an eighteenth-century cliché that luxury is a blessing and a curse whose effects are most evident in women: "Luxury in the fair sex, while it inflames perhaps the passion for enjoyment, seems always to weaken, and frequently to destroy altogether, the powers of generation." In considering the Highlands, though, Smith embraces luxury as a necessary risk. The consequences otherwise seem altogether too morbid: "It is not uncommon, I have been frequently told, in the Highlands of Scotland, for a mother who has borne twenty children not to have two alive" (83).[4]

In this (punningly) pregnant passage, Smith evokes Highland women as iconic figures of Highland savagery and romance. Metonymically signifying Highland Scotland as a whole, these women's fortitude represents an admirable though tragic necessity; the specter of their suffering authorizes progress. In this respect, Highland women correspond to the category of labor in Smith's description of commercial society, which subsists on surplus value. The logic here recalls his model of sympathy in *The Theory of Moral Sentiments*. There, as we saw in the last chapter, Smith's impartial spectator refines the material generated by individual human subjects into exemplary and exchangeable units of feeling. In *The Wealth of Nations*, surplus value—"capital"—takes the place of sympathy, abstracting itself less from subjects seeking fellow feeling than from laborers in the material process of production. But, as we saw in the case of Smith's moral philosophy, individual human subjects never obtain the sympathy they seek because they only acquire it as impartial spectators—that is, as something other than themselves as sympathy-seeking subjects. Likewise, laborers per se do not accumulate capital; rather, they produce it. In this light, Smith's reference to Highland women appears more poignant. Like laborers, Highland women are excluded from the fruits of their labor. Cutting peat, milking cows, making butter, baking, brewing, spinning, mending, and so on (see Symonds 98)—and, for Smith, childbearing—all fail to generate any appreciable return, any "surplus." This renders them primitive, deprived. But as we will see below, it also accords them and all they symbolize a romantick aura of nature.

Before analyzing the explicit connection in Smith's treatise between the Highlands and labor we might think a bit more closely about the consummate image of that liaison in the form of the "half-starved Highland woman." Maternal labor provides Smith with a point of contrast between the arid Highlands and the fertility of the British empire elsewhere, and between capitalists and laborers in a commercial society. But the power of the image derives as much from its pathos as from its metonymic status. Smith clearly expects his readership to feel sorrow for Highland women, even in some ways to sympathize with them. Recalling Smith's logic of sympathy, this means that the pain these women purportedly experience bears a collective, iconic quality: through them we experience the travail of our human condition. In personifying this universal sorrow, and in helping us name it (as "barrenness," or "disappointment"), the "half-starved Highland woman" aids our understanding. Hence, though Smith gives her no literal voice, he does not render her speechless, either. Indeed, by helping us synthesize our sadness she serves as a kind of balladeer of mass society. As anonymous—but, also, as universal—as the collective body which she represents, she sings the sorrows "we moderns" cannot name without her.

Though it takes striking form in this late text, Smith had elicited this image of romantick balladry before. In his university *Lectures on Rhetoric and Belles Lettres* which he delivered at Glasgow in the late 1740s and '50s, he extolled "the superiority of Poetry over prose." He spoke specifically of "Erse [i.e., Highland Scottish, and perhaps Irish Gaelic] poetry," claiming that "we never heard of any Erse prose," and arguing in the same vein that "Prose is naturally the Language of Business; as Poetry is of pleasure and amusement."[5] This was tantamount to arguing that Highland literary artifacts might be deemed superior in their artfulness or sublime pathos, but that they ultimately did not figure into the practical aims of a rhetorical education, which aimed to endow Scottish students with expendable cultural capital for an urban English and imperialist British marketplace.[6] Hugh Blair formulated a similar argument in his university lectures at Edinburgh in the 1760s. On the one hand, he claimed, "poetry is more ancient than prose" inasmuch as "all language must have been originally . . . tinctured with that enthusiasm, and the descriptive metaphorical expression, which distinguishes poetry." Furthermore, the Gaelic language that "now subsists only in the mountains of Wales, in the Highlands of Scotland, and among the wild Irish" is without question "[t]he language of the first inhabitants of our island" of Great Britain, and hence may be said naturally "to be very expressive and copious." Highland poetry thus evokes the misty past from whence we derive. And yet, on the other hand, advancement into the more prosaic language of English "may, indeed, be assumed as one mark of the progress of society towards its most improved period."[7] The institutionalization of a literary curriculum will thus attend to this civilizing aim, though necessarily at the expense of some of the "expressive" felicity native to earlier generations.[8]

Associations of primitivism, passion, and poetry are quite common throughout the eighteenth century, emanating most notably from Thomas Blackwell's famed *Enquiry into the Life and Writings of Homer* (1735), where these associations acquired further substance through their connection to such material factors as the political structure of society. Smith and Blair took these materialist associations one step further by coordinating them to the economic logic of improvement in the elaboration of a literary curriculum. Smith's figure of the Highland woman in *The Wealth of Nations* evokes this subject, but this time with the effect not only of authorizing the logic of improvement but also of adumbrating what improvement leaves behind—specifically labor, the Highlands, and (as we will see below) witness experience. To this extent, his reference to Highland women might be considered a corrective to his earlier enthusiasm. Indeed, and commensurate with the logic of improvement, it converts his *Lectures on Rhetoric and Belles Lettres* into the "poetic" effusions of "passionate" youth. But this reference also resembles the recuperative projects undertaken by the most renowned ballad collectors of the period, in which women singers figured so prominently.

Smith's gesture becomes more consequential if we bear in mind the social context of balladry in the eighteenth century. In step with the antiquarian movement which took hold in a variety of ways, ballads began to serve as sources not only of pleasure, but also of cultural self-reflection. Several collections of traditional ballads—Allan Ramsay's *Evergreen*, Thomas Percy's *Reliques of Ancient English Poetry*, John Pinkerton's *Scottish Tragic Ballads*, and dozens of others—emerged during this period, each purportedly opening a window onto the deep past. Balladeers were both performers and composers, creatively adapting extant oral and, later, written traditions.[9] Commentators typically identified ballads with the oral traditions of "the north" and the bardic effusions of Ossian, but the most famous female balladeers actually hailed from northeastern Scotland. Percy and Ramsay credited Elizabeth Halket, later Lady Wardlaw (1677–1727), as the principal source of such famous ballads as *Hardyknute, Sir Patrick Spens*, and *Gil Morrice*. Later, nineteenth-century collectors like Walter Scott, Robert Chambers, and Francis James Child relied heavily upon Anna Gordon, later known as Mrs. Brown of Falkland (1747–1810), in compiling their editions.[10] Commenting on these collections, Mary Ellen Brown remarks that the preponderance of attention devoted there to such topics as love, marriage, and family conflicts underscores the major role women played in transmitting and adapting these ballads, and also serves to create a profile of "women's life situations."[11]

One such ballad, *The Cruel Mother*, seems especially provocative in light of Smith's evocation of the bereft and "half-starved" Highlander. Child's authoritative compilation locates this ballad in eighteenth- as well as nineteenth-century collections; it is most prominent in the Scottish tradition, though variants also appear in English, Irish, German, and Danish cultures. This ballad tells of a young woman who becomes pregnant out of wedlock (some editions say by her father's clerk), gives birth (either to a single child or to twins), kills the child with a penknife, and then returns home. Some indeterminate time later, she sees a child playing, feels drawn toward it, and tells it that were it hers she would deck it out in the finest clothing. The child then denounces her, saying that when it was hers she put it to death and that she shall suffer in hell for what she has done.[12]

Infanticide was a common theme in eighteenth-century balladry, and *The Cruel Mother* was by no means the most popular of these works (a distinction more rightly held by *Mary Hamilton* [see Symonds 56–67]). Nevertheless, *The Cruel Mother* distills a number of central issues which pertain to our discussion of Smith and experience. From a critical standpoint, this ballad presents a fairly typical blend of the mundane, the supernatural, and the moral. It functions partly as a cautionary tale, warning that one's actions return to haunt one. However, the ballad's power derives principally from the protagonist's encounter with the uncanny. Whether the child has returned from the dead or whether the young woman is simply seized with a crisis of conscience is not entirely clear, but in either case the object of desire (i.e., the beautiful child whom the woman observes) turns against her, as indeed her earlier sexual desire had punished her in the form of an unwanted pregnancy. Hence, more than merely conveying a message about karma, *The Cruel Mother* tells a story about unhappy returns: the life one desires (e.g., with one's beloved, or with a beautiful child) becomes a source of misery, and the child's testimony against the mother functions as an indictment of conscience.

From Smith's perspective, this is the tale of Highland improvement: prosperity in other corners of Britain incites a desire for the same in the remote region of northwestern Scotland, but efforts toward that end are likely to end badly as the Highlands lack the infrastructure to generate capital. For that matter, and even more alarmingly, wage laborers are found similarly lacking, producing wealth but enjoying no surplus value, no "improvement." The Highlands, then, vividly illustrate the more pervasive (indeed, as in *The Cruel Mother*, the more uncanny) problem of labor on which capital and improvement are predicated. The "half-starved Highland woman" typifies and rhetorically configures this problem. Only two of her twenty children are alive, making her a "cruel mother" *par excellence*, even if unintentionally (e.g., even if she means to care for them, or if she herself is the victim of others' sexual desire). Indeed, in this respect, Smith's image at least gestures toward the stories of abuse and suffering on which the ballad is silent. Of course, if we reimagine the mother as "Mother England," then the "child" whose life it terminates after reaching lustily for improvement returns uncannily in the form of Highland indigence and the urban working class.

The dynamics of witness testimony underscore this connection between the Highlands and labor as the mutual victims of "cruel" desire. Smith resorts to the image of testimony (and of ballad culture) in his description of "the half-starved Highland woman": he has "been frequently told" of something in that remote region which, though "not uncommon," nevertheless contradicts the pulse of ordinary experience in, say, Smith's Glaswegian home (*Wealth of Nations* 83). It would not always be this way, of course, as Glasgow would soon become with Manchester one of the most famous sites of proletarian misery in Britain. At the time when Smith was writing in 1776, Glasgow had not yet become the embattled center of "Red Clydeside," although the town was increasingly flooded with immigrant Highlanders looking for work.[13] The Highlands thus haunted Glasgow, becoming both an emblem of labor and the exception that proves the rule: it is because we (i.e., "we British," a nationality many Lowland Scots claimed) cannot impose programs of economic improvement onto every social milieu that we gain an appreciation of our own historicity—that is, of the progress of which we are capable in our more advanced stage of social development. The Highlands thus acquire the status of an anachronism, of a remote and uncanny space which evokes the past but is still alive in the present, making the region a perpetual curiosity that must be seen—perhaps most disturbingly for Smith in the form of immigrant laborers flooding his home town—in order to be believed.

The testimonial difference of which the Highlands and labor are exemplary works its way into the very heart of *The Wealth of Nations*. If we recall the criticisms leveled by Anderson and Marx against Smith's working concept of equivalence, and if we consider that the improbable prospect of Highland improvement causes Smith to suspend this concept outright in discussing that "primitive" region (which is incapable, supposedly, of sponsoring the improving logic of equivalence), then Smith's references to the Highlands become the key to understanding the forces which haunt "equivalence" even when it appears to be fully active. In other words, the Highland references in *The Wealth of Nations* point toward a deeper ambivalence in Smith's political-economic program, an ambivalence that makes it something different from the ideological apology for *laissez-faire* that it is often taken to be.

This issue returns us to the concept of labor as Smith's threshold of the "real." This threshold never pertained strictly to commerce alone, as Istvan Hont and Michael Ignatieff remind us, but was consumed with matters of justice, and especially "with finding a market mechanism capable of reconciling inequality of property with adequate provision for the excluded."[14] In discussing social tensions between rich and poor, Grotius, Pufendorf, Locke, and others had sought to explain either how the property rights of the rich were suspended in times of economic crisis and food shortage—temporarily bringing all property and goods into common—or else how the rich bore a moral obligation to utilize their inalienable property to aid the poor. "Rights" here oscillated between, on the one hand, the needs of the poor for adequate subsistence and, on the other, the claims of the rich to legal protection of their property. It was these conflicting interests that Bernard Mandeville would bring into unsettling harmony early in the eighteenth century by arguing that private aims served public ends; and yet, even Mandeville pessimistically linked this union with "vice" and corruption. The Scottish philosopher Francis Hutcheson, a strong influence on Smith, defended a similar notion of social harmony, but maintained that such ends were achieved not by vice but rather by a universal moral sense of virtue and beauty.

The concept of labor figures so importantly in *The Wealth of Nations* because it allowed Smith to shift the legal issue of rights onto more properly economic ground. According to Hont and Ignatieff, Smith wanted to demonstrate that "because modern economies were the first capable of sustained 'improvement'" due to the division of labor, "the share of the labourer could continue to grow in absolute terms, even though the oppression of the superior orders might prevent it from increasing in relative terms."[15] Disparities between rich and poor, Smith believed, did not erase the fact that economies which multiplied the division of labor seemed to meet the basic needs of everyone, even the poor, thereby allowing all citizens to share in the abundance of wealth. "The 'invisible hand' passage[s]" in *The Theory of Moral Sentiments* and *The Wealth of Nations* thus "explained the paradox of commercial society as an outcome of unintended consequences—the subsistence of the needs of the poor being served through a machine kept in motion by the blind cupidity of the rich."[16]

However, the concept of labor as "real" value parallels Smith's reflections concerning the Highlands in that it punctures a hole in the smooth lining of the system in which it signifies. This becomes apparent as we follow the system's logic. If we reason that Smith attends to labor as a way of addressing questions of justice, then, adopting Smith's parlance, we might regard his evocation of labor as a "nominal" symptom of his argument's "real" concern, which is to explain how the commercial system is capable of administering even to the needs of its lower classes, laborers, and wage earners. "Labor," in short, is symptomatic of a deeper problem, as Anderson and Marx each realized; if Smith's concept of labor fails in their estimation to reflect on its basis in abstraction, then this failure (of which Smith, supposedly, should have been aware) functions rhetorically to accentuate the issue which to him was of deepest philosophical concern, namely, the rights authorizing the distribution of resources. Labor functions in Smith's treatise, in other words, as what Žižek calls a sublime object of ideology: inhering at the edge of the conceptual system in which it figures, labor also reveals the fissures that shatter the illusion of consistency (or, in the terms of "improvement," the illusion of universality and progress).

How, exactly, does this occur in Smith's text? If we entertain the idea that *The Wealth of Nations* rhetorically reflects Smith's preoccupation with questions of justice, then a curious contradiction opens up between the form and content of his argument. We should recall, first, Smith's contention that European peasants enjoy greater material prosperity than "an African king, the absolute master of the lives and liberties of ten thousand naked savages" (18). In substance, Smith argues that an unrestrained market economy supersedes any need to suspend property rights in times of crisis, since commerce guarantees a measure of equality which oversees the needs of rich and poor alike. This system is said to be adequate even though "equality" consists less in subjects' equal enjoyment of wealth than in their universal participation in a system of commerce. However, if Smith suggests that legislation need not suspend the natural course of the commercial system, then this begs the question as to why, methodologically, Smith effectively suspends this system himself by fetishizing the significance of labor as real value. Why, in other words, does Smith not allow labor to be subsumed (as an "equivalent") by the system that he promotes? Why is he compelled instead to suspend this argument in order to call special attention to the system's adequacy in meeting the needs of laborers?

In answer to these questions, we may read Smith's erring fixation (according to Anderson and Marx) on labor as "real" value as a displacement of his argument's ostensible focus from the equivalencies of improvement to the plight of the laborer. This seems especially to be the case with laborers whose lot may not have improved along with the advancement of the economy. Perhaps most vividly for Smith, this seems to be the case with the displaced peasantry of the Highlands, or with those who were "butcher[s], baker[s], and brewer[s]" all at once—at least, until the failed attempts at improvement, which forced individuals and families into villages, cities, or emigration. Hence, in Smith's political economy, Highland peasant labor simultaneously and paradoxically fosters economic speculation and improvement by serving as the grist of capital while also frustrating such speculation by suspending its natural course (i.e., by resisting the logic of equivalence). In the case of Highland peasant labor, the (evidential) logic of equivalence breaks down. Smith's appeal to labor thus amounts to a "testimony" that the economy of his own argument (and its logic of systematic "value") appears to contradict when cross-examined by Anderson and Marx.

The remote and arid Highlands thus haunt Smith's *Wealth of Nations*, and incite him to the kind of testimonial position that his *Theory of Moral Sentiments* sought to exclude. In the Highlands, he reasons, there can be no improvement; but this then calls attention to the limitations of capitalist rationalization in adequately meeting the needs of laborers.

Hence, the Highlands function as the "return" of what Smith's labor theory of value—and, more generally, the system of equivalencies—"represses," as they did other programs of improvement in the latter half of the eighteenth century. Whereas, at mid-century, Highland intractability had been most vividly associated with the Jacobite Rebellion, the region's sluggish economic output in the later eighteenth century took the form of a preternatural strangeness, irreducible as it was to the commercial dogmas of speculation and probability. No longer "other" *to* prevailing systems of economy and law in Britain, the Highlands came to signify alterity *from within* these systems. Highland romance not only authorized the ideology of progress, but it also testified against it, much as the declamatory children in *The Cruel Mother*. Highlandism helped to articulate an unsettling structure of feeling concerning the social inequity of commercial society's system of equivalencies. For Smith, as for so many other observers, Highland romance configured the experience of difference.

Highland Testimonies, Continued: Marx's Specters of Time and Landscape

Smith's Highland testimony is figural to the extent that he does not literally bear witness in court to his unresolved concerns regarding labor. But these concerns, vividly portrayed in the figures of the "half-starved Highland woman" and the peasant who serves as "butcher, baker, and brewer," implicitly take the form of testimony. They do so inasmuch as they call into question the presumptions of the logic of equivalence whose early expression in Smith's philosophy takes the form of evidence (i.e., in the deliberations of the impartial spectator). Marx would eventually pay homage to this testimony in *Capital*. For him, however, Highland romance figures less as the remainder of a failed system of equivalencies than as the latter's graveyard, evinced most clearly in the quintessential product of that system—that is, the product of the commodity.

Marx refers to Highland romance in a provocatively self-reflexive moment in *Capital*: "what 'clearing of estates' really and properly signifies, we learn only in the Highlands of Scotland, the promised land of modern romantic novels."[17] By "modern romantic novels," Marx invokes the category of romance as it was redefined by such figures as Walter Scott, for whom modern romance "distinguish[es] works of pure fiction" from historical accounts purporting to record reality.[18] In the eighteenth century, *romance* and *history* were fungible terms which bore a reciprocal relation to each other. "Romance" typically designated the modern world's imaginary relation to its own history, such that tales of the supernatural were believed to have formed the credulous basis of Gothic and medieval historiography: in essence, what now appeared to be fiction was once taken for fact.[19] At the same time, in poems like "The Bard" and "Ode to a Friend on his Return," Thomas Gray, William Collins, and others proposed the inverse proposition, namely that a modern appreciation of the ancient past could only be achieved through a feat of imagination. In effect, the eighteenth-century theory of romance postulated that the past's facts were the present's fictions, and vice versa. In the Scottish Highlands and Islands, and in the living portraits presented there of primitive customs, the signifiers of romance, and hence of this historicist dialectic between present and past and between fiction and fact, appeared most vividly. This was so even given (indeed, especially given) the evanescence of the local culture that presumably legitimated and sustained these associations. In the vacuous wilds of Highland Scotland, an ascendant British empire caught a virtual glimpse of its own historical origins even as these origins seemed to fade from view.[20]

The Highlands were compelling, then, not because they were empty, but rather because they seemed *uncanny*—in Freud's terminology, un-home-like[21]—inspiring visions of past and future in the process of their emptying. Such visions were both enticing and alarming: if the Highlands functionally signified the British past, then the eventual desolation of the Highlands—the specter that so unnerved Smith, especially in its structural proximity to the problem of labor—made the future loss of tradition appear imminent. The haunting spatial emptiness of Highland Scotland thus attained broad social significance in Britain from the relative emptiness, the abstract calculability, of time that sustained the visions of eventual Highland vacuity.

Walter Benjamin, Reinhart Koselleck, Benedict Anderson, Stuart Sherman, James Chandler, and others have discussed how the concept of "homogeneous, empty time" came to insinuate itself into the epistemological and institutional fabric of Britain and western Europe from the late seventeenth through the early nineteenth centuries.[22] "Homogeneous, empty time" signified a temporality purged of foreshadowings and fulfillments (such as those prominent in the Judeo-Christian tradition), with time measured instead by clock and calendar. The parameters of this argument have become increasingly familiar in recent years: empty time provides a common, contemporaneous ground whereby individuals who have no other tangible or immediate relation to each other may imagine themselves into vast communities or nations (see Benedict Anderson). Or again, empty time inscribes itself into new diurnal prose forms such as the diary, the newspaper, the travelogue and, in subtler ways, the novel, and hence shapes structures and contents of representation (see Sherman). Or again, a concept of empty time aids historians in accounting for cultural difference by delineating alternative conditions of agency and possibility at different spots on the globe in the same historical moment (see Chandler, *England in 1819*). Or again, and most portentously for the late eighteenth-century Highlands, empty time enables a hegemonic mastery over the future by the present, and as a consequence over social peripheries by a dominant core, by subjecting contingent events to calculations of probability that conform to a logic of investment and return, and hence that infinitely extend the socioeconomic axes of power deployed by advanced nations (e.g., Britain). The British government and a younger generation of profit-driven landlords tamed the refractory Highlands, this argument would have it, by instituting a logic of temporal abstraction (and, by extension, of investment and return) in the place of clan ancestry.

In their (for Marx, commercially inflected) vacuity, and in their sponsorship of an attendant nostalgia, the cultures and romance of the late eighteenth-century Scottish Highlands and Islands appear thoroughly implicated in empty time. However, such culture and romance also impelled a provocative and nascent critique of empty time in the theory of the four stages of social progress. Propounded by a host of Scottish literati, from Smith and Adam Ferguson to John Millar and William Robertson, the four-stage theory shared with the popular nostalgia a mythic belief in the inexorability of progress, but maintained in lieu of a strictly empty and calculable time a materially constitutive notion of temporal unfolding according to which social development corresponds with a society's dominant mode of subsistence, whether hunting, pasturage, agriculture, or commerce. If conditions in London or Glasgow, for instance, represent a commercial stage of development, then the Highlands and Islands, by contrast, seem to belong to an earlier, agricultural stage. Calendrical time charted these social differences, but to borrow from Benjamin's famous phrase, if time itself were "empty" in this one respect it certainly wasn't "homogeneous." For instance, 1776, the year Smith published his *Wealth of Nations*, abstractly calibrated vestiges of feudalism in the Highlands, a more advanced agrarian society in the American colonies, and a commercial society in Glasgow and London.[23]

The stagist theory and explicit mention of the Highlands would find one of its most provocative and powerful echoes in Marx's concept of uneven development. And Marx's most sweeping use of that concept occurs in Volume I of *Capital*. This is where, in expounding on what he calls "primitive accumulation" and on the "expropriation of the agricultural population from the land"—that is, on the conversion of subsistence farms to profitable ventures in line with the historical course of capital—Marx declares that "what [the] 'clearing of estates' really and properly signifies, we learn only in the Highlands of Scotland, the promised land of modern romantic novels. There the process is distinguished by its systematic character, by the magnitude of the scale on which it is carried out at one blow . . . [and] by the peculiar form of property under which the embezzled lands were held" (890). The Highlands and their rapid social transformation are crucial, Marx asserts, to an elaboration of progress as well as the materialist dialectic which apprehends "progress" as ideology. In effect, then, the Highlands function for Marx in a manner similar to "labor" for Smith—that is, they undermine the system in which they are employed.

Unlike Smith, however, Marx wrote nearly a century after the *Ossian* phenomenon, and a generation or two after Highlandism had exerted its impact on Goethe, Herder, and burgeoning German concepts of aesthetics and nationalism. Marx also wrote in the wake of Scott's historical novels, and their appeal to the Highlands as a land of wonder and difference. For Marx, therefore, even more than for Smith, Highland Scotland represented a "promised land of *modern* romantic novels" ["*die modernen Romanliteratur*"] whose aura conspicuously betrays the cultural contours of the present. Indeed, the "primitive" Highlands that served nostalgically for the improvers to justify industrial progress and imperial law also illuminated primitive Highland society for Marx as a "late" stage of civilization in two interrelated senses. First, the Highlands presented a region that had been effectively devastated by legal, moral, and economic programs of "improvement," most recently the clearances; the Highlands bore the scars of modernity. Second, the Highlands appeared as an outpost whose primary commodities—culture, history, and literary romance (e.g., Macpherson's *Ossian*)—seemed inherently fetishized, bearing disturbing traces of the erasure of their means of production. (In Macpherson's case, as we will see in Chapter 5, Samuel Johnson contended that this erasure took the form of absent or nonexistent supporting manuscripts from which Macpherson had effected his translations.) By calling attention to these two "modern" features of Highland romance, Marx identifies how the Highlands were coming in the late eighteenth and early nineteenth centuries to symbolize and dramatize the larger plight of the Scottish nation which, as David Hume claimed, became the "most distinguish'd for Literature in Europe" despite the loss of its "Princes, [its] Parliaments, [its] independent Government," its pride in its language or, in short, any material basis that might explain Scottish literary productivity.[24]

As Marx implicitly recognized, then, the Highlands were a region where western society might perceive (or witness) itself in an uncanny way that defied "homogeneous, empty" probabilism. Temporality in the "romantick" Highlands thus reverted to a form of figural typology which calculations of "empty time" purportedly had succeeded. The Highlands literally turned back the clock. Such typological fulfillment, though, took the form less of such campy icons as Bonnie Prince Charlie than of the commodity itself, of a burgeoning culture industry, and also of a potentially critical demystification of emptiness, both in time and in the Scottish landscape. In primitive Highland romance, that is, and in the proximal geographical relation between the insular Highlands and the metropolis of London, an expanding British empire beheld the uncanny lineaments of its own reflection, less in the ideological image of historical progress, however, than in the spectral and ruinous image of the commodity.

Highland Testimonies, Continued: Back to the Future

Walter Benjamin would later underscore the connection between commodities and ruin, citing the immediate fossilization of products by compulsive consumerist demands for novelty.[25] Still later, in the late 1980s and early '90s, Fredric Jameson would decry the reduction of history to the status of a commodity (and, by extension, to ruin). He specifically attacked new historicism for adopting Marxist terminology even as it reduced dialectical materialism to a play of homologies, or equivalencies, between categories.[26] In its place, Jameson elucidated a dialectical "aesthetic of cognitive mapping," invoking the Scottish Enlightenment as the model for a thoroughgoing critique of postmodern society. And here, once again, Highland romance returned.

The structure of this return recalls Marx's critique of empty time and the correlative effort to dissolve the obscurity of abstraction by recovering the materiality—in Smith's and Marx's terms, the "labor"—of production. If late capitalist society obfuscates historical, cultural, and class differences behind the monolithic form of the commodity—for instance, in the period piece in cinema, which drapes present-day values in the garb of the past, making the past less discernible as the past per se—then criticism must reinstill the ability to make meaningful distinctions. Jameson's preferred method of cognitive mapping thus demands the provisional tracing of social and historical differences between otherwise self-same commodities, places of production, corporations, and consumers. But the specific contours of cognitive mapping are of less interest to me than the precedent Jameson finds for it in Enlightenment Scotland. "The brilliance of [eighteenth- and early nineteenth-century] Edinburgh," he argues, was "owing to the strategic yet ec-centric position of the Scottish metropolis and intellectuals" with respect to the primitive outback of the Scottish Highlands on the one hand and the cosmopolitan world of London on the other. This liminal position granted Scottish literati a perspective onto the "virtually synchronic coexistence of distinct modes of production," the agrarian and the commercial, "which it was uniquely the task of the Scottish Enlightenment to . . . conceptualize." In eighteenth-century Edinburgh, the exigencies "of thinking a new reality and articulating a new paradigm for it," which the Scottish literati did with the four-stage theory of social progress, "seem to demand a peculiar conjuncture and a certain strategic distance from that new reality, which tends to overwhelm those immersed in it." This "conjuncture" and this "distance" coalesced in eighteenth-century Scotland in ways that were subsequently elided by the "universalization of capitalism" (405). To proceed to the post-postmodern moment of cognitive mapping, Jameson suggests, we must therefore somehow reproduce the intellectual peculiarity of Enlightenment Edinburgh. The Scottish Enlightenment takes us back to the future.

Jameson's historical project derives strength from its supposed congruity with eighteenth-century intellectual culture in Scotland. However, we might ask whether Jameson is not merely reproducing the logic of the period piece in cinema. His ingenious observations regarding the "ec-centric" position of Scottish intellectuals are predicated on a contradiction in that Jameson anchors his critique of commodification in an already commodified image of the past—the image, that is, of the primitive Highlands and their affective difference from "modern" Britain (i.e., primarily from England and Lowland Scotland), a notion which circulated amongst the Scottish literati whom Jameson idealizes. For Scottish stagist philosophers, a usable past animated the present. To cite one example, James Macpherson's epic ideal of ancient Caledonia (which I address in Chapter 5) conjured a nationalistic image in the present, specifically of a future moment when he imagines Scotland acquiring greater prestige throughout Europe as a seat of literature and learning, if not of (Jacobite) political power. This prophecy would be partly fulfilled by Macpherson's peers—for example, Blair, Smith, and others—and seemed fully to realize itself with Walter Scott, who converted Scottish legend and customs into cultural and liquid capital. For Jameson, in a similar manner, the generative stagist philosophy of the Scottish Enlightenment foreshadows Marx's theory of uneven development, gesturing toward a "future" (i.e., the present) when a similarly generative stagist theory (i.e., Jameson's own "aesthetic of cognitive mapping") will once again transcribe the hieroglyphs of postmodernism into historical terms.

Macpherson's and Jameson's formulations function analogously to the extent that they posit a congruity between discrete entities as well as between past, present, and future. Ancient Caledonia and eighteenth-century Scotland become interchangeable in Macpherson's work, as do eighteenth-century Scotland and postmodern society in Jameson's. For Macpherson, to read *Ossian* is to experience ancient Gaelic culture and Scotland's glorious future; for Jameson, to perceive the cartographic impulses in Enlightenment Scotland is to discern the contours of late capitalism via a "romantick" critique of the same.

In terms of speech act theory, Jameson's analysis is performative rather than constative: rather than capturing the historical particularity of Scottish Enlightenment historicism, it converts the philosophical history of eighteenth-century Edinburgh into the framework for a transhistorical cultural critique. In the language employed by Paul de Man, Jameson's historicism thus takes the form of a *promise*; it is "future-oriented and prospective," a "promissory [note] in which the present of the promise is always a past with regard to its realization."[27] Reconceiving of Macpherson's case in light of de Man's insights, we might say that to read Macpherson credulously is to bind the past to an image of the present. The past will become, in memory or in "history," what the present suggests it might have been. Likewise, in Jameson's case, the Marxist concept of uneven development, which Jameson takes as his starting point, will enable us to "read" its prefiguration in Enlightenment Edinburgh; meanwhile, the hypothetical congruity of Enlightenment Edinburgh with our own postmodern moment will then project onto historical criticism the "aesthetic of cognitive mapping" which Marx's motivating concept will have taught us to deploy. The present (i.e., "uneven development") will configure the past (i.e., Enlightenment Edinburgh) for the purpose of realizing a future (i.e., a revision of new historicist criticism in light of Jameson's "aesthetic of cognitive mapping").

Residues of eighteenth-century Scotland are everywhere in this formulation. They inflect the method—that is, the stagist historicism—and also the motive of a proper historical analysis. Jameson refers to this motive in discussing the "figure" of his old (i.e., Marxist), new (i.e., post-postmodern) historicism. This historicism will take the specific form, he says, of "a figure that runs through [Marx's] *Grundrisse*, connecting the 1844 manuscripts in an unbroken line to *Capital* itself"—the figure of "separation," which Marx describes by referring to "enclosure." "There has not yet . . . been a Marxism based on this particular figure," Jameson portentously observes. "But the logic of separation may have become even more relevant for our own period, and for the diagnosis of postmodernism" (398–99). Old/New historicism must realize this promise—must realize, that is, the figure of "enclosure." In *Capital*, uncannily, it is Highland Scotland that Marx expressly identifies as the archetypal *topos* of clearance, the corollary of enclosure: "what 'clearing of estates' really and properly signifies, we learn only in the Highlands of Scotland, the promised land of modern romantic novels." These are "romantick" Highlands, to be sure, as there were very real differences between, for instance, the local experience of the Highlands for Macpherson, the native Highlander, and Smith, the distant commentator. Beyond that, and employing Marx's vernacular, the contours of enclosure in the Highlands and Islands were radically "uneven" in the eighteenth century: enclosures occurred in varying degrees and at different times, depending on the specific locale. But it is these "romantick" Highlands, and the image of mass enclosure, Jameson suggests, which point the way out of postmodernism. Highland Scotland acquires new meaning—or rather, it recovers its old meaning—as Marx's "promised land," which now lies beyond the borders not of modernity and Britain, but of postmodernity and the West.

Jameson's "aesthetic of cognitive mapping" thus functions, we might say, according to a figural typology of romance, which Northrop Frye distinguishes "by its extraordinarily persistent nostalgia, its search for some kind of imaginative golden age in time or space."[28] Far from rejecting this characterization of his Marxian project, Jameson embraces it. He commented on this romantic typology in *The Political Unconscious*: "The Marxian vision of history . . . has sometimes . . . been described as a 'comic' archetype or a 'romance' paradigm. What is meant thereby is the salvational or redemptive perspective of some secure future." The prospects of romance are especially important to historical criticism: "Romance now again seems to offer the possibility of sensing other historical rhythms, and of demonic or Utopian transformations of a real story now unshakably set in place."[29]

Jameson's advocates and critics alike have commented on this feature of his work, perceiving in it a powerful narrative economy which overcomes the inertia of history, and not always for the better. Jameson's work, some argue, adopts the strategy of the homologies he claims to despise in new historicism.[30] Highlandism, these critics might argue, comprises one such homology, erasing the historical difference (in this case, between the late eighteenth and the late twentieth centuries) which Jameson nominally celebrates. However, such "aesthetic" projections of history have become the responsibility of criticism, Jameson argues. Moreover, it is a task which demands above all the analysis and, potentially, the restoration of the quality of experience which Marx, Benjamin, Adorno, and others perceived to be decaying in modernity: "one of our basic tasks as critics of literature is to track down and make conceptually available the ultimate realities and experiences designated by [rhetorical] figures . . ." (*Postmodernism* 411–12). This is the charge of criticism because, as we discussed in the Introduction, Jameson interprets the split between experience and knowledge as one which makes experience untrue and scientific understanding inauthentic (411). This situation is not only logically untenable, Jameson implies; it is also ethically corrupt. It reflects the logic of improvement (and evidence) and the correlative reign of the commodity—a dynasty which is turning the world to ruin.

In taking up the crisis of experience, Jameson preserves not only Marx's dialectical methodology (and, less directly, Smith's virtual balladry), but also the emblem of Highlandist critique. Jameson's Highlandism may be problematic in its contradictory homologizing, much as Smith's Highland romance perturbed Anderson and Marx for its apparent lack of self-reflection. But the significance of Highland romance as a critical category may consist less in the problems it successfully resolves than in its illumination of the more elusive dilemma of experience which it symptomatically displays. In both the Enlightenment and after, Highland romance became a key figure of the rupture of experience from knowledge. The "testimonies"—the counter-equivalencies—of Smith, Marx, and Jameson, while displaying and delineating the limitations of improvement as the evidential logic of economics, are at root meditations on this rupture. "Experience" in these testimonies forms the shadow haunting enlightened configurations of knowledge, including (in Jameson) the knowledge of history *and* the critique of the same. But, as we will see in Part II, the Highlands came not only to mark the limits of "enlightenment," but also to signify potential (if problematic) resolutions to its exile of experience.

Part Two
Feeling

Chapter 5

The Compulsions of Immediacy
Macpherson, Wilkomirski, and Their Fragments *Controversies*

Their stories are strikingly similar in some key respects. Each felt drawn toward a historical catastrophe by whose ghosts he felt haunted. Each labored diligently and in relative obscurity in piecing together the fragments of this past. From these fragments, each cobbled together a mosaic of images which he declared was intended for him alone and perhaps for those closest to him. Each had the good or ill fortune to come into contact with people of social influence at a time when these narrative mosaics might find a wide and voracious audience. Each professed reticence at the thought of publishing his findings, then relented at the urging of his instigators. Each subsequently embraced his sudden celebrity, and adopted (whether as moniker or legally) the name of the person he depicted in his work. Each reacted with initial fervor and then with growing diffidence at the accusations that his work was fraudulent. Most importantly from my perspective, each continued to testify to the authenticity of the work, placing peculiar epistemological and aesthetic emphasis on the value and fragility of witness testimony in the work itself as well as in its defense.

The similarities mostly end here, because James "Ossian" Macpherson and "Binjamin Wilkomirski," *né* Bruno Grosjean, emerge from and circulate within worlds that are otherwise quite foreign to each other. Macpherson, the Highland-born, Lowland-educated Scot, arrived at his fame in the early 1760s as the reputed translator of the ancient Caledonian bard Ossian. Wilkomirski, a natural-born Swiss who claims he was born into a Jewish family either in Latvia or in southern Estonia, burst onto the scene in the mid-1990s with his childhood memoirs of time spent in the concentration camps of Majdanek and Birkenau. Of Macpherson's translations, critics raised serious questions concerning their authenticity within months of their initial appearance as *The Fragments of Ancient Poetry*; nonetheless, readers celebrated these translations as monuments of ancient civilization and Scottish cultural supremacy for some four decades before coming gradually to a different and less favorable opinion. With Wilkomirski's *Fragments: Memories of a Wartime Childhood*, the case was accelerated: initially greeted with real enthusiasm as a record of Jewish persecution reputedly on par with the work of Primo Levi, Elie Wiesel, and Anne Frank, the cheers for Wilkomirski's memoirs abated some four years after their publication, when lengthy articles in *Die Weltwoche* and *The New Yorker* divulged the fraudulence of Wilkomirski's identity. In addition to the myriad differences of their historical eras, one principal point of contrast lies most simply in the authors' fundamental claims: Macpherson vehemently attested to have translated the work *of* someone else; Grosjean, a.k.a. Wilkomirski, defends his memoirs by maintaining that he *is* someone else.

Given the preponderance of differences, the works' similarities seem almost uncanny. And, with respect to the legacy of the "ruins" of experience, their sensational claims to immediacy are what link them most instructively. The word "sensational" here carries a double charge: on the one hand, it describes the cultural furor these texts incited; on the other, it designates the unit of perception which, since the Enlightenment, has historically been arrogated to witness testimony, which in turn is the modality of meaningful knowledge in these texts. Macpherson's *Poems of Ossian* and Wilkomirski's memoirs promote sensationalist immediacy as a marginalized but supreme medium of truth, and in that respect they each exhibit the symptoms of the longstanding dilemma of experience.

After addressing the pervasive logic of evidence in and outside the law in the first four chapters, I turn in these next three chapters to a closer examination of the paradox inhering in claims to both experiential immediacy and mediation. As we will see, immediacy and mediation make a fungible pair. They conspire to shape trauma theory, one of the key sites for reflecting on the problem of experience in modernity. Originally devised in the 1860s as an offshoot of neurology, then revised by Freud in the 1920s and '30s to account for the rupture of experience from consciousness and the mind's libidinal economy, and finally resuscitated in the 1980s as a means of registering the effects of social horrors (e.g., the Holocaust, Vietnam, spousal and child abuse, etc.), trauma theory is widely recognized to manifest the condition it attempts to explain. This dynamic was evident in Freud's seminal study *Beyond the Pleasure Principle* (1920), in which he concluded that a compulsion to repeat—an impulse toward mastery, a need for quiescence, a death instinct—overpowers sexual drives toward the aleatory and the unexplored. The irony implicit in such a conclusion, of course, is that Freud's theory of trauma exemplifies the death-like desire for meaning which he associates with traumatic symptoms. By its own logic, trauma theory itself appears traumatized, or else it promotes trauma.

Trauma theory's critics often note this mimetic feature. Mark Seltzer, for instance, perceives in trauma theory a voyeuristic taste for the psychical violence which it pretends to detoxify in the experience of its victims.[1] Trauma theory's most rigorous historian, Ruth Leys, explains these mimicking features within trauma theory as a reflex of hypnotic imitation, the most persistently perceived problem of trauma. Since the nineteenth century, most theorists have attributed the trauma victim's compulsive tics to an originary "experience that . . . appear[s] to shatter the victim's cognitive-perceptual capacities, [making] the traumatic scene unavailable for a certain kind of recollection."[2] Unable to apprehend the psychic wound itself, the victim compulsively repeats its symptoms on her body—either that or she enacts the suggestions of the analyst, whose interventions may create the symptoms which he then interprets, reproducing the scene of trauma in the course of treatment. As Leys sees it, trauma theory thus historically revolves around the problem of individual agency, which allegedly is overwhelmed by experiences that break through the mind's mediating, protective shield.

As powerful as Leys's analysis is, and as fluent as it is in clinical terminology, there are some key premises in her study which pass unreflected. One such premise concerns the dominant model of consciousness, which trauma theorists present as mediated by psychical processes (e.g., Freud's unconscious, preconscious, perceptual consciousness, and so on), and which thus apprehends immediate experience as a problem. As a result of this governing assumption, the other premise which Leys partly overlooks is the normative conception of experience which the psychoanalytic model presumes. As we have seen, the nature of mediation has changed over time. During the Enlightenment, purportedly direct (or immediate) experience became both requisite and inadequate to the demands of knowledge. Scholastic authority yielded to a disinterested, investment-and-return conception of likelihood. In psychoanalytic terms, the contradictory injunction demanding direct experience and objective remove created an epistemological climate of disavowal, which was nowhere more vividly displayed than in the shifting theory and practice of legal evidence, specifically in the formalized division of labor between witnesses (as repositories of immediate, sensuous experience) and jurors (as exemplars of mediated but more probabilistically truthful experience). To the extent that the jury position has continued to displace the authority of witness experience across a variety of social constellations, including the Freudian model of consciousness, Highlandism and trauma each function as artifacts of the residual allure of immediacy.

They are not alone. As we will see below, and then again in Chapter 6, the instrumentalization of testimony within an economy of evidence has not succeeded in purging knowledge of witness-like contingency. In a hypercomplex world, each of us comes to rely on the testimony of experts, even for rudimentary things: labels inform me that my television was manufactured in Japan and that my breakfast cereal was packaged in Ohio; custom informs me that the button on the console will illuminate my computer and that a plane weighing several tons will lift into the air if it reaches a certain velocity; highly placed intelligence officials warn me, the voter, that there are WMDs in Iraq. Alas, as this last example indicates, testimony is not always equal to truth. Still, what should one do? The speed of life, as well as its complexity, demands belief as a matter of course; there is not sufficient time to deliberate over the details. But this means that testimony and its claims to immediacy suffuse the modern world, invading it from the margins, the Highland peripheries, to which Enlightenment rationality purportedly banished it. Highland romance and its correlative figures haunt modernity.

Highlandism also haunts modernity in more literal ways, and the results are not always happy. This is a matter I take up in this chapter by juxtaposing Macpherson and Wilkomirski across their vast cultural and historical divides, magnifying the structure of experience in which they are mutually implicated. Macpherson's and Wilkomirski's respective *Fragments* depict enlightened modernity as a tale of the traumatized witness—the witness who, in terms of consciousness, was never there, or never at the site about which he reports. However, this figure of the absent witness also describes the role of the jury in modern evidential law, inasmuch as jurors must decide the truth of things they have neither directly seen nor heard. The proximity between witnesses and jurors in this figure paints trauma as a general condition of modernity, a condition of ineluctable mediation perpetually haunted by the specter of immediacy.

These are the specters the respective *Fragments* both promise and deliver. Macpherson's work, which is so provocative from the perspective of experience, becomes especially portentous by adopting the logic of experiential purity. After analyzing the testimonial dynamics of Macpherson's *Ossian* and the criticism he wrote in its defense, I take up Wilkomirski's memoirs and, with them, the theories of witness testimony that have emerged out of studies of the Shoah. Here, we will see, the dream of immediacy morphs into a racialized phantasm. Adorno serves here as the principal object of my discussion, mostly because he implicitly organizes a narrative about the devolution of witness-like immediacy from Enlightenment ideal to fascistic, racialized nightmare. This narrative will not be the last word on immediacy, as we will see with Chapter 6. Still, it usefully recalls Highland-romantick motifs, and it forcefully communicates one of the most problematic legacies of witness experience in modernity.

Ossian and the Testimony of the "Echoing Heath"

Macpherson's *Ossian* translations have presented readers with a crisis of evidence since they were first published in 1760. For Macpherson's peers and modern critics alike, this crisis has usually revolved around the third-century Celtic epics' status *as* evidence, or their presentation of facts that point toward probable truths concerning fraud or authenticity, ancient or modern history, British or Scottish nationalism, and so forth. Skeptics like Samuel Johnson correctly surmised, for instance, that Macpherson had taken liberal (and, to Johnson's taste, unfortunate) poetic license with the material, even going so far as to invent much of what he claimed merely to have translated. In the eyes of many modern scholars, however, Macpherson exonerates himself from accusations of forgery by having produced works that creatively adapted extant traditions in Gaelic poetry.[3] Evoking another set of facts, enthusiastic eighteenth-century readers detected a different truth in *Ossian's* orotund prose, treating the sentimental rhetoric of the *Fragments, Fingal* (1761), and *Temora* (1763) as proof of a native literary grandeur that exalted Scotland and Britain as ancient seats of "politeness, humanity and Enlightenment." Subsequent generations of readers, though, would discern in those same epics the all-too-familiar traces of eighteenth-century literary tastes, seemingly disproving the poems' ancient origins.[4] A few years ago, yet another evidential conflict arose over the nationalistic implications of Macpherson's work. Do the poems of Ossian "forge a common [British] identity," as Leith Davis argues, through their presentation of the Highlands as "the cradle of civilization from which all the inhabitants of Britain emerged"? Or, do they and other bardic poems of Britain's Gaelic peripheries give what Katie Trumpener calls "new emphasis to the social rootedness and political function" of distinctively Scottish, Irish, or Welsh literature?[5]

The composite whole of the issues surrounding *Ossian* is arguably greater than the sum of its parts. After all, what the questions of authenticity, history, and nationalism share is a mutual implication in the epistemology of evidence that was forged during the Enlightenment; that is, they each rely on truth claims that entail a deliberative consideration of sources and facts, and that therefore demand the implementation of a logic of probability. For instance, based on an examination of Macpherson's sources, *it is likely that* his translations are (in)authentic. Or again, the nostalgic tenor of *Ossian* forges a *circumstantial link* to the ambivalent national imaginary—"Scottish" in one register, "Highland

Jacobite" in another, "British" in a third—which defined Scottish identity after the Union of 1707. Hence, for all the potential diversity of inquiries into the cultural contexts of *Ossian*, the sheer redundancy of the epistemic economy sustaining them makes "evidence" in some ways the master key to them all. It reminds one of Derrida's declaration in *Of Grammatology* that the problem of language has never been simply one problem among others.[6] Neither has the problem of evidence; not since the Enlightenment.

Because of the unusual weight Macpherson's *Ossian* places on this problem of evidence, we may interpret it as a touchstone of the epochal rupture of experience from knowledge. In Chapter 3, we saw how this rupture directly impacted the Highlands in the evidentially inflected form of "improvement." Macpherson's translations thematize and criticize improvement, specifically the epistemological and institutional configuration of evidential knowledge which improvement entailed. Hence, more than as a repository of empirical facts, the *Ossian* poems may be read as a critical commentary on the social as well as conceptual ramifications of evidential thought.

FIGURES OF WITNESSING IN FINGAL

The story of how Macpherson's translations first came into public consciousness is well known. Macpherson was toiling in obscurity as a private tutor when he met the Scottish playwright John Home in the spa town of Moffat in the fall of 1759. Born into and raised by a Highland family, Macpherson had been nurturing an interest in the idea of native Highland poetry since listening to lectures on poetry in primitive societies delivered by Thomas Blackwell, his professor at the University of Aberdeen from 1752 to 1755. Home's fascination with Highland culture dated back at least to 1749, when his conversations on the subject with William Collins had inspired the latter's "An Ode on the Popular Superstitions of the Highlanders of Scotland, Considered as the Subject of Poetry." In Macpherson, Home was thrilled to find someone who could provide him with greater insights into Gaelic poetry. He urged Macpherson to translate a few verses, and was taken by what he heard. Home then shared these findings with his literati friends in Edinburgh. Fiona Stafford, Macpherson's biographer, remarks that "[t]he man who took the greatest interest [in the poems] was Hugh Blair, who . . . sent for Macpherson at once, eager to see further examples of the Highland poetry and to publish them, if possible."[7] Macpherson first resisted the invitation, then reluctantly agreed to produce a few verses for publication, and then tried to back out of the agreement. Nevertheless, his *Fragments of Ancient Poetry* appeared in June of 1760, followed eighteen months later by the epic *Fingal.* Blair accepted a post as Chair of Rhetoric and Belles Lettres at the University of Edinburgh in 1760. Macpherson's translations and his own famous "Critical Dissertation on the Poems of Ossian" (1765) soon worked their way into the curriculum as Blair began shaping a discipline that makes him perhaps the first Professor of English Literature in a British university.

Meanwhile, *Fingal,* published in December of 1761, was later republished with *Temora* (first printed in 1763), a second epic, in 1765. These two works, Stafford remarks, "were to make Ossian famous throughout the world. By 1763 the Abb[é] Cesarotti had translated *Fingal* into Italian, and from here, the vogue for *Ossian* spread across Europe and even to America, as the poems were published in Swedish, German, French, Spanish, Danish, Russian, Dutch, Bohemian, Polish and Hungarian."[8] The poems would eventually extend forward into history as easily as they had initially traversed national boundaries, inspiring a later generation of Romantic politicians, poets, and philosophers from Napoleon and Thomas Jefferson to Goethe and William Blake.

From the outset, Macpherson's *Ossian* embroiled itself in a standoff between witness testimony and probabilistic evidence. The public prosecution of the translations based itself on the need for circumstantial proofs independent of human testimony, demanding such "facts that cannot lie" as actual manuscripts. Samuel Johnson groused most famously that "[t]he editor, or author, never could shew the original; nor can it be shewn by any other; [and] to revenge incredulity, by refusing evidence, is a degree of insolence, with which the world is not yet acquainted." James Boswell concurred that "when no ancient manuscript, to authenticate the work, was deposited in any publick library, though that was insisted on as a reasonable proof, who could forbear to doubt?" Another polemicist, William Shaw, argued against Macpherson (and supposedly with Johnson's aid) that "[w]hen the proposition to be proved is a fact, and not mere speculation, or matter of opinion, facts alone, not internal evidence, which always give[s] latitude to conjecture and uncertainty on both sides, can be a reasonable proof; and nothing less can procure the assent of the dispassionate and unbiassed mind."[9]

The public defense of *Ossian,* on the other hand, based itself on what Dr. John Pringle, a friend of David Hume's, called "a cloud of witnesses," mostly from the Highlands. To many participants in the debate, these witnesses seemed all the more compelling for defying the mandates of probability. The English poet Thomas Gray confided to a friend in 1760 that "I continue to think [Ossian's poetry] genuine, tho' my reasons for believing the contrary are rather stronger than ever: but I will have them antique, for I never knew a Scotchman of my own time, that could read, much less write, poetry; & such poetry too!" Even Hume, who eventually expressed his own doubts about the authenticity of Macpherson's translations, initially urged Hugh Blair, Macpherson's primary public defender, to authenticate the poems through "testimonies. People's ears are fortified against [arguments]; [but testimonies] may yet find their way, before the poems are consigned to total oblivion."[10]

The poems reflect in their narrative and linguistic structure the evidential controversy they aroused publicly. This becomes apparent on a close review of *Fingal*. The Preface to the *Fragments* announced optimistically that "there is reason to hope that one work of considerable length, and which deserves to be styled an heroic poem, might be recovered and translated, if encouragement were given to such an undertaking."[11] An epic in six "books," *Fingal* recounts the assault on a northern Irish kingdom by the forces of a Norse invader, Swaran. Cuchullin, chief of the Irish tribes, tries to resist Swaran's attack, but eventually he is forced to rely on the beneficent prowess of the Highland king and mighty warrior, Fingal. The text foregrounds its testimonial instability in a number of ways, from the conventions of character and plot through its narrative voice and choice of tropes. The character and plight of Cuchullin, for instance, almost typologically represent the evolving status of the legal witness. In the epic's first two (of its six) books, we behold Cuchullin receiving the testimony of scouts and fellow warriors with skepticism. "Rise, said [Moran], Cuchullin rise; I see the ships of Swaran. Cuchullin, many are the foe. . . . Moran! replied the blue-eyed chief . . . [t]hy fears have much increased the foe" (*Poems* 55). When told of a foreboding message delivered to another comrade by a ghostly portent, Cuchullin retorts that "it was the wind that murmured in the caves," else "why didst thou not force him to my sight . . . [where m]y sword might find that voice, and force his knowledge from him" (65–66). As Cuchullin finds his forces routed by Swaran's, however, his position and attitude begin to change. When Moran descries "the ships of the lonely isle" that carry Fingal and his army (68), Cuchullin retires in dejection from the fight. Ossian, the narrator, reports that "[t]he winds came down on the woods. The torrents rushed from the rocks. Rain gathered . . . [a]nd the red stars trembled. Sad, by the side of a stream whose sound was echoed by a tree, sad by the side of a stream the chief of Erin [i.e., Cuchullin] sat" (69). The refrain of his sadness underscores the melancholy of Cuchullin's recession from battle, a withdrawal that, combined with his subsequent view of Fingal's conquests, lays the basis for the latter's glory. Cuchullin retires to a cave, where he communes with ghosts. "For never more," Ossian tells us, "shall Cuchullin be renowned among the mighty in the land. . . . [He is] like a mist that has fled away, when the blast of the morning came" (88).

Ossian's allusion to the rising sun foreshadows the displacement of Cuchullin by Fingal along lines that retrace the marginalization of legal witnesses. The trope implicitly evokes Fingal, whose battle standard "was distinguished by the name of *sun-beam*" (431), an important figure in the ballad tradition from which Macpherson drew.[12] Contrasting with Fingal's ascension, Cuchullin's communion with ghosts (which Macpherson elsewhere associates with those "*improbable tales* . . . which we meet with in the highlands" [502, my emphasis]) places him in the same testimonial company as the portents and visionaries whose reports he had previously dismissed. Fingal, by comparison, personifies justice, arriving climactically on the scene "like the sun in a storm, when he shines on the hills of grass." As I mention above, Fingal's arrival all but banishes Cuchullin, who, "bending, weeping, sad, and slow . . . sunk in Cromla's wood . . . fear[ing] the face of Fingal, who was wont to greet him from the fields of renown." Fingal even mournfully pronounces Cuchullin's death: "The battle is over . . . and I behold the blood of my friends. Sad is the heath of Lena . . . the son of Semo [i.e., Cuchullin] is no more" (75–76). Cuchullin is not dead, but has been reduced to being a mere witness to Fingal's conquests. And yet, precisely *as* such a witness he has become dead to the action of battle, or to direct involvement in the determination of justice. In Ossian's narrative the improvers decide the course of right; accordingly, Fingal's triumph relegates Cuchullin to the narrative's peripheries.

The significance of Cuchullin's position and of the general status of testimony in *Fingal* comes more clearly into focus if we bear in mind the contextual field of legal evidence in the eighteenth century. One consequence of the preference for a removed and contemplative rather than a direct relation to the events in question in a particular trial was that witness testimony was becoming all the more incidental to evidential truth for occupying a position all the more immediate (indeed, all the more im-probable) with respect to the facts at issue. Reduced to being merely one of many elements in a deliberative process, testimony came to play an increasingly peripheral role in the determination of justice. Macpherson's text inscribes this judicial history into its narrative by marginalizing Cuchullin, transforming him as ruler and chief into a passive observer who gazes on as Fingal restores the proper balance of power. As with legal witnesses during this period, the more Cuchullin becomes a spectator of the conflict, the less he is allowed to participate in the battle with, or ultimate judgment of, the antagonistic Swaran.

Critically, however, the same improbability that attends Cuchullin (and his hallucinatory visions from "the cave of his sorrow," [88]) might also be said to infect Ossian's narration of these events. The son of Fingal and "king of many songs," Ossian pronounces himself "the first and bloodiest in the war" with Swaran (87, 85). And yet he composes his epic at a much later time, after the death of Fingal and the extinction of the Celtic golden age. Now "mournful and blind . . . dark and forlorn" (83), Ossian's perspective is as riddled by the "ghosts" of "former years" as the dubious Cuchullin's (99). Indeed, the narrative of Fingal's arrival and conquest is largely Cuchullin's own. The narrative that tells us about a witness thus reflexively models itself after that witness, as Ossian falls into the fiction he describes, multiplying improbability on improbability.[13]

Eighteenth-century Scottish antiquarians stigmatized bardic history for this very trait. Thomas Innes, an influential mid-century antiquarian, reasoned that since the bards' "subsistence [in the clans] depend[ed] on their flattering great men, no credit [can] be given to" their historical accounts.[14] And yet, Macpherson's expressed aversion in a 1765 "Dissertation" to "systems of history [built on] probabilities" suggests that our access to the Celtic past must contend with these testimonial ruins (*Poems* 43). In one sense, then, Macpherson's epic tacitly confirms the common privilege accorded to probability by identifying testimony with loss. However, more importantly than rehearsing the defeats suffered by Cuchullin and, eventually, Ossian, Macpherson emphasizes testimonial loss in order to recover or at least point toward the types of social histories, Scottish and legal, that were being implicitly occluded by "probable" truths.

The judicial tensions in Macpherson's text reflect those that had been building in the Highlands since the defeat of the Jacobite army on Culloden Moor in 1746, when the British government sought to ensure permanent victory by passing a series of prohibitive and proactive laws designed to abolish the region's feudal particularity, from illegalization of the bagpipes to the seizure of estates by government factors. Probability transformed evidence in the same fundamental way that improvement altered the Highland economy: in each case, speculation either replaced or heavily supplemented a system that heretofore had operated ostensibly according to principles of subsistence. In court, this subsistence had manifested itself in the relative tangibility of evidence, or its traceability to a concrete testimonial source (i.e., to witnesses, whether on the jury or not). Circumstantial evidence, by comparison, educed a kind of surplus value, as facts—such as the iconic "bloody knife" or "smoking gun"—now acquired the capacity to "speak for themselves." And yet, the more emphatic division of labor between witnesses and jurors, coupled with the emergence of lawyers, made this speech the product of a system in which neither witnesses, jurors, nor lawyers were wholly accountable for the facticity of the fact. A complex legal process increasingly came to speak in addition to and ultimately in the place of persons. In essence, this new evidential economy alchemized facts into a species of capital: lawyers and juries appropriated testimony and reinvested it in such a way that its facts and their interpretations might multiply themselves endlessly.

Born into a Highland Jacobite clan in 1736, Macpherson witnessed the failure of the rebellion and the onset of improvement, and the "facts" he presents in *Fingal* bear traces of this turbid social complexity. A decade after the publication of *Fingal,* he continued to argue of Celtic history that "[b]eyond the reach of records is a gloom which no ingenuity can penetrate."[15] We have seen how aspects of character, narrative, and voice reenact this "gloom" in *Fingal* by conspicuously and regressively mediating our access to Celtic history through a series of witnesses: Cuchullin as onlooker, Ossian as bard, Macpherson as translator, and so forth.[16] The epic's sonorous language, which permeates Ossian's Highland landscape, only amplifies this effect.

The text embellishes the tenuousness of its facts by consistently subordinating tropes that appeal to sight to those which evoke sound, thus suggesting the dependence of visuality on aurality, or (by implication) of evidential conviction on testimony. At the epic's opening, Cuchullin sits beside "the tree of the rustling leaf," and he is incited to action, like the narrative itself, by his scout's testimony of the approaching Norsemen.[17] Cuchullin instructs Moran to "strike [a] sounding shield" to alert the Irish forces. "Moran went and struck the bossy shield. The hills and their rocks replied. The sound spread along the wood. . . . Curach leapt from the sounding rock; and Connal of the bloody spear" (*Poems* 55). The sound of the shield acts here as an incantation, animating the landscape from which the chiefs emerge. Thus, from the outset of the epic we experience a sonorous multiplication of voices: Cuchullin (whose name etymologically signifies "the voice of Ullin," [419]) responds to a (scout's) voice in a place of "rustling" sounds and then commands the scout to strike a shield, to which "the hills and their rocks repl[y]." Finding his own imagination stimulated by this polyphony of voices, the narrator, Ossian, describes the summoned chiefs in similarly aural terms: "Now I behold the chiefs in the pride of their former deeds. . . . They came like streams from the mountains; each rushed roaring from his hill. . . . The sounds of crashing arms ascend. The grey dogs howl between. Unequally bursts the song of battle; and [the] rocking [region of] Cromla echoes round" (56). Book II perpetuates this aural motif by opening in like fashion: "Connal lay by the sound of the mountain stream, beneath the aged tree. . . . Shrill thro' the heath of Lena, he heard the voice of night." Approached by a specter, Connal asks, "What green-headed hill is thy place of rest? Shall we not hear thee in the storm? In the noise of the mountain-stream?" (65).

Sound in *Fingal* acts as an impetus in two principal ways. First, and most obviously, the text's aurality is supposed to indicate its orality as a bardic work "handed down by tradition" and "adapted to music" (49). Second, and perhaps more provocatively, tropes denoting sound serve as the dominant medium through which objects come into focus. Blood "sounds" from an expiring maiden's side (58); war's "noise is like the blast of winter" or like "streams from high rocks" that are noted less for their cascading splendor than for the way they "meet, and mix and *roar* on the plain" (59; my emphasis). In addition then to reproducing the structure of legal witnessing in the interaction between the characters, *Fingal* invites its readers to a (literal) hearing in which the resonance of the language underscores the relation between objects and voice and hence between objects and the speakers, or witnesses, who behold them.[18] Sound here resides not so much in the landscape as in the implicit testimonies of those who describe it to us. When Ossian speaks of "the silent sunshine of heaven" (67) and thus portrays the source of light in relation to (its lack of) sound, he also attunes us to the testimony of those who, Macpherson says, "have been in the Highlands" and are familiar with the "gloominess of th[ose] scenes . . . [that] beget [a] melancholy disposition of mind" (425, 502). Sound becomes the sign less of objects than of subjects who appear in silhouette against the thickness of their words.

In *Fingal*, such witnesses are often invoked in terms of an expiring sonority, a "voice of music d[ying] away" (84). Numerous references are made to the "echoing heath," or to the virtual emptiness of the landscape, lending the latter's sounds, scenes, and figures a haunting quality. In defending the authenticity of *Ossian*, Hugh Blair distinguished between two contrasting valences of attenuating Highland resonance. In one sense, "the silence of a whole country" toward Macpherson's translation might be taken as "positive" proof of the poems' validity, since no outcry was raised in opposition (402). In a more somber register, however, this silence also intimated that "the manners of the inhabitants . . . [had] of late undergone a great change. . . . The introduction of the busy and laborious arts [i.e., commerce] [had] considerably abated . . . poetical enthusiasm" (404). Macpherson proposed a similar explanation for the deepening silence: "The genius of the highlanders has suffered a great change within these few years. . . . [T]he introduction of trade and manufactures has destroyed that leisure which was formerly dedicated to hearing and repeating the poems of ancient times. Many have now learned to leave their mountains" (51).[19]

John Barrell alludes to this condition while discussing the erosion of comprehensive knowledge and social unity in eighteenth-century British society. He ascribes the growing sense of fragmentation to a proliferating market economy that was dividing and subdividing labor into increasingly discrete and minute particles. As a result of this extensive division of labor, "no one could thenceforth claim to have a complete view of society." Analyzing this phenomenon through landscape painting and poetry (and in a manner evocative of the sonorous Ossian), Barrell says that if "we cannot grasp the design of the landscape, that is because we are a part of it—we are the trees, the hills, the light, the shade. To discover its proportions and unity, we must occupy, as it were, a position outside the landscape."[20]

Such exteriority is repeatedly undermined and even criticized in *Fingal* by the sounds—the voices, the testimonies—reverberating through the landscape, as waves of resonance transport and engulf our literal point of view. In the eighteenth-century era of legal evidence, a limited purview meant that determinations of truth could pretend to little more than conjectures of probability. As we have seen, probable conviction came to be valued all the more for what it professed *not* to see, or for the echoes—the testimonies—it was able to reinvest as reasonable judgment. Witness testimony provided the court with those resources, "the trees, the hills, the light, the shade," from which the evidential truth might be cultivated. In Chapter 3, we discussed how this process took on a more transparently economic dimension in the Highlands, as speculative programs of improvement altered the face of the landscape and the profile of its inhabitants. The outright failure of so many of these projects to stimulate commerce or make living conditions more hospitable served in a different sense to imbue the Highlands with an air of recalcitrant primitivism that acquired a double significance in later eighteenth-century British culture. The region became at once the ideological reservoir of a less fragmented social past and a vivid index of the failure of commercial progress and the complacency of its nostalgia. Hence, whereas commerce sought to transform the Gaelic wilderness into an industrial arcadia much as evidentiary codes sought to refine blindness into insight, Macpherson's Highlands, through their improbable and professedly impoverished echoes, served instead to unsettle the philosophical foundations of improvement by suspending the evidential parameters of legal knowledge.

ROMANCE, "RACE," TRAUMA

The evidentiary codes subtending *Fingal* suggestively frame the epic's Highlandism in terms of the attractions of experience in modernity. Macpherson and his supporters seemed archly aware that the poems comprised a tenuous source of historical evidence. Hugh Blair's Preface to the *Fragments of Ancient Poetry,* written "in consequence with the conversations

[he] had held with Mr Macpherson," opened by announcing that "[t]he public may depend on the following fragments as genuine remains of ancient Scottish poetry"; but, of course, if either the poems' authenticity were obvious or the public trust assured, no such announcement would have been necessary (*Poems* 415, 5). Five years later, in a "Dissertation" appended to the third edition of his *Works of Ossian, the Son of Fingal* (1765)—which contained the *Fragments* as well as the two longer epics, *Fingal* and *Temora*—Macpherson sublimated this particular anxiety regarding his own translations into a general theory regarding the status of all historical evidence: "Inquiries into the antiquities of nations afford more pleasure than any real advantage to mankind. The ingenious may form systems of history on probabilities and a few facts; but at a great distance of time, their accounts must be vague and uncertain" (*Poems* 43). Then, in another "Dissertation" written eight years later, Macpherson further inflated this "uncertainty" into a normative condition of antiquity itself:

Destitute of the use of letters, [the ancient Highlanders] themselves had not the means of transmitting their great actions to remote posterity. . . . The traditions and songs to which they trusted their history, were lost, or altogether corrupted in their revolutions and migrations, which were so frequent and universal, that no kingdom in Europe is now possessed by its original inhabitants. Societies were formed and kingdoms erected, from a mixture of nations, who, in process of time, lost all knowledge of their own origin. (*Poems* 205)

In this self-reflexive passage, the ancient Highlands are presented as opaque not only to us in retrospect, but also contemporaneously to themselves. For this reason, Macpherson suggests, whether considered historically or culturally, discussions of Highland Scotland are not conducive to "systems of . . . probability," or to the estimations of likelihood driving evidential inquiry—a claim which helps his own testimonial case.

One of the more provocative aspects of Macpherson's treatises was their virtual reversal of Blair's position in the *Fragments*. In defending the poems' authenticity, Blair had implicitly undermined the evidential strength of Macpherson's translations without impugning the intrinsic nature of such evidence. In the later editions, however, especially his 1773 "Dissertation Concerning the Poems of Ossian," Macpherson argued that it was the nature of such historical proof—and *not* his translations per se—that had fallen into disrepute. In most nations, he claimed, ancient traditions fell into "corrupt[ion]" through "revolutions and migrations. . . . If," therefore,

tradition could be depended upon, it is only among a people, from all time, free of intermixture with foreigners. We are to look for these among the mountains and inaccessible parts of a country: places, on account of their barrenness, uninviting to an enemy, or whose natural strength enabled the natives to repel invasions. Such are the inhabitants of the mountains of Scotland. We, accordingly, find that they differ materially from those who possess the low and more fertile parts of the kingdom. Their language is pure and original, and their manners are those of an antient and unmixed race of men. Conscious of their own antiquity, they long despised others, as a new and mixed people. (205–6)

Macpherson's argument for "unmixed race" resolves itself into an appeal to testimony, and hence to witness experience. Not all defenders of Ossian appealed to the category of race in this way: the minister John Macpherson, among others, made a more biological claim for the poems' Caledonian (as opposed to Irish) origin.[21] Later, and echoing the enthusiasm for Ossian expressed by his German Romantic forebears, Friedrich Nietzsche struck this chord in mentioning "Fin-Gal" as the exemplar of a "blond race."[22] However, Nietzsche's labile argument actually turns less on race per se than on religiously motivated turpitude, to which he opposes a brazenly aesthetic attitude toward matters of truth. James Macpherson hardly resembles Nietzsche's Zarathustra, but he does articulate similar skepticism toward the claims of evidence. The Ossianic record is true, Macpherson argues—we have its word in the form of local tradition—even though (or, perhaps, precisely because) we cannot verify it; *Ossian* trails clouds of witnesses, but leaves scant trace of hard facts.

The purity of testimony, the immediacy of what is seen and heard, appealed to Johann Gottfried von Herder, who enthusiastically regarded *Ossian* as a window onto ancient Caledonia on the basis of "*innern Beweise*" ("internal proof," from *Weise*, meaning "way" or "tune"—the testimony of the "echoing heath" in *Ossian*). He did so even in the face of the "*inneres Zeugnis*" ("inner testimony," from *Zeuge*, witness, but also *Zeug*, meaning material, stuff, or things: hence, the testimony of things, or circumstantial evidence) presented by those who claimed *Ossian* was a fraud.[23] For Herder, as for Macpherson, testimony designated a distinctive quality, in this case an unmediated, unmixed relation to objects of knowledge. *Ossian* compels attention, Macpherson and Herder agreed, less because it is true than because it is distinctive, presenting and inciting an experience of truth in an alternative, testimonial register.

Ironically, the "racial" quality of this argument is mixed, uneven, anything but pure. While we should not overlook Macpherson's possible Celtic tribalism and corresponding xenophobia toward Saxon (read: "British") society—Howard Weinbrot's argument here is compelling, Colin Kidd's mitigating view notwithstanding[24]—we should at least recall that nation, culture, and religion were all associated with the term "race" in the eighteenth century, rendering the category inherently ambiguous. As we now realize, biological inquiry would soon turn the category

of race toward very different ends.[25] While this helps present a more var-
iegated portrait of Macpherson, it also prompts the question of whether
Freud may not have been, in his way, a man of the eighteenth century.
It almost appears so given the palimpsest in his late work on trauma of
Macpherson's blend of race, culture, and experience.

In his 1939 text *Moses and Monotheism,* Freud broached the issues he
had raised nineteen years earlier in *Beyond the Pleasure Principle.* This
time, rather than addressing trauma from the perspective of the individual, Freud reflected on the dispersion of traumatic neurosis throughout
an entire society. The concept of monotheism historically derived, he
argued, from the Israelites' murder of their tyrannical liberator, Moses.
Harrowed by this deed, the Jews displaced the image of Moses onto a
thundering, austere deity. The murder, which the Jews repressed, thus
returned in such forms as the strictness of the Torah, the mandate
demanding circumcision, and persecution by other societies who
unconsciously discerned the traces of the Jews' repressed act. This persecution was most vivid for Freud in the escalating savagery of Nazi political policy, which had incited Freud to seek asylum in London as he was
working on his essay. In his "Prefatory Notes" to Part III, Freud writes:
"[i]n the certainty of persecution—now not only because of my work,
but also because of my 'race'—I left, with many friends, the city [i.e.,
Vienna] which from my early childhood . . . had been a home to me."[26]
Cast into exile like the Israelites of old, Freud reflected on how he may
have inherited his circumstances as much as he experienced them:
"there probably exists in the mental life of the individual not only what
he has experienced himself, but also what he brought with him at birth,
fragments of phylogenetic origin, an archaic heritage" (125).

Freud's scare quotes in referring to his "race" divulge a playful determination to redefine the term. His aim here was partly to escape the
biological confines of the individual human body expressed in previous
theories which explained trauma as a neurological condition. Freud's
"phylogenetic" observations concerning the Jews do not devolve on biological determinism as much as on the blurry region of culture, and on
the kinds of social symptoms, inherited as ritualistic practices, which cause
history compulsively to repeat itself. Jews, he argued, "have a very good
opinion of themselves, think themselves nobler, on a higher level, superior
to others. . . . They really believe themselves to be God's chosen people"
(134). For Freud, this confidence is grounded, however, on the distortion
of a primal deed, murder, dispersed into the vortex of everyday life.

While the cultural implications of the Jewish "race" evoke Ossian's
Highlanders, Freud diverges from Macpherson in nullifying any suggestion of experiential immediacy. Neither Jews nor their persecutors directly perceive or exhibit any obvious connection between primal murder

and monotheism; rather, the connections to that primal experience are scattered, fragmentary, and oblique. But, as we have discussed in earlier chapters, such mediated experience betrays the image of its opposite—the image of an experience that is collective instead of alienated, full rather than fragmentary. Marx's (and later Benjamin's) observations concerning labor apply to Freud's notion of modern Judaism as well: universal alienation (or, in this case, mediation) conduces to solidarity (or, here, to a phylogenetic inheritance).

The vivid color of Freud's topics—Judaism, Nazism, primal murder—should not distract us from perceiving the "distorted traces" of the Enlightenment dilemma of experience. Theodor Adorno, Freud's near contemporary and close reader, commented in trenchant ways on similar intersections between experience and race. His most poignant reflections concerning the transference between these categories may be found in his reflections (with Max Horkheimer) on Judaism. As a prelude to that discussion, we should first consider Adorno's argument regarding the evidentiary drive to uncover tangible facts, a drive which secretly harbors the same desire for "epic naïveté" exhibited by Macpherson's translations. Epic naïveté "emerges from the enlightenment-oriented and positivist effort to adhere faithfully and without distortion to what once was as it was," or from the desire to see things in their true character. An unmediated relation to an object, a culture, or a historical period represents "thought's innermost yearning" to arrive at "something real that would no longer be enclosed by social domination and the classificatory thought modeled upon it."[27] Modern Western thought, Adorno regretfully notes, constitutionally forecloses this kind of immediate relation to objects. The concept and practice of science place us at a double remove from objects—first, in their mediation to us by way of tools and procedures (e.g., the microscope; the scientific method), and second, in the displacement of a social perspective onto objects—a socially derived relationship to objects (e.g., as one finds in magic)—with bare "fact," or with a knowledge which divorces us as subjects from the objects under investigation. In a fallen world like this one, Adorno reasons, immediacy and the integration of society and nature come to seem almost supernatural.

But, in typically Adornian fashion, a dialectical reversal accompanies this unfortunate fall into abstraction. Precisely because of the gross unlikelihood of immediacy, "[a] critique of bourgeois reason," or instrumental, means-end reason, implicitly "dwells within epic naïveté. It holds fast to a possibility of experience that is destroyed by the bourgeois [i.e., probabilistic, profit-driven] reason that ostensibly grounds it" (26). In other words, the critique implicit to epic naïveté adheres to an ideal of witnessing that regards the experience of objects as being sufficient to a knowledge of them—an experience that is independent of the type of inferential calculation which began to count as "evidence" during the eighteenth century. Adorno thus claims that primal impulses toward immediacy—toward im-probability—haunt the process of enlightenment and its technologies of probabilistic calculation.

It is axiomatic in Adorno's work that every benevolent operation in spirit finds a cruel parody in practice. And so it is here: the dream of a pure, immediate relation to the world—the dream of "race," as Macpherson (partly) imagines it—attained its ugliest possible expression in Nazi conceptions of Aryan supremacy and anti-Semitism. There, the Enlightenment ideal of an immediate relation to objects deteriorated into a crass biologism, a horrific caricature of an epistemology of belonging. Below, I reflect on the insidious raciological repercussions of experiential purity, as well as on Adorno and Horkheimer's conception of Judaism as a source of trauma for fascistic modernity. Here, I would only underscore that such insights are significant to the *Ossian* controversy because they cast Macpherson's translations as an unusually enlightened endeavor to arrive at a more immediate experience of objects (in this case, the "object" of ancient Caledonia) while showing how the translations' promotion of testimonial "naïveté" intuited a necessary critique of Enlightenment rationality. "It is easy," Adorno remarks, "either [to] ridicule [epic] simplicity . . . or deploy it spitefully in opposition to the analytic spirit. . . . But again, only this kind of naiveté permits one to tell the story of the fateful origins of the late capitalist era"—or, in the case of the Highlands, the story of "improvement"—in such a way that it fosters "a kind of remembrance of what cannot really be remembered [anymore]" (26). To this extent, Macpherson's Highlands metonymically name the overdetermined, Enlightenment dream of unmediated, improbable experience that typified the eighteenth-century legal conception of the witness.

Evidence after Auschwitz

A blurb on the book jacket of the American edition of Binjamin Wilkomirski's *Fragments: Memories of a Wartime Childhood* attests to how much baggage the concept of experience has accumulated since Macpherson's *Ossian*, and also to the concept's enduring implication in the Enlightenment evidential model. This blurb exclaims enthusiastically that the commodity it promotes is "not to be read but experienced." Intended as high praise, this comment reiterates the seminal difference between a witness's direct and a jury's more mediated experience, privileging the former. To read is to reflect, to deliberate; Wilkomirski's memoirs promise something more immediate—in Macpherson's words, less "mixed."

Indirectly and in negative, the blurb echoes Adorno's famous dictum that "[t]o write poetry after Auschwitz is barbaric." Adorno formulates this enigmatic phrase in his essay "Cultural Criticism and Society" as a commentary on modernity's absorption of raw experience by mediating codes of understanding, and of these codes in turn by the massification of culture. "The more total society becomes, the greater the reification of the mind and the more paradoxical its effort to escape reification on its own." After all, such escape would reproduce the appearance of novelty, which was the desideratum of all commodities. In modernity, novelty is the norm, reducing extremes of intellect and anguish to equations of value. Under these conditions, "[e]ven the most extreme consciousness of doom threatens to degenerate into idle chatter" in that it only perpetuates an industry already feeding off the appetite of its consumers for the sensational (e.g., the end of the world). Sensation here devolves to sensationalism and reflection to instrumental reason. In Adorno's estimation, poetry exhibits this degenerate condition in almost archetypal fashion. Succinctly captured by Wordsworth as feeling (sensation) recollected in tranquility (reflection), poetry had served for Hegel as the fusion of the sensuousness of music with the conceptual possibilities of philosophy, and hence as the summit of artistic achievement. For Adorno, however, poetry's status as a cultural emblem of modernity divulged a more harrowing social reality. He saw it as "the final stage of the dialectic of culture and barbarism," the process of modernity's reification of experience as sensation. In Adorno's mind, poetic beauty masked a horrific social ugliness; this made poetry reprehensible as a commemorative medium of the Shoah.[28]

To Adorno's way of thinking, the practice of culture as the transmission of values had become barbaric; hence, paradoxically, only the epic naïveté of projects like Macpherson's (which mimic barbarism—all too literally for critics like Johnson) seemed to provide the utopian image of a regenerative culture. The blurb on Wilkomirski's book jacket unconsciously reiterates this dialectic of barbarism and redemptive naïveté, this promise of raw experience. (The irony that this redemption is promised on a book jacket as a commodity and in the form of an advertisement would certainly not have been lost on Adorno.)

The blurb echoes a second dictum that is pertinent to studies of the Shoah and of experience, and which raises the question of what exactly "experience" signifies in Wilkomirski's book. This second dictum, ironically, is one whose history we have already traced—namely, that facts should "speak for themselves." In his 1990 study *Act and Idea in the Nazi Genocide*, Berel Lang confirmed Adorno's injunction by lamenting that "literary representation imposes artifice, a figurative mediation of language, and the contrivance of a persona—that is, a mask—on the part of the writer." Literary writing thus "obtru[des] on its subject." Lang's argument echoes the logic of evidential probability: language, or testimony, obscures a clear understanding of objects, or facts. And, when the "facts" which testimony obscures are those which pertain to the Nazi genocide, such testimony becomes complicit with the Nazi apologists who denied the reality and the magnitude of the crimes that were committed. Accordingly, Lang counterpoises to the poetics of experience a style of writing in which "the facts 'speak for themselves.'"[29] Consistent with the legal ideology of the Enlightenment, Lang's larger aim in sponsoring this evidential ideal is to incite a heightened degree of critical judgment in studies of the Shoah, and to impress on readers and writers alike a juror's grave responsibility for their conceptions.

However, as Thomas Trezise notes, one unfortunate consequence of this critical-evidential program is the silencing of testimony. "Lang implies that the proper response to the Holocaust would consist not only in representing but also in *re-enacting*, through the obliteration of personal voice, the depersonalization that characterized the Final Solution."[30] To experience something by way of "facts speaking for themselves," Trezise observes, would be commensurate with not experiencing it at all. This is because experience, filtered (as Trezise imagines it) through the lens of one's cultural inheritance and perceptions, ineluctably taints any pure contact with the facts themselves. Hence, to condemn figurative language is to condemn testimony and experience alike; and this condemnation of testimony and experience is structurally homologous to the Nazi genocide that Lang urges us to abhor, but seems drawn in some ways silently to repeat. The Enlightenment dilemma of experience returns here as an ethical conundrum: how is one to represent (or mediate) the unrepresentable (or the experience of immediacy)?[31]

As we recall, eighteenth-century juries posed this question all the time, sometimes in overtly violent ways (as in the Stewart Trial). Lang and Trezise perhaps overdramatize this type of violence by formally likening it to the Final Solution, but their arguments resonate with the history of Enlightenment experience.[32] Still, neither Lang nor Trezise seem fully attuned to the violence inscribed into the concept of experience as a mediated phenomenon—that is, in Trezise's account, as a by-product of an experiencing subject's cultural inheritance and perceptions. To be sure, the concept of mediated experience confirms current theories of memory, models of trauma, notions of common sense, and conceptions of a postmodern media state. However, the acceptance of mediated experience as a fact of nature also erases the historical and ideological origins of that idea in Enlightenment conceptions of evidence. The conversion of mediation into a truism thus conforms historically to the Enlightenment devaluation of witness experience. In decrying the Shoah—or, more properly, studies of the Shoah—Lang and Trezise thus testify (in the very premises of their arguments *for and against* it, similarly to the pursuers and defenders in the Stewart Trial vis-à-vis circumstantial evidence) to the decay of experience that Adorno laments, the kind of decay that manifests itself in predigested claims about mediation.

We have seen that such claims possess long and complex histories. In fact, the lineaments of Nazi raciology and the reduction of experience to the body reenact in perverse fashion the logic of eighteenth-century legal testimony. Witness experience deteriorated during this period to an experience of the body—to sensory, bodily impressions—as opposed to the mediated, rational experience of jurors. This reduction to bodily sensation implicitly informs the ideal of racial and evidential purity which Macpherson evokes as the "tradition . . . [of] a people," a cloud of witnesses, "free from intermixture with foreigners" (*Poems of Ossian* 205). In *Fingal*, this purity manifests itself in the epic's narrative structure, its characters, and its sonorous tropes as the valorization of a witness's experience that no jury reasonably can judge. Witnesses in *Ossian* are a race apart. As we saw, Adorno defends the legitimacy of such claims as a kind of "epic naïveté," the secret dream of immediate experience set against the nightmare of endless probabilistic mediation. However, it is also this notion of experiential purity that Adorno deprecates elsewhere as "the idol of pure original experience"; "a hoax."[33] In theory, that is, "immediacy" calls attention in negative to the debased condition of a thoroughly mediated, decayed experience; in practice, however, the notion of immediacy fetishizes bodily sensation, which is precisely the state of experience in modernity's rationalized public sphere.[34] "Epic naïveté" thus applies both to the kind of experiential immediacy which Macpherson's translations evoke and also to the inverse ideal, the positivistic immediacy of the "facts which cannot lie" to which Lang aspires. More desirable as an emblem of unachievable ideality than as social praxis, "epic naïveté" functions for Adorno as a negative dialectic, a "consistent sense of nonidentity" that undermines enlightenment presumptions of purity, whether conceptual or, in a broader sense, "racial" (*ND* 5). But this negative function would all but disappear in Wilkomirski's implicit revival of *Ossian*.

WILKOMIRSKI'S TEARS

Macpherson made a fortune by persuading readers to believe Ossian's testimony precisely because it was improbable. The "Wilkomirski affair" resets this issue for our time, not only in the phenomenon of his memoirs themselves but also, more importantly, in the evidentiary debates these memoirs have incited. In fairness to Macpherson, scholars have shown that the *Ossian* translations are creative adaptations of extant Gaelic poetry, and not utter fabrications. The same, though, might be said of Wilkomirski's *Fragments*: many people suffered the kinds of atrocities Wilkomirski describes, even if he himself did not, or not exactly in the same way.[35]

Wilkomirski's story is that of a young boy ripped from his family at the beginning of World War II. Hiding on a farm with his brothers after being separated from his parents, young Binjamin is eventually discovered by the authorities and taken to the concentration camps of Majdanek and then Birkenau, witnessing horrors of wide variety and intense magnitude. After the war the state places him in an orphanage in Kraków, from where he is smuggled into Switzerland and eventually adopted by upscale parents who urge him to forget his past as though it were nothing more than a nightmare. He rejects this plea, and years later he begins the process of reconstructing the childhood images that had incessantly haunted him. From this process of circumstantial reconstruction, the *Fragments* are born.

There is another version of the story. Bruno Grosjean was born out of wedlock to a young woman who had been partly disfigured by a bicycle accident. This woman had trouble making ends meet, eventually lost interest in her baby, and was forced to place him in foster care. Moving every few weeks from home to home, the boy was finally taken in by a foster mother who suffered from mental illness and was abusive toward young Bruno, as well as her own son. After a time, an upscale family adopted Bruno, giving him the name of Bruno Dösseker. Resisting his parents' efforts to shepherd him into the medical profession, he took up music and, for years, prospered as a clarinetist before producing the *Fragments* in his mid-fifties.

Grosjean-Dösseker-Wilkomirski's unwanted biographer, Stefan Maechler (who Wilkomirski's publisher solicited to unearth the "true" story of the man), regards the *Fragments* as the product of "cumulative trauma" coupled with a vibrant imagination. Sympathizing with Wilkomirski's pathos if not his factual claims, Maechler argues that in the Shoah Wilkomirski "found a meaningful story for an inexplicable and inaccessible past. The dark side of his metamorphosis was that he lost himself in the role written for him. In that sense he was indeed horribly victimized. . . . Wilkomirski, an outsider to his own society, became a Jew, the prototypical outsider in the modern world."[36] Defying the *prima facie* mandate of Adorno's famous proscription, Wilkomirski expressed his angst by making "poetry" of Auschwitz.

Of course, so did Adorno. In his late work, Adorno acknowledged that "[p]erennial suffering has as much right to expression as a tortured man has to scream; hence it may have been wrong to say that after Auschwitz you could no longer write poems" (*ND* 362). Equating poetry with a kind of primal scream, and finding a case of "perennial suffering" in the state of modernity at large, Adorno attempts something quasipoetic in his own right. "Negative dialectics," he argues, entails "a thinking against itself" in the manner of "epic naïveté." "If thought is not measured by the extremity that eludes the concept," or if rationality is permitted to proceed unimpeded toward its own dehumanizing ends, then such thought "is from the outset in the nature of the musical accompaniment with which the SS liked to drown out the screams of its victims" (*ND* 365). The Shoah here provides Adorno with an analogy by which he characterizes the dire condition of Western society; more specifically, reference to the Shoah aids Adorno in modeling his critique of enlightenment after survivor testimony.

On speaking tours to promote the *Fragments*, Wilkomirski too played music, though less to "drown out" than to enhance the "screams" of the victims he pretended to be.[37] Often, Wilkomirski had actors read parts of his narrative. Maechler argues that these productions were compelling to the general public when Wilkomirski's experience was believed to be authentic, but, "[o]nce the professed interrelationships between the first-person narrator, the death-camp story he narrates, and historical reality are proved palpably false, what was a masterpiece becomes kitsch." Originally functioning as signifiers of the ineffable, the music and dramatic pathos of these performances wilt into mere sensations: "The text, which . . . has previously circled an empty core" of forgotten or unutterable horrors, "is mercilessly reduced to its sheer material value. What remains is" less the traumatized speech of childhood memory than "childish speech."[38]

The attractions of kitsch, however, reside precisely in its sensationalism. The book-jacket blurb gushing that Wilkomirski's was "a book that is not to be read but experienced" acquires a second life in this context as an advertisement for scandal. In fact, the controversy surrounding the *Fragments* only magnifies the sensationalistic violence which was originally promoted by the publisher as enticement. This is where we are left: the victims of the camps once indubitably suffered unspeakable brutality; but now, either Grosjean-Dösseker-Wilkomirski has done violence to history, or else his skeptics compulsively repeat the violence wrought upon him as a boy (with Wilkomirski becoming Freud's quintessential Jewish subject). As Maechler reports, "Wilkomirski's defenders argued that to put the burden of proof on him was to repeat past injustice and traumatize him again" (295). Wilkomirski speaks to this trauma, and to the dismemberment of experience from reality, in assailing his critics: "Each time it's as if someone wanted to kill us because they are taking away our identity" (quoted in Maechler 294).

The book's uneven—traumatic—reception mirrors its traumatic content, which is less a coherent narrative than a motley sequence of gruesome images that are, in Dominick LaCapra's words, oddly "sentimentalizing and comforting" given Wilkomirski's "child's-eye approach."[39] Lang would seemingly be pleased by the narrator's claim that his "childhood memories are planted . . . in exact snapshots of [his] photographic memory," and that they possess the quality of "[s]hards . . . with knifehard edges. . . . I'm not a poet," Wilkomirski declares, echoing Lang's reading of Adorno. "I can only try to use words to draw as exactly as possible what happened, what I saw . . . with no benefit of perspective or vanishing point."[40] In other words, Wilkomirski purports to present his readers—whether imagined as his fellow witnesses or his disinterested jurors—with facts which cannot lie. His testimony is that of a witness reduced to a receptacle of sensations.

These alleged facts, these sensations, are alluring and repugnant largely because of their gross (and acknowledged) improbability. In his lengthy investigative article on Wilkomirski in *The New Yorker*, Philip Gourevitch remarks that "[t]he antiheroic realization that remaining alive usually required a series of inexplicable chances, even for those who were best equipped to evade death, has been a central theme of Holocaust literature. Yet Wilkomirski [goes] further, arguing that survival was such an anomaly that the survivor's existence could be represented only as otherworldly."[41] For instance, the narrator survives not one but two camps (Majdanek and Auschwitz); he survives the kick of a "black boot" that hurtles him into the air (Wilkomirski 55), as well as extremes of cold and heat, a train wreck, a temporary loss of self-control in which he actually attacks a "bull-neck[ed]" guard and "bite[s him] with all [his] strength" (Wilkomirski 78–79), and so on. Wilkomirski intersperses these episodes with sentimental scenes that are, in their way, equally improbable: one in which the narrator is taken clandestinely through Majdanek to meet his mother, a word ("mother") whose meaning he could not even remember; or again, another in which, as a child of ten now living safely in Switzerland, he encounters Mila, a girl he had known in the camps, who imagines with him that the ski lift on which they are sitting is transporting them to the place of their execution. "A brief feeling of happiness came over me," he relates of that experience. "We were the only children who knew the truth, and we could rely on each other absolutely, and we were ready to hold hands as we went toward the end." "This must be what people call love," he decides (Wilkomirski 143).

Later, after the *Fragments* were published and Wilkomirski was on a speaking tour, his American publisher Arthur H. Samuelson shared his uncanny impressions of the author's sentimentality: "He cried everywhere we brought him. . . . I told him if he didn't stop crying I'd send him home. . . . Maybe it was insensitive of me, but I've published Primo Levi, Elie Wiesel, Aharon Appelfeld—I know a lot of survivors—and one thing they have in common is that they don't cry. This guy couldn't stop. I thought that was odd" (Gourevitch 51). Wilkomirski's tears, perceived by some as signs of inexpressible suffering, and functioning on tour as lubricants of public catharsis, also served as emblems of kitsch, of hollow sensation. In this respect, they testified to the problem of evidence, casting doubt on the authenticity of Wilkomirski's testimony even as they underscored the sensationist reduction of truth to the rhetoric of "facts which cannot lie."

Perhaps the most graphic episode in the *Fragments* is the one that now best exemplifies the book's enigmatic relevance to issues of evidence and experience. Wilkomirski relates how a cart would come to the barracks daily to carry off the fresh heap of dead bodies. One day it doesn't come, and the narrator finds himself staring at "the mountain of corpses" in a corner of the large room. Then, starting, he asks himself, "didn't something just move over there?" He walks over to the heap and gazes at a woman lying on the top. "She's on her back, her body hanging down a little, her arms wide open, and her breasts are tipped to one side like little sacks above her ribs, which stick out a lot, and her belly seems all swelled up" with "a big wound on one side." He then sees her belly move, and recalls a conversation with one of the older girls in another barrack about how children are born. Curious, he says, he positions himself to where he "can see it better. I poke my head forward, and at this very moment the wound springs open, the wall of the stomach lifts back, and a huge, blood-smeared, shining rat darts down the mound of corpses. . . . I saw it, I saw it! The dead women are giving birth to rats!" (85–86).

This image and others of its ilk continue to make *Fragments*, even given its gross unlikelihood, "a powerful testimony to events that are unavailable to those who were not there," Michael Bernard-Donals argues, "and that are available as open wounds to those who were."[42] Precisely because they are so graphic, so over-the-top, the *Fragments'* images and episodes capture the unimaginable (and profoundly improbable) realities of the camps. For some interpreters, this quality alone lends Wilkomirski's *Fragments* an air of authenticity. Bernard-Donals cites Israel Gutman, "a survivor with serious doubts about the historical veracity of the book," who "says nonetheless that 'Wilkomirski has written a story that he has experienced deeply, that's for sure.'"[43]

Gutman's comment returns us to the interface of experience and race as it is evoked by Macpherson and Adorno. That is, Gutman again insists on the purity of Wilkomirski's experience, if not his biological identity.

Indeed, if Wilkomirski never in fact spent time in the camps, then the episode with the rat may be interpreted as a would-be portrait of the artist, with the female corpse giving birth literally to the metaphor— the Nazi racial slur—the author figuratively claims himself to be.[44] *Who* is the subject of Wilkomirski's memoirs? S/he is the ultimate victim, Maechler replies, whose Jewishness seemingly appeals to its author precisely because it is the supreme image of abjection. And *what* then is the nature of Wilkomirski's experience in this abjection, and what about this experience makes the image of abjection so appealing to his readers (who "experience" rather than "read" his memoirs, as the book's blurb suggests)?

Horkheimer and Adorno address this latter question by placing the image of the Jew "at the limits of enlightenment." This image recalls Macpherson's defense of *Ossian* in its ambiguous connotations of "race." On the one hand, Horkheimer and Adorno remark how the Nazis viewed the Jews biologically and dialectically "as an opposing race, the embodiment of the negative principle." Liberals, on the other hand, claimed during the war "that the Jews have no national or racial characteristics and simply form a group through their religious opinions and tradition."[45] "Neither doctrine is wholly true or wholly false," Horkheimer and Adorno argue. "The first is true to the extent that Fascism . . . made it true. . . . The other, liberal, theory is true as an idea" (*DE* 168), or rather, in Louis Althusser's famous dictum, as ideology, or as an imaginary representation of individuals to their real conditions of existence. The fascists created the racial history which they imagined to be inherent, whereas the liberals imputed to the Jews a cultural power in the effect of their religious customs. In some ways, this latter, liberal perspective struck Horkheimer and Adorno as more insidious because it unconsciously adopted and accommodated the productivist notion of history. Such ideology, they argued, the power of culture to make real, bolsters the self-perception of "the modern bourgeoisie, which was moving inexorably toward . . . reorganization as a pure 'race,'" that is, toward a naturalization of its own contingent social circumstances, or of the belief in absolute self-determination. Historically, this belief has proceeded by way of Enlightenment rationality—indeed, by the logic of evidence and the latter's conversion of blindness into insight, and uncertainty into truth. This would be more acceptable, Horkheimer and Adorno imply, if the risks of such rationality were more widely recognized, and perhaps checked (e.g., by "epic naïveté"). But the sacralization of progress as the "racial" destiny of the bourgeoisie struck Horkheimer and Adorno as pernicious—an extension of Nazi fantasy, albeit in sheep's clothing.

This is where the image of Jewishness to which Wilkomirski appeals becomes important to the question of experience. In a complex analysis of the relationship between sensation and reflection, Horkheimer and Adorno locate authentic experience (*Erfahrung*) in the exchange between "the true object" as it is conceived by the rational faculty "and the undisputed data of the senses," or essentially, between that which occurs "within" the mind and that which occurs "without" (*DE* 188). Only through this exchange, through this perpetually renewed "possibilit[y] of reconciliation," is "the pathological loneliness which characterizes the whole of nature overcome" (189). This principle of reconciliation (e.g., with the Messiah and the Holy Land, and hence to the ideal and to nature) "is the highest notion of Judaism," they argue (199). This largely explains for them why the Jews became the scapegoats of progress, because the process of enlightenment is one of domination in which the rational faculty cancels out the contingent perceptual sphere and the interplay between sensation and reflection. The erasure of this interplay is in fact the "dialectic of enlightenment": technology enables humans to predict and control the external world to the point where they become the slaves to the tools, and the perceptions, which they have created. This process constitutes Horkheimer's and Adorno's version of the devaluation of experience. In this state, anything that promises or holds out for reconciliation—anything that purports to offer the possibility of *Erfahrung*—becomes the enemy to progress. Culture, which mediates the lessons of nature as well as history, becomes a self-enclosing reality, a "commodity disseminated as information. . . . Thought [becomes] restricted to the acquisition of isolated facts" in a manner that defies the possibility of synthetically unifying these facts into a coherent whole (197). In this type of society, "[e]xperience is replaced by clichés, and the imagination active in experience by eager acceptance" (201).

Judaism, on the other hand, bears "the features to which totalitarian domination must be completely hostile: happiness without power, wages without work, a home without frontiers, religion without myth" (199). In other words, Judaism becomes the uncanny emblem of holistic (i.e., sensationistic *and* reflective) experience, and hence of the kind of social formation which modernity must suppress in order to sanctify the mission of progress and to bring the dialectic of enlightenment to its logical end. This is the end at which the taming of nature turns into the anesthetizing of experience and the subjugating power of technology against other human beings. For Horkheimer and Adorno, anti-Semitism is the ultimate expression of this dialectic; Auschwitz is thus the quintessential metaphor of the decay of experience.

In appealing to Jewishness as the ultimate image of abjection, to abjection as a desideratum, and to this desideratum as his own personal history, Wilkomirski implicitly reiterated the arguments made by Horkheimer and Adorno half a century earlier. Moreover, in recasting the Horkheimer-Adorno arguments as fragments of memory that could no longer be suppressed, and that he was compelled to repeat, Wilkomirski thus attested to the paradoxical insistence and inadequacy of experience—that is, in Wilkomirski's words, to the irrepressible "shards that keep surfacing against the orderly grain of grown-up life and escaping the laws of logic" (4). Wilkomirski claimed that over the course of his life these testimonial fragments had found little place "in a time and in a society that didn't want to listen, or perhaps was incapable of listening" (153). Such willful deafness must therefore have seemed miraculously cured when his published testimony caused such a sensation.

Wilkomirski's *Fragments* appealed here in like manner to Macpherson's: Wilkomirski specifically conceived of himself as a witness who "knows" things no jury ever could: "Legally accredited truth is one thing—the truth of a life another" (Wilkomirski 154). His memoirs thus implicitly recall Stevenson's character David Balfour, who inscribed his novels *Kidnapped* and *Catriona* as testaments to the kind of experience that was occluded in the Stewart Trial. Wilkomirski himself claimed to write "with the hope that perhaps other people in the same situation would find the necessary support and strength to cry out their own traumatic childhood memories, so that they too could learn that there really are people today who will take them seriously, and who want to listen and to understand. They should know that they are not alone" (155). When his book's jacket gushes that these memories are "not to be read but experienced," it picks up on Wilkomirski's own expressed desire for a more collective form of experience, or *Erfahrung*. Hence, fraudulent though the book's specific claims of experience may be, Adorno and Horkheimer would recognize it as a book which intuits and documents (albeit in garishly immodest form) the more general problem of experience in a post-Enlightenment era. The *Fragments* recreate Horkheimer and Adorno's concept of Judaism as *sensation*—that is, as the debased emblem of a (nevertheless) genuinely collective social condition. This is postmodernism, perhaps as nobody would desire it.

Ultimately, it may be fair to claim that the Wilkomirski *Fragments* are no more (and perhaps no less) about the death camps than Macpherson's *Ossian* was about ancient Caledonia. Nevertheless, we should underscore a couple of key differences. For one thing, whether we regard Macpherson and Wilkomirski as impostors, authentic witnesses, or agents of more complex phenomena which fall somewhere between these poles—poles which seem almost raciological to the extent that they devolve on conceptions of purified and self-same identity—Macpherson's and Wilkomirski's cases are in one respect as different as are the genres of translation and memoir, and in another as the mid-eighteenth- and late twentieth-century cultural spaces in which they were produced.

If I have focused less on these seminal differences than on the uncanny correspondences between these texts, it is because whatever objects we imagine these respective *Fragments* ultimately to represent (e.g., ancient Scotland or Scots' upward mobility in the 1760s; the horrors of the death camps or voyeuristic fascination with the same), Macpherson's and Wilkomirski's texts tell a remarkably consonant story about the dilemma of experience in modernity. In each case, the enthusiastic expressions of testimony as the possibility of "real" experience reveal something far less consoling—namely, the implication of "enlightenment" in the unsated hunger for immediacy and in the epistemological (more than simply the ethical) complications of race. As Horkheimer and Adorno argue, the promise of testimony accedes to the practice of violence. In the literal, racial sense, this type of violence is pervasive in today's world in the form of ethnonationalist identities (e.g., Serb *versus* Croat; in Rwanda, Tutsi *versus* Hutu). From the perspective pursued by Horkheimer and Adorno, a similarly racialized violence inscribes even the "liberal" recognition of culture as the historically contingent and self-generated nature of identities. In modernity, it would seem, "race" is as difficult a category to avoid or supersede as "enlightenment."

However, as we will see in the following chapter, there is an alternative outcome to the inexorably degenerative dialectic of enlightenment. At least, this is an implication which we may intuit in the eighteenth-century Highland Gaelic poetry of Donnchadh Bàn Mac-an-t-Saoir (Duncan Bàn Macintyre), which transports us in dialectical fashion from the pits of abject experience to the prospects of its social redemption.

Chapter 6
Of Mourning and Machinery
Contrasting Techniques of Highland Vision

Raymond Williams persuasively, if somewhat fancifully, argues that the modern concept of literature emerged as compensation for "the socially repressive and intellectually mechanical forms of a new social order: that of capitalism, and especially industrial capitalism."[1] By this logic, the "romantick" Highlands of the late eighteenth century foreshadowed the modern conceptual space of literature in their popular differentiation from "the socially repressive and intellectually mechanical" schemes of progress imported into the region by the improvers. From this perspective, Highland romance originated as a nostalgic image of the receding past, compensating as "literature" and "culture" for what was irretrievably lost with the onset of "science" and "industry."

Martin Heidegger tells a different story, not about the Highlands per se, but rather about the meaning of primitive romance. In his view, the industrialization to which Williams refers did not so much proceed from the advent of technology as from its seizure, its stagnation, during the Enlightenment. Heidegger operates here with a different notion of technology, one which denotes less the intricate engines of modernity than a way of seeing.[2] In ancient Greece, he argues, *techne* signified a mode of revealing, of labor as a means of engaging the flux of being. Technology in this context assumed the form of *poeisis*, or "poetry" in its etymological sense of "making" and craftsmanship. He contrasts this sophisticated ontological activity with the probabilistic calculation which rose to the fore during the Scientific Revolution of the seventeenth century, when technology devolved into instrumental mastery of the earth and its resources. Here, according to Heidegger, the tasks of "regulating and securing" became technology's chief characteristics; probabilism froze the perpetual flow of being in its medusa-like gaze, locking the future into schemes of expectation. Ever since, technology has existed primarily in this debased and debasing form despite its sublime intricacy.[3]

Something residually romantic inhabits Heidegger's account, evoking as it does a fall from plenitude into the alienating conditions of modern life. This residue seems consistent with Heidegger's well-known fancy for primitivism, and is a taste rendered all the more odious for its proximity to fascistic programs which dreamed of utilizing technology in the production of a national culture (allegedly as the primitive spirit of the *Volk*). But, in a different sense, Heidegger's argument concerning technology complicates the *mythos* of consolatory romance to which Williams refers. It does so by interpreting the past less as the casualty of modernization than as the wizard of high tech. By the terms established in Heidegger's essay, Highland romance would not have originated during the eighteenth century as a cultural reaction against burgeoning industry; rather, Highlandism would have emerged as the *repression* of technology, not in England and Lowland Scotland so much as in the Highlands and Islands themselves.

In this chapter I address aspects of technology in the eighteenth-century Highlands, less in the form of "improving" tools like the spade and hoe, or of the intricate networks of roads and canals, than of modalities of vision. I am particularly interested in the implicit dialectic of romance and antiromance which Williams and Heidegger each conjure. In relation to the Highlands, this dialectic consists, on the one hand, in a probabilistically motivated narrative of progress and compensation and, on the other hand, in a disclosure of complex social and epistemological (in Heidegger's terms, "technological") features already extant in eighteenth-century Highland society. I engage this dialectic by juxtaposing Samuel Johnson's observations concerning second sight in his *Journey to the Western Islands of Scotland* (1775) with the visions of his contemporary, the Highland Gaelic poet Donnchadh Bàn Mac-an-t-Saoir (Duncan Bàn Macintyre). Second sight is a form of supernatural vision which entitles its recipient either to peer into the future or to uncover secrets from the past. During the eighteenth century, it was widely associated with the Highlands, and was held by some to inhere less in the seers themselves than to flow primordially from the Highland landscape.

As one would anticipate in comparing an erudite English traveler with an illiterate Highland bard, the visions of Johnson and Mac-an-t-Saoir are marked by substantive differences. Less expected, however, is the nature of these differences, which turn less on ontologies of identity— "imposing outsider" *versus* "authentic native"—than, as Heidegger would have preferred, on more elusive qualities of experience and ways of seeing. At root, Johnson and Mac-an-t-Saoir present contrasting models of Highland vision. What these models share is an understanding of vision (of both the supernatural and natural variety) as an intrinsically technological phenomenon; in contrast with Macpherson and Wilkomirski, they also interpret the experience ensuing from vision as a mediated phenomenon, evoking more the normative image of juries than witnesses.

Each writer also conceives of Highland vision as redemptive, a perception of the prospective transfiguration of adverse circumstances, of ruin. This is where the comparisons leave off, however, for redemptive experience in Johnson's *Journey* takes the form of improvement and consolation, whereas in Mac-an-t-Saoir's poetry it highlights a collective process of mourning that conduces less to romance than to critical self-consciousness.

A couple more prefatory notes may be helpful here. Johnson's *Journey to the Western Islands* has been widely discussed in recent years. My aim in revisiting it briefly is not to rehearse the oft-told tale of Johnson's tour, but rather to illuminate the logic of perhaps his narrative's richest section, the excursus on second sight. As I see it, this logic coincides with the ideology of improvement, and Johnson emerges in my critique as something of an apologist for progress. In itself, this is neither terribly surprising nor enlightening; Johnson's affirmation of improvement was more rule than exception. If I appeal to Johnson, it is because of the intricate modality of second sight in his account. Reminiscent of Smith's impartial spectator, Johnson conceives of second sight as a quasimechanical process of perception and reflection—that is, of evidence—which shapes the experience of its witnesses. His logic provides a rich context in which to consider the mnemonic devices and other oral-poetic conventions encrypted into Mac-an-t-Saoir's poetry. These poems also attest in their own way to a kind of techno-logic, but here technology acquires a "use value" which recasts the meaning of the relationship between technology and the ruins of experience. In Mac-an-t-Saoir's poetry, we discover a prototype of the dialectic which Marx and Benjamin later deployed—the dialectic in which technology promotes alienation only to convert alienation into the basis for heightened consciousness and solidarity.

At its limits, and consistently with previous chapters, I am suggesting here that the modern interplay between *Erlebnis* and *Erfahrung*, the "short" experience of sensation and the "long" experience of holistic reflection, arrives at compelling cultural expression in the romantick Highlands. If Johnson's musings on second sight symptomatically portray the Highlands in light of the decay of experience, then Mac-an-t-Saoir's vision of etiolating Highland society nonetheless draws upon the collective experience that makes the widespread nostalgia of "decay" possible. Read in conjunction with Johnson's *Journey*, Mac-an-t-Saoir's poetry thus articulates a provocative antithesis to the conventional terms of post- or late-Enlightenment despair. In contrast to Heidegger, the "question concerning technology" in Mac-an-t-Saoir's poetry rebuts the thesis of degenerative modernization, prompting us to reimagine the "ruinous" nature of the rupture of experience from knowledge.

After analyzing Johnson's reflections on second sight, I will discuss two of Mac-an-t-Saoir's poems, including two translations of his most famous poem from the 1760s, "Praise of Ben Dobhrain" one a literal translation of the original, the other a poetically rendered translation by Iain Crichton Smith, the respected twentieth-century poet, critic, and novelist from the Isle of Lewis. Smith's translation will prove to be most provocative, teasing out the techno-logic of Mac-an-t-Saoir's original and bespeaking the nostalgia of Highland romance even as it reaffirms a positive legacy of Enlightenment experience in the period following the advent of modern evidence.

Johnson's Highland Romance

Notoriously caustic toward most things Scottish, Johnson nevertheless made little secret of his enthusiasm at the idea of venturing into the primitive Highlands. He opens his *Journey to the Western Islands* by professing that he "had desired to visit the Hebrides . . . so long, that [he] scarcely remember[ed] how the wish was originally excited."[4] In his *Journal* of this tour, James Boswell invokes Martin Martin's *A Description of the Western Islands of Scotland* as a more specific provenance of Johnson's desire. Johnson "told [Boswell] . . . that [Johnson's] father put Martin's *Account* into his hands when he was very young, and that he was much pleased with it." Inspired by Martin, Johnson and Boswell imagined that in the Highlands and Islands they might "contemplate a system of life almost totally different from what [they] had been accustomed to see," a "system" rendered more tantalizing by its proximity "to [their] native great island. . . ."[5] All of this is well known, as is Johnson's crestfallen reaction to the reality awaiting them: "We came too late to see what we expected, a people of peculiar appearance, and a system of antiquated life. . . . Of what [Highlanders] had before the late conquest of their country" following the Jacobite Rebellion "there remain only their language and their poverty" (*Journey* 73).

However, there was for Johnson something undismissably "romantick" about Scotland in general, and the Highlands in particular. Johnson vigorously trafficked in Highlandism. Eithne Henson and others have detailed the *Journey*'s implication in the tropes and motifs of medieval romance, with Johnson playing the role of Quixote. The *Journey*'s romantic episodes range from a pastoral scene "such as a writer of Romance might have delighted to feign" where Johnson "first conceived the thought" of compiling his narrative (61), and from Johnson's recurrent expressions of perplexed interest in ruins (especially of sacred edifices—e.g., the ruined cathedral in St. Andrews [36–37] and "the ruins of Iona" [140–42]), to the pathos of defeated Jacobitism (e.g., the respect shown for the "virtues," if not the cause, of Flora Macdonald [80]) and other instances.[6]

That said, from my perspective, the relics of Highland romance which Johnson sought to discredit are of greater interest than those which he fetishized. Johnson's disgust with Macpherson's *Ossian* figures principally among these scandalous remnants (see 118–19).[7] And yet, Johnson mounts an even more compelling case against oral history than he does against Macpherson—compelling inasmuch as traces of oral historicizing inflect Johnson's own written account. He avows that over the course of their adventure he and Boswell "were willing to listen to such accounts of past times as would be given [them]. But [they] soon found what memorials were to be expected from an illiterate people, whose whole time is a series of distress" (113). Poverty and the specter of famine prohibited most native inhabitants from cultivating a disinterested love of knowledge, making their narrative chains of cultural transmission particularly susceptible to decay. However, Johnson powerfully identified with this condition, conflating the oral-historical erosion of memory with the problem of travel writing:

An observer deeply impressed by any remarkable spectacle, does not suppose, that the traces will soon vanish from his mind, and having commonly no great convenience for writing, defers the description to a time of more leisure, and better accommodation.

He who has not made the experiment, or who is not accustomed to require rigorous accuracy from himself, will scarcely believe how much a few hours take from certainty of knowledge, and distinctness of imagery; how the succession of objects will be broken, how separate parts will be confused, and how many particular features and discriminations will be compressed and conglobated into one gross and general idea. (139)

This is "second sight" in a belated rather than a vatic sense. While Johnson's reflections ratify common sense, they also conform to the logic he deploys against oral history. The "distress" corroding oral chains of transmission mirrors the absence of "leisure" and "accommodation" afflicting the traveler, whose mind condenses into one afternoon the degenerative course of Highland oral history.[8] One significant facet of the phenomenological reduction of history which Johnson's text performs is the privilege it arrogates to sight (i.e., the "distinctness of imagery") to the detriment of alternative modes of experience (like oral/aural transmission). This ocularcentric element of the *Journey* reaffirms the tenets of rationalism and empiricism—tenets which Johnson questions as much as defends, but which nonetheless figure into the techno-logic of his account, as I discuss below.[9] Highland history here is effectively reduced to the features of its landscape, which becomes an assemblage of unreconstructed fragments which the anthropological traveler (i.e., Johnson-cum-Lévi-Strauss) arranges into a systematic table, location by location. However, when the traveler's record evinces mnemonic lapses similar to the oral history it disclaims, then it too devolves to the nominal status of romance. Hence, for Johnson, the Highlands not only safeguard a culture of romance, they generate it anew; no longer a relic of the past, Highlandism uncannily informs everyday life.

Johnson's reflections on second sight are acute, but they were not new. In certain respects, Johnson's record cobbles together other accounts of the subject, perhaps most prominently Martin's *Description of the Western Islands of Scotland* (c. 1695, published 1703).[10] Like Johnson in his later travelogue, Martin professes devotion to empirical observation. He claims to take advantage of recent developments in "[n]atural and experimental philosophy," which is "much improved" since the time of sixteenth-century Scottish historians like George Buchanan. However, despite this commitment to the concrete, Martin devotes significant attention to second sight, at least to the extent that "the nature of the thing will bear."[11] For Martin, this "nature" unfolds as a narrative of the receding witness, with one testimony yielding to another—his own reporting on others (in the form of what eighteenth-century jurists began to classify as hearsay), which in turn are based on the visions related by the rustic seers themselves. The following example is illustrative:

Four men of the village Flodgery in Skye being at supper, one of them did suddenly let fall his knife on the table, and looked with an angry countenance; the company observing it inquired his reason, but he returned them no answer until they had supped, and then he told them that when he let fall his knife, he saw a corpse, with the shroud about it, laid on the table which surprised him, and that a little time would accomplish the vision. It fell out accordingly, for in a few days after one of the family died, and happened to be laid out on that very table. This was told me by the master of the family. (331)[12]

Martin's story signifies in several registers. It melds mundane and perfectly "likely" circumstances (e.g., the supping of four villagers) with dramatic details (e.g., the "angry countenance" of one of the men), romantic elements (e.g., the vision of the "corpse, with [a] shroud about it"), and testimony ("This was told me by the master of the family").

Such shifts of narrative register were typical of accounts of second sight which circulated early in the eighteenth century, reflecting the challenge of negotiating fact and fancy, observation and hearsay.[13] Johnson's discussion of this phenomenon exemplifies this challenge. His three-page discussion of second sight comprises a relatively small but symbolically crucial portion of his book's longest section, "Ostig in Sky." After touching briefly on the climate, agriculture, and fauna native to that corner of the island, Johnson takes up four abstract subjects of a rather more philosophical nature, upon which he expounds at some length: the value of the social structure of lairds and peasantry that was still prevalent in the Highlands, with special attention devoted to the attenuating role of tacksmen, or leaseholders; the problems attending the importation of imperial law into the Highlands; the popular superstition of second sight; and the imposture of Ossian, and the corresponding improbability of any genuinely bardic history.[14] Essentially, Johnson enunciates a pocket history of Highlandism: schematically speaking, he places second sight on a four-stage continuum that begins with scenes from contemporary Hebridean life and then devolves from the degeneration of traditional social roles and the introduction of extrinsic legal policy to, ultimately, the propagation of an allegedly counterfeit history and culture (i.e., the romantick "invention of tradition"[15]). By dint of its position in this chronicle, second sight connects "true" to "false" (i.e., the historical fact of imperial law to the effusions of Ossianic bombast), and "real" to "symbolic" (i.e., everyday Island life to a fabricated epic history). From a formal standpoint, and in prototypically "romantick" fashion, second sight in Johnson's narrative links truth and falsehood, the real and the symbolic, and the empirical and the imaginary.

As for second sight itself, Johnson's definition echoes those provided by Martin and others. He makes it out to be

an impression made either by the mind upon the eye, or by the eye upon the mind, by which things distant or future are perceived, and seen as though they were present. A man on a journey far from home falls from his horse, another, who is perhaps at work about the house, sees him bleeding on the ground, commonly with a landscape of the place where the accident befalls him. Another seer, driving home his cattle, or wandering in idleness, or musing in the sunshine, is suddenly surprised by the appearance of a bridal ceremony, or funeral procession, and counts the mourners or attendants, of whom, if he knows them, he relates the names, if he knows them not, he can describe the dresses. Things distant are seen at the instant when they happen. Of things future I know not that there is any rule for determining the time between the sight and the event. (110)

The content of these paranormal visions supposedly consists of actual circumstances—accidents, weddings, funerals—that bear a spectral relation to their seers; these events are "seen *as though* they were present," but they cannot therefore be said to be either present or absent.[16] Johnson makes an additional, etymological connection between second sight and spectrality, expounding that "[b]y the term second sight, seems to be meant a mode of seeing superadded to that which Nature generally bestows. In the Erse [or Gaelic] it is called *taisch*; which signifies . . . a spectre, or a vision" (111).

Crucially, within the epistemological context of the Enlightenment, these specters would have haunted not only supernatural visions, but also empirical objects themselves. Lorraine Daston has shown that from the late seventeenth through the eighteenth centuries, jurists, scientists, and theologians increasingly viewed this median, spectral position between the quotidian and the supernatural as the optimal position of objective facts, or of those curiosities which, abstracted of taint from religious dogma but deemed worthy of special attention, might come to speak for themselves.[17] "Evidence" in its modern form thus begins as animism, which itself was a source of perpetual fascination throughout the eighteenth century.[18] Animistic tropes attested not only to positivistic desires to discern the truth of material things on their own terms, but also to the bewildering oddity accruing to objects in the new (scientistic) public sphere.

For Boswell, whose images of Johnson typically melded monstrous peculiarity to tragic humanity, Johnson's attraction to spectral vision reflected the wider animistic anxieties of the age. In particular, Boswell intuited that Johnson's interest in supernatural phenomena of all varieties, and especially in second sight, furnished him with desirable "evidence of spirit, in opposition to the groveling belief of materialism." This paradoxical desire for "evidence of spirit," or for reasonable proof of things which elude the strictures of reasonable proof, drove Johnson, Boswell argues, "to inquire into the truth of any relation of supernatural agency" (*Life of Johnson* 288). The inquiry occasionally took sublime forms, as when it inspired Johnson's moving reflections on divine revelation in the sermon he wrote (but never preached) for the funeral of his wife: "All those to whom the supernatural light of heavenly doctrine has never been imparted, however formidable for power, or illustrious for wisdom, have wanted that knowledge of their future state, which alone can give comfort to misery, or security to enjoyment. . . ."[19] On the other hand, this inquiry occasionally appeared ridiculous, never more notoriously than in the case of the Cock Lane ghost. Here, Johnson believed with several others that a woman named Fanny Lynes had returned fifty-six years after her death to testify, through knocking and scratching sounds, to her murder by poisoning in 1706.[20] Consistent with this incident, Boswell believed that it was this interest in the supernatural, and hence in second sight (articulated so effusively in Martin's *Description*), which inspired Johnson to undertake his voyage into Scotland in the first place.

Johnson's attraction to second sight is conspicuous in light of certain well-noted items that he claimed *not* to see while on his journey. He judged the region and its inhabitants to be wanting in many things: its society lacked civility, its cottages lacked windows, its landscape lacked trees, and its popular literary traditions—most notably Ossian—lacked the ring of true authenticity. More disturbingly, however, its culture and society seemed bereft of historical continuity:

There was perhaps never any change of national manners so quick, so great, and so general, as that which has operated in the Highlands, by the last conquest [of "improvement"], and the subsequent laws [that were passed. Boswell and I] came too late to see what we expected, a people of peculiar appearance, and a system of antiquated life. . . . Of what they had before the late conquest of their country, there remain only their language and their poverty. Their language is attacked on every side. Schools are erected, in which English only is taught, and there were lately some who thought it reasonable to refuse them a version of the holy scriptures, that they might have no monument of their mother-tongue. (73)

In effect, what Johnson perceived when surveying Highland society was the presence of ghosts, or of what Francis Bacon had called "idols"— specters of the imagination—and of what Jacques Derrida, in a more modern setting, has described as the generative or creative power of memory as the "attraction or provocativeness of [a] past . . . which has never been fully present."[21] Johnson's virtual memory of prosperous Highland societies which he had never actually witnessed conjured for him and Boswell a complex and overdetermined image of the feudal clans—of what they once were—laboring under the encroaching shadow cast by Britain's empire. "The phantoms which haunt a desert are want, and misery, and danger," Johnson stated. This was the spectacle which the Highlands presented to the modern tourist. The clans' "pride has been crushed by the heavy hand of a vindictive conqueror, whose severities have been followed by laws, which, though they cannot be called cruel, have produced much discontent, because they operate upon the surface of life, and make every eye bear witness to subjection" (97).

I have discussed the laws to which Johnson refers in earlier chapters: they included prohibitions against the bearing of arms, the wearing of plaid, and the playing of bagpipes, and initiatives regarding the instruction of English, the introduction of commerce, and the structure of the legal system. Of more interest to me here than these laws themselves is Johnson's reference to them by means of witness experience. Imperial laws have brought about cosmetic changes which, he says, "make every eye bear witness to subjection." The implication following from Johnson's evidential logic, however, is that the motivating force behind these changes—a force which might be deduced by juries, but which cannot be perceived by witnesses—passes unobserved. In Chapter 3, I discussed some of the motives behind improvement, as well as (via Adam Smith's concept of sympathy) the judicial form these motives took. In Johnson's account of second sight, the judicial spirit recurs, as we will see, though Johnson seems less concerned to ferret out improvement's hidden sources than to show how jury disinterestedness takes up residence within the dimensions of witness experience itself. In other words, Johnson effectively argues that our engagement of what he calls "the surface of life" is already informed by mediating processes of probability.

The lineaments of probability in Johnson's account of second sight become apparent in his description of rustic Highland visionaries. Here, Johnson reifies and complicates the formalized split between witnesses and jurors. On the one hand, second sight for Johnson denotes a passive registration and reportage of mere data, such as that which was required from legal witnesses: "This receptive faculty, for power it cannot be called, is neither voluntary nor constant. The appearances have no dependence upon choice: they cannot be summoned, detained, or recalled. The impression is sudden, and the effect often painful" (111). On the other hand, however, Johnson's visionaries seem to possess a privileged relation to the substance of their experience—a privilege of deliberative interpretation that English and Scottish courts increasingly arrogated to jurors: "The foresight of the seers is not always prescience: they are impressed with images, of which the event only shews them the meaning. They tell what they have seen to others, who are at that time not more knowing than themselves, but may become at last very adequate witnesses, by comparing the narrative with its verification" (112). Such belated reconstructions transform the truth of the events in question into probable inferences concerning signs whose meanings remain opaque at the moment of perception. In other words, these seers begin as mere witnesses, but within the social framework of their experience they become in time rather "more adequate" witnesses, or jurors, weighing narrative against its circumstantial verification.

This "more adequate" position of the juror is one toward which Johnson seems predisposed in his assessment of Highland second sight, although it is also a position about which he expresses genuine ambivalence:

To collect sufficient testimonies for the satisfaction of the publick, or of ourselves, would have required more time than we could bestow. There is against [the case of second sight] the seeming analogy of things confusedly seen, and little understood; and for it, the indistinct cry of national persuasion, which may be perhaps resolved at last into prejudice and tradition. I never could advance my curiosity to conviction; but came away at last only willing to believe. (112)

The judicial division of labor between witnesses and jurors provides Johnson with an eloquent institutional expression of the epistemological dilemma he describes as he refers to "sufficient testimonies" he can neither bear nor summon as well as to the "conviction" he can neither muster nor enforce. His "willing[ness] to believe" indicates a prevailing attitude of probabilistic, reasonable certainty, though not without also attesting to the ultimately unsatisfying conclusions that are to be drawn from such inferential chains of circumstantial reasoning. Hence, while Johnson admits that "[s]trong reasons for incredulity will readily occur" when evaluating the phenomenon of second sight, and while he himself assumes the role of a lay judge or juror in weighing its evidentiary value, he also insists "that where we are unable to decide by antecedent reason, we must be content to yield to the force of testimony" (111–12).

Johnson's account of second sight thus problematizes—but ultimately reaffirms—the forensic logic of moral certainty, or likelihood. Eighteenth-century courts of law, like Johnson's queries about paranormal vision, circumscribed the authority of testimony, even though strictly *probable* judgment was by definition incapable of determining anything more than presumptive actuality. David Hume traced this epistemological territory in *A Treatise of Human Nature* (1739–40) by arguing that "all knowledge degenerates into probability" on the reasoning, first, that human fallibility frustrates attempts at perfect judgment, and second, that the mind itself is an aggregate of impressions whose only connection to one another is imaginary.[22] The most radical conclusion ensuing from this line of argument consisted for Hume in the disclosure of the factitious relationship between cause and effect, which he shows to be "a fiction of the imagination" (251), thus transmogrifying knowledge, as a probabilistic chain of reasoning, into a work of romance. (This, we may recall, is how the defenders in the Stewart Trial portrayed the pursuers' circumstantial case.) Hume's serpentine hypothesis inevitably bites its own tail, however, inasmuch as it implicates its own conclusions as mere "fictions," thereby making *testimony* rather than probability the "degenerative" condition of knowledge, begging the enlightenment it describes.[23]

Hume essentially outlines an argument that has persistently framed the problem of experience, and more specifically the role of technology in exacerbating this problem. This argument anticipates Johnson's account of second sight, and this account finds in turn a provocative present-day echo in Paul Virilio's critique of technology. Writing from the phenomenological perspective articulated by Maurice Merleau-Ponty, who anchors experience in the sensibilities and rhythms of the body, Virilio argues that technology has so warped our frames of perceptual reference that we find ourselves condemned to perpetual illusion, the mere specter of actuality. Even presumably direct experiences of the external world are marked by "war[s] of images and sounds, rather than objects and things," traumatically impacting our understanding of what we perceive.[24] "The will to see all, to know all, at every moment, everywhere, the will to universalised illumination" which one encounters in twenty-four hour news networks, amounts to "a scientific permutation [of] the eye of God which would forever rule out the surprise, the accident, the irruption of the unforeseen" (70). Virilio envisions technology as a kind of perceptual prophylactic, gumming us from direct experience of the world and eradicating the possibility of anything unanticipated or im-probable. Provocatively, and implicitly recalling Johnson, Virilio attributes this decay of experience to what he calls the technocratic "will to second sight" (70). Supernatural vision manifests itself here in media technology, which acquires paranormal properties in eradicating the lag between the transmission and reception of images and information. But such second sight also overwhelms our natural cognitive faculties, which process perception at a more moderate pace. Moderation, Virilio argues, is what modern, mediated society lacks; indeed, the latter is so suffused with technologically enhanced images that second-sighted realities—like Baudrillard's simulacra—achieve almost total presence. Hence, romantic notions of nature and natural experience begin to haunt the world from which they are exorcised.

Virilio's dystopian vision of telesurveillance places Johnson's relatively benign observations regarding second sight under electronic magnification, so to speak. The logic in each case is remarkably similar: the figure of second sight describes a process which frames and mediates experience through a system of perception. For Johnson, this system is the jury; for Virilio, it is electronic media. Accordingly, the experience of "seers"—for Johnson, witnesses; for Virilio, human subjects—is effectively occluded by the technologies shaping it. Additionally, second sight comes to serve a higher explanatory cause: for Johnson, it ratifies the ideology of evidence, whereas for Virilio it indicates the technological reduction of experience to mere illusion. In this way, Virilio accentuates with Johnson the transformative power of second sight to educe "more adequate witnesses" for objects of simple perception.[25]

And yet, as Hume argues, the logic of mediated perception ultimately warps into a reaffirmation of testimonial immediacy. Johnson asserts as much in his defense of second sight.[26] Conceding the "[s]trong reasons for incredulity" in evaluations of second sight, Johnson nonetheless argues that

by presuming to determine what is fit, and what is beneficial, [we] presuppose more knowledge of the universal system than man has attained; and therefore depend upon principles too easily complicated and extensive for our comprehension; and that there can be no security in the consequence, when the premises are not understood; that the second sight is only wonderful because it is rare, for, considered in itself, it involves no more difficulty than dreams, or perhaps than the regular exercise of the cogitative faculty; that a general opinion of communicative impulses, or visionary representations, has prevailed in all ages and all nations; that particular instances have been given, with such evidence, as neither

Bacon nor Boyle has been able to resist; that sudden impressions, which the event has verified, have been felt by more than own or publish them; that the second sight of the Hebrides implies only the local frequency of a power, which is nowhere totally unknown; and that where we are unable to decide by antecedent reason, we must be content to yield to the force of testimony. (112)

In this rhetorical cascade of clause upon clause, we should note the way in which Johnson begins and ends his philosophical defense of second sight—namely, by proclaiming that rational estimations of propriety or likelihood easily swell to irrational and improper proportions, and by reaffirming that in cases in which we are able to recognize the limits or limitations of reason "we must be content to yield to the force of testimony." This "force of testimony" seems all the more compelling here given Johnson's own force of argument, and given his eminently reasonable attack on the use of reason in determining the validity of second sight. Paradoxically, it is the epistemological inadequacy of such ratiocination—and the possible reality of phenomena too "extensive for our comprehension"—which second sight and forceful testimony purportedly impress upon consciousness. Like Hume, Johnson here weds skepticism and credulity, with the effect of reinforcing our reliance upon the authority of experiences whose epistemological force seems wanting. Hence, like Hume's, Johnson's argument here is not contradictory as much as self-reflexive: as rational determination, Johnson's claims are of limited value by his own admission; but, as forceful testimony, these claims emit a more compelling charge.[27]

Ultimately, forceful testimony notwithstanding, Johnson's defense of second sight resets the ideology of improvement, converting a singularly strange phenomenon into a believable one. That is to say, Johnson reaffirms the privilege of the jury even in reducing the reasonable certainties of that position to a form of testimony. He hints in his analysis as to why this conflation between witness and juror should occur in this case: "By the term second sight, seems to be meant a mode of seeing, *superadded* to that which Nature generally bestows" (111, my emphasis). Second sight denotes a secondary form of vision, one whose supplementary relation to quotidian experience improves upon the meaning typically associated with those scenes by placing them in unfamiliar or extraordinary contexts. For instance, Johnson reminds us, a petty farmer "driving home his cattle, or wandering in idleness, or musing in the sunshine, is suddenly surprised by the appearance of a bridal ceremony, or funereal procession, and counts the mourners or attendants, of whom, if he knows them, he relates the names . . . " (110). Neither cattle driving, nor weddings, nor funerals are all that remarkable until they are experienced in such settings. Second sight makes over the mundane. In literary language, second sight defamiliarizes quotidian experience; in legal terms, it not only inspires witness experience of novelty, but it also converts such experience into evidence by referring it to "truths" whose veracity cannot be determined within the context of the experience itself. This is why Johnson argues that vatic witnesses become in time "more adequate witnesses," or jurors, deciding upon the truth of previously alleged facts.

Second sight thus supplements the Highland life that Johnson claims he and Boswell arrived "too late" to see; in that way, second sight *improves upon* the torpor of Highland existence. "In the Erse [second sight] . . . is called *taisch*; which signifies . . . a spectre, or a vision" (111). While directing its gaze toward the future, second sight evokes the ghost, or memory, of events (such as weddings or funerals) which are quite common in other settings or at other times while also conjuring the spirit of Highland lore that Johnson found so lacking in the region's desolate clime. Second sight is thus an uncanny form of repetition, a supplement to nature; it shapes its visionaries' (or, more accurately, its listeners', or jurors') understanding of the future even as it validates their place in the present. Second sight is genuine, therefore, not only because it might actually occur in nature—Johnson suspends his judgment here—but also, primarily, because its form suggests an origin in synthetic human production. In the spirit of improving programs and technologies, and the evidential logic which they exhibit, second sight as the literal power of revision projects an image of future Highland prosperity— of the accidents of (witness) experience become the assurance of (judicial) progress. Second sight makes the Highland miracle which Johnson and Boswell were otherwise "too late" to find.

The Visions of Donnchadh Bàn Mac-an-t-Saoir

In his account of second sight, Johnson converts a ghost from the past into the apparition of progress. In doing so, he travels in the footsteps of his near contemporary, the respected Welsh topographer and naturalist Thomas Pennant, who embarked on landmark tours of the Highlands in 1769 and 1772. Professing his devotion to the rigors of empirical observation, Pennant consistently dismissed local Highland superstitions as "tales founded on impudence and nurtured by folly."[28] And yet, on leaving the Hebrides, Pennant tells of a confrontation he had with one of the "heroes immortalized in the verse of Ossian" who "seemed of no common size, and spoke the former strength of the hero. A graceful vigor was apparent in his countenance, notwithstanding time had robbed him of part of his locks, and given the remainder a venerable hoariness" (364, 365). Over the next few pages, this spectral figure assures Pennant that Pennant's "purpose is not unknown to [him]," and that he has "attended [Pennant] (invisible) in all [his] voyage; ha[s] sympathised with [him] in the rising tear at the misery" of Highland Scotland. "[S]ighs, such as spirit can emit, have been faithful echoes to those of [Pennant's] corporeal frame" (365). The spirit implores Pennant to improve the latter's native Wales, and by implication the Highlands as well, by "[b]ringing them instructors . . . [t]each[ing] them arts adapted to their climate . . . [s]end[ing] them materials for coarser manufactures," and so forth (368). Mixed in with these admonitions, however, are contradictory criticisms bemoaning primitive society's "degenerate progeny," whose "features and habit are changed . . . effeminated . . . become ridiculous by adopting the idle fashions of foreign climes: lost to the love of their country!" (368).[29]

Pennant's vision is at once enigmatic and engaging. In some key respects, it anticipates Smith's simultaneous denunciation and expressed admiration for the Highlands in *The Wealth of Nations*. The apparition enjoins Pennant to carry on the work of improvement, and yet the spirit's deprecations of modern society dull improvement's luster. Echoing standard eighteenth-century moral-philosophical platitudes, ancient Highland society is portrayed as "manly" and noble, in contrast with the "effeminated" state of civilization and luxury. In terms of its overall effect, the vision reaffirms the ideology of consolation and improvement, but with a caveat. The Highlands may be a region drowning in poverty and lost potential, and they may require the miracle of progress, but they are also glorified as a place of wonder, a proto-Marxian "promised land" of modern romance, where pundits of normative views of improvement acquire "otherworldy" perspectives concerning the problems introduced by improvement and its probabilistic methodology. In other words, and via the medium of Highland testimony, empiricist observation in Pennant's *Tour* morphs into something like cultural criticism.

A similar process occurs in the poetry of Pennant's (and Johnson's) contemporary, Donnchadh Bàn Mac-an-t-Saoir (1724–1812), though in a different, subtler way. In a literal sense, Mac-an-t-Saoir traces an inverted circuit from Pennant by emigrating out of the Highlands instead of journeying into them, moving from his native Glen Orchy in Argyll to Edinburgh in 1766, when he was in his forties. Closer to Pennant, Mac-an-t-Saoir was a supporter of the noted improver the Duke of Argyll, though Mac-an-t-Saoir himself repeatedly expressed ambivalence regarding the effects of progress. But there is another, figurative difference from Pennant in the converse movement of some of his poetry. Whereas Pennant's tour and his views concerning improvement culminate with a supernatural experience, effectively moving from the progressive position exemplified by the jury to the anachronistic perspective of the

witness, some of Mac-an-t-Saoir's poems move in the opposite direction—
namely, from the private experience of a solitary witness to the collective
vision associated with the jury. One of his more renowned poems, the
"Oran nam balgairean," translated into English as "The Last Adieu to
the Hills" (and literally meaning "Song of the Fox," a hunting song, as
well as "Song of the Mean Man"), illustrates this process and resonates
with other nostalgic tributes to Highland Scotland that became popular
after the onset of improvement. I quote the poem here at some length:

> Yestreen I stood on Ben Dorain, and paced its dark-grey path,
> Was there a hill I did not know—a glen or grassy strath?
> Oh! gladly in the times of old I trod that glorious ground,
> And the white dawn melted in the sun, and the red-deer cried around. . . .
>
> Oh! wildly, as the bright day gleamed, I climbed the mountain's breast,
> And when I to my home returned, the sun was in the west;
> 'Twas health and strength, 'twas life and joy, to wander freely there,
> To drink at the fresh mountain stream, to breathe the mountain air. . . .
>
> Yestreen I wandered in the glen; what thoughts were in my head!
> There had I walked with friends of yore—where are those dear ones fled?
> I looked and looked; where'er I looked was naught but sheep! sheep! sheep!
> A woeful change was in the hill! World, thy deceit was deep!
>
> From side to side I turned mine eyes—Alas! my soul was sore—
> The mountain bloom, the forest's pride, the old men were no more.
> Nay, not one antlered stag was there, nor doe so soft and slight,
> No bird to fill the hunter's bag—all, all were fled from sight!
>
> Farewell, ye forests of the heath! hills where the bright day gleams!
> Farewell ye grassy dells! farewell, ye springs and leaping streams!
> Farewell ye mighty solitudes, where once I loved to dwell—
> Scenes of my spring-time and its joys—for ever fare you well![30]

Like Johnson's *Journey*, Macpherson's *Ossian* Dissertations, and dozens
of other works, this poem expressly thematizes the social transformation of the Highlands in the latter half of the eighteenth century. Like
those other works, the poem paints a nostalgic picture of loss (in this
case, within an elegiac, counter-pastoral mode) and identifies modern
forces (e.g., "sheep! sheep! sheep!") and the attendant emphasis on
improvement as the culprits. Another common, though less noted, feature of Mac-an-t-Saoir's poem and many of these other works (like
Pennant's) is the poem's adoption of the perspective of the witness.
The poet places the emphasis on his personal experience—what he
sees, what he knows and has known, and how he feels. One obvious distinguishing feature of the poem when compared with travel narratives
like Johnson's or Pennant's is that the poet regards the rugged hills, its

"glen[s and] grassy strath[s]," as his home rather than as an exotic land of primitive wonder. However, like Marx's *Capital* and numerous eighteenth-century English and Lowland Scottish accounts of the Highlands, the poet evokes an apocalyptic vision: not only are his friends and kinsmen gone, and not only have the deer been displaced by sheep, but "the mountain's bloom" itself has faded. Hence, the poet's valediction denotes not only his own departure from those once-familiar scenes, but it also decries their absence when he would return and try to relive them.

These common features are significant because they help delimit the wide appeal of Highlandism. As a language of loss and critique, a language of experience, Highlandism inflected Highland as well as Lowland, native as well as foreign accounts of the region. In this respect, Mac-an-t-Saoir's poem strikes a further note demanding our attention. Significantly, the poet seems to have anointed himself the lone source of stability in his fallen world: he is still present on his native ground, and has not yet fled to the cities or to the New World (even though the poem would be published in an Edinburgh edition in 1768, when Mac-an-t-Saoir was living there). It is rather, he implies, the ground itself that has disappeared. In this sense, the poet's vision apprehends a degenerative condition or an experience of death whose arrival the poem defers by keeping alive the image of a world that may no longer be seen. In effect, the poet converts himself into a figure like Pennant's specter, who continues to hold a primeval sphere before his (and, vicariously, our) eyes.

The vicariousness of this experience, however, intrinsically alters its nature by sequestering a virtual body of juror-readers. The poet witnesses a scene that is redolent of death, but he dispels the horror of this vision by adopting a recognizable poetic form and lyrical voice that reestablishes a connection with his listeners (or, in the print form that Mac-an-t-Saoir—an illiterate—never achieved independently, his readers).[31] In other words, the formal constraints of elegy serve a ritualistic function that averts the ravaging effects of death by enabling a collective experience of mourning. If the poet's beloved Ben Dorain is particular to him, elegy nonetheless is a form that prospectively fits any loss. Once, the poet implies, the land was pristine; then, it fell; now, we hold it alive in memory—all of us. This is a mythic structure with which anyone, presumably, may identify; it is certainly one with which Mac-an-t-Saoir's native community identified.[32] In effect, Mac-an-t-Saoir's poem implies that the poet-as-witness perceives a fact of death that only its articulation, and the resonance of that articulation with its auditors or readers, is able to forestall. Hence, the specific object of mourning passes away in the poet's testimony, becoming virtual, or true-to-life, in his readership.

Mac-an-t-Saoir's poem exhibits a tendency similar to Johnson's account of second sight, which presents the testimony of seers to a judicial body of readers. Here, in "The Last Adieu to the Hills," the poet-witness becomes reliant on the auditor-jurors who help transform the primeval past into an incorruptible—and, in that sense, an improved—future. In this way, the Highland witness invokes a judicial body that nullifies the singularity of his experience and the uniqueness of his land by performing improvements to each. The poet's testimony endures as a function of its own declarations of finitude, or death, transforming the particularities of its vision into an experience with which others—jurors—may identify. Ironically, then, the poet hastens the transformation he purports to abhor by leveling his experience to the status of a commonplace. And, in the process, the seer's unique vision and emphatic testimony become mere items of verisimilitude, or probable likeness.

Probability, we recall, is a concept with a long and evolving history. Medieval juries too convicted on grounds of probability, but the concept had not yet acquired its connotations of disinterested objectivity, replete with an assumption of distance and a necessary calculation of likelihood. Mac-an-t-Saoir's elegy is thus all the more compelling for the social context in which it appeared in the late 1760s. Recalling our discussion in Chapter 2, we may say that the poet's elegy strikes the chord which Benjamin echoes in "The Storyteller," suggesting that if the poet's literate audience is no longer the *ceilidh*-house community of his native Argyll, then communal experience (for Benjamin, *Erfahrung*) is still possible if only as the collective experience of loss.

With Mac-an-t-Saoir's "Last Adieu" in the air, we might ask whether modern juries too are conceivable as communities founded on the oral-historical principle of traditions held in common. This is essentially what Derrida suggests in his 1996 essay "Faith and Knowledge: The Two Sources of 'Religion' at the Limits of Reason Alone." Testimony is fundamental to modernity, Derrida argues, because it perpetually promises a knowledge which it cannot quite deliver, or make entirely evident. "In testimony, truth is promised beyond all proof, all perception, all intuitive demonstration." This is most true from the perspective of the jury, of course; but Derrida's aim is not merely to reaffirm this modern conceit, but also to show how testimony reflects the state even of judicial knowledge in the modern world, a world whose technological hyper-complexity returns even its most sophisticated human subjects to a relatively "primitive," "archaic" sphere. "[I]n a growing disproportion between knowledge and know-how, the space of . . . technical experience tends to become more animistic, magical, mystical," as well as "increasingly primitive and archaic."[33] That is, technological hyper-complexity illuminates the widening abyss between the full understanding of an issue and the practical expertise of knowing how to access something (or some-one) that can. Internet search engines, for instance, provide any user possessing the technical understanding of access with virtually instanta-neous information on any given subject. But information here takes the form of testimony—at some level, users must take it (or a competing information source, or simply the medium itself) at its word. Our tech-nical experience of information transforms us all into witnesses.

It is this capacity of testimony to "speak for" the modern world of tech-no-power which makes it emblematic for Derrida of the social fabric in which it signifies. The experience of testimony—of radical uncertainty—is what "we" "moderns" share. For Derrida, unlike for eighteenth-centu-ry jurists, testimony is thus the rule of knowledge, not the means to a morally certain end. That is, witness experience reflects not only the state of truth to which nobody has anything more than partial access, but such experience also carries in tow the institutional forums in which witnesses are called, heard, and interpreted. Witnesses are thus at once singular and collective; in attesting only to what they see and hear, they speak for and about the wide extent of the system which summons them. Experience acquires heightened relevance in modernity as the return of repressed, improbable contingency.

This dynamic, joining the modern and the primitive, juror and wit-ness, underscores a theme we discussed in relation to Macpherson and Wilkomirski. There, the insistence on witness testimony morphed into a reliance on sensationist experience which, Adorno persuasively argues, reflects the probabilistic fabric of enlightenment. Sensationism does so to the extent that it is born from the biases of modern science, whose immediate relation to objects is always highly mediated (e.g., through procedures and instruments—the scientific method and the micro-scope). Hence, testimony born of alleged immediacy actually reflects the image of its (mediatory) opposite. With the situation Derrida describes, conversely, probabilistic determinations of evidential fact ulti-mately devolve on the type of witness experience they endeavor to sup-press; knowledge becomes testimonial to the extent that it becomes authoritative, exceeding the limits of user verification during the moment we process it and put it into action.

This dialectic of (im)mediacy plays out in the visions of Pennant and Mac-an-t-Saoir. In Pennant's case, the enlightened traveler's conception of improvement harbors an ecstatic vision of the same. Mac-an-t-Saoir's poem reflects an inverse process, as the claim to privileged experience divulges the normative fabric in which his testimony signifies. Pennant, an improver like Smith, unwittingly serves (like Smith) as a Highland witness, whereas Mac-an-t-Saoir, like Macpherson-Wilkomirski, tacitly promotes the median norm against which his testimonies appear to chafe. This paradox—that testimony refines itself into evidence even as evidence reverts to testimony—plays up the dilemma of experience that has been with us since the Enlightenment. Experience is at once requisite and inadequate to the demands of knowledge, marginalizing witness testimony; however, such testimony returns precisely when mediation appears to achieve total presence.

The Haunted Fringes of Empirical Detail

The bi-vocal quality of Mac-an-t-Saoir's poetry—its resonance in the voice of witness and juror—makes it a provocative counterpoint to Johnson's techno-logic of second sight. For Johnson, this logic converts witness experience into probabilistic judgment; despite Johnson's critique of reductive rationalism, he creates a scenario in which passive observers, and even vatic seers themselves, come away "only willing to believe" the testimony of immediacy. Ultimately, the seers' visions project little more than probable images of imminence, or spectral evocations of what improvement may yet "superadd" to Highland Scotland. Johnson's interpretation of second sight thus redounds on empiricist ideology: direct experience yields something less than knowledge; truth implies a process of speculation.

In his most famous poem, "Praise of Ben Dobhrain" (the Gaelic spelling of "Dorain"), Mac-an-t-Saoir delimits a Highland location that likewise avails itself to empiricist observation, devalues the epistemological claims of experience, and conjures a spectral reality. This poem, however, casts a different light on these processes. Mac-an-t-Saoir's 554-line description of a mountain from his home in the west Highlands, composed sometime between 1751 and 1766, evokes an image of the traditional *ceilidh*-house audience for whom it was composed; it also implicitly narrates the decline of the collective experience (Benjamin's *Erfahrung*) which such a community presupposed.[34] In doing so, however, "Praise of Ben Dobhrain" distills a similarly, if less nostalgically, collective basis of decayed experience.

These spectral communities, at once eroding and undead, filter themselves through Mac-an-t-Saoir's poem and compel close attention. Traditionally serving as media of history and genealogy, bardic poems like Mac-an-t-Saoir's often celebrated the accomplishments and munificence of the clan chiefs who personified the spirit of the particular clans. John MacInnes refers to the elaborate strictures of this poetry as the "panegyric code." Evocative of the structuralist methodology applied to folklore by Vladimir Propp, the panegyric code represents a systematic attempt to account for references to such features as the chief's background, social roles, household recreation, personal endowments, destiny, and so on.[35] Ronald Black comments that "Macinnes's work represents an act not of discovery but of recovery—although it had never previously been laid out in writing, the principles and *topoi* of the panegyric code were well known to the poets, patrons, and *ceilidh*-house audiences of the past, and indeed this familiarity allowed traditional verse to be highly allusive and succinct in expression."[36] By this logic, it follows that the codified tradition in which Mac-an-t-Saoir was working predicated itself on the collective experience of its adherents. Any deviation from the code would only become perceptible against the backdrop of such shared experience and expectation; indeed, this rule applies to any generic formation.

"Praise of Ben Dobhrain" is noteworthy precisely for such deviations, specifically in its detailed attentiveness to nature and in the corresponding absence of any reference to the clan chief in sections of the poem where such references would have been expected. One passage exhibits Mac-an-t-Saoir's deviations from the code most poignantly. In a section extolling the deer that inhabit the mountain, and in which the poet speaks effusively about the chase, he fails to mention the chief as a renowned hunter. Instead, he focuses on the deer in flight:

> Ged thig Caoilte 's Cù Chulainn,
>   'S gach duine de 'n t-seòrs' ud,
> Na tha dhaoine 's a dh' eachaibh
>   Air fasdadh Rìgh Deòrsa,
> Nan tèarnadh a craiceann
> O luaidhe 's o lasair
> Cha chual' is chan fhac' i
>   Na ghlacadh r' a beò i . . .

> (Though there came Caoilte,
> Cuchulainn and all such,
> all the men and horses
> in King George's service,
> if her [i.e., the deer's] skin should escape
> from lead and from flame,
> she neither heard of nor saw one
> that would soon seize her alive . . .)[37]

Studies of the poem debate the significance of this passage. Is the passage symbolic? Do the deer represent clan members and Jacobites fleeing from Hanoverian forces? Interestingly, the presence or absence of symbolic content means little when read in conjunction with the panegyric code. On the one hand, if the passage is symbolic, then the focus on the flight of the deer—the flight of the clans—speaks to the disintegration of Highland clan society after the '45. If, on the other hand, the passage is devoid of symbolism (which is the claim of Iain Crichton Smith, one of

Mac-an-t-Saoir's modern translators), and if all we have is a description of nature, and of the flight of the deer regardless of who chases them, then the failure of the poet to mention the prowess of the clan chief also speaks to the disintegration of Highland clan society.[38]

The relative insignificance of what presumably should figure as a key item of interpretation—the symbolic status of Mac-an-t-Saoir's subject—is precisely what makes the erosion of clan society a matter of thematic priority in this poem. In this respect, there is a significant interface between the Highlandism of the Highlander, Mac-an-t-Saoir, and that of relative outsiders like Johnson. For both Highlander and tourist, the region affords a view that the storyteller provides for Benjamin: the Highlands become "a concomitant symptom of the productive forces of history, a concomitant that has removed [primitive clan society] from the realm of [modern life] . . . making it possible to see a new beauty in what is vanishing" (Benjamin, "Storyteller," 146). Johnson turns to second sight, we recall, only after he first attends to the flora and fauna of Skye, and after he discusses the social deterioration of the Highlands. Preserving these associations in inverse order, the poet in "Praise of Ben Dobhrain" turns to a discussion of nature once clan society seemingly erodes past the point of repair. In each case, Johnson's and Mac-an-t-Saoir's, the Highlands figure as a place in which nature and society, empiricism and culture, past and future dwell in haunting relation to each other. Here, it seems, nothing exists in full; everything appears as the shadow of its others.

At this point, it might be helpful to accentuate a subtle difference between the two poems I have cited by Mac-an-t-Saoir. As with "The Last Adieu to the Hills," "Praise of Ben Dobhrain" is partly an elegiac tribute to a locale whose absence is compensated for by the poet's ecstatic vision: "Precedence over every ben/has Ben Dobhrain;/of all I have seen beneath the sun,/I deemed her loveliest . . . " (ll. 2766–69). Unlike "Last Adieu," however, "Praise of Ben Dobhrain" signals this elegiac vision *through* (and not in transcendence of) its attention to empirical detail: "a long, unbroken moor,/covert where deer are found;/the brightness of the slope/I noted specially" (2770–73). Such vivid detail comes into view precisely as a function of that which does *not* appear—specifically, the clan chief and an attendant sense of social solidarity. Close attention to details in and for themselves is what remains when such details no longer inhere within an epic tapestry according them secondary meaning (e.g., the deer as symbols of the clan). The poem thus situates itself somewhere between the conventions of traditional bardic poetry and the "improved" empiricism of Highland accounts like Martin's, Pennant's, and Johnson's.

"In Praise of Ben Dobhrain" opens a liminal space (rather than the elegiac space elicited in "The Last Adieu to the Hills") which inverts the professed quality of experience. If obeisance to the panegyric code effectively signals a tradition which both bard and audience share, and if manipulation of the code indicates an erosion of traditional values, then it follows that Mac-an-t-Saoir's poem anticipates the dialectic which Benjamin (following Marx) elucidates in his discussion of storytelling. On the one hand, the poet's liberation from the clan chief accentuates the singular, even alienated nature of his experience; experience thus deteriorates here to the status of *Erlebnis*, a private reality of empirical details which assumes, at its limits, a break between perception and reality (i.e., between Ben Dobhrain as it appears to the untutored swain, and the mountain as it is revealed in its true, though non-self-evident, geological nature). On the other hand, the poem's bardic echoes situate it, despite its pointed deviations from the panegyric code, within the type of integrated community that would register and understand the poet's digressions; the poem's violation of its listeners' expectations accentuates the social fabric in which such expectations are woven in the first place. This persistent presence of traditional bardic forms in the poem, even given the ostensible breakdown of clan society, attests to the residues in the poem of experience as *Erfahrung*, or of an integrated relation to the world. This may signify either the endurance of tradition, or the restitching of a new social fabric, or both.

With respect to Mac-an-t-Saoir's tourist contemporaries Pennant and Johnson, we might put it this way: if one of the things "Praise of Ben Dobhrain" describes is a decline of experience, a reduction of *Erfahrung* to *Erlebnis*, then it also suggests the "universal" quality of this decline, within the Highlands as well as outside them; it testifies, we might say, to the collective experience (*Erfahrung*) of alienation (*Erlebnis*) for native and tourist alike. In the Highlands, presumably, "we" (i.e., native and tourist; Mac-an-t-Saoir and Johnson) collectively experience our alienation; in the Highlands, "we" achieve community by mourning its passing.

A TECHNO-ELEGY OF SPEED: MAC-AN-T-SAOIR IN MODERN TRANSLATION

Mourning, for Freud, occurs through a process of ruin. Faced with loss, the libido withdraws "bit by bit, under great expense of time and cathectic energy." The force of living and torrents of new impressions gradually erode the subject's attachment to the deceased. Dust (i.e., the dead) breeds dust (i.e., the crumbling libidinal attachment).[39] For Derrida, by contrast, mourning activates memory as a kind of technology. Memory "preserves an essential and necessary relation with the possibility of the name," including, per force, the name of the deceased; and yet, "[i]n calling or naming someone when he is alive, we know that his name can survive him and already survives him; the name begins during his life to get along without him. . . . [T]he structure of the name . . . is in advance 'in memory of.'"[40] Mourning, memory, name—all speak to a projective apparatus fashioning future presents. In this respect, they forge a structural and spectral bond with the techno-logic of improvement.

Mourning as ruin, mourning as techno-logic: Iain Crichton Smith's 1969 translation of Mac-an-t-Saoir's "Praise of Ben Dobhrain" provocatively links these notions while converting the consolation of "mourning" into something more foreboding, like melancholy. For Crichton Smith, Mac-an-t-Saoir's descriptive poem emerges in a provocative if paradoxical space of technically induced immediacy whose sensations we moderns are barred from fully experiencing. Crichton Smith was not the first Scottish poet to idealize and translate Mac-an-t-Saoir's poem; Hugh MacDiarmid published his own translation in 1940 as a testament to the strength of what he called the "Gaelic Idea" (which I discuss in Chapter 7). The richness of Crichton Smith's translation thus partly devolves on its deep historicity—its multivalent source of origin in Mac-an-t-Saoir and MacDiarmid. At once a testament to the technical virtuosity of eighteenth-century Gaelic poetry (underscored through Crichton Smith's technological metaphors), an homage to a bygone era, and a tribute to MacDiarmid's "Idea," Crichton Smith's translation charts a general decline of experience: forces of improvement, hastening the deterioration of Mac-an-t-Saoir's *ceilidh*-house community, now mass-produce ruin in modernity. This ruin manifests itself in the uncanny immediacy of Mac-an-t-Saoir's poetic vision, and in the implicit contrast between this perspective and the modern gaze in which everything acquires a depth of meaning precisely because its truth remains perpetually inaccessible to experience. Ultimately, the comparative "ruin" of modern experience generates a kind of solidarity of its own, though it is one in which experiential immediacy recurs in pathological form.

Crichton Smith understands that translation and interpretation mutually implicate each other; nevertheless, and implicitly recalling Heidegger's concept of technology, Crichton Smith did not set out to update Mac-an-t-Saoir's work for a modern era by putting a new spin on the poem as much as he sought to underscore the poem's inherently modern ethos by remaining as faithful as possible to the original. He saw the poem as trafficking in "information" (a technocratic buzzword) and in presenting an un-sentimentalized, un-Wordsworthian, more frankly realistic view of the eighteenth-century Highlands. "The deer" in Mac-an-t-Saoir's poem, for instance, "are not aesthetic objects. They are real. The dogs" that chase them down and destroy them at the poem's end "too are real and equally lovingly described. . . . This is violence. This is the real world. [Mac-an-t-Saoir] would never have dreamed of using the deer as symbols for anything."[41] The significance of this alleged realism consists in highlighting the materiality of eighteenth-century Highland culture: "It is the Gaelic language at its peak. It is the poet writing before morality," before sentimentality, before the politicization of loss (e.g., in nationalism). "Never again would a Gaelic poet write like this. Never again would the Gaelic ethos allow him to" (7). This materiality, in turn, inspires the poem's bereaved tone—bereavement for a world that has been rendered increasingly obsolete.

Crichton Smith, a native of the Hebridean Island of Lewis, struck this note in a number of poems he composed and published in the late 1960s and early '70s, around the time when he translated "Praise of Ben Dobhrain" (restoring the anglicized "Dorain"). One such poem, "Ceilidh," has villagers entering a communal space "to listen to their past":

> The music starts. Exile begins again.
> They leave the mountains and the glens in song. . . .
>
> The common dream unites them as they gaze
> into the tender surfaces. They hear
> the bagpipes playing from the wars they've lost
> historically, daily. . . .
>
> Their souls return to what their souls have prized
> too little against exile and decay
> and they set out to real glens and hills
> depleted townships and the gathering roar
> of midnight streams, the moonlight on the sea.
> They come together—Art and what they see. . . .[42]

Though beleaguered by their struggle against the elements and poor labor conditions, the Highlanders here purportedly share a communal experience which unites them to each other (in "common dream"), to their past (in "the wars they've lost / historically, daily"), and to their media of representation ("They come together—Art and what they see"). Such experience is not easily reduplicated in modernity, however, outside the auspices of the *ceilidh*—at least, not simplistically so.

This was an ongoing theme across the body of Crichton Smith's work. In some of his most poignant short fiction, he situates the Highlands and Islands on a delicate border on which sensations of immediacy and communal experience haunt forces of modernization. His 1973 story "An American Sky" tells of an emigrant Islander, John, who returns to his home after many years in America only to find abundant traces of what we would now call globalization (i.e., a Chinese restaurant downtown; the enthusiasm of his niece and nephew for science and American culture, and their corresponding indifference to native traditions) resting cheek-by-jowl against the kind of painful, exquisitely presentist experience described in the poem "Ceilidh." In the reflective moment that marks the climax of the story, John acknowledges to himself that "he had felt his return as a regression to a more primitive place, a more pastoral, less exciting position, lower on the scale of a huge complex ladder. Now he wasn't so sure. Perhaps those who went away were the weaker ones, the ones who were unable to suffer the slowness of time, its inexorable yet ceremonious passing."[43] Experience—*Erfahrung*—is presented here as difficult, even psychologically agonizing, but still possible; the supposedly "primitive" Highlands, which really aren't so primitive, John realizes, represent a fund of experience from which "America" and modernization provide shelter.[44]

All of this is to say that Crichton Smith, like Mac-an-t-Saoir, embraced the Highlandism of his native home, interpreting it as a channel of witness experience whose relative improbability was largely a function of the "improved" (i.e., evidential) public sphere against and out of which Highland romance had entered modern consciousness.[45] "Technology" in the Heideggerian mode of *poeisis* is an important, if often subtle feature of this romantic image and of Crichton Smith's work, including his translation of Mac-an-t-Saoir's poem. In a negative sense, technology represents the calculating, improvement-oriented forces that Heidegger traces to the rise of modern science in the seventeenth century (and which manifests itself most vividly in Mac-an-t-Saoir's poem in the form of the firearms that destroy the deer). In a more positive sense, however, technology also provides a lens onto the secret springs of experience. There are places in his translation, for instance, when Crichton Smith resorts to technological metaphors in order to capture the kinetic energy of Mac-an-t-Saoir's original. One such passage describes the swift movements of the deer. I cite the original, a literal translation, and then Crichton Smith's:

'N uair a shìneas i h-eangan
'S a théid i 'na deannaibh,
Cha saltradh air thalamh
Ach barra nan ìngnean:
Có b' urrainn g' a leantainn
A dh' fhearaibh na rìoghachd?

(when she stretches her limbs
and breaks into a gallop,
nought but the hoof tips
would tread on the ground;
of the men of the kingdom,
who was fit to pursue her? [2846–51])

(Accelerant, speedy,
when she moves her slim body

> earth knows nought of this lady
> but the tips of her nails.
> Even light would be tardy
> to the flash of her pulse. [11])

All three versions describe the light step of the deer. The more literal of the two translations expresses this step through the phrase "hoof tips," Crichton Smith's through "the tips of her nails," and the original through an assertion that not even the briny slime at the tip of a fishing spear clings to the deer's hooves. Mac-an-t-Saoir's original then punctuates this image by asking who in the kingdom would have the power of remaining beside her, with the "who" denoting not only royal suitors but also, etymologically, evoking the diffusive limits of the atmosphere (from the Gaelic *aibheis*, embedded in the phrase "*A dh'fhearaibh na rìoghachd*"). In essence, this line suggests that nobody—nothing human—is capable of staying with and thus perceiving the type of speed the deer represents; nobody is able to experience the deer in its essential quality of speed. The more literal of the translations codifies this question in terms of "the men of the kingdom," a faithful if colorless rendition of the original that occludes the latter's implicit focus on rapid movement. Crichton Smith's translation is the more engaging, concerning itself less with suitors than with the inadequacy even of "light" itself to keep pace with "the flash of [the deer's] pulse." Here, the poet recodifies the deer as a species of phototechnology, "flash[ing]" more rapidly than unaided perception can detect. For Crichton Smith, the deer do not evoke technology as much as technology makes it possible for us to conceive—precisely through what we fail to perceive—of the elusive essence of the deer. In Crichton Smith's translation, unlike in Virilio's phenomenology, technology does not precipitate a decline of experience; rather, technology helps us experience collectively a vision of what we have already lost.

Other passages play upon this same dynamic. Mac-an-t-Saoir describes the sound of a hind as *binne geum* (a "harmonious low"), rendered literally as a "young hind of sweetest low" (l. 2914). Both the original and this translation portray the hind answering a stag lustfully (*Gu deòthasach*; "so yearningly" in the translation [l. 2917]). Crichton Smith focuses less on the relation of the deer to each other than to nature: "The sweet harmonious hind—/with her calf behind—/elaborates the wind/with her music" (14). The focus shifts here to the technical virtuosity of music, and to the close relationship between such technique and nature (whose "wind" the hind "elaborates"). It is this technical, musical quality for which Crichton Smith extols eighteenth-century Gaelic poetry, and Mac-an-t-Saoir's poem in particular: "What distinguishes 'Ben Dorain' is its gaiety and its music" (3). This music and the poem's "absolutely superb use of assonance" is one of the most acute pleasures of the poem (5), a pleasure which lends oneself the impression of being "in the hands of an expert. And we like that" (5). The hind's "elaborations," her harmony with and technical channeling of nature, thus evoke Crichton Smith's depiction of Mac-an-t-Saoir's poetic virtuosity, a symbiotic space of nature and culture (evocative of Coleridge's *Eolian Harp*) and hence of integrated experience from which we in modernity are purportedly severed.

There are still other pointed technological metaphors in Crichton Smith's translation which accentuate the problem of experience. In a subsequent passage to those cited above, Crichton Smith refers to a small buck as "a clever machine" which is "as swift as your vision/with speed and precision" (17). Mac-an-t-Saoir's original is "machine"-like only in the repetitive nature of its syntax: "*Gun sgiorradh gun tubaist/Gun tuisleadh gun dìobradh*" ("without mishap without accident [a synonym of "mishap"]/without stumbling without break-down" [modified translation of ll. 3004–5]). The "speed and precision" to which Crichton Smith refers thus pertain to the poet's staccato-light musical touch as much as to the movements of the deer. Here, as in the passages we surveyed above, techno-speed actually helps us catch a glimpse of what would otherwise pass unnoticed. In Crichton Smith's translation, this happens not through super-slow-motion as much as what Virilio calls a sensation of disappearance: technology crystallizes the nature of an experiential immediacy which we know (collectively and intuitively—through *Erfahrung*) that we cannot know.[46] Only this sort of collective realization, Crichton Smith implies, can enable us to appreciate Mac-an-t-Saoir's poetry and the world in which it was created.

The techno-logic of Crichton Smith's translation thus underscores the experience of what we cannot experience. In this respect, it partly reiterates Virilio's phenomenological critique of technology. In *The Aesthetics of Disappearance*, a book whose title plays on Merleau-Ponty's posthumous *The Visible and the Invisible* in exploring unperceived facets of perception, Virilio argues that technology (especially phototechnology) is generating "a kind of dissolving view," expelling humankind "from the world in which it has lived." "With [technological] speed, the world keeps on coming at us, to the detriment of the object, which is itself now assimilated to the sending of information. It is this intervention that destroys the world as we know it, technique finally reproducing the [perpetual] violence of the accident. . . ." The declining quality of our experience, its reduction to sensation (and sensationalism), renders us permanent exiles: "The development of high technical speeds would thus result in the disappearance of consciousness as the direct perception of phenomena that inform us of our own existence."[47]

Virilio is not alone in striking this refrain. Indeed, he might be considered one oracle amidst a cadre of technology critics that includes Weber, Benjamin, Adorno, Marcuse, Heidegger, McLuhan, Ong, Baudrillard, and many others. It is seemingly against the nostalgic pathos of this critique that Derrida argues for the spectral interface between technology and religion, for the technological features of memory and representation, and hence for the implication of technology in the pasts and mentalities that deny it. Given this wider critical context, I find Virilio's phenomenological critique less significant for its uniqueness or lucidity than for its affect, its resonance with the historical tenor of Highland romance. It certainly accords with Crichton Smith's Highlandist vision across the body of his work, and with Crichton Smith's interpretation of Mac-an-t-Saoir's poetry. Technically, "Praise of Ben Dobhrain" is a descriptive poem; however, for Crichton Smith, it functions as the elegy of a Highland society and a quality of experience that call to us from an ethos of decline, forever fading but never entirely extinguished. From Crichton Smith's perspective, and adopting Virilio's critical vernacular, Mac-an-t-Saoir's poem is an elegy of speed: its rapturous, almost supernatural vision of Ben Dobhrain, whose social value purportedly is eroding at the instant in which it is conjured, finds appropriate modern expression in technological tropes. Technology, Virilio insists, degrades all "real" experience into an encounter with ghosts; technological metaphors (for Crichton Smith) and movement (in Mac-an-t-Saoir's poem) likewise impress upon consciousness the spectrality of the poet's visionary experience.

Derrida's declension of technology and mourning seems at first too consoling for an experience like this. Upon closer inspection, however, something hopeful emerges from Crichton Smith's translation—namely, the possibility of arriving at critical self-consciousness, revealing, for better or worse, the survival of integrated experience in modernity. From this perspective, the ghostly quality of Man-an-t-Saoir's poem and the "materiality" (as Crichton Smith has it) of his vision accommodate what eighteenth-century critics called the joy of grief. That is, "Praise of Ben Dobhrain" may not fetishize the picturesque erosion associated with "ruin," but neither does it devolve to the mechanical dysfunctionality of trauma, of compulsive repetition. In Mac-an-t-Saoir's portrait of the Highlands, as in Crichton Smith's, holistic experience (*Erfahrung*) endures, even if in debased form; as such, it generates images of the redemption for which its poets long in the very act of bemoaning its impossibility.

TECHNOLOGY AS A STRUCTURE OF FEELING

This reference to trauma recalls our discussion of Macpherson and Wilkomirski in Chapter 5, and of the pathologies associated with "immediate" experience. In a slightly different vein, it also brings to mind our discussion of Johnson. Johnson's grave disappointment at the belatedness of his vision derived primarily from the inevitably mediated quality of his Highland romance. From the perspective of direct experience, little appeared to his view other than an arid and "hopeless sterility." Hence, reflecting the dimensions of this experience, the *Journey* is peppered with figures of mediated vision, most strikingly in the case of second sight. What Johnson purportedly desires to find in second sight is nature in its purer, untrammeled—for that reason, its supernatural—form. Wordsworth would seemingly follow Johnson's path a generation later when, citing the "savage torpor" of life due to "the encreasing [*sic*] accumulation of men in cities," he undertook his iconic return to nature.[48] And yet, as we have seen, Johnson champions "improving" mediation by conceptualizing second sight as evidence. Similarly, while outwardly disdaining industrial progress, Wordsworth promotes a circuit of improvement—in this case, of feeling by thought (as "the representations of all our past feelings" [157–58]), and of thought by feeling. Eventually, he believes, virtuous "habits of mind will be produced . . . by obeying blindly and mechanically"—industrially— "the impulses of those [improving] habits . . ." (158).

Still, as they do in *The Wealth of Nations*, phantoms of immediacy haunt Johnson's text, for instance in the form of travel notes which professedly devolve to the kind of oral history—the kind of undiscerning, witness-like credulity—they purport to criticize. Heidegger would doubtlessly delight in the way that Johnson's account thus recovers a different brand of technology in these moments. (He might say the same thing about the "wreaths of smoke/Sent up, in silence" by the displaced vagrants in "*Tintern Abbey*" as the counter-image to burgeoning British industrialization.) In Mac-an-t-Saoir's "Praise of Ben Dobhrain," and in Iain Crichton Smith's translation of that poem, witness-like immediacy takes the form of a collective experience of what we claim no longer to be able to experience. Crichton Smith's translation, especially, elucidates Highland romance—high-tech primitivism—as neither true nor false as much as a structure of feeling, attesting across more than two centuries to the haunting return of experience programmed into the latter's supposed decay.

During the eighteenth century, the epistemological gap widened between experience and understanding. For all the division it promoted, this widening gulf also unites such diverse souls as Johnson and Mac-an-t-Saoir—and, more recently, Paul Virilio and Iain Crichton Smith. The solidarity forged here, common today under the rubric of globalization, involves a quality more than a geography, a way of seeing more than a place of supernal vision. According to Heidegger and Derrida, the power to reflect on this solidarity is the more sophisticated—if also, historically, the more primitive—meaning of technology. This meaning is redemptive, Benjamin might say; it restores a sense of the integrated quality of experience in modernity. Just as important, for us, it sheds light on the enigmatic and perpetual return to experience, to ruin, as a reflex of our impulse toward progress, especially via epistemic and mechanic technologies.

This may seem like quite a mouthful for the oral poetry of an illiterate Highland bard. But while Man-an-t-Saoir may not have known how to read letters, he was a canny reader of his native Highlands. And in his best, most lucid verse, he nullifies not only the question of poetic symbolism, but also superficial distinctions between Highland reality and Highland romance. In an age of progress, the Highlands become an elegiac land of promise to native and tourist alike.

Chapter 7

Highland Romance in Late Modernity

Amid a larger discussion of the virtual death of the humanities in the Information Age, Alan Liu's *The Laws of Cool* resets the narrative of the decay and redemption of experience. Not that Liu sees it exactly in this way: he imagines, rather, a story about the decay of this redemptive possibility. It was not always thus, he recognizes. A notion of experiential reality accompanied emergent ethnic and class identities during the industrial era. Consistent with the dynamics of Mac-an-t-Saoir's complex elegies, individuals within these ethnic- and class-based communities drew strength from their identification as "part of a 'people' or 'tribe'" despite—indeed, partly because of—dehumanizing conditions in the workplace.[1] "Exile from one's humanity simultaneously created the sense of a whole working-class neighborhood away from neighborhood, a community with so much potential for solidarity that it could have its own after-hours hangouts, charities, bowling leagues, youth subcultures, and so on" (53). However, Liu laments, such compensatory, collective experience has effectively been flattened by a business paradigm which vitiates historical and class identities, replacing the richness of "culture" with the capital-driven hegemony of the "team." Here, we find all the hallmarks of the Adornian concept of fascism—the devolution of historical difference into presentist sensation, the atomization of individuals into composites of discrete technical skills, and the triumph of a vast "monoculture of diversity" which is a contradiction in terms (58). *Erfahrung* in this context signifies universal degradation: "Whether we turn our gaze upon identity groups or class in this corporatism, the 'same' look of simulated identity thus stares out at us—the same composite, repixelated, and endlessly mutable monoculture of diversity backed up by no more history than a daily backup of the hard drive" (63).

However, and as we have seen elsewhere, even this brave new digitized world harbors a romantick dream of experience. Cultural identity may have lost its edge in the era of the "team"—"diversity" may have refined itself into an expression of traits possessing little more meaning than a difference between competing commodities—but "hunger for identity . . .

survives within the [techno-capitalist] pipeline as a craving for a restorative ethos . . . able to withstand the [matrix] of postindustrialism" (71). Liu describes this "hunger" as "something like what Raymond Williams called a 'structure of feeling' that, if it can no longer be identity or class in customary ways, can nevertheless reconstitute the basis for a renewed folk identity" (71, emphases deleted). This "hunger," this "ethos," this "structure" "at once cleaves from and to inchoate social experience (72n.). Indeed, the desire here is for something like witness experience in an era of evidence. Accordingly, Liu situates the humanities at the (Highland) border of the neo-Enlightenment monoculture, "already in the pipeline alongside—but profoundly separated from—the . . . contemporary ethos of disenchanted knowledge" (72). Hence, without naming the Highlands, Liu reproduces their "structure of feeling"—literally—in his romantick narrative about a newly redemptive promise of experience following on the heels of the latter's decay as a function of ongoing capitalist improvement.

Liu's discussion animates the modern dilemma of experience for a postmodern, postliterary, even a posthuman age. No Highlandist, Liu nevertheless underscores the historical significance of Highland romance by invoking the Information Age as the "New Enlightenment." In this "new" moment, the "old" dialectic of experiential decay and redemption returns with such vengeance that it almost falls outside all history and acquires the status of a modern "human" universal for an era which no longer believes in such things (except, perhaps, at the level of genetics, updating La Mettrie's *L'Homme Machine*). David Simpson comments on this strange universality in his provocative 1995 study *The Academic Postmodern and the Rule of Literature*. He rehearses Walter Benjamin's famous pronouncement in "The Storyteller" that "the art of storytelling is coming to an end" and then asks, incredulously, "What . . . has happened? Benjamin was writing about the end of an oral tradition whose fullness we have certainly not recovered. Nonetheless, it now seems that everyone is telling stories, and professing the ability to exchange experiences."[2] This latter phenomenon, the "exchange" of "experiences," rests at the heart of the matter, for we have seen that Benjamin treated storytelling as a palimpsest of experience, whose quality he believed had been decaying since the Enlightenment. No longer deemed adequate to an understanding of the complexities of modernity, experience increasingly reflected for Benjamin a general condition of alienation, both between and within individuals. As Simpson remarks, this is a condition which, by the mid-1990s, had begun paradoxically to serve as an impetus rather than an impediment to storytelling. "Literature" had become commensurate with a certain type of knowledge—"half-knowledge," as he puts it; the knowledge of "cool," in Liu's vocabulary.

"Half-knowledge," "cool knowledge," is the oxymoronic knowledge of experience, the authority accruing to witness testimony. As we have seen, this is not knowledge in the fully legitimated, "enlightened" sense of the term, but it also possesses an aura of something which supersedes knowledge, an allure of the improbable. In this concluding chapter I discuss this allure in two pairs of twentieth-century Highland-romantic narratives. Selected from the early and later ends of the century (even, in one instance, the early twenty-first century), these pairs—Virginia Woolf's *To the Lighthouse* (1927) and Neil Gunn's *Morning Tide* (1930), and Alan Warner's *Morvern Callar* (1994) and Sophie Cooke's *The Glass House* (2004)—present intricate portraits of Simpson's half-knowledge in a Highland setting. Knowledge and experience do not merge into each other in these texts as much as sit side by side—forever linked, but irreconcilably, in a relationship of core and periphery.[3] As Liu and Simpson indicate, and as I suggest in the Introduction, the Enlightenment binary of knowledge and experience—historically conflated in empiricist epistemology, and never as rigid as the division of witness and juror has made it appear—seems in some ways to have eroded in postmodernity. And yet, to the extent that this conviction reiterates the logic of romance (i.e., "once upon a time" knowledge superseded experience), it intrinsically retraces the (Highland) periphery of what no longer counts as knowledge (and, hence, which signifies merely as experience).[4] Hence, though perennially dubious, the conflict between knowledge and experience continues to inform modern thought. The four texts I discuss in this chapter attest to the evolution and endurance of this conflict, and hence to the alluring improbability, the Highland romance, which continues to haunt us.

Woolf and Gunn: Irony and Its Double

To the Lighthouse is considered Woolf's most autobiographical novel. In it, via an exposé of individual and familial angst, Woolf reportedly presents her own background in defamiliarized form: the Ramsay house in the Hebrides is "really" the Stephen family's holiday residence on St. Ives; Mr. Ramsay—"petty, selfish, vain, egotistical"—is "really" Woolf's father, the Victorian man of letters Leslie Stephen; and Mrs. Ramsay is "really" Woolf's mother, Julia Jackson Duckworth, who died when Woolf was in her early teens.[5] Of course, as Woolf was to demonstrate with her novel *Orlando*, "biography" in her fiction is typically doubled by a self-reflexive commentary on the medium of narrative. So it is, I argue, with *To the Lighthouse*, which weaves a commentary on the historical associations of Highland romance into its reputedly autobiographical narrative. It does so via the novel's titular icon, a Hebridean lighthouse.

Set provocatively on the romantick periphery of the novel's action, the lighthouse acquires its significance by emblematically configuring and mediating the novel's fixation with lost plenitude.

The novel's focal character, Mrs. Ramsay, embodies this motif. Widespread attention to the novel's autobiographical details has incited some critics to theorize Mrs. Ramsay as an absent mother, a crucial figure in psychoanalysis. From this perspective, the three sections of *To the Lighthouse* ("The Window," "Time Passes," and "The Lighthouse") correspond to Jacques Lacan's tripartite schema of subject formation: the Imaginary, the Real, and the Symbolic.[6] Drawing upon Melanie Klein's theory of drives, Lacan argues that individuation and signification devolve on an impossible quest for plenitude which originates with the child's weaning from the mother. As Julia Kristeva explains, "Drives involve pre-Oedipal [or primordial] semiotic functions and energy discharges that connect and orient the body to the mother. . . . The mother's body is . . . what mediates the symbolic law organizing social relations," functioning as the image of primordial fullness which the subject vainly strives to (re-)obtain. The mother becomes "the addressee of every demand"; she "takes the place of all narcissistic, hence imaginary, effects and gratifications."[7] Her absence, therefore, is less contingent than constitutive; it motivates the subject formation and the process of signification: the absent mother names the subject's desire and spectrally anchors cognition.

To the Lighthouse lends itself to a Lacanian reading inasmuch as it thematizes the obsessive fixation of its characters with objects of desire and lost plenitude, and with the unnamable presence—the (m)other—which haunts them.[8] In this respect, Woolf's novel presents a biography not only of the Stephen family, but also of the aesthetics of modernism, in which loss figures so self-consciously. Accentuating this fixation with plenitude, little actually "happens" in most of the novel: we spend a day with a family, the major event in which is the evening meal; then several years pass; then we return to the family, its circumstances having changed, as the father and two children (finally) make their way to the lighthouse. Mostly, the narrative self-reflexively engages dynamics of loss and desire, and their permeation of quotidian circumstances. Lily Briscoe, a family friend and the narrative's surrogate artist, reflects on these dynamics when seated one evening at the dinner table: "Nothing need be said; nothing could be said. There it [i.e., plenitude] was all around them. It partook . . . of eternity" (105). Lily feels the proverbial vibes. Articulating them, however, is another matter: "if they knew, could they tell one what they knew?. . . [Lily] imagined how in the chambers of [Mrs. Ramsay's, the mother's] mind and heart . . . were stood, like the treasures in the tombs of kings, tablets bearing sacred inscriptions, which if one could spell them out, would teach one everything, but they would never be offered openly, never made public" (50–51).

What Lily (and, by extension, the free-indirect discursive voice of the narrator) expresses so vividly here—and what the fixation with lost plenitude divulges throughout the novel—is the modernist sensibility of alienation, the conviction of an incommunicable reality shaping our lives but resisting our efforts at full comprehension and expression. This is a conviction which a number of prominent discursive models share in the early part of the twentieth century, from the Freudian unconscious and Heideggerian Being to Proust's memory and Kurtz's "horror." As we have discussed in previous chapters, especially by way of Adorno and Benjamin, these models all reflect the "decay of experience" in the rupture of individuals from each other and of experience from knowledge: the Freudian unconscious posits the inequality between conscious experience and unconscious reality; Proustian memory struggles to fill the gaps created by truncation from its objects; etc. And so it is, significantly, that Lily elsewhere remarks to herself that "it was not knowledge but unity that [she and the other characters] desired, not inscriptions on tablets, nothing that could be written in any language known to men, but intimacy itself, which is knowledge" (51). Integrated experience functions here as the object of desire, the lost mother, whose presence is at once immanent, ethereal, and haunting.

It is this sense whose absence sends the characters searching for lost plenitude, uniting them in their collective lack. Hence, in contemplating this pervasive desire, Lily reflects that "[o]ne need not speak at all. One glided, one shook one's sails (there was a good deal of movement in the bay, boats were starting off) between things, beyond things. Empty it was not, but full to the brim. . . . [S]ome common feeling held the whole" (192). It is this sense of experiential fullness—*Erfahrung*, both as fullness and as the collective search thereof—which Mrs. Ramsay comes to personify; indeed, it/she sits at the seat of desire in the novel even prior to her death in the novel's second section, "Time Passes." In Lacanian language, Mrs. Ramsay's death belatedly "symbolizes" the "lost (m)other" whose "real" character in the novel is less a figure than an ethos of belonging and understanding—the romantick ideal of integrated experience. And as critics like Perry Meisel have observed, it is this ideal which makes even the novel's first section, when Mrs. Ramsay is still alive, feel so profoundly elegiac.[9]

Woolf, of course, presents this ideal self-consciously as a myth: the decay of experience and the search for plenitude were standard icons of modernist aesthetics. This is a myth, however, which delimits the familiar, enlightened dimensions of witness and juror. I draw here upon Ann Banfield's excellent discussion of Woolf's novel. She shows how the preoccupation with distance exhibited by the characters and narrative of *To the Lighthouse* ("so much depends, [Lily] thought, upon distance" [191]), and also their concern with the passage of time (most famously in the novel's shortest but most enigmatic section, "Time Passes"), critically frames the early twentieth-century debate concerning the relationship between experience and artistic form. On this score, Woolf admired but sought to "distance" herself from Katherine Mansfield's witness-like, impressionistic documentation of the individual moments of experience. Woolf observed that in Mansfield's diary "we have 'the spectacle of a mind—a terribly sensitive mind—receiving one after another . . . haphazard impressions. . . . [N]othing could be more fragmentary; nothing more private.'" As Banfield remarks, "The language [of this passage] is familiar. It is that of Woolf's essay 'Modern Fiction,'" in which she rehearses and critically reflects on the impressionistic aim of "record[ing] the atoms as they fall upon the mind. . . ."[10] The higher aim of art, Woolf argues there, is not merely to report on experience, but rather to "trace the pattern, however disconnected and incoherent in appearance, which each sight or incident scores upon the consciousness" (MF 107). This can only be done if the writer achieves a measure of distance from her subject matter.

Woolf's poetics of distance resembled the postimpressionistic technique adopted by Paul Cézanne, whose work superseded the daubs of paint associated with Monet, Manet, and others. It was a technique also embraced by Woolf's friend Roger Fry, who in turn influenced Woolf. In postimpressionism, Fry argued, "we [pass] from the complexity of the appearance of things . . . to the geometrical simplicity which design demands."[11] It was a technique predicated not only on spatial distance, but also on a holistic sense of temporality. Cambridge philosophers like Bertrand Russell had begun appealing to such temporality as a critique of the impressionistic atomism preferred by continental phenomenologists like Henri Bergson, and enunciated in Britain by John McTaggart. Bergson had famously insisted that true temporality proceeds according to a logic of "duration," which is the time of consciousness as it processes diverse impressions. Duration was to time what impressionism was to space. Russell, Fry, and Woolf believed that, as Banfield puts it, "[g]iven the discontinuity of experience, one must get a distance from it, just as one must step back from the Impressionist canvas to grasp its formal continuity. . . ."[12]

We have seen this will-to-distance before. Indeed, *mutatis mutandis*, postimpressionism recapitulated the evidential position elaborated over the course of the eighteenth century, in which circumstantial narrative became the privileged mode of proof. As we have discussed in previous chapters, jurors rather than witnesses were granted legal authority to decide the truth of a case based on the overall "design" of the evidence presented in court. *To the Lighthouse* most clearly enables such design in its brief middle section, "Time Passes," which removes us from the intimate thoughts of its characters in order to relate a series of momentous events, each of which will impact the phenomenological status of the characters who are left behind. A daughter, Prue, is "given in marriage" (131) and then dies in childbirth; a son, Andrew, dies in the war; Mr. Carmichael, a family friend, becomes a well-known wartime poet; and, most cataclysmically, Mrs. Ramsay dies. Banfield argues that our distance from the characters' consciousness is what enables the pulse of individual moments to transcend the chaos of description and attain the coherence of design, of narrative.

Minus these events, much still feels familiar in the novel's concluding section. Mr. Ramsay is still pathetically self-absorbed; Lily remains something of a voyeur with respect to her host family; and the narrative still weaves in its free-indirect-discursive manner in and out of the minds of its subjects. True, young James, now a teen, will finally make it to the lighthouse, and Lily, the fledgling artist, will finally have her "vision" (209). But these achievements seem secondary to the novel's persistent exploration of the limits of individual experience, and of narrative's ability to "record the atoms as they fall." *To the Lighthouse* presents us less with a story about these "atoms" per se, or with a full resolution of the characters' diverse desires, than with a method for negotiating this diversity and for achieving distance from it. In the terms of our discussion in previous chapters, Woolf seems less concerned with witness experience than with a jury's abstraction from it. Depicting full experience per se as an inherently lost cause, her novel seemingly seeks it less than it does a way of extricating us from the hopelessly mythic quest for it. Woolf doubles and hence displaces romantick experience. Hence, whereas Lily and the other characters mystify plenitude, Woolf, establishing an ironic distance from them, portrays the idea of plenitude as source of collective longing. In this respect, Woolf's gesture recalls Mac-an-t-Saoir, who did not mystify clan society as much as comment on its deterioration while showing how clannish solidarity survived even if only as an extended, all-inclusive feeling of fragmentation.

Woolf's peer, the Scottish Renaissance novelist Neil Gunn, similarly addresses the insatiable desire for meaningful experience. However, unlike Woolf, Gunn does not depict this desire ironically, as a mere convention; rather, he sanctifies it by proposing Highland myth as its healing balm. In this respect, he resembles Mac-an-t-Saoir less than Macpherson, or perhaps Stevenson. Such myth takes the form in his work of what Roderick Watson calls "Celtic Platonism," an archetypal infrastructure underlying modern experience; as John Burns puts it, this archetypal element enables the characters in Gunn's fiction to experience "direct contact with a culture that is wholly integrated."[13] The persistence of this motif across the body of Gunn's work inspired Kurt Wittig to proclaim him more "modern" than any other Scottish novelist; Douglas Gifford goes a step further, arguing that Gunn is "the writer who stresses more than anyone else" of any literary tradition "the need of humanity for warmth and loyalty of community."[14]

In doing so, Gunn accentuates a prominent feature of the Scottish literary tradition. Cairns Craig remarks that after Walter Scott, Scottish fiction began to move away from the theme of progressive history, asserting in its stead "a knowledge more ancient than civilisation, one which is inscribed in and maintained by the particular qualities of its landscape."[15] That is, Scottish fiction began to reflect less on the exigencies of evidence than on the pulsations of experience (most notoriously in the excesses of Kailyard fiction). The mythic energies of this experiential movement reached a peak during the Scottish Renaissance of the 1920s and '30s. Even as Edwin Muir vilified Scotland for the vacuity of its national tradition (most notoriously in *Scott and Scotland* [1936]), Gunn and Hugh MacDiarmid were espousing what the latter called the "Gaelic Idea" as a fertile source of preclassical heritage. The "Gaelic Idea" emerged partly as a radical revision of Matthew Arnold's ideas of the Celt—ideas which had been enfranchised in the defeatist "Celtic Twilight" fiction of such writers as "Fiona Macleod" (i.e., William Sharp) and Neil Munro. Modeled partly on Irish folk nationalism (including, for MacDiarmid, its militancy), but drawing on the reputedly richer folk traditions of Scotland, the "Gaelic Idea" inspired feelings of national unity in a manner evocative at once of socialism on the left and fascism on the right. As Murray G. H. Pittock remarks, the so-called Celtic Communism enunciated first by W. F. Skene in *Celtic Scotland* (1880) and embraced later by Gunn and MacDiarmid "provided a vision of Celtic society not as savage or disorganized, but rather collectivist and ideal."[16] More than merely "collectivist," Pittock and others add, this "ideal" was racialized; indeed, MacDiarmid praised Hitler's Germany in the early 1930s as a model for Scottish Nationalism, before recanting the tribute as he watched Germany grow more volatile.[17]

In Gunn's fiction, this "Celtic-Platonist," "Celtic-Communist," racialized "Idea" most often materializes in the form of heightened experience. In his semiautobiographical work *The Atom of Delight* (1956, the last book he ever published), Gunn essentially presents a manifesto on the search for lost plenitude—the search which Woolf ironically attributes to Lily and the other characters of *To the Lighthouse*. Reflecting on the modern(ist) fascination with the past, Gunn reflects that "research into lost times is a search for delights, for the particular moment, the arrested scene, that holds a significance difficult to define." When we uncover such moments, they have an oblique, "by the way" quality which eludes concentrated thought. That is, they are moments of genuine and heightened experience: "What happens by the way is not a matter of philosophy but of life, of universal experience."[18]

Such experience forms the subject of Gunn's fiction, especially his semiautobiographical novels *Morning Tide* (1930), *Highland River* (1937), and *The Silver Darlings* (1941). The latter two are generally considered Gunn's masterpieces, though it is *Morning Tide* that makes for the most provocative comparison with *To the Lighthouse*. Like Woolf's narrative, Gunn's consists of three parts, is largely characterized by impressionistic detail, and partly centers around a powerful and even somewhat haunting mother figure. However, unlike *To the Lighthouse*, the mother in *Morning Tide* falls ill but does not die. Also, there is no section like "Time Passes" in which we achieve real distance from the impressionistic "moments" which dominate the narrative. And, lastly, we do not venture outward into the sea (literally, to the lighthouse); instead, the desired beacon returns to us from the sea (when the protagonist's father and brother make their way perilously to shore through heaving, storm-tossed waves). In short, compared with Woolf's novel, Gunn's resists absence, distance, and deferral, respectively; its focus remains squarely on notions of fullness, especially the fullness of experience. If *To the Lighthouse* thematizes plenitude lost, *Morning Tide* presents us instead with plenitude regained.

It is important here that we resist Woolf's gesture whereby we immediately cast the image of such plenitude as naïve. Like Woolf, Gunn was intently aware of the mythic quest for integrated experience in modernist aesthetics; however, rather than taking an ironic view of that quest, Gunn approached it more earnestly, and with striking power. In *The Atom of Delight* he aligns it with contemporary advancements in particle physics, with Darwin's reflections concerning the "primal horde," and with Freud's narrative of primordial angst in *Totem and Taboo*. With respect to Freud, Gunn observes that psychoanalytic theory exhibits a measure of the repression which it seeks to explain. Freud tells a mythic narrative around a tyrannical father and a group of harrowed sons who conspire to put the father to death. Once the father dies, he acquires even greater power in the form of conscience, through which he continues to harass his sons. However, Gunn argues that Freud's narrative, like the primal horde in eradicating the father, effects an erasure of its own: "When I begin to probe into [Freud's myth] an astonishing change takes place. It is as if its backcloth were removed to disclose a still earlier drama where the central figure is not the old man of the horde," the tyrannical protagonist of Freud's drama, but rather an "old woman." Indeed, Gunn anticipates Kristeva in arguing that matriarchal orders preceded those of patriarchy: "the first gods were female" (AD 51). By this account, Woolf's tale of the deceased mother and her ironic commentary on the modernist quest for lost plenitude is Freudian, all too Freudian and, hence, inherently repressive. Indeed, the irony through which Woolf implicitly belittles the quest for integrated experience functions as an emblem and tool of patriarchy—in Lacanian language, of the Name-of-the-Father or Symbolic register which defines human subjects in terms of distance and desire, thus dividing them from plenitude, from the mother. According to Gunn, to mock the quest for plenitude is to champion the "No" of the father.

These convictions ramify in Gunn's fiction. Indeed, each of *Morning Tide*'s three sections—about the fishing expedition, the brother's emigration to Australia, and the mother's brush with death—revolve around a drama of heightened, full experience which plays out in Hugh, the young protagonist. The first section illustrates this preoccupation most vividly. It opens with Hugh collecting mussels on the beach in a locale modeled on Gunn's own native Dunbeath, a rugged coastal area in the northern Highland region of Caithness. But this remote setting is dense with the mood of modernism, as we soon realize: "The loneliness of the bouldered beach suddenly caught [Hugh] in an odd way. A small shiver went over his back. The dark undulating water rose from him to a horizon so far away that it was vague and lost."[19] Though only a boy, Hugh is already natively familiar with the effects of alienation and the uncanny, and hence with the strange distance dividing human subjects from their environment. However, the boy's Highland habitat also harbors an archetypal world of spiritual presences, such that even in the barren heath or the scarring wind "there was somehow more to it than that, an incommunicable something extra" (99). (This, we recall, is what Woolf's Lily Briscoe remarks as she sits at the dinner table.)

Accordingly, the local culture is given to second-sighted visions and storytelling. In the novel's opening section both Hugh and his older sister Kirsty receive "involuntary intuition[s]" and "divination[s]" (47, 50). And, when Hugh is woken in the middle of the night by the howling wind, the pounding surf, and the realization that his father and brother are out at sea, he recognizes something primordial in the figure of his frightened sister: "'Oh, Hugh—they'll never come home—through this,'" she lamented. "At that moment Kirsty had for Hugh the voice of the story-teller and the story-teller's imagination. Her tone was not mournful: it was sweet as the honey of woe; its intimacy went down through the personal to the legendary where the last strands of being quiver together" (68). As we have already seen in Chapter 2, this was the type of image on which Benjamin would draw in his landmark essay about the decay and uncanny return of experience. For Hugh, however, unlike for Benjamin, there is no "beauty in what is vanishing," for nothing has truly vanished; the collective-experiential features of his local Highland culture have endured into the present day.

In the emotional climate of *Morning Tide*, in which the effects of alienation are offset by feelings of attachment to ancestry and to the *genius loci* of the Highland region, the actual return of the fishing boats becomes almost secondary; indeed, one gets the sense that even if the father and brother perish, they will be enshrined through their mythic involvement with the elements. Hugh's thoughts suggest as much when the first boats begin making their way to shore: "out of this orgy of drunken movement" in the waves, "out of this supreme sport of chance, tossed aside, buried, staggering and wallowing . . . the slim bow [of the first boat] rose again, quivering, indomitable. The thrill of its purpose was heroic" (84). This is why Craig remarks that at one level Gunn's novels seem less committed to overcoming the effects of distance—such distance is finite—than "the structures of fear which have permeated the Scottish imagination." Here, Hugh stanches his visceral fear that his father and brother are lost. It is a battle he wins. Craig remarks, accordingly, that "Gunn's novels are a quest beyond that fear, [a quest] to find an alternative way of relating the imagination to the world."[20] Other critics note this motif in Gunn's fiction as well. His biographers Francis Russell Hart and J. B. Pick relate that "[o]ne day on a visit to Dunbeath, Neil and his brother John sat in the unused harbourmaster's hut at the quay wall. While a storm raged outside, they talked of 'the elemental shudder of fear and terror and insecurity', of how a chuckle of security could turn to 'a subtle primal defiance, to something not unlike a snarl of exultation, a shouting back.'"[21] Hart observes elsewhere that this attitude had strong political overtones: "The sudden Nationalist upsurge of these years [i.e., the early 1930s] called for 'shouting back' at despair, and Neil wrote three shouting novels, spokesman novels that arise from the unique time when he felt with uneasy exhilaration a part of a communal movement. The public situation cried out for a 'Morning Tide', and a Scottish press would publish it."[22] Hence, from this perspective, the drama of the fishing boats is less one of experience—such is already assured—but rather one of fear. Hugh's determination to stare down the surging sea is an effort to "shout back" at the (political, nationalistic) threat of loss.

However, while the boats may devolve on the motif of fear, the dark waves are their medium; and these waves are the agents of modern anomie. In Gunn's description, the waves take on the sinister, almost allegorical mien of unchecked industrialization: "Out of the murk each roller came, a wall of water, deliberately gathering volume, massing itself, steadily advancing, gaining speed, curling all along the line to a smoking crest, onrushing, uprising, curving over—till its baffled speed thundered crest-first on the beach" (78). It isn't the water as much as its speed and "smoking" power (familiar technological metaphors) that seem calibrated to crush individual human subjects. "[F]ar as [Hugh's] eye could reach, nothing lived in that tumbling waste" (92). Through it, however, single two-man boats begin to make themselves visible to the tight-knit community waiting for them on the dark beach. "Even when the first boat was no more than an elusive dark nucleus of the murk, a great cry went along the waters of the beach. Bodies drew taut and a shivering ran like cold fire over the skin. 'Here she comes!'" (82) Hugh's brother's boat eventually comes to shore, his brother almost drowning in the process. Then, when the father's boat finally appears on the black horizon, and when one man exults "And as I said—trust John MacBeth [i.e., Hugh's father] at the tiller!" Hugh reflects on the heroic nature of his father's return: "it was a strange and thrilling thing to have his father praised not merely for fine seamanship, but for the seamanship that conquers come what will" (95). The "thrilling" nature of the strangeness suggests that the latter does not denote the alienation born by experiential decay as much as the mythic integration of people to their community, their history, and their environment: "'He's managed it!' said Kirsty breathlessly to Hugh. Managed it! Managed it!! He turned from the woman, his soul a flame. 'Oh, Father! sang the flame to generations of Norsemen and Gael. [Hugh] saw [a character he calls] the Viking mutter huskily, 'God, that's uncanny!' his blue eyes the colour of fluting green sea-water" (101).

Integrated experience—*Erfahrung*—of this nature is a dominant motif in Gunn's fiction, and in later novels like *Highland River* it moves up a level from myth to metaphysics. There, in the protagonist's (Kenn's) quest to find the mouth of the river which ran by his childhood home, community per se seems less at stake than the source of life itself. But for this very reason, Kenn's "experience" begins to reflect not only the balm of commonality (in Benjamin's terms, redemption) which Hugh feels, but also the specter of something more ominous, isolating, and totalizing, even totalitarian. That is, and as Pittock remarks in commenting on this phenomenon in the history of Celtic nationalism, communal experience at this metaphysical level takes the form less of territory than blood, less of circumstance than (the human) race.

The corollaries to fascism are subtle in *Highland River*, but if we bear in mind our earlier discussion of Wilkomirski, and more importantly Adorno's expansive description of fascism as the shadow perpetually haunting "enlightenment," its aura is unmistakable. For Adorno, we recall, fascism consists less in a form of government than in a totalization and reduction of experience to the status of sensation, and in the latter's rupture from reflection. Imprisoned in atomized moments and impressions, "experience" becomes the product of a system which massproduces fragments, converting collective energy into ruin. The traces of such ruin are subtle in *Highland River*, but they are present nevertheless. Early in the novel, Kenn (whose name onomastically designates a special knack for understanding), reflects that "[t]he little Highland community in which [he] lived was typical of what might be found anywhere round the northern and western shores of Scotland." Whatever the contingencies of circumstance, its inhabitants "were never greatly dissimilar over a whole year or over ten years. Thus in the course of centuries there had developed a communal feeling so genuine that the folk themselves never thought about it. They rejoiced and quarrelled, loved and fought, on the basis of social equality."[23]

While this is a *Volksgeist* that any socialist would love, we should note that it is not one which Kenn shares. "[T]he folk themselves never thought about" their collectivity, their sense of integrated experience, *Erfahrung*. The narrator, however, does; with Kenn acting as his surrogate, he is more conscious than they are. To Kenn, the world and his own experience have always been a mass of secrets, as the novel compulsively reminds us. As Kenn ventured to school as a boy, "his eyes had quick glances . . . for moors and distant hills whence the river came. They were secret glances, almost unconscious; little entranced flicks of vision that caught a loneliness and secrecy and magic, at which in a silent internal way he laughed back" (19). His own thoughts shroud him in mystery, such that even "the hidden glimmer" twinkling in his eye and noticed by his friends is taken as a sign "that Kenn had a deep secret" (20). Prior to receiving one of his two schoolboy thrashings, Kenn reflects that his schoolmaster's smile "was hardly so much a smile as a glimmer that shone in the eyes and brought a warmth to the delicate features; there was a secrecy in it and memory and remoteness" (21). And on and on it goes. When Kenn grows up he becomes a scientist in order to better understand nature's bounteous secrets. It is in this scientific frame of mind that he reflects on the distinguishing characteristics of his community, a group to which he was once more deeply attached.

Hence, for Kenn, experience has something private about it, something evocative of *Erlebnis*, or inner experience. This is why, in contemplating the river running through the village, the narrator remarks that its "communal importance had little interest for [Kenn]. In all his outings, by himself and with his companions, the river was an adventure often intense and always secretive" (33). That is, the river possesses for Kenn, as for Macpherson and Wilkomirski, the "intense" quality of sensation, or of the immediacy associated with witness experience. But such experience is also the normative logic of modernity. Here, then, in a remote Highland region, as with *Morning Tide*'s allegory of industrialization in the power and speed of the surging waves, we recover the lineaments of alienation, urbanization, and the modernist aesthetic. Kenn is less a beneficiary of full experience, Benjamin's *Erfahrung*, than the exemplar of its decay and romanticization as *Erlebnis*. And it is his doubling of that experience through reflection, his ability to note it without being at one with it, which sets him apart. In the place of "communal feeling," Kenn is left with the sensation of his own experience.

Christopher Whyte has insightfully addressed this Macpherson-like, unwittingly sensational aspect of Gunn's work. He observes that Gunn, who spoke no Gaelic, found in Macpherson a key precursor in the exploitation of "his public's ignorance of Gaelic culture." Such ignorance made it easier for Gunn to assert a mythical realm of primitive Highland (and, indeed, human) experience. But Whyte intuits in Gunn's Celtic archetypes the trace of gender stereotypes which mar the former's peaceable images of plenitude. Instead, Whyte maintains, the "seductive rhetoric of blood, ethnicity and gender stereotypes" in Gunn's work approximates that of "European fascism."[24] Gunn himself was sensitive of the threat of fascism, and of the shadow it cast over his thought and work. His allegorical tale *Green Isle of the Great Deep* (1944) conjures what Gunn takes to be a quintessential Highland community as an oppressive police state; Gunn spun this allegory so as better to imagine a totalitarian state brought close to home. In a 1936 essay, Gunn complained that many of his fellow Scots had confounded his socialist objectives with fascistic sympathies.[25] In truth, Gunn himself was not a fascist in any literal sense, but as Pittock remarks, the so-called "Celtic Communist" tradition which Gunn's work invoked derived its mythos from impulses similar to those of fascism. But for this reason, Kenn's secretive, sensationist retirement from his Highland community foreshadows Gunn's own retreat from the polemics of political nationalism. In effect, Gunn's consternation toward his compatriots reflects Kenn's position vis-à-vis his Highland community.

Of course, consciousness of the problem was one thing; resolving it, another. Adorno would observe that the critique of fascist dogma via a display of atomistic sensationism only expands the reign of fascism. Political fascism created a sense of community through a racialized fantasy of biological destiny rather than collective experience. The splintering of this community may have subverted this biological fantasy, but it also failed to generate solidarity on the basis of experience. In fact, anarchic though it may appear, sensation remains inherently racialized to the extent that it reduces experience to the body. *Highland River* inadvertently falls into this morass, converting *Erfahrung* into a private sensation which permeates and transmogrifies "primitive" Highland society, causing virtual expatriates like Kenn to reimagine experience as a private, internal phenomenon.

But again, just as we defended Gunn above from facile comparisons to Woolf's Lily Briscoe, so should we here remember that the relationship of experience to fascism is complex. In reality, Gunn is one of the twentieth century's most astute thinkers about experience, and about the latter's problematic allure. In *The Atom of Delight* he reflects at length on the quality of this allure as a universally privative phenomenon. In a moment of heightened experience, the Kenn-type figure who serves here as Gunn's autobiographical stand-in "sees his fellows more distinctly, more in the round. They are separated from him, with peculiar habits of their own. . . . They are real people, he observes, with faces. But this does not occupy him much except in the sense that he is detached from it, for all the time he is on his own way" (181). Such detachment becomes the basis of a different quality of understanding: "this detachment helps him to understand better those whom he thought he knew well. . . . [There is s]omething delightful about this, because now they cannot touch him, he has won free of them, need not think about them, and in the next moment doesn't" (181). "Experience" here functions as the secretive double of everyday life. In such moments of experience we ostensibly "know" something higher about ourselves; we "know" that life is indelibly laced with the mystery of experience, of "delight." But such experiential understanding is not knowledge, at least not in the scientific sense which Kenn is trained to reproduce. Such delight devolves on the sensation of the witness, not the deliberation of the juror.

However, in Woolf's *To the Lighthouse*, such "delight" also doubles as the medium of ironic voice, of the free indirect discourse of the narrative. This voice may be most clearly discerned in the novel's enigmatic middle section, "Time Passes." Here, in detaching itself from the characters themselves, the voice reflects, like Kenn, on the aura of plenitude which the Ramsay residence (like Kenn's community) still possesses: "The house was left; the house was deserted. It was left like a shell on a sandhill to fill with dry salt grains now that life had left it. The long night seemed to have set in; the trifling airs, nibbling, the clammy breaths, fumbling, seemed to have triumphed" (137). The passage achieves its haunting effects not only through what it describes, but also through the lyrical grace of its alliterative lines—lines which connect together diverse phrases, thoughts, even sections of the novel. Though divided from the "human" subjects it inhabits in the novel's first and third sections, voice here is the medium of memory, thus converting the "shell" of the house—its "airs" and "breaths"—into a repository of human presence, a shelter of integrated experience. This is a shelter, however, from which the voice detaches itself, as Kenn does from his community; it ranges over and around it, abstracted from it. To this extent, we might say that Woolf's narrative is manifestly more self-conscious than Gunn's in the ironic distance it achieves from the myth of plenitude; and yet, the effect it generates is largely the same. In style if not in substance, *To the Lighthouse* draws upon the myth of experience as assuredly as *Highland River*. And that myth is one of "delight," of sensation—in Adorno's vocabulary, the residual traces of fascism.

It seems fitting that Woolf's novel is set in the Hebrides, the historic locale (along with the mainland Highlands) of "romantick" experience in its rupture from objective (or, in terms we used earlier, postimpressionistic) knowledge, replete with all the complexities which that rupture entails.[26] In "Time Passes," the lighthouse—set on a small Hebridean island off the coast of Skye, and thus the quintessential icon of remoteness— hypostatizes the haunting, doubling quality of the narrative voice as it dances across the walls of the empty house: "Only the Lighthouse beam entered the rooms for a moment, sent its sudden stare over bed and wall in the darkness of winter, looked with equanimity at the thistle and the swallow, the rat and the straw. Nothing now withstood them; nothing said no to them" (TL 138). Here, the lighthouse doubles Woolf's narrative voice. The effect of this doubling is ambiguous. On the one hand, it further reduces experience to sensation, to a scientistic gaze of "equanimity" on "the thistle and the swallow, the rat and the straw." However, on the other hand, the lighthouse's narrative gaze enables the remote Highlands emblematically to display the logic of sensationist experience in a way which generates solidarity. These are "our" aesthetics, Woolf's self-conscious conventionality implies; these are the media through which "we moderns" arrive at meaning, however atomistically. It is a modality which, considered in the light(house) of romantick Highland experience, is uncannily familiar.

Warner and Cooke: The Poetics of Postsensationism

In some ways, Alan Warner's hipster novel *Morvern Callar* could not be further from the earnestly romantic work of Neil Gunn, especially in its portrait of community. Where Gunn's village seems quaintly indigenous, Warner's "Port" (a thinly veiled double of his native West Highland town of Oban) feels anonymously globalized, dispirited, ruinous. Furthermore, Morvern's first-person narrative takes Kenn's solipsistic reflections and Woolf's ironic voice to a whole new level; it dissolves any residual trace of communal spirit, *Erfahrung*, through an intensely alienated/alienating deluge of sensation (e.g., in descriptions of the rave scene and, more persistently, in an intensely presentist narrative style, which I discuss below). In that respect, *Morvern Callar* literalizes and exaggerates the subtle complexities unfolding in Gunn's and Woolf's work: where Gunn and Woolf evoke the Highland landscape—its seas, rivers, hills, and lighthouses—as signs of their characters' auratic experience (e.g., the mystical presence on which Lily Briscoe reflects), Warner's spare portrait of earth and water (e.g., "Breeze in leaves. Birds.") blankly denies any mystical presence of any sort. Or, where Gunn and Woolf unfurl a series of experiential doubles by way of figure and voice (e.g., Kenn here, the lighthouse there), Warner inflates these doubles to comic proportion: autobiographically, "Port" derives from Oban and Morvern's experience with rave culture models itself on Warner's; diegetically, or plot-wise, the suicide of Morvern's writer-boyfriend surpasses mere doubling to create a narrative ménage à trois with the dead boyfriend, Morvern, and Warner all sitting in the seat of author(ial)ity. In this latter respect, Warner presents Gunn (and, to a degree, Woolf) on ecstasy.

But, precisely because *Morvern Callar* literalizes the subtler features of Gunn's and Woolf's work, it vividly elucidates the "romantick" course of experiential decay and return—that is, of Adorno's convictions regarding a sensationist state expanding beyond all borders, and also of David Simpson's documentation of a postmodern age's renewed impulses toward storytelling. Morvern Callar pays homage to Adorno and Simpson simultaneously. She is an iconic, Adornian anti-hero of late modernism, but she also has stories to tell us. These stories concern her own strange, surprising adventures, to be sure, but they also recount the ongoing legacy of the romantick Highlands with respect to the long-standing dilemma of experience.

It is this latter tale which is of greatest relevance here. With Gunn and Woolf serving as important precursors, *Morvern Callar* recounts the inadequacy of doubling as a technique for promoting consciousness and resolving the dilemma of experience. Indeed, Warner's novel moves in the opposite direction, deploying its doubles to expand the empire of sensation, and thus "flattening . . . experience," Cristie L. March observes, by celebrating "the instant-gratification, sound [byte], youth culture" which Morvern inhabits.[27] In this respect, *Morvern Callar* seems almost gothic, recounting the decay not of tyrants or hysterics, or even of bodies per se, but rather of experience.

There are indeed some strikingly gothic aspects of Morvern's tale. The novel opens when the protagonist awakens two days before Christmas to find that her boyfriend has committed suicide. Though Morvern weeps, her narrative is strangely detached:

I stopped the greeting [i.e., "crying"] cause I couldn't breathe and was perished cold. I slowed down the speed of the flashing Christmas tree lights. I put on the scullery light then the immersion heater then the bar fire but I didn't put a record on. . . . I couldn't get past Him without stepping in His blood and I was

scared to go too nearish so's I got my things in the bedroom. I took the last pill
in that cycle. . . . I did a number-one then a number-two remembering always to
wipe backwards. Though he was dead I used the air freshener spray.[28]

This autistic, serialized account ("I stopped . . . I slowed down . . . I put
on . . . I got . . . I took . . . I did . . . I used") continues over the long of
the narrative. It alone speaks to Morvern's quality of experience—or the
lack thereof—as I discuss below. Here, at the outset, we should note that
while Morvern is hardly introspective, she does gradually reveal aspects
of her life which may explain such detachment. Psychologically speaking, she is an orphan with a vaguely abusive past (as her letter to her
stepfather in Warner's follow-up novel *These Demented Lands* suggestively
indicates); from a socioeconomic standpoint, she possesses a rudimentary education, undesirable employment, and bleak prospects. None of
this is a recipe for sentimental involvement. Moreover, we learn,
Morvern is capable of violence: rather than reporting the suicide, she
hides and then eventually cuts up and buries the body, sends "His" novel
off to a publisher under her name (eventually collecting the advance
when it is published), and empties "His" bank account. With "His"
money she twice departs for the Mediterranean rave scene, where she
revels in narcotically induced states of self-obliteration. She is pregnant
when she returns to the vicinity of Port the second time, seeking to find
work but also to avoid her past and the people in it. In essence, she has
become a specter, bearing mysterious Mediterranean adventures and
seeming both present and absent to her former life.
    This spectrality manifests itself most provocatively in the form of
Morvern's doggedly sensationist experience. "[A]cutely alive," in
Douglas Gifford's words, "to physical detail,"[29] Morvern's experience is
also replete with the traces of all that sensation alone cannot grasp, like
the material forces which have shaped her world and the "romantick"
aura which continues to haunt it. This aura gradually impresses itself on
us by way of what Gifford hauntingly calls Warner's "strange, dark poetry
of place."[30] It does so, moreover, as the palimpsest of all that Morvern's
sensationist experience fails to name. Such sensationism, such fixation
with empirical detail, is the *modus operandi* of her narrative. We have
already witnessed it in her dispassionate discovery of "His" body. It also
informs her description of her dismemberment of it: "I cut away the still-
hanging hand and sliced into the first arm." She literally dons rose-col-
ored goggles, which "helped take away the reality of what you were up to
and you didn't smell a thing with those tight noseclips . . . " (86). The
rhetorical slippage into the second-person singular magnifies Morvern's
detachment: "What you do is divide the limbs and wrap them in a good
few layers of binliner and absorbent hessian sacking bound again and

again with strips of thick parcel tape. . . . You dont [*sic*] get difficulty with the head or limbs, it's the organs pushing out from the torso sodden through with blood. The two torso packages needed almost twice as much wrapping but I made a good job of them" (86). Modeled by Warner on Camus's quintessentially alienated anti-hero Mersault in *L'Etranger*, such violent detachment persistently characterizes Morvern's "voice." Later in the novel, after a lengthy, sensationist description of a typical day lounging on a Mediterranean beach (including an episode of an old lady "pulverising" a cicada [204]), Morvern summarizes her experience by linking its fixation with successive sensationist details to existential satisfaction: "I closed my eyes there in the quietness just breathing in and breathing in. I hadnt [*sic*] slept for three days so I could know every minute of that happiness that I never even dared dream I had the right" (222).

Some critics seem to have taken Morvern at her word, regarding her not only as a happy raver but also as a kind of Celtic goddess destroying such idols as conventional language patterns, gender roles, and national boundaries.[31] Others, including Warner himself, are more skeptical. Carole Jones discerns in Morvern (and in the specter of her dead, dismembered boyfriend and his hocked novel manuscript) the symptom of a crisis in Scottish male hegemony and identity.[32] Warner perceived in Morvern the natural expression of "political realities . . . in the Scottish Highlands," not that he intended this to be either soothing or romantic.[33] He regarded the "popular music" to which Morvern was so addicted to be "a tool [of] 1990s monopoly capitalism," with March adding that Morvern's "music choice reveals the emotional insufficiency of rave culture as a substitute for 'real' life," attesting less to anarchic energy than to "vast internal emptiness."[34] In a published interview, Warner further disavowed the utopian associations of the rave scene, and also bemoaned (in Adornian fashion) "the 'dumbing down' [of] culture."[35] The picture that emerges here is one less of happiness than abjection, of rebellious strength than vitiation.

This picture is born out by Morvern's own fantasies of dissolution. The rave scene provides Morvern with one obvious expression of this desire. Dancing in a club "with the pound-pounding of hardcore all around you," Morvern relates that "[y]ou [i.e., she] felt the whole side of a face lay against my bare back, between shoulder blades. It was still part of our dance. If the movement wasnt [*sic*] in rhythm it would have changed the meaning of the face sticking there in the sweat. You didnt [*sic*] really have your body as your own, it was part of the dance, the music, the rave" (215). Later that night, swimming alone in the sea, she experiences the feeling all over again: "I sucked in air deep and dived down sharply in the nightwater. . . . I jerked eyes open in the nothingness. . . . I blew out to

stop me rising and when my bubbles were gone, then there was silentness. My ears squeaked, I opened my legs wide, yanked my head back and
threw out my arms to keep me down in those waves and layers of cold
thick-seeming water" (221).

For Adorno, empty sensation was not all it was cracked up to be. For
Morvern, however, it is pure bliss. And yet, the rave scene in itself may
not provide Morvern with the consummate sensation of "silentness" and
"nothingness." Provocatively, such feelings seem even more available in
the Highland hills near her home. Earlier in the novel, as she takes
"His" body into nature to bury it, she reflects (in her typically serialized,
sensationist fashion) on the Highland landscape:

From up there you could see all that land; from the Back Settlement westwards
where the railway moved into the pass, following the road toward the power station, the village beyond where the pass widened out towards the concession
lands. Birches clustered in sprays where the dried-up burns dipped into the
streams. One stream ran under the concrete bridge by the sycamore where sweet
primroses were spreading thickly. Flickers were coming off the loch and the massive sky seemed filled with a sparkling dust above those hot summer hills, fattened with plants and trees. You could hear the waterfalls down in the gulley.
They would be spraying onto ferns there and drops of water would be hanging
from their tips. I looked out at the landscape moving without any haste to no
bidding at all. I yawned a big yawn. Two arms and a leg were buried on the cliff
above the sycamore tree and higher up the torso and leg would be helping
flower the sheets of bluebells below the dripping rocks. All across the land bits
of Him were buried. (95–96)

This scene exemplifies the quality which Gifford describes as "Warner's
strange, dark poetry of place." Although our gaze merely shifts, like
Morvern's, from one object to another (from "the railway" to "the village" to "[b]irches" to "stream[s]" and so on), the adjectives are telling
of Morvern's heightened attention—the "thickly" spreading primroses,
the "fattened" hills, the "massive" sky, and so on. There is a fulsomeness
to these phrases which belies their states as mere sensations.
Furthermore, like Macpherson's Ossian, the sound of "waterfalls down
in the gulley" incites Morvern to a visualization of what she cannot simply see: "They would be spraying onto ferns and drops of water would be
hanging from their tips." A "leg would be helping flower . . . sheets of
bluebells below the dripping rocks. . . ."

Although it is subtle, something important and connected—
something important *because* connected—occurs here. Unlike the body
of her boyfriend or her sensationist narrative, the landscape here is
more than the sum of its parts. If we add to these heightened (non)sen-
sations the sacramental image of "His" body broken and buried "All
across the land," a "romantick" picture emerges. Later in this scene,
Morvern describes deer and even her own movements in ways which

recall both Donnchadh Bàn Mac-an-t-Saoir and Iain Crichton Smith (the latter of whom Warner read with great admiration). Further down, she describes to her friend Lanna her affection for nature in a way which again recalls these Gaelic poets and their "inhuman" deer: "This place, it doesn't care, it's just *here*. It helps that this place is here just a few hours' walk away. All this loveliness. It's just silence isnt [*sic*] it?" (110).

"This place," "silent" like her nighttime swim and indifferent like the melding bodies of the rave scene, effectively doubles the existential bleariness of Morvern's life and its degenerate quality of sensationist experience. If the Mediterranean is Morvern's place of escape, then the hills are her place of regeneration, both before she ventures south and also after she returns, now pregnant with the "child of the raves" (242). In their blank indifference, the hills also double Morvern's emotional detachment. This is no ordinary detachment, however. Indeed, doubled and hence dissociated from her flat-lining account of events, the hills dialectically negate her sensationist experience, inciting in its stead something more auratic and evocative, as indicated by her image of "drops of water" trickling from unseen ferns. Essentially, the Highland landscape connects Morvern with a world of which she has no immediate sensation. The effect is one of reversal: detached from detachment, Morvern's narrative reacquires an aura of romance. Amidst the Highland landscape, sensation becomes something more than itself.

This episode potentially alters our perception of Morvern's narrative. The hills reflect but then also negate the blankness of Morvern's existence, restoring to it something like meaning and connection from the far end of sensation (indeed, much as Mac-an-t-Saoir educed communal feeling from the decay of clan relationships). With the regenerative effects of the Highland landscape in mind, Morvern's behavior acquires an almost ideal character as a supplement to its apparent abjection: the raves become less the instrument of facile dissolution than a figure of limit-experience—the limits of the flesh, and of sensationism, at the far or peripheral regions of modernity.

I will have more to say about this below. It may be a point best made by way of Sophie Cooke's recent novel *The Glass House*, which further adumbrates Warner's "romantick" geography. Like Warner, Cooke does not invoke romance simplistically or straightforwardly. But she lights on similar themes and techniques, and might even be said to exaggerate Warner's novel in the same way that the latter hyperbolizes Neil Gunn. Gunn, we recall, unwittingly doubles the supposedly integrated experience of the Highland village with a deeply modernist, sensationist celebration of private experience, *Erlebnis*. Warner begins from here and does not return to community as much as find something redemptive and prospectively integrated in Morvern's alienation. For her part,

Cooke doubles the detached Morvern with a teen-aged protagonist who lives in deep denial and almost pathological dissociation. Likewise, Cooke distends the "romantick" aspects of Morvern's comportment—namely, its resemblance to the Highland landscape—into a sentimental portrait of a family falling into ruin. *The Glass House* thus paints post-modern experience with a broader brush. Compared with Morvern, that is, Cooke's teenaged Vanessa seems almost too conscious of her need for intimacy. Hence, her gestures (e.g., her appeal to her boyfriend, the aptly named Alan [Warner?], as well as to the landscape) have something contrived about them. This is not to belittle Cooke's intelligent novel as much as to underline the "romantick" conventions within which it operates, and which accentuate for us the enduring legacy of the Highlands as a place of heightened experience.

Set in a location northwest of Perth and over a period of four years, *The Glass House* tells a story about a troubled teen, her equally troubled sisters, and their neurotic and suicidal mother. The father works in Saudi Arabia and is rarely home, as much from a desire to defer divorce and thus keep the family nominally bound as from the exigencies of his job. As the mother grows more and more desperate (commencing an affair, having an abortion, then growing hysterical when her lover refuses to leave his wife), the façade of family security becomes increasingly impossible to maintain. Vanessa personifies this dysfunctionality. Expelled for vandalism from a ritzy boarding institution, she becomes an outsider in her new school, wins and then rebuffs a new boyfriend, and converts her literate education into a janitorial job in a youth hostel. Throughout, Cooke plays up Vanessa's detachment, even in her physiognomy: "Sometimes mum wonders if I'm her daughter. I've got no feelings, and those horrid little eyes."[36] However, as with Morvern, Vanessa's cool exterior belies a deeper level of emotional concern, and Vanessa comes to feel increasingly responsible for her mother's well-being, even remaining behind with her when her father comes to remove Vanessa's older sibling Lucy and younger sister Bryony (who has fallen into anorexia and despondency). Mary, the mother, persistently abuses Vanessa verbally and physically and finally succeeds in taking her own life. With no reason to remain around home, Vanessa departs, like Morvern, for Spain.

Vanessa's first-person narrative resembles the coldly probing beam of Woolf's lighthouse, sweeping across the home and its inhabitants—in this case, however, with only apparent indifference. As with Morvern, whose abusive past filters to us from behind closed blinds, Vanessa's detachment is born partly from the violence she has suffered. This detachment manifests itself not only in her expulsion for vandalism, and not only in her disjointed rapport with siblings and schoolmates, but also in her willfully myopic (almost sensationist) perspective onto her own family. When Alan, her boyfriend, asks her to confide in him over her troubles at home, Vanessa "start[s] feeling anxious about it. There really isn't anything wrong, and Alan is building up this big thing in his head. [She feels] guilty for the care it elicits. What's going to happen when he finds out that everything really is fine?" (90). In addition to her denial, and also like Morvern, Vanessa likewise derives pleasure from feelings of self-obliteration. Her mother, seeking sympathy, exclaims, "It's a terrible thing. To understand you're going to disappear." But to Vanessa this thought "sounds quite nice" (171).

Perhaps most significantly, and here most expressly recalling Morvern, Vanessa takes solace in the majestic blankness of the Highland landscape. This is apparent from the beginning of the novel, which opens with Mary's voice "going like a kettle, faster and faster, higher and higher, a squawking song. I do not like her face when she does this," Vanessa tells us. So she takes for the hills: "I pass through a gap in the mossy dyke at the back of the garden and take the path up the hill. It is quite steep, which is good because you don't have to walk far to feel like you've come a long way. The house is quickly far below you . . . " (1). The allure of the high, barren landscape soon establishes itself as a motif, as when things begin to grow tense between Vanessa and Alan:

We sit outside, leaning against the wall of the bothy and leaning into each other. I let him shelter me, for a while.

"I don't understand you," says Alan.
I wish he would stop saying that. I look out across the high land and it is empty. It swells and dips in folds of rock and scrubby grass. Wind blows clean across it. . . . The wind blows right into my soul, calms it. There is nothing here. Nothing, I realise. This is an empty place. A kind of gratitude flows over my tear-wrecked innards. (54)

In this episode, the "high land[s]" provide Vanessa with a gratifying (if somewhat melodramatic) means of escape. They also furnish Vanessa with a vehicle of self-reflection. During her stint as a janitor at the hostel, she steps outside her house one day and makes a tacit connection between the landscape and herself: "A fine rain falls in the afternoon, like a lank mop sweeping over the grass and rock. You hear it dripping into puddles as it flops on the terrace below. The light is dimmed, the outline the hills weeping into the sky. Having a good cry. . . . You know the rain won't last long. It's just a midsummer tantrum . . . " (167). Here functioning vicariously to purge Vanessa's sorrows, elsewhere the landscape promotes the impression of meaning: "I'm feeling relaxed, looking out at the waves, feeling elated and in control. I feel as if I am out on the horizon, out on that line where the sea meets the blue and gold sky. The line is dead straight, like a string hung with lead. It is true because it is far, far away from the beach, away from the human edge of things. The straightness of the line will last for ever" (120). The "straightness" of the horizon corresponds with Vanessa's belief that there is a secret mathematical order to things: "I sometimes think there is a perfect logic to life, like in maths, an underlying logarithm, if you can just find it. It flows along, making sense, and you can understand it. But the trouble with this maths is that every little part is essential. If you take away pi then circles just stop making sense" (100). Highland earth- and seascapes embody this "perfect logic," explaining why Vanessa feels drawn to them, and compelled to see herself doubled and represented in them.

Hence, the Highland landscape in *The Glass House* incites feelings of reflection, negation, and transcendence. Essentially reproducing the dialectical features of thesis, antithesis, and synthesis associated with German philosophers like Friedrich Schiller and G. W. F. Hegel (for whom the dialectic resolved the experience of the present with the knowledge of history), Cooke's Highland landscape serves in her novel as the "romantick" vehicle of understanding and meaning. Moreover, and also in dialectical fashion, inasmuch as the landscape reflects Vanessa's feelings back to her in the conventional form of the pathetic fallacy, it partly sutures the rupture between sentiment and actuality— what Vanessa tells herself and what is really happening—which her detached persona dramatizes. From here, it is but a short step for us to see the novel implicitly engaging the dilemma of experience in addition to the emotional lives of its characters. The peace Vanessa feels when involving herself with the Highland surroundings hardly resolves this complex dilemma, but it underlines the historical connection between the Highlands, romance, and heightened experience. It does so, more-over, despite the novel's self-consciously present-day setting. The Highland landscape gives to Vanessa what her own family cannot—or, for that matter, what (post)modernity fails adequately to provide its human subjects. In the "romantick" Highlands, though not (for Vanessa) at home, a fractured individual may feel whole.

As we have seen, the romantick aura of experience laced through the Highland landscape is also what appeals to Morvern. In Warner's novel it is not spelled out quite so explicitly; but this in turn leads us to an important point, both about the relationship of all four novels to each other and also about their relationship to the Enlightenment dilemma of experience. In relation to *Morvern Callar*, *The Glass House* literalizes some of Warner's subtler explorations of experience—as, for instance, in the contrast between Morvern's characteristic attention to sensationist detail in her quotidian existence and the more integrated quality of that detail in her experience of the Highland landscape. (We should add that while this literalization is unconscious on Cooke's part, it was self-conscious on Warner's in *These Demented Lands* [1997], otherwise known as the Further Adventures of Morvern Callar. In that second novel, the Hebridean landscape literally harbors heightened—in truth, surreal—experience as Morvern makes her way to the millennial rave to end all raves on the island where her foster mother is buried. Along the way, she encounters a variety of bizarre characters and topographical features, all of which conspire to create a kind of pomo *Tempest*. *These Demented Lands* reads like *Morvern Callar* on Quaaludes, with Morvern's sensationism peaking at hallucinogenic levels.) But just as Cooke implicitly literalizes Warner's Morvern, so does Morvern literalize Gunn's character Kenn, whose purportedly communal experience actually reveals itself to be more consistent with the private, inner experience of *Erlebnis* than the holistic feeling identified with *Erfahrung*. Continuing with this train of associations, Kenn exaggerates certain features of Gunn's earlier character Hugh in *Morning Tide*. Meanwhile, Hugh's sensations of plenitude in awaiting the mythic return of his father and brother distend Lily Briscoe's reflections concerning ineffable fullness around the Ramsay dinner table. And Lily, in turn, serves as Woolf's caricature of the modernist conviction of the transcendent nature of heightened experience.

I do not conceive of this genealogy extending from Woolf to Gunn to Warner to Cooke as one of influence. Its effect is rather more impressionistic—or, perhaps, in Woolf's terminology, postimpressionistic. It illustrates the dual persistence of Highland romance in late modernity—the persistence, that is, of the association of the Highlands and witness experience which comes to prominence during the eighteenth century, and also of the consistency of this "romantick" quality in texts falling into categories as different as high modernism (Woolf's, Gunn's) hipster postmodernism (Warner's), and pomo neo-realism (Cooke's). The pseudo-genealogy linking these texts thus underscores a point which has been made in various ways over the course of this book, which is that Highland romance has been a surprisingly ductile category across a variety of disciplines (e.g., legal history, political economics, literature, memoir, critical theory), literary genres (e.g., fiction, poetry, travel literature), national identities (Highland, Lowland, English, other), and literary periods (Macpherson's, Scott's, Stevenson's, Woolf's, Warner's).

How do we account for the remarkable resilience of Highland romance? As I have argued, this resilience emerges from the very inception of Highland romance during the eighteenth century as a figure of and partial compensation for the problem of experience in modernity. Enlightenment insistence on a direct contact with objects yielded the paradoxical division of experience from knowledge, witness from juror. The epistemic authority of witnesses did not entirely disappear during the eighteenth century; instead, it took a variety of new forms, Highland romance being one of the most vivid. As we have seen, witness authority has long haunted pretensions to objective understanding. Today, in the form of what David Simpson calls "half-knowledge," it endures as the indelible allure of the improbable, a beckoning "ruin of experience."

Enduring Icons

Though not a Highlander or Islander by birth, Alan Riach understands something about peripheries, having taught British and postcolonial literatures for many years in New Zealand before accepting his current position at the University of Glasgow. In 1994, from Coromandel in northern New Zealand, he wrote a poem entitled "Clearances." Eventually published as part of a collection of poems bearing the same title, the poem imagines a family's (apparent) departure from home in terms of the Highland clearances.

The poem begins as Morvern or Vanessa might—namely, by interacting with nature. Here, however, unlike the Warner and Cooke novels, it is not the poet who ventures into nature, or who turns to it for transcendence; rather, it is nature which forces its way into the space of consciousness:

> The clouds go over
> singly, or in fleets, trailing
> raggedly back, against a sky
> where looming vaults of rain
> come over too. Then the sky lets loose:
> the shades of grey become uncountable,
> the rain comes down on everything, diagonal, banks:
> the windows, roof, the wooden deck,
> the trees around, the green slopes run
> with mud, the fields below are soaked and fill;
> the road becomes a grey and moving river.[37]

The intensity of the deluge, accentuated by a treble stress as "the *sky lets loose*," transforms the multitude of raindrops into a maze of mottled grays, and the well-traveled roadway into a body of moving water. The "windows, roof, the wooden deck"—all has returned to a virtual state of nature. This gets the poet thinking: "It must be time to leave. The weather is an actual farewell" (45). But his thought involves more than simple valediction, making instead a more mythic and disturbing parallel:

> I used to think the old Gaels of Ireland,
> or the west of Scotland, knew

so little of our modern world.
It seemed they were a pastoral people
and burdened with a culture of conservatism.
But clearances are always strong on the mind,
the images recurrent, the rubble of ruined homes,
the ghosts of children, animals, and men
and women helpless in the face of the event. (45)

The lyrical tetrameter of the third line underscores the iconic image of the primitive Highlanders: they know "so little of our modern world." However, the equally iconic and perennial nature of the Highland clearances—they "are always strong on the mind"—transforms them from a historical event into a language, a convention for negotiating the present, even in circumstances so apparently disparate from, say, the clearances of Highland peasantry in Sutherland during the early nineteenth century. This, in turn, makes "the old Gaels of Ireland,/or the west of Scotland" prototypes for our time.

But what kind of time is this, exactly? Partly, it seems to be a timeless moment, a moment of universal human experience: "Farewells and birth, there are some things/no clues or forms of knowledge alter/in themselves" (45). And for such experience, beyond the pale of abstract knowledge, the image of displaced Highlanders is indispensable: "They knew about departure, those old people,/and the kinds of life we deal with here/require that inherited wisdom" (45). They had, in essence, the knowledge of experience, a union which seems so much more elusive and yet indelible in a modern age. The poet imagines modernity as something of a clearance, uprooting us from—but, hence, revitalizing—intimate connection with our pasts: "It's time to pack what we have and can carry./It's time to take what we can, and go. The boy/will not remember this, the landscape/of his parents, unless we do" (46). While the concept has a more sloganeering ring to it here than it does in Jameson, Adorno, or others whom we have discussed, the sentiment is largely the same: enlightened modernity diminishes the quality of existence, primarily by atomizing experience into "rubble" and "ruin," or into concrete units of sensation. And yet, either our consciousness of this degradation, or else its sheer universality, somehow exclude us from it. Redemption is universal, but perpetually elusive; it is formal rather than substantive. The memory for which the poet pleads thus pertains more to a form than to any actual content. More than a recollection of Highland heritage, the poet implores aid in emulating it; what he professedly needs—therefore, paradoxically, what he already possesses by virtue of this plea—is a "romantick" way of experiencing the world.

The dynamic which Riach richly traces bears a long and wide history. Throughout this book, we have discussed how the modern phenomenon of legal witnessing emerges in concert with the epistemological focus on concrete particulars. It does so, moreover, in a way which both confirms (e.g., in Macpherson and Wilkomirski) and challenges (e.g., in Mac-an-t-Saoir) the dominant concept of probabilistic understanding, which reportedly instigates the decay of experience. "The ruins of experience" describe the enduring attractions of witness experience as something other than such understanding, something other than likely knowledge. The "romantick" Highlands represent one especially powerful form this allure took during the Enlightenment, an allure which increasingly delimits the structure and concerns of everyday life. Indeed, this book's most important argument concerns the pervasive nature of this alluring situation, a situation in which experience returns as a limit condition (including in the vivid and increasingly common portraits—like Alan Liu's, with which we opened this chapter—of a posthuman world.) Riach's "clearances" thus amplify far beyond the borders of Highland Scotland, and function as icons for more than simply those of literal Highland heritage. Highlandism tells a powerful story about modernity and its compulsions. In a real if elusive way, it helps us to better recognize the historical meaning of experience, and our enduring romance with it.

Notes

Preface

1. See, for instance, Aamir R. Mufti, "Critical Secularism: A Reintroduction for Perilous Times."

2. Avery F. Gordon, *Ghostly Matters: Haunting and the Sociological Imagination*, 7, my emphasis.

3. Womack, *Improvement and Romance*, esp. 1–3; Trumpener, *Bardic Nationalism*, esp. 3-34; Davis, *Acts of Union*, ch. 3; Sorensen, *The Grammar of Empire in Eighteenth-Century British Writing*, esp. 16–20.

4. *Improvement and Romance*, 102, 108.

5. *Bardic Nationalism*, xi, 70.

6. Catherine Gallagher and Stephen Greenblatt characterize this shift as emblematic of new historicism. See *Practicing New Historicism*, 9.

7. *Acts of Union*, 1–2.

8. See *Grammar of Empire*, 16–20 and Hechter, *Internal Colonialism*, 4–5.

9. I borrow this phrase from Gallagher and Greenblatt, *Practicing New Historicism*, ch. 1 (see esp. 20–21).

10. *The Identity of the Scottish Nation*, 6–7.

11. *The Invention of Scotland*, 102. Pittock's chapter here is entitled "Reality and Romance."

12. *Celtic Identity and the British Image*, esp. ch. 4.

13. *Improvement and Romance*, 3.

14. *The Mirror of Production*, 17, 19.

15. Though I generally agree with Baudrillard's contention, productivist humanism has clearly energized Scottish studies. In addition to the books I have already discussed by Womack, Trumpener, Davis, and Sorensen, see also Saree Makdisi, *Romantic Imperialism*, ch. 4; Christopher Harvie, *Scotland and Nationalism*, esp. 1–33; Tom Nairn, *Faces of Nationalism*, esp. 179–81; Robert Crawford, *Devolving English Literature*, esp. ch. 1; and David McCrone, *Understanding Scotland*, esp. 26–32.

16. See *The Laws of Cool*, esp. 1–10.

17. *The Order of Things*, 383.

18. "Thing Theory," 5.

19. See Womack, *Improvement and Romance*, 179–80.

20. Foucault, *The Order of Things*, 383–84.

21. For an exemplary recent instance of such work, see Paul Hamilton, *Metaromanticism*, esp. the Introduction.

Introduction

1. *The Works of William Collins*, 56–57.
2. See *Truth and Method*, esp. 65–81. Subsequent references will be cited in the text.
3. This is the view enunciated of Collins's poem specifically, and of the Highlands generally, in David Hill Radcliffe's "Ossian and the Genres of Culture," 216–18 and Peter Womack's *Improvement and Romance*, 87–101.
4. Ermarth, *Wilhelm Dilthey*, 99.
5. "Experience without a Subject: Walter Benjamin and the Novel," *Cultural Semantics*, 49. Cf. Jay, *Cultural Semantics*, chs. 3 and 5; Jay, "Is Experience Still in Crisis?"; and Shusterman, "The End of Aesthetic Experience." For more on Benjamin's conception of experience, see Caygill, *Walter Benjamin: The Colour of Experience*, esp. ch. 1.
6. Munier, as quoted in Lacoue-Labarthe, *Poetry as Experience*, 128.
7. On the profound impact of Sartre on French phenomenology and deconstruction, see Tilottama Rajan, *Deconstruction and the Remainder of Phenomenology*, esp. ch. 3.
8. *The Long Revolution*, 63. Williams professed that he "took over" the term of experience from F. R. Leavis, whose "strength was in reproducing and interpreting what he called 'the living content of a work.'" But Williams found Leavis "very weak in all consideration of formal questions, particularly when it was a question of deep formal structures which had undergone historical change." Hence he organized the concept of "structures of feeling," a materialist-experiential category that "was designed to focus a mode of historical and social relations which was yet quite internal to the work, rather than deducible from it or supplied by some external placing or classification." *Politics and Letters: Interviews with New Left Review*, 163–64.
9. Jay, "Roland Barthes and the Tricks of Experience," 469.
10. See Jay, *Songs of Experience*, ch. 9.
11. Tilottama Rajan describes Foucault's conservation of the category of experience as "not an origin, a foundation for knowledge, but simply a point of resistance . . . to the positivity of knowledge." *Deconstruction and the Remainders of Phenomenology*, 163. In what I will describe as Highlandist fashion, Foucault situates experience at the limits of enlightened knowledge.
12. I discuss some of this work in Chapter 6.
13. William Beatty Warner anticipated and theorized this resurgent interest in the irreducible strangeness of experience by linking experience to the play of chance. See *Chance and the Text of Experience*, esp. 14–17.
14. See *Provincializing Europe*, esp. Part I.
15. "The Evidence of Experience."
16. See Shapiro, *A Culture of Fact*, esp. ch. 1, and Shapin, *A Social History of Truth*, esp. chs. 1–3.
17. Williams discerns a similar formation in the emergence of a modern concept of literature as creative writing in the late eighteenth and early nineteenth centuries. He argues that dehumanizing working conditions in the commercial and industrial spheres reconfigured literature into the repository of creativity and "human" "experience"—a radical cultural development that would assume the form of conservative humanist values after Matthew Arnold. See Williams, *Marxism and Literature*, 45–54.
18. "The Method of Natural Philosophy," 5. On the power of this notion in a French Enlightenment context, see O'Neal, *The Authority of Experience*, esp. Part I.

19. "Preface of 1800," 153.

20. See Hacking, *The Emergence of Probability*, esp. ch. 4; Shapiro, *Probability and Certainty in Seventeenth-Century England*, esp. ch. 2; Patey, *Probability and Literary Form*, Part I; Daston, *Classical Probability in the Enlightenment*, esp. the Introduction; and Poovey, *A History of the Modern Fact*, esp. ch. 1.

21. Steven Shapin and Simon Schaffer coined the phrase "virtual witnessing" to describe this phenomenon. See *Leviathan and the Air-Pump*, 60–65.

22. On these shifts, see Shapiro, *"Beyond Reasonable Doubt" and "Probable Cause"*, esp. ch. 1; J. M. Beattie, *Crime and the Courts in England, 1660–1800*, 352–62; and Alexander Welsh, *Strong Representations*, ch. 1.

23. These ideological factors, which held during the eighteenth century in a great number of ways, have persisted into the twentieth century. They inform the economist J. M. Keynes's argument for a "constructive theory" of probability in his *Treatise on Probability*, especially in his concluding remarks on the widening sphere of theories of chance in physics and biology, 427–28. These views also remain dominant in the field of statistics. Theophilos Cacoullos alludes to them and their limitations by pronouncing the "supremacy of chance" as the first of his "Ten Commandments for a Statistician," reminding his readers in the fourth commandment that they must "stochasticize," or distinguish between statistics and predictability. See Charalambides et al., *Probability and Statistical Methods with Applications*, xxxviii.

24. This is an axiom of French phenomenological and postphenomenological thought, informing even such apparent sites of "immediate" experience as bodily touch. See Derrida, *Le Toucher: Jean-Luc Nancy* (esp. 11–17, when Derrida advances the paradox that in touching we make contact only with the surface of things, and thus that the essential remains beyond our grasp even as it seemingly touches us) and Kelly Oliver, *Witnessing: Beyond Recognition*, esp. ch. 4.

25. Felman and Dori Laub, *Testimony*, 5.

26. Anthony Giddens speaks to this point in *Runaway World*, 43–44.

27. T. J. Clark alludes to this paradox when he speaks of the "two great dreams" that lay "at the heart of the symbolic order" of modernity: "The first proposed that the world was becoming modern because it was turning into a space inhabited by free individual subjects, each dwelling in sensuous immediacy. The world was becoming a pattern of privacies—of appetites, possessions, accumulations. . . . In the realm of economy, they gave rise to markets. . . . The second [dream of modernity] . . . was hard to separate from its twin. The world, it said, is more and more a realm of technical rationality, made available and comprehensible to individual subjects by being made mechanized and standardized. The world is on its way to absolute material lucidity." Hence, sensuousness meets up with bureaucratization; the dogmatically empirical and the dogmatically rational intersect. "Modernism, Postmodernism, and Steam," 164–65.

28. *Celtic Identity and the British Image*, 6. Pittock appeals here to Michael Hechter's influential analysis of the "Celtic fringe" in *Internal Colonialism*. I further discuss Hechter's book in "Of Probability, Romance, and the Spatial Dimensions of Eighteenth-Century Narrative."

29. Devine, *Clanship to Crofters' War: The Social Transformation of the Scottish Highlands*, 84.

30. Pittock persuasively refutes this popular view by dislocating Jacobitism as a nationalist movement from the Highlands proper. See *The Myth of the Jacobite Clans*, esp. the Introduction and ch. 1.

31. Devine, *Clanship to Crofters' War*, 86, 98. Devine is echoing the title of the well-known book edited by Eric Hobsbawm and Terence Ranger, *The Invention of Tradition*.

32. The impetus for much of this work seems to have come politically from the Scottish drive toward devolution and expanded legislative independence, and academically from Tom Nairn's powerful 1977 argument that Scotland historically represented the last of the first world nations and the first of the third world nations, and thus served as a harbinger of a modern nationalist spirit even if it failed fully to develop a national identity of its own in the late eighteenth century. See Nairn, *The Break-Up of Britain*, chs. 2 and 3. Benedict Anderson modifies (but also largely reconfirms) Nairn's thesis in his landmark *Imagined Communities*, 88–90. Nairn then revises his materialistic analysis of nationalism (and of Scottish contributions to the modern concept of nationalism) in his later book *Faces of Nationalism*. See also Christopher Harvie, *Scotland and Nationalism* and David McCrone, *Understanding Scotland*. In literary studies, the definitive works on Scottish nationalism are Robert Crawford's *Devolving English Literature*, Katie Trumpener's *Bardic Nationalism*, and Leith Davis's *Acts of Union*.

33. *Marxism and Literature*, 131.

34. Althusser, "Ideology and Ideological State Apparatuses (Notes towards an Investigation)," *Lenin and Philosophy and Other Essays*, 162.

35. Foucault rejects "ideological" analyses on similar grounds. See "Truth and Power," 60.

36. *Politics and Letters*, 168, 172. For a more detailed history of the embattled status of Williams's "structures" in the Marxist context of the 1970s and '80s, see Jay, *Songs of Experience*, 199–205.

37. Spanos, *The End of Education*, 26.

38. Williams, *Marxism and Literature*, 132, Williams's emphases. For Williams's elaborations on the concept of experience, see his heading "Empirical" in *Keywords*.

39. Kevis Goodman discusses the relevance and limitations of Williams's "structures" in the rather different eighteenth-century context of georgic poetry. See *Georgic Modernity and British Nationalism*, esp. the Introduction.

40. This point is made most forcefully by Ian Duncan in *Modern Romance and Transformations of the Novel*, ch. 2.

41. For excellent criticism of Scott which strikes this note, see Duncan, *Modern Romance and Transformations of the Novel*; James Chandler, *England in 1819*, ch. 5; Saree Makdisi, *Romantic Imperialism*, ch. 4; and Paul Hamilton, *Metaromanticism*, ch. 5.

42. *The Achievement of Literary Authority*, 133.

43. See Trumpener, *Bardic Nationalism*, esp. ch. 3, and Siskin, *The Work of Writing*, esp. ch. 8.

44. *The Achievement of Literary Authority*, 119.

45. See Žižek, "Introduction," *Mapping Ideology* (New York: Verso, 1994).

46. *Romantic Returns*, 35. Subsequent references will be cited in the text.

47. On the subject of ideology, White discusses how the "Ode" constructs a historical narrative against which it chafes. "To call this version of 'history' ideology would not be inaccurate, and to find it at work in Collins's poetry suggests a great deal about poetry. It is not, however, the point at which one can conclude one's reading. Collins takes one further, or, more precisely, he interrupts himself before taking one so far" (51). Ian Duncan arrives at a similar conclusion regarding Scott's *Waverley*, in which the chief cartographic project involves less the Highlands in themselves or even the historical progress of the British nation than the protagonist's identity as a modern subject. See *Modern Romance and Transformations of the Novel*, ch. 2.

48. White sees the "[i]magination—and therefore a certain relation to the 'other'—[a]s constitutive of the self" (14). Though she does not expressly make

this connection, she implicitly reiterates Michel Foucault's influential exploration of the invention and death of "man" during this same period of the late eighteenth and early nineteenth centuries in *The Order of Things*.

49. Jameson, *Postmodernism*, 410–11.

50. *The Prison-House of Language*, 50–51.

51. Though not addressing the Highlands or experience per se, Jan-Melissa Schramm addresses the status of legal testimony relative to literary discourse in the nineteenth century. For Schramm, however, testimony is primarily a rhetorical category; her approach is thus less oblique than mine, focusing on the ongoing dependence of evidence on testimony, and hence on romance. See *Testimony and Advocacy in Victorian Law, Literature, and Theology*, esp. ch. 1.

52. While it seemed a bit far afield for this project, I discuss the counterintuitive "posthuman" preoccupation with experience in "Terror's Abduction of Experience: A Gothic History."

Chapter 1. A Musket Shot and Its Echoes

1. Carney, *The Appin Murder*, 1.

2. Clyde, *From Rebel to Hero*, 182.

3. Mackay, *Trial of James Stewart (The Appin Murder)*, 109. Subsequent references will be cited in the text.

4. The defense argued that laws in both England and Scotland prohibited such action, while the prosecution countered by citing exceptions to this rule within those laws alluded to by the defense, and by defending the sovereignty of Scottish law from English custom: "With regard to the old law books mentioned . . . they are generally believed to have been transcribed from the laws of England, at a time . . . when many salutary alterations are thought to have been introduced into our practice from thence, but . . . it is by no means admitted that they were ever engrossed into the body of our laws, or that every part of them has been confirmed by our practice" (Mackay 108).

5. As quoted in Carney, 29.

6. Langbein, "Historical Foundations of the Law of Evidence," 1170. Reflecting on the relatively primitive status of legal evidence in the seventeenth and the eighteenth centuries, the legal historian William Twining observes that "for a remarkably long time the main methods by which disputed questions of fact were dealt with did not require a system of evidence." However, numerous hallmarks of modern evidentiary codes were beginning to emerge during this period. For instance, "the conclusiveness of documents under seal was an early development; the rules concerning the competency of witnesses . . . were largely established in the sixteenth century; . . . [and] the hearsay rule . . . did not become firmly established until after 1600." "The Rationalist Tradition of Evidence Scholarship," in Twining, *Rethinking Evidence*, 34.

7. Wigmore, *The Principles of Judicial Proof*, 1.

8. *Lord's Journal*, February 25, 1794; as quoted in Twining, "The Rationalist Tradition," 34.

9. Langbein, "The Criminal Trial before the Lawyers," esp. 307-16; cf. Shapiro, *"Beyond Reasonable Doubt" and "Probable Cause,"* 25–29.

10. Langbein, "Shaping the Eighteenth-Century Criminal Trial," 2.

11. Landsman, "The Rise of the Contentious Spirit," 502. For more on the role of lawyers in the eighteenth century, see Langbein, "The Criminal Trial

before the Lawyers," and "Shaping the Eighteenth-Century Criminal Trial," 123–34; cf. J. M. Beattie, *Crime and the Courts in England 1660–1800*, 352–56.

12. Twining, "The Rationalist Tradition," 34.

13. Twining, "The Rationalist Tradition," 39.

14. On the role of probable estimations of likelihood in English legal history, see Barbara J. Shapiro, "Classical Rhetoric and the English Law of Evidence."

15. Newsom, *A Likely Story*, 19.

16. Shapiro, *Probability and Certainty in Seventeenth-Century England*, 5.

17. Hume, *A Treatise of Human Nature* (1739–40), 251.

18. Locke, *An Essay Concerning Human Understanding* (1689), IV.15, 654–55 (Locke's emphases deleted); on the degrees of assent, see IV.16, 657–68.

19. Gilbert, *The Law of Evidence*, 1–2. On the relatively ante-modern quality of Gilbert's treatise, see Landsman, "From Gilbert to Bentham: The Reconceptualization of Evidence Theory," 1149–86.

20. Sprat, *The History of the Royal Society*, 115.

21. Daston "Baconian Facts, Academic Civility, and the Prehistory of Objectivity," 342.

22. Newton's reflections concerning the design of the universe form a notable exception to this rule, but they were often derided in subsequent decades, most famously by David Hume in *Dialogues Concerning Natural Religion* (1776).

23. Francis Bacon, *Novum Organum*, 195, 196. We should note that witnesses remained vital components of empiricist "factuality." The authentication of facts required the personal testimony of credible witnesses—usually men of birth and education. Steven Shapin, Mary Poovey, and Barbara Shapiro, however, have argued persuasively that these opaque facts required and, indeed, already referred to systems of interpretation which classified the facts and authenticated the testimony of those who spoke in their defense. Ideally, the witnesses were gentlemen, for instance, free from the burdens of manual labor that might coarsen their senses. Their accounts should be simple, tending toward plainness; the witnesses should be Christian; etc. See Shapin, *A Social History of Truth*, esp. ch. 3; Poovey, *A History of the Modern Fact*, 7-16; and Shapiro, *A Culture of Fact*, ch. 1.

24. Daston, *Classical Probability in the Enlightenment*, 19.

25. Ogden, *Bentham's Theory of Fictions*, 118.

26. Ogden, *Bentham's Theory of Fictions*, 55; cf. Bender, *Imagining the Penitentiary*, 34–35.

27. Morano, "A Re-examination of the Development of the Reasonable Doubt Rule," 508 (emphases in original). For a more comprehensive survey of the formation of this rule, see Shapiro, *"Beyond Reasonable Doubt" and "Probable Cause,"* 1–41.

28. In *The Expedition of Humphry Clinker* (1771), Tobias Smollett's acerbic Scottish character Lismihago denounces English juries for their typical unreasonability: "Juries are generally composed of illiterate plebeians, apt to be mistaken, easily misled, and open to sinister influence. . . ." He finds conditions more favorable, however, in Sweden, and also in Scotland. *Humphry Clinker*, 241–42. On the control exerted over juries by judges, see P. J. R. King, "'Illiterate Plebeians, Easily Misled': Jury Composition, Experience, and Behavior in Essex, 1735–1815," 254.

29. Roughead, *The Trial of Mary Blandy*, 103.

30. Nelson, *The Law of Evidence*, 7.

31. Alexander Welsh, *Strong Representations*, 8.

32. It is important that we recognize the change this wrought in the traditional conception of the jury. Shapiro relates that prior to this modification, juries "brought to the courtroom precisely what a Westminster judge could not: personal knowledge of the facts surrounding the alleged crime" (*"Beyond Reasonable Doubt" and "Probable Cause,"* 241). In the eighteenth century, however, the difference between "jurors as witnesses" and "jurors as hearers of witnesses" was still relatively fluid. In what is considered to be the inaugural treatise on evidence, published in 1717, the jurist William Nelson declared that "[b]eing return'd of the Vicinage, whence the Cause or Action ariseth, the Law supposeth [jurors] thence to have sufficient Knowledge to try the Matter in Issue . . . ; but to this Evidence the Judge is a Stranger. They [i.e., the jurors] may have Evidence from their own Personal Knowledge, by which they may be assured, and sometimes are, that what is deposed in Court is absolutely false; but to this the Judge is a Stranger, and he knoweth no more of the Fact than he hath learned in Court, and perhaps by false Depositions; and consequently knows nothing" (*The Law of Evidence,* 2). Hence, in the early eighteenth century, it was customary that jurors might conclude that a given "Deposition" or testimony is false in a manner to which "the Judge is a Stranger"—namely, by a more direct, witness-like relation to "the Matter in Issue." Another contemporary jurist confirmed the prerogative of jurors to testify in court as late as 1728, even extending this privilege to judges by professing that "[a]ny of the Judges may come down from the Bench, and give Evidence as Witnesses. Also a Juror may be a Witness, as well as any other Person" (Hawkins, *A Summary of the Crown-Law,* 423).

33. On the contention that "circumstances cannot lie" and its place in eighteenth-century jurisprudence, see Welsh, *Strong Representations,* 15–17. On the endemic connection between witness testimony and the possibility of error, see Wigmore, *The Principles of Judicial Proof,* 312–13.

34. Sir John Hawles, *The English-Man's Right,* 11 (Hawles' emphasis).

35. Ehrlich, *Ehrlich's Blackstone,* 679. See also Gilbert, *The Law of Evidence,* 60, and Wigmore, *The Principles of Judicial Proof,* 426–27.

36. Dear, *Discipline and Experience,* 4.

37. Shapiro reiterates this point by relating that "[a]ll the fact-oriented disciplines [such as science, law, and history] exhibited a preference for personal observation and a belief that the testimony of credible witnesses under optimum conditions could yield believable . . . 'facts'" (*A Culture of Fact,* 211).

38. *Leviathan and the Air-Pump,* 56 (my emphasis).

39. Schaffer, "Self Evidence." *Questions of Evidence,* 56–91; cf. Strickland, "The Ideology of Self-Knowledge and the Practice of Self-Experimentation."

40. Shapin, *A Social History of Truth,* 6, 15; cf. Giddens, *Consequences of Modernity,* ch. 3.

41. See Golan, *Laws of Men and Laws of Nature,* ch. 1.

42. To take this problem even one step further, when Stewart was finally permitted to seek counsel, he and his friends found that many of Edinburgh's finest attorneys had been "retained" or employed elsewhere by the pursuers so as to be unavailable for Stewart's cause. And, crowning the pursuers' chicanery, Stewart and his defense were not permitted to see a copy of the libel which detailed the specific charges on which he was tried. It was only at the eleventh hour that a copy fortuitously fell into the hands of a sympathetic stranger, who shared it with the defenders. A later commentator observed that had Stewart "been tried at Edinburgh, he, in all human probability, would have been acquitted, unless, which is not to be supposed, uncommon pains had been taken to pack a jury,"

which is precisely what happened in Inveraray. John Maclaurin, Lord Dreghorn, *Arguments and Decisions, in Remarkable Cases, before the High Court of Justiciary, and Other Supreme Courts, in Scotland*, xxviiin.

43. Although Scottish law in almost every instance forbade the testimony of family members, one pursuer sophistically justified this exception by claiming that "[w]hen the murder was committed all was confusion and ignorance," and Stewart's family was questioned as a procedural formality. "So . . . his wife and children were not really examined with any view to him," the pursuers reasoned; instead, they were summoned in court only to repeat what they had said to investigators when initially interrogated (Mackay 97–98). Perhaps most ironically (and gallingly), this justification was uttered by Simon Fraser, the son of the notorious Jacobite Lord Lovat, who had been hanged for treason only a few years earlier.

44. While English law is usually seen as accommodating circumstantial evidence earlier than Scottish law (which, in conformity with other Roman legal systems on the continent of Europe, was known as a system of trial-by-witnesses), Scottish law was actually quite open to such evidence. This is less surprising when it is considered as a reflection of an epistemological climate rather than simply as a legal fact. The nineteenth-century Scottish jurist David Hume maintained that shifts in evidential law were universally "grounded . . . in reason and necessity, and the law and practice of all other civilized realms." *Commentaries on the Laws of Scotland Respecting Crimes*, 2: 385.

45. Hugo Arnot, *A Collection and Abridgement of Celebrated Criminal Trials in Scotland*, 225.

46. See Welsh, *Strong Representations*, ch. 1. On this "system" of evidence, see Bentham, *Rationale of Judicial Evidence*, esp. 1: 1-15; cf. Twining, *Theories of Evidence*, 1–108; and Terence Anderson and William Twining, *Analysis of Evidence*, 446.

47. While the rules against hearsay were not yet formalized, the ideological position being sketched out for witnesses by Blackstone and others was already tending to discourage hearsay as a more traditional and less enlightened evidentiary custom.

48. John Breck's testimony bears out these gendered implications, especially inasmuch as Katharine Maccoll's feminized perspective—or indeed, the limited evidential purview afforded to virtually all witnesses almost by definition—portended the contagion of "frighting the women of the town," or those who were susceptible to the same sensuous limitations (thereby disrupting their cattle-tending responsibilities and unsettling the fine balance of the local economy). Thinking along with (and partly foreseeing) the stereotypical notion of women as delicate creatures bound to their senses, the renowned Scottish jurist Sir George Mackenzie explained in 1678 that "the reason why women are excluded from witnessing, must be either that they are subject to too much compassion, and so ought not to be received in Criminal cases, then [*sic*] in any Civil cases; or else the Law was unwilling to trouble them, and thought it might learn them too much confidence, and make them subject to too much familiarity with men, and strangers, if they were necessitated to vague up and down at all Courts, upon occasions." *The Laws and Customes of Scotland in Matters Criminal*, 531.

49. Johnson, *A Journey to the Western Islands of Scotland* (1775), 69.

50. An anonymous "Bystander" (who published "A Supplement to the Trial of James Stewart" in London in 1753, and who may well have been Brown himself) argued that the pursuers' zeal in arguing their case actually promoted the antipathetic Highland traits that they had ostensibly been working to eradicate.

Commenting on Argyll's virulent speech to Stewart after the verdict had been pronounced (in which Argyll reviled Stewart for having acted "according to the malice always prevailing in uncivilised parts of the Highlands," among other things—see Mackay 290–91), the "bystander" leaves "it to the reader to consider, whether this speech, together with the whole tenor of these proceedings, does not furnish ground to apprehend, that the late acts of parliament for abolishing the spirit of clanship, may contribute in a great degree to confirm the evil they meant to destroy. For, by appointing circuit-courts to be held at Inverar[a]y in the country of Argy[ll], and under the very walls of the castle, where the majorities at least of juries must be composed of Campbells, his Grace, who, by his office of Justice-General, is intitled [sic] to preside at these courts, has thereby an opportunity of exerting that spirit of clanship in so much stronger manner than before, as the authority of judge is added to the influence of chief" (as quoted in Mackay 339).

51. Neil Philip has preserved a version of the local legend of the Stewart Trial in his edition of Scottish folktales. See *The Penguin Book of Scottish Folktales*, 255–79.

52. On Benjamin's concept of the dialectical image, see Susan Buck-Morss, *The Dialectics of Seeing*, esp. ch. 3.

Chapter 2. Aftershocks of the Appin Murder

1. "The Storyteller," *Walter Benjamin: Selected Writings*, 3: 143–44. Subsequent references will be cited in the text.

2. Adorno remarks that Benjamin "never wavered in his fundamental conviction that the smallest cell of observed reality offsets the rest of the world. To interpret phenomena materialistically meant for him not so much to elucidate them as products of the social whole but rather to relate them directly, in their isolated   singularity,   to   material   tendencies   and   social   struggles." "A Portrait of Walter Benjamin," 236.

3. On the connection between Poe and Benjamin, see most recently Cutler, *Recovering the New*, ch. 3.

4. "Scott and the Classical Form of the Historical Novel," 131.

5. *Kidnapped* and *Catriona*, 474–75. Subsequent references to this edition will be cited in the text.

6. See "Translation and Tourism."

7. See Susan Buck-Morss, *The Dialectics of Seeing*, esp. ch. 3: "Natural History: Fossil."

8. This narrative motif actually more closely models the historical reality of the eighteenth century. See Withers, *Urban Highlanders*. I discuss this phenomenon more fully in Chapter 3.

9. "*Rob Roy* and the Limits of Frankness," 379.

10. *Waverley; or, 'Tis Sixty Years Since*, 296.

11. "*Rob Roy*," 122.

12. Alexander Welsh remarks that "[f]or a century and a half readers have scorned the plot of *Rob Roy* as either unimportant or unintelligible." Welsh concurs, but to a lesser degree: "Apart from its topographical contrast, ranging the civil state against the state of nature, the construction of *Rob Roy* is weak. But a wealth of suggestion compensates for this weakness." *The Hero of the Waverley Novels*, 123, 125.

13. "Introduction" to *Rob Roy*, 74. Subsequent references to this edition will be cited in the text.

14. See, for example, Hutcheson's *Essay on the Nature and Conduct of the Passions and Affections*, which speaks "of computing the Quantities of Good" and "proportion[ing] the *Number* of Persons to whom the good Event shall extend," defining "In general, the Strength of publick Desire [as] a Compound Ratio of the *Quantity of the Good itself, and the Number, Attachment, and Dignity* of the Persons" (39, Hutcheson's emphasis).

15. Scott underscores this connection in his Introduction, where he tells of Rob venturing in the cattle trade. "Unfortunately, that species of commerce was and is liable to sudden fluctuations," and Rob was "rendered totally insolvent." It was then that Rob "exchanged his commercial adventures for speculations of a very different complexion." This was when he retreated "farther into the Highlands, and commenced the lawless sort of life which he afterwards followed" (*Rob Roy* 17). In effect, then, Rob only became a stereotypical Highlander belatedly, and only by taking the commercial logic of "exchange" to a more extreme level.

16. *Modern Epic*, 52.

17. *Power and Punishment in Scott's Novels*, 47. Subsequent references will be cited in the text.

18. Benjamin's "Critique of Violence" is perhaps the most strident and, to Jacques Derrida, disturbing. See "Critique of Violence," *Walter Benjamin: Selected Writings*, 1: 236–52 and Derrida's later reflections on this essay, "Force of Law" in *Deconstruction and the Possibility of Justice*, 3–67. For Lyotard's intervention into this issue, see *The Differend*; Lyotard defines the differend "a case of conflict, between (at least) two parties, that cannot be equitably resolved for lack of a rule of judgment applicable to both arguments" (xi). Violence was a major theme of Girard's work; he connects it to rituals of religion as well as law. See most famously *Violence and the Sacred*, esp. ch. 1.

19. "Scott and the Classical Form of the Historical Novel," 96. Subsequent references will be cited in the text.

20. "Scott and Empire: The Case of *Rob Roy*," 43. Subsequent references will be cited in the text.

21. Lincoln shows how Scott expounds especially on the Campbells, who were such key players in the Stewart Trial. See "Scott and Empire," 55.

22. Following the sentence of death pronounced upon Stewart, the Duke of Argyll, the Lord Justice General exclaimed to the condemned man that "[i]f you had been successful in that rebellion you had been now triumphant with your confederates trampling upon the laws of your country, the liberties of your fellow-subjects, and on the Protestant religion. You might have been giving the law where you now have received the judgment of it; and we, who are this day your judges, might have been tried before one of your mock Courts of judicature, and then you might have been satiated with the blood of any name or clan to which you had an aversion." Mackay, *Trial of James Stewart (the Appin Murder)*, 291.

23. Duncan refers to other scholarly discussions of Scott which make a similar case: Welsh in *The Hero of the Waverley Novels*, 118–33; Millgate in *Walter Scott: The Making of the Novelist*, 134–50; Wilt in *Secret Leaves*, 51–70; and Elam in *Romancing the Postmodern*, 107–10.

24. Welsh, *Strong Representations*, 8.

25. Welsh suggests as much by claiming that "there are too many sources of interest" in the novel's plot, mirroring its scattered narrator, and that none of

these sources "commands the whole" as a lawyerly narrative would. *The Hero of the Waverley Novels*, 183; cf. Howard, "The Symbolic Structure of *Rob Roy*," 72.

26. "*Rob Roy* and the Limits of Frankness," 379.

27. See Barrell, "Fire, Famine, and Slaughter" on the regisidal associations of imagination in the late eighteenth century.

28. This is Millgate's point: "Though the novel is filled with voices and peopled by characters who love to talk—all faithfully rendered by the ventriloquial powers of the narrator—it is, in fact, the silences that reverberate in the reader's mind, those agonized moments within the action when the words will not come, those still places in the narration when the clear opportunity for retrospective amplification remains unexploited." "*Rob Roy* and the Limits of Frankness," 380–81.

29. Scott's ability to weave semicoherent narratives from the tattered strands of culture and history inspires Jerome McGann to dub Scott a "postmodern" novelist. See "Walter Scott's Romantic Postmodernity."

30. "Stevenson and Scotland," 26.

31. *Robert Louis Stevenson: A Literary Life*, 56.

32. Stevenson confided to friends that he considered "the best of all [his] designs . . . a History of the Highlands from the Union to the Present day; social, literary, economical and religious." Quoted in Swearingen, *The Prose Writings of Robert Louis Stevenson*, 106.

33. The novel even bore this title in its first American edition. In Britain, and in subsequent American editions, it was packaged and sold as *Catriona* to prevent readers from confusing it with *Kidnapped*.

34. Douglas Gifford, "Stevenson and Scottish Fiction: The Importance of *The Master of Ballantrae*," 67.

35. "Writing *Kidnapped* in 1886, Stevenson realized that he wished to and could carry David Balfour's adventures well beyond David's return to Edinburgh; and by late May 1886 he had accepted Sidney Colvin's suggestion to conclude the novel in Edinburgh but leave room for a sequel," *Catriona*. The novels were thus published serial-style (which is how *Kidnapped* first appeared in print). Swearingen, *The Prose Writings of Robert Louis Stevenson*, 167.

36. *The Rise of the Novel*, 31.

37. Bender, "Enlightenment Fiction and the Scientific Hypothesis," 9.

38. Karl Popper most famously distinguished fictive from factual discourse, adducing the maxim that aesthetic objects are not "true" because they are incapable of being proved false. See *The Logic of Scientific Discovery*, esp. 78–92.

39. *The Political Unconscious*, 104.

40. *The Origins of the English Novel*, 120.

41. *Modern Romance and Transformations of the Novel*, 2.

42. Critics have remarked that *Catriona* in particular self-consciously bears the hallmarks of an eighteenth-century novel. See Robert Kiely, *Robert Louis Stevenson and the Fiction of Adventure*, 90–93; J. R. Hammond, *A Robert Louis Stevenson Companion*, 130–32; and Frank McLynn (who quotes Gosse making a similar observation), *Robert Louis Stevenson*, 268.

43. Stevenson, "Preface by Way of Criticism," *Familiar Studies of Men and Books*, 7.

44. Alan Sandison has recently commented on how this aspect of *Catriona* amounts to David's education in *Realpolitik*. *Robert Louis Stevenson and the Appearance of Modernism*, 190.

45. Quoted in Hammond, *A Robert Louis Stevenson Companion*, 140.

46. Carlo Ginzburg discusses this matter in *No Island is an Island*, ch. 4.

47. "A Plea for Gas Lamps," *"Virginibus Puerisque" and Other Papers*, 150–52.
48. Benjamin, *Charles Baudelaire*, 50.
49. See Benjamin's letter of August 28, 1938 in *Theodor Adorno and Walter Benjamin: The Complete Correspondence, 1928–1940*, 273–74.
50. *The German Ideology*, 92, authors' emphasis.
51. "Paris, the Capital of the Nineteenth Century," *Walter Benjamin: Selected Writings*, 3: 33–34.
52. "Experience and Poverty," *Walter Benjamin: Selected Writings*, 2: 731–32. Subsequent references will be cited in the text. These expressions are repeated almost verbatim in "The Storyteller."
53. "The Handkerchief," *Walter Benjamin: Selected Writings*, 2: 658.
54. "Little Tricks of the Trade," *Walter Benjamin: Selected Writings*, 2: 729.
55. Adorno doesn't name fascism in his correspondence with Benjamin, but this concern manifests itself in his objection that Benjamin's work was insufficiently dialectical and that it was thus, first, being swallowed up in a kind of transhistorical dream consciousness and, second, becoming impenetrable in its failure explicitly to enunciate its ideas. In essence, Benjamin's work seemed to Adorno to be becoming increasingly impressionistic, making it more of a reflection of insidious modern forces than a critique of the same. See Adorno's letters to Benjamin of June 2, 1935; August 2–5, 1935; and November 10, 1938, *Theodor Adorno and Walter Benjamin: The Complete Correspondence, 1928–1940*, 92–94, 104–15, and 280–87.
56. "The Storyteller," 147. For a more extensive materialist analysis of Benjamin and Lukács on the novel, see Vincent P. Pecora, *Self and Form in Modern Narrative*, 7–11 and 31–35.
57. Benjamin, "The Work of Art in the Age of Mechanical Reproduction," *Illuminations*, 241. I cite this version of Benjamin's essay rather than the revised essay which appears in Volume 3 of *Walter Benjamin: Selected Writings* because in that later version Benjamin submerges aesthetics into the rhetoric of "property relations"—more amenable, certainly, to Adorno's criticism of his work, but less resonant with his cultural criticism in "The Storyteller."

Chapter 3. Evidence and Equivalence

1. I am referring here, respectively, to Womack, *Improvement and Romance*; Trumpener, *Bardic Nationalism*; Davis, *Acts of Union*; and Makdisi, *Romantic Imperialism*.
2. A short list of accounts of Highland improvement would include Alexander Mackenzie's classic nineteenth-century *The History of the Highland Clearances* and more recent historical analyses such as Richards's *The Highland Clearances* and *A History of the Highland Clearances*, Devine's *Clanship to Crofters' War*, and Dodgshon's *Chiefs to Landlords*. For the impact of Highland improvement on the cultural image of Scotland, see Womack, *Improvement and Romance* and Clyde, *From Rebel to Hero*.
3. *Life of Johnson*, 443.
4. Clyde, *From Rebel to Hero*, 21.
5. *A Journey to the Western Islands of Scotland* (1775), 100.
6. These changes are most famously documented and analyzed by Williams in *The Country and the City*.
7. *Integration, Enlightenment and Industrialization*, 5–6.

8. *Clanship to Crofters' War*, 32.

9. See Devine, ed. *Scottish Emigration and Scottish Society*, esp. chs. 1 and 5.

10. *After the Forty-Five*, 26.

11. Quoted in Youngson, *After the Forty-Five*, 27.

12. *A History of the Highland Clearances*, 1: 114.

13. *After the Forty-Five*, 29.

14. Clyde relates that "[t]he outside agencies that intervened in the Highlands and Islands after the 'Forty-Five to bring order and economic prosperity to the region believed their success to be dependent upon the concurrent spiritual and moral rehabilitation of the Gaels. In their eyes, the transformation of the Gaels from rebellious and indolent barbarians to loyal and industrious Presbyterians required the supplanting of Gaelic by English and the elimination of the non-juring Episcopalian and Roman Catholic clergy whose influence prevented the instilling of 'proper' beliefs, morals and habits. The task of educating the Gaels was left for the most part to the SSPCK [the Scottish Society for the Propagation of Christian Knowledge], an evangelical society which saw the promotion of literacy as a means of saving souls rather than as aiding the development of a skilled and well-informed citizenry, and which operated on the premise that 'civilization' was something the Lowlands could pass on to the Highlands." *From Rebel to Hero*, 90.

15. *General View of the Agriculture of the Northern Counties and Islands of Scotland*, 69–70.

16. See Knox, *A View of the British Empire* and Anderson, *The True Interest of Great Britain*.

17. Clyde, *From Rebel to Hero*, 25. The Revered Doctor John Walker was perhaps the first to introduce the idea of canals in the Highlands, remarking in 1764 that "[t]he Industry of these Countries is greatly damped by their remote Situation, from a proper Market for their Commodities. . . . This Obstacle would be effectually removed was there a Navigable Communication cut. . . . [A] Canal though Navigable only for open Boats of the largest Size, would be an Undertaking of great Expence, if it can be called great, when compared with the beneficial Consequences it would produce." *The Rev. Dr. John Walker's Report on the Hebrides of 1764 and 1771*, 107.

18. Quoted in Youngson, *After the Forty-Five*, 36.

19. Quoted in Clyde, *From Rebel to Hero*, 34, original emphasis.

20. James Buzard discusses the connotations of the notion of "finish" as termination and polish in Walter Scott's fictive portraits of the Highlands in "Translation and Tourism."

21. *From Rebel to Hero*, 132. John Anderson's *Essay on the State of Society and Knowledge in the Highlands of Scotland* (which won the 1827 prize from the Northern Institution, a society dedicated to the celebration and advancement of science and literature in the Highlands) elaborates on the two Highland societies. The Highland Society of London was "directed to the preservation of the language, music, poetry, and garb of the Highlands, and along with these some of the best traits of the ancient characteristics of the people. It was followed by the association of a Highland Society at Edinburgh in 1784. The attention of this body is turned to the present state of the Highlands and Islands of Scotland, and the condition of the inhabitants; the means of their improvement by the erection of towns and villages; formation of roads and bridges; advancement of agriculture, and extending of fisheries; introducing useful trades and manufactures; and an endeavour to unite the efforts of the proprietors and the attention of government to these beneficial purposes" (125–26).

22. *Bardic Nationalism*, 30.

23. "The Market of Symbolic Goods," 16.

24. *A Critical Dissertation on the Poems of Ossian* (1765), 345, my emphasis.

25. "The Field of Cultural Production," 311.

26. *A History of the Highland Clearances*, 1: 172–73.

27. Youngson, *After the Forty-Five*, 153, 151.

28. James Anderson, for instance, claimed that industry, and activity of body and mind, are the qualities that contribute in the highest degree to the happiness of every civilized nation: those circumstances, therefore, which tend to promote these in the highest degree, ought to be attended to with the greatest care.

"If a grasing-country has its chief dependence upon cattle, it is attended with this peculiar inconvenience, that as the inhabitants have no necessary inducement to industry, they naturally abandon themselves to idleness. And a habit of indolence being once acquired, it must be extremely difficult to get it eradicated." *Observations on the Means of Exciting a Spirit of National Industry*, 47–48; cf. Youngson, *After the Forty-Five*, 36–37, 52, 191–92.

29. Anderson, *Observations on the Means of Exciting a Spirit of National Industry*, 185. The father of Walter Scott's protagonist Francis Osbaldistone rehearses this idea in *Rob Roy*: Commerce "connects nation with nation, relieves the wants and contributes to the wealth of all, and is to the general commonwealth and civilised world what the daily intercourse of ordinary life is to private society, or rather, what air and food are to our bodies." However, Scott's novel begins with the protagonist rejecting a place in his father's firm and eventually heading into the Highlands in search of adventure. *Rob Roy*, 75.

30. Anderson, *Observations*, 5–6.

31. Such reports of squalor became *de rigeur* in the travel literature on the Highlands. In his *Diary* of 1813, Nathaniel Wraxall noted that "a young Woman, very well dressed in white, but without Shoes or Stockings, came out of a House not far distant; & squatting down on the side of the 'Burn', quite unconcealed, proceeded to perform her Devotions to Cloacina in the most expeditious Manner. Having dispatched her Sacrifice, she shifted her situation about a Foot on one Side, continuing still however in the same attitude for a few seconds, when she rose, let drop her cloathes, & returned very quietly to the House." Quoted in Malcolm Andrews, *The Search for the Picturesque*, 210–11.

32. Marx, for one, inveighed against the complicity between English law and the interests of capital in Chapter 28 of *Capital*, "Bloody Legislation Against the Expropriated, from the End of the 15th Century. Forcing Down Wages by Acts of Parliament." For a historical overview of such legislation in the late eighteenth and early nineteenth centuries, see E. P. Thompson, *The Making of the English Working Class*, 497–521.

33. "The Rehabilitation of Sir James Steuart," 6.

34. *A History of Modern Fact*, 239, emphases deleted. One of the more poignant discussions of how Smith subordinates empirical description to systematic theorizing may be found in Kathryn Sunderland's analysis of how Smith's text served as an ideological construct shaping the world it purported to describe. Sunderland's example is Smith's dismissal of female labor. See "Adam Smith's Master Narrative: Women and *The Wealth of Nations*."

35. Richards, *A History of the Highland Clearances*, 2: 18.

36. *Inquiry into the Causes of the Wealth of Nations*, 17–18. Subsequent references will be cited in the text.

37. "Adam Smith and the Classical Concept of Profit," 19.

38. *Wealth of Nations*, 351–52, my emphasis; cf. *The Theory of Moral Sentiments*, 184–85. Subsequent references will be cited in the text.

39. See *Observations*, 355–56. For Anderson's critique of Smith, see 358: "the value of every commodity, through all the possible variations of price it may be made to undergo, will at all times be equal to the quantity of labour it can purchase; or, in other words, the value, that is, the price[,] will be equal to the price. But this would be a play upon words, or rather a jingling of words, without meaning, that we cannot supposed Dr Smith could be capable of employing."

40. *Principles of Political Oeconomy*, 25–26.

41. One of Steuart's modern commentators, Andrew S. Skinner, elaborates that in the "agricultural stage," the stage following pastoral barbarism and preceding commercial society, "those who lacked the means of subsistence could acquire it only through becoming dependent on those who owned it; in [the commercial stage, however, Steuart] noted that the situation was radically different in that all goods and services command a price." "Sir James Steuart: Economic Theory and Policy," 119.

42. *Capital*, 1: 128. Subsequent references are cited in the text.

43. Tellingly, Marx traces this mystification from Ricardo through Smith back to Bernard de Mandeville, whose disclosure in *The Fable of the Bees* of the commercial economy as the production of "publick virtue" through "private vices" incited Francis Hutcheson and Smith to create a "providential" version of this same phenomenon. Marx labels Mandeville "an honest, clear-headed man," in contrast with those, like Smith, who followed him. *Capital*, 764–65.

44. *Postmodernism*, 231, 232.

45. "Hence the origin of Polytheism, and of that vulgar superstitions which ascribes all the irregular events of nature to the favour or displeasure of intelligent, though invisible beings, to gods, daemons, witches, genii, fairies. . . . Fire burns, and water refreshes; heavy bodies descend, and lighter substances fly upwards, by the necessity of their own nature; nor was this *invisible hand* of Jupiter ever apprehended to be employed in these matters. But thunder and lightning, storms and sunshine, those more irregular events, were ascribed to his favour, or to his anger. . . . And thus, in the first ages of the world, the lowest and most pusillanimous superstition supplied the place of philosophy." "The Principles which Lead and Direct Philosophical Enquiries; Illustrated by the History of Astronomy," 49–50.

46. "Look No Hidden Hands," 141; Dwyer, *The Age of Passions*, ch. 1.

47. See Caygill, *Art of Judgement*, esp. chs. 1 and 2; Guillory, *Cultural Capital*, ch. 5; and Poovey, *A History of the Modern Fact*, ch. 4.

48. *The Theory of Moral Sentiments*, 22.

49. On the juridical implications of Smith's moral system, see Bender, *Imagining the Penitentiary*, 218–28.

Chapter 4. Improvement and Apocalypse

1. *Inquiry into the Causes of the Wealth of Nations*, 24. Subsequent references will be cited in the text.

2. "[A]s soon as the distribution of labour comes into being, each man has a particular, exclusive sphere of activity, which is forced upon him and from which he cannot escape. He is a hunter, a fisherman, a shepherd, or a critical critic,

and must remain so if he does not want to lose his means of livelihood; whilst in communist society, where nobody has one exclusive sphere of activity but each can become accomplished in any branch he wishes, society regulates the general production and thus makes it possible for me to do one thing today and another tomorrow, to hunt in the morning, fish in the afternoon, rear cattle in the evening, criticise after dinner, just as I have a mind. . . ." Marx and Engels, *The German Ideology*, 53.

3. Symonds, *Weep Not for Me: Women, Ballads, and Infanticide in Early Modern Scotland*, 211. Subsequent references will be cited in the text.

4. On constructions of female virtue that inhabited and haunted the discourse of luxury, see Felicity A. Nussbaum, *Torrid Zones*, esp. the Introduction and ch. 1; Clery, *The Feminization Debate in Eighteenth-Century England*; and Kathryn Sunderland, "Writings on Education and Conduct: Arguments for Female Improvement," 25–45.

5. Smith, *Lectures on Rhetoric and Belles Lettres*, 118, 136, 137.

6. On this subject see Duncan, "Adam Smith, Samuel Johnson and the Institutions of English." Sorensen discusses this phenomenon from the perspective of factitious British nationhood in *The Grammar of Empire in Eighteenth-Century British Writing*, ch. 4.

7. Blair, *Lectures on Rhetoric and Belles Lettres*, 61, 86, 85, 9.

8. Franklin E. Court discusses the literary programs instituted by Smith and Blair in *Institutionalizing English Literature*, ch. 1.

9. On the logic and method of ballad composition, see William Bernard McCarthy, *The Ballad Matrix*, esp. the Introduction.

10. On the powerful ballad tradition of northeastern Scotland, see David Buchan, *The Ballad and the Folk*, ch. 7.

11. "Old Singing Women and the Canons of Scottish Balladry and Song," 52.

12. *The Cruel Mother*, 1: 218–26.

13. See Withers, *Urban Highlanders*, esp. chs. 3 and 4.

14. Hont and Ignatieff, "Needs and Justice in the *Wealth of Nations*," 2.

15. "Needs and Justice in the *Wealth of Nations*," 6.

16. "Needs and Justice in the *Wealth of Nations*," 11. Hont and Ignatieff argue that Smith's theory marks a break from the jurisprudential tradition of Grotius, Pufendorf, et al. For a different view, see Samuel Fleischacker, *On Adam Smith's Wealth of Nations*, 209–26.

17. *Capital*, Vol. 1, 890. Subsequent references will be cited in the text.

18. Scott, "Romance," 1: 560. Duncan addresses this term at length in *Modern Romance and Transformations of the Novel*, esp. the Prologue and ch. 2.

19. For a thorough compilation of eighteenth-century resources on this subject, see Ioan Williams, *Novel and Romance*.

20. See esp. Makdisi, *Romantic Imperialism*, ch. 4.

21. "The Uncanny," 21–30.

22. See Benjamin, "Theses on the Philosophy of History," in *Illuminations*; Koselleck, *Futures Past*; Anderson, *Imagined Communities*; Sherman, *Telling Time*; Chandler, *England in 1819*.

23. On this subject, see esp. Chandler, *England in 1819*, esp. 127–35.

24. Greig, *The Letters of David Hume*, 1: 255. In truth, there were certainly material and largely institutional-bases for Scottish literary productivity during the eighteenth century. See Robert Crawford, ed., *The Scottish Invention of English Literature* and Clifford Siskin, *The Work of Writing*, esp. ch. 3.

25. See Buck-Morss, *The Dialectics of Seeing*, esp. chs. 3 and 6.

26. Jameson, *Postmodernism*, 181–217. Subsequent references will be cited in the text.

27. *Allegories of Reading: Figural Language in Rousseau, Nietzsche, Rilke, and Proust*, 273.

28. *Anatomy of Criticism*, 186.

29. *The Political Unconscious*, 103, 104. Jameson refers to Hayden White's characterization of Marxism in *Metahistory*, 281–82. He also evokes Adorno's praise of the attitude of romance in Benjamin: "Everything that Benjamin said or wrote sounded as if thought, instead of rejecting the promises of fairy tales and children's books with its usual disgraceful 'maturity,' took them so literally that real fulfillment itself was now within sight of knowledge." Adorno, "A Portrait of Walter Benjamin," 230.

30. For instance, Perry Anderson converts Jameson into an archetypal romantic hero who has succeeded in "capturing" the cultural category of postmodernism for the Left. See Anderson's homage to Jameson in *The Origins of Postmodernity*. Jameson's critics, however, regard Jameson's aesthetic turn in much the same light as Jameson viewed new historicism. For instance, Alex Callinicos admires Jameson's "brilliantly and imaginatively executed" study, but he concludes that the linkages Jameson establishes between cultural phenomena look "a lot more like a relationship of homology than one of structural difference. . . . Jameson's discussion of Postmodern art, despite its many felicities, does tend to involve forcing into a single mould a diversity of cultural phenomena which do not obviously belong together" (*Against Postmodernism*, 129, 131). Similarly, scholars like David Harvey and Terry Eagleton back away from Jameson's aesthetic turn into a more precise, materialist analysis of the political, economic, and ideological bases of postmodernism. See Harvey, *Condition of Postmodernity* and Eagleton, *Illusions of Postmodernism*. Even Anderson implicitly reflects critically on Jameson's aesthetic turn by providing a more thorough history of postmodernism than Jameson before bestowing his praise.

Chapter 5. The Compulsions of Immediacy

1. "Wound Culture: Trauma in the Pathological Public Sphere."

2. Leys, *Trauma: A Genealogy*, 8–9.

3. When asked whether "any men of a modern age" could have composed the Ossianic poems, Johnson is said to have replied, "Yes, Sir, many men, many women, and many children." Boswell, *Life of Samuel Johnson*, 280. The key source for the modern scholarly defense of *Ossian* is Derick Thomson's *The Gaelic Sources of Macpherson's "Ossian"*; cf. Donald E. Meek, "The Gaelic Ballads of Scotland: Creativity and Adaptation," 19.

4. John Dwyer, "The Melancholy Savage: Text and Context in the Poems of Ossian," 166. For an assessment of the poems as eighteenth-century creations, see Malcolm Laing, *The History of Scotland*, 2: 377–453.

5. *Acts of Union*, 77, 84; Trumpener, *Bardic Nationalism*, 6.

6. "However the topic is considered, the *problem of language* has never been simply one problem among others." *Of Grammatology*, 6.

7. Stafford, *The Sublime Savage*, 78.

8. Ibid., 163.

9. *A Journey to the Western Islands of Scotland*, 118; Boswell, *Life of Johnson*, 581–82; Shaw, *An Enquiry into the Authenticity of the Poems Ascribed to Ossian*, 28.

10. Pringle, quoted in David Raynor, "Ossian and Hume," 152; Toynbee and Whitley, *Correspondence of Thomas Gray*, 690; Hume to Blair, September 19, 1763, *The Letters of David Hume*, 1: 399.

11. *The Poems of Ossian and Related Works*, 6. Subsequent references will be cited in the text.

12. See Donald E. Meek, "The Gaelic Ballads of Scotland," 42–44.

13. John Smith, one of Macpherson's later public advocates, attributed the poems' power to Ossian's position as an archetypal witness: "[Ossian's] compositions are marked with a signature which they could never receive from the lamp or from the closet: a signature which he alone could impress, who saw before him, in that apartment in which he mused, those objects which he describes; who bore a part in those expeditions which he celebrates; and who fought in those battles which he sings." *Gaelic Antiquities*, 91.

14. *A Critical Essay on the Ancient Inhabitants of Britain, or Scotland*, 373.

15. Macpherson, "A Dissertation Concerning the Aera of Ossian," 56.

16. Henry Home, Lord Kames, defended the authenticity of Ossian through a more properly evidential argument, contending that "[o]ne, at first view, will boldly declare the whole a modern fiction; for how is it credible, that a people, rude at present and illiterate, were, in the infancy of their society, highly refined in sentiment and manners? And yet upon a more accurate inspection, many weighty considerations occur to balance that opinion." *Sketches of the History of Man*, 1: 422.

17. "Leaf" was changed to "sound" in the 1773 edition. See *Poems* 419.

18. In a landmark essay on the philosophical concept of light, Hans Blumenberg postulates that historically "'seeing' is oriented toward the *repetition* of eyewitness experience, most clearly in the restoration of the phenomenon itself in all experimental methodology. The demand for the *presence* of the object under study is a point of departure for the modern idea of science, and in Bacon and Descartes, this demand is formulated in opposition to the validity of *auctoritas*," or the authority of witness testimony. "Light as a Metaphor for Truth: At the Preliminary Stage of Philosophical Concept Foundation," 48.

19. Ted Underwood interprets spectrality in the Ossian poems as an emergent historicist sensibility, the testimony of difference between present and past. See "Romantic Historicism and the Afterlife."

20. John Barrell, *English Literature in History*, 65–66, 31.

21. See *Critical Dissertations on the Origin, Antiquities, Language, Government, Manners, and Religion, of the Ancient Caledonians*, 199–225. On the numerous eighteenth-century writers on the Celtic "race," see William Ferguson, *The Identity of the Scottish Nation*, ch. 10. On the more conventionally "racist" (or, at the very least, xenophobic) dimension of Macpherson's work, see Howard D. Weinbrot, "Celts, Greeks, and Germans: Macpherson's Ossian and the Celtic Epic," and also *Britannia's Issue*, 516–25. For a contrasting view which portrays Macpherson embracing a Germanic, Saxonist heritage, see Colin Kidd, *British Identities Before Nationalism*, 200–203.

22. See *On the Genealogy of Morals*, 30–31. On Nietzsche's implication in (mostly German) Romanticism, see Adrian del Caro, *Nietzsche Contra Nietzsche*, ch. 2 and, for a slightly broader historical context, George S. Williamson, *The Longing for Myth in Germany*, ch. 7.

23. Herder, "*Auszug aus einem Briefwechsel über Ossian und die Lieder alter Bölter*," 150.

24. See note 21.

25. On the emergence of modern racial codes during the eighteenth century, see Roxann Wheeler, *The Complexion of Race* and Felicity A. Nussbaum, *The Limits of the Human*, esp. Part II.

26. *Moses and Monotheism*, 69–70. Subsequent references will be cited in the text.

27. Adorno, "On Epic Naïveté," 1: 25–26. Subsequent references will be cited in the text.

28. Adorno, "Cultural Criticism and Society," 34.

29. *Act and Idea in the Nazi Genocide*, xi.

30. "Unspeakable," 49, Trezise's emphasis.

31. This concern resonates with the poetics of Holocaust testimony enunciated by Shoshana Felman and Dori Laub in *Testimony* and Giorgio Agamben in *Remnants of Auschwitz*. Felman, Laub, and Agamben all associate testimony with poetry, to wit: "Poets—witnesses—found language as what remains, as what actually survives the possibility, or impossibility, of speaking" (Agamben 161).

32. Dominick LaCapra discusses the disturbing conflation of the experience of the survivors of the Nazi genocide with the assault on quotidian experience in a hypercomplex world. While Byzantine technological systems and a globalized marketplace have effectively rendered it impossible for individual human subjects to reconcile their experience with the material conditions of their existence, and while this corresponds with the structural coordinates of trauma, we must continue to insist on the difference of Auschwitz from everyday bewilderment lest we lose the ability to make meaningful critical and ethical distinctions. See *Writing History, Writing Trauma*, esp. ch. 2.

33. *Negative Dialectics*, 368. Subsequent references are annotated *ND* and are cited in the text.

34. See, for instance, the passage entitled "Late Extra" in *Minima Moralia*, where Adorno denigrates the aesthetics of "the new" (the "Baudelairean *nouveau*") precisely for its conformity to sensation, which is, among other things, the logic of the commodity. Rather than undertaking a labyrinthine analysis of the Parisian arcades, Benjamin would have been better served, Adorno argues, "to analyse the change in the meaning of the word sensation" from the Enlightenment into the twentieth century (235–36).

35. Mary Jacobus makes this point in her reading of Wilkomirski, whose "child's-eye view is inevitably mediated by other writings on the Holocaust, by generic aspects of Holocaust testimony. . . ." In her later postscript to this discussion, however, written after the disclosure of Wilkomirski's likely fabrications, Jacobus revises this position: "Holocaust memory risks losing its historicity when it becomes a metaphor for object loss. To paraphrase Adorno, after Auschwitz there can be no metaphor untouched by the event." *Psychoanalysis and the Scene of Reading*, 134, 160.

36. *The Wilkomirski Affair*, 269, 272, 278.

37. One of Wilkomirski's speaking partners was a woman named Laura Grabowski, whom Wilkomirski claimed to have recognized from his childhood in the camps. It was later revealed that Grabowski was in fact Laurel Wilson, also known as Lauren Stratford, a woman who had written another book about her harrowing childhood experiences as a victim of Satanic worship. See Maechler, *The Wilkomirski Affair*, 204–10.

38. *The Wilkomirski Affair*, 281.

39. *Writing History, Writing Trauma*, 208.

40. *Fragments: Memories of a Wartime Childhood*, 4–5. Subsequent references will be cited in the text.

41. Gourevitch, "The Memory Thief," 52. Subsequent references will be cited in the text.

42. "Beyond the Question of Authenticity: Witness and Testimony in the *Fragments* Controversy," 1303.

43. Ibid.

44. This makes *Fragments* potentially an even more graphic exhibition than Art Spiegelman's ironic *Maus*, in which the characters—including the author's father, who was a survivor, and the author himself—are visually illustrated as rodents.

45. *Dialectic of Enlightenment*, 168. Subsequent references are annotated *DE* and are cited in the text.

Chapter 6. Of Mourning and Machinery

1. *Marxism and Literature*, 50.

2. I borrow this phrase from John Berger's book *Ways of Seeing*.

3. See "The Question Concerning Technology."

4. *A Journey to the Western Islands of Scotland*, 35. Subsequent references will be cited in the text.

5. *The Journal of a Tour to the Hebrides*, 161. Subsequent references will be cited in the text.

6. Henson, "Johnson's Quest for 'The Fictions of Romantic Chivalry' in Scotland." Late in his journey, Johnson describes his arrival on the small Hebridean island of Inch Kenneth in these words: "Romance does not often exhibit a scene that strikes the imagination more than this little desert in the depths of western obscurity, occupied not by a gross herdsman, or amphibious fisherman, but by a gentleman and two ladies, of high birth, polished manners, and elegant conversation . . ." (136).

7. Trumpener, for instance, complains that whereas Macpherson's *Ossian* "had turned the Highlands into one enormous echo chamber" by accentuating both the formal richness of a Gaelic oral tradition and the imaginative fecundity of the mountain scenery, "Johnson, by contrast, insists on the desolation of the Highlands and describes his decision, during the journey, to write an account of Scotland as motivated by the silence of its landscape, empty of history and cultural referents." *Bardic Nationalism*, 70–71. Boswell acknowledges that he was "uneasy when people [were] by, who [did] not know [Johnson] as well as [he did], and may [have been] apt to think him narrow-minded" (*Journal of a Tour*, 228). Mary Ann Hanway was scathing in her indictment of Johnson's *Journey*: "The event of his publication has confirmed his fear, as all who read that strange medley regret, that, a man, who has justly acquired great literary merit by his other publications, should so much fail in this—Pity for that fame, so dear to authors, he had not contented himself with *writing Ramblers*, instead of *taking a ramble*." *A Journey to the Highlands of Scotland*, 157, Hanway's emphases. Karen O'Brien adds that Johnson's *Journey* is equally contemptuous toward the "Lowland improvers and Scottish Enlightenment literati." Recognizing that the myth of Highland primitivism "underpins the Lowland construction of [English] historical identity[,] Johnson's text works against this mythologizing tendency in order to recreate" a more barren vision of Scotland in need of English cultural resuscitation. "Johnson's View of the Scottish Enlightenment in *A Journey to the Western Islands of Scotland*," 59, 64.

8. This moment in the *Journey*, and its equation between Johnson-as-traveler and his conception of oral history corresponds implicitly with Boswell's description of Johnson's "spirit of a highlander": "One night, in Col, [Johnson] strutted about the room with a broad-sword and target, and made a formidable appearance; and, another night, I took the liberty to put a large blue bonnet on his head. His age, his size, and his bushy grey wig, with this covering on it, presented the image of a venerable *senachi* [or bard]: and, however unfavourable to the Lowland Scots, he seemed much pleased to assume the appearance of an ancient Caledonian." Boswell, *Journal of a Tour*, 359–60. Ian Duncan relates this passage to Macpherson's *Ossian* in "The Pathos of Abstraction: Adam Smith, Ossian, and Samuel Johnson," 52.

9. For an overview of ocularcentrism in various permutations since the seventeenth century, see David Michael Levin, ed., *Modernity and the Hegemony of Vision*. Samuel Taylor Coleridge famously played up the ocularcentric emphasis in Johnson's work by parodying the first two lines of his *Vanity of Human Wishes* ("Let Observation, with extensive view, / Survey mankind, from China to Peru") as "Let observation with extensive observation observe mankind." *Coleridge's Miscellaneous Criticism*, 439.

10. See Thomas Jemielity, "Samuel Johnson, the Second Sight, and His Sources."

11. *A Description of the Western Islands of Scotland, Circa 1695*, 61, 65. Subsequent references will be cited in the text.

12. Edmund Burt, another early traveler through the Highlands, disapproved of what he took to be either Martin's gullibility or his overindulgence of the marvelous: "We had the other day, in our coffee-room, an auction of books, if such trash, and so small a number of them, may go by that name.

"One of them I purchased, which I do not remember to have ever heard of before, although it was published so long ago as the year 1703.

"It is a *Description of the Western Islands of Scotland*, and came extremely *à propos*, to prevent my saying anything further concerning them.

"I have nothing to object against the author's (Mr. Martin's) account of those isles, with respect to their situation, mountains, lakes, rivers, caves, etc. For I confess I was never in any one of them, though I have seen several of them from the mainland. But I must observe, that to furnish out his book with much of the wonderful (a quality necessary to all books of travels, and it would be happy if history were less tainted with it), he recounts a great variety of strange customs used by the natives (if ever in use) in days of yore, with many other wonders; among all which the second sight is the superlative." *Burt's Letters from the North of Scotland*, 273–74.

13. For a succinct compilation of accounts of and theories on second sight see Norman Macrae, ed., *Highland Second Sight*.

14. Johnson imagined the tacksmen as mediative agents between the educated and the ignorant, the wealthy and the poor: "If the tacksmen be taken away, the Hebrides must in their present state be given up to grossness and ignorance; the tenant, for want of instruction, will be unskillful, and for want of admonition will be negligent" (96). Not every traveler held the tacksmen in such high esteem, however. The Reverend John Lane Buchanan, who lived on the Island of Harris from 1782 to 1790, made a number of scathing remarks about the tyranny perpetrated by the tacksmen: "[I]n the absence of the great proprietors, the power and influence of the laird is transferred to a few tacksmen, who, in some instances, of late, squeeze [the tenants] without mercy. . . . [These tenants] must approach

even the tacksmen with cringing humility, heartless and discouraged, with tattered rags, hungry bellies, and down-cast looks, carrying their own implements of husbandry for ten or twelve miles backward and forward, over hills and mountains, to do the work of their tacksmen." *Travels in the Western Hebrides, from 1782 to 1790* (1793), 21. Buchanan later draws a number of compelling comparisons between the condition of the poor tenants and the black slaves of the West Indies and United States, in which he claims that the Highlanders in most ways fare more poorly. For instance, "[t]he negroe works only from six o'clock in the morning to six in the evening; and out of that time he has two complete hours for rest and refreshment. The scallag [or peasant farmer] is at work from four o'clock in the morning to eight, nine, and sometimes ten in the evening." Moreover, "many a negroe, I am well assured, has been known to clear, besides many comforts for his own family, by the produce of his little property, from twenty to thirty, and even forty pounds a year so that there is a fair probability, that any negroe would soon be enabled to gain the price of his liberty, if he desired and deserved it. Of relief from bondage, and woe, the scallag has not a single ray of hope on this side of the grave" (86–87).

15. I am referring here to the famous volume edited by Eric Hobsbawm and Terence Ranger, and to Hugh Trevor-Roper's equally famous essay on Scottish kilts: "The Invention of Tradition: The Highland Tradition of Scotland."

16. In a modern analysis of spectrality, Jacques Derrida argues that ghosts efface "the border between the present . . . and everything that can be opposed to it: absence, non-presence . . . virtuality . . . and so forth." *Specters of Marx*, 39.

17. See "Marvelous Facts and Miraculous Evidence in Early Modern Europe," 243–74.

18. Christopher Flint relates how narratives and satires giving voice to gold coins, corkscrews, atoms, and other objects articulated the challenge of consolidating human and social identity (including epistemological identity, or the authority of knowledge) in a commercializing society inundated with new commodities. "Speaking Objects: The Circulation of Stories in Eighteenth-Century Prose Fiction."

19. "Sermon 25," 261–62. I thank Howard Weinbrot for reminding me of these sermons and their relevance to this chapter.

20. For a detailed account of the ghost in Cock Lane, see E. J. Clery, *The Rise of Supernatural Fiction*, 13–17.

21. "The Art of *Mémoires*," in *Mémoires for Paul de Man*, 64–65.

22. *A Treatise of Human Nature*, 231. Subsequent references will be cited in the text.

23. Hume later reiterated this position in his essay "Of Miracles," in which he first disqualified testimony as a valid source for the belief in miracles before averring at the conclusion of his essay that the greatest, most indisputable miracle of all is that we go on believing in them, and in the testimonies that assert them. James Chandler comments here that "Hume's tone is notoriously labile, and the irony of the passage especially cuts both ways; enthusiastic self-deception figures here as a kind of second order miracle, the continued miracle in one's own person of one's susceptibility to believe miracles. . . . [T]his credulity seems more than a matter of interest to [Hume]; it seems to inspire Hume's own reluctant sense of wonder." "Proving a History of Evidence," 279. As in the *Treatise*, then, a testimonial position is reconfirmed after having been demonstrably shown to be inadequate to the exigencies of reason and evidence.

24. *The Vision Machine*, 70. Subsequent references will be cited in the text.

25. Roland Barthes appeals to second sight in a similar manner, likening it to what he calls the *punctum* in photography, the supplement decomposing the intended effects of certain images. "The Photographer's 'second sight' does not consist in 'seeing' but in being there." *Camera Lucida*, 47.

26. Ten years prior to his voyage into Scotland, Johnson had confessed to Boswell that "Every thing which Hume has advanced against Christianity," meaning Hume's arguments against miracles on the same probabilistic grounds outlined in his *Treatise*, "had passed through [Johnson's own] mind long before [Hume] wrote." Johnson, however, professed to have rejected such ideas. Boswell, *Life of Johnson*, 314. For more on the intellectual compatibility between Johnson and Hume, see Adam Potkay, *The Passion for Happiness: Samuel Johnson and David Hume*, esp. the Introduction. Potkay discusses Johnson's *Journey* in relation to Hume on 31–37.

27. In essence, Johnson's forceful argument devolves to the status of testimonial anecdote—a move which infoms not only Johnson's prose but also Johnsonian studies. See esp. Helen Deutsch, *Loving Dr. Johnson*, esp. 1–70.

28. *A Tour in Scotland and Voyage to the Hebrides, 1772*, 280. Subsequent references will be cited in the text.

29. Elizabeth Bray summarizes the significance of Pennant's vision in the context of Highland improvement in this way: "Pennant, through the mouth of his dream figure, attacks the rapacious exploitation of the Highlands and Islands by anglicized lairds, who drained their estates dry in order to match the lifestyle of their models, the English aristocracy. The tragedy was that the wealth of the English landowner was sustained by advances in agriculture; in the Islands no such advances had been made. And when they came, they took the form of the clearances, with the burning of houses, and the introduction of sheep." *The Discovery of the Hebrides: Voyages to the Western Isles, 1745–1883*, 87.

30. Quoted in Dugald Mitchell, ed. *The Book of Highland Verse*, 132–34.

31. Scholars of oral history devote considerable attention to the strictures of genre as a means whereby speakers create horizons of expectation with their audiences. On this point, see Elizabeth Tonkin, *Narrating Our Pasts*, ch. 3. Derrida shows how the collective experience implied in what he calls "the law of genre" ultimately accedes to a type of witness experience. See "The Law of Genre" and "Before the Law" in *Acts of Literature*.

32. The poem was intended for recital to a *ceilidh*-house audience. Scholarship on *ceilidh*-houses is abundant, but somewhat diffuse. For a fairly concentrated discussion of their role as communal places of storytelling and entertainment in Gaelic-speaking communities, see Michael Newton, *A Handbook of the Scottish Gaelic World*, 101–5.

33. "Faith and Knowledge: The Two Sources of 'Religion' at the Limits of Reason Alone," 56.

34. Ronald Black notes how the *ceilidh* became "the power-house of eighteenth-century Gaelic culture" after the "virtual collapse of chiefly patronage after 1715. . . . In twentieth-century terms, the *ceilidh* was school and university, CD and video, council chamber and concert hall, cinema and newspaper, night-class and parliament, radio and television, internet and technical college. . . ." "Introduction," xii.

35. See John MacInnes, "The Panegyric Code in Gaelic Poetry and its Historical Background."

36. *An Lasair*, xix.

37. "Praise of Ben Dobhrain," in MacLeod, ed. *The Songs of Duncan Ban Macintyre*, 211, ll. 3034–41.

38. See Smith's introductory essay in his *Ben Dorain*.

39. "Mourning and Melancholia," 154.

40. *Mémoires for Paul de Man*, 49.

41. *Ben Dorain*, 6–7. Subsequent references will be cited in the text.

42. In Crichton Smith, *The Notebooks of Robinson Crusoe and Other Poems*, 34–35, ll. 3, 13–14, 19–22, 29–34.

43. In Crichton Smith, *The Black and the Red and Other Stories*, 61.

44. Elsewhere, Crichton Smith remarks that modernization is not necessarily "progress, it is the sick turning-back of progress itself. . . . It is against such a failure that one can set the idea of community," the kind of close-knit society exemplified for Crichton Smith in the Hebrides. "[W]ho would care to say that the islanders have turned their backs on a world that is viable and worth preserving?" "Real People in a Real Place," *Towards the Human*, 43.

45. Crichton Smith seemed engaged in a perpetual dialectic between the particularities of his sense of his native island Lewis and the more general pathos associated with the Highlands at large (and manifest in his most famous novel *Consider the Lilies*, which recounts the early nineteenth-century clearances in Sutherland, a northern Highland region on the mainland of Scotland). Crichton Smith addresses this motif in his work in "The Double Man," 136–46.

46. I discuss Virilio's concept of this "sensation" below; for a discussion of this phenomenon in terms of the slow motion effect, see Mark Hansen, "The Time of Affect, or Bearing Witness to Life."

47. *The Aesthetics of Disappearance*, 37, 76, 101, 104.

48. "Preface of 1800," 160.

Chapter 7. Highland Romance in Late Modernity

1. *The Laws of Cool: Knowledge Work and the Culture of Information*, 53. Subsequent references will be cited in the text.

2. *The Academic Postmodern and the Rule of Literature*, 22.

3. I refer here tacitly to Michael Hechter's pathbreaking study *Internal Colonialism*. See also the cluster of essays devoted to this theme by Sorensen, Matthew Wickman, Ian Duncan, and Charlotte Sussman in *Eighteenth-Century Fiction*.

4. For more on this subject in a high modern and postmodern context, see my essay "Terror's Abduction of Experience: A Gothic History."

5. Critics who refer to the autobiographical component of *To the Lighthouse* are too numerous to mention. The quotation is from *To the Lighthouse*, 24. Subsequent references are to this edition, and will be cited in the text.

6. See especially James M. Mellard, *Using Lacan, Reading Fiction*, 140–94.

7. "Revolution in Poetic Language," 95, 101.

8. On Woolf's shrewd negotiation of the modernist quest for lost origins, see Perry Meisel, *The Myth of the Modern*, esp. 1–10, 182–92.

9. See Meisel, *The Myth of the Modern*. Kristeva gestures toward this dynamic in her reference to Woolf as an image of the death which would accompany any attainment of lost plenitude, and hence cessation of the economy of desire and signification: "I think of Virginia Woolf, who sank wordlessly into the river, her pockets weighed down with stones. Haunted by voices, waves, lights, in love with colours-blue, green-and seized by a strange gaiety that would bring on . . . fits of strangled, screeching laughter. . . ." "About Chinese Women," 157.

10. "Time Passes: Virginia Woolf, Post-Impressionism, and Cambridge Time," 488; Woolf, "Modern Fiction," 107. Subsequent references to Woolf's essay will be designated MF and cited in the text.

11. Quoted in Banfield, "Time Passes," 484.

12. Ibid., 490–91.

13. Watson, *The Literature of Scotland*, 394; Burns, *A Celebration of the Light*, 81.

14. Wittig, *The Scottish Tradition in Literature*, 388; Gifford, *Neil M. Gunn and Lewis Grassic Gibbon*, 15.

15. *The Modern Scottish Novel*, 150.

16. *Celtic Identity and the British Image*, 75.

17. See MacDiarmid, "The Caledonian Antisyzygy and the Gaelic Idea," 70: "Hitler's 'Nazi's' wear their socialism with precisely the difference which post-socialist Scottish nationalists must adopt."

18. *The Atom of Delight*, 2–3.

19. *Morning Tide*, 14. Subsequent references will be cited in the text.

20. *The Modern Scottish Novel*, 71.

21. *Neil M. Gunn: A Highland Life*, 94.

22. "Neil Gunn's Drama of the Light," 4: 89.

23. *Highland River*, 17. Subsequent references will be cited in the text.

24. "Fishy Masculinities: Neil Gunn's *The Silver Darlings*," 56, 66.

25. "Scotland: A Nation," *Left Review*, 2:14 (1936), quoted in Price, "Whose History, Which Novel? Neil M. Gunn and the Gaelic Idea," 97.

26. Recently, "The List: Glasgow and Edinburgh Events Guide" proclaimed *To the Lighthouse* one of the 100 best "Scottish" books of all time. Katie Gould, who wrote up this particular entry, acknowledged that "Woolf is not a name immediately synonymous with Scottish writing." However, she reasoned, "as a depiction of a place passionately longed for, Woolf's novel resounds with the echoes of the Hebridean landscape." Maley, ed. *One Hundred Best Scottish Books of All Time*, 57.

27. *Rewriting Scotland: Welsh, McLean, Warner, Banks, Galloway, and Kennedy*, 66.

28. *Morvern Callar*, 1–3. Subsequent references will be cited in the text.

29. "Contemporary Fiction I: Tradition and Continuity," 601.

30. Ibid., 602.

31. See for instance David Leishman, "Breaking Up the Language? Signs and Names in Alan Warner's Scotland"; John LeBlanc, "Return of the Goddess: Contemporary Music and Celtic Mythology in Alan Warner's *Morvern Callar*"; and Catherine Claire Thomson, "'Slainte, I goes, and He Says His Word': Morvern Callar Undergoes the Trial of the Foreign."

32. See "The 'Becoming-Woman'—Femininity and the Rave Generation in Alan Warner's *Morvern Callar*."

33. Quoted in March, *Rewriting Scotland*, 75.

34. March, *Rewriting Scotland*, 65, 66.

35. "Existential Ecstasy," *Spike Magazine* 2001 (www.spikemagazine.com/0300alanwarner.php).

36. *The Glass House*, 3. Subsequent references will be cited in the text.

37. *Clearances*, 45. Subsequent references will be cited in the text.

Bibliography

Adorno, Theodor. "Cultural Criticism and Society." Translated by Samuel and Shierry Weber. In *Prisms*. Cambridge, Mass.: MIT Press, 1967.

———. *Minima Moralia*. Translated by E. F. N. Jephcott. New York: Verso, 1978.

———. "A Portrait of Walter Benjamin." Translated by Samuel and Shierry Weber. In *Prisms*. Cambridge, Mass.: MIT Press, 1967.

———. "On Epic Naïveté." Translated by Shierry Weber Nicholsen. In *Notes to Literature*, edited by Rolf Tiedemann. New York: Columbia University Press, 1991.

———. *Negative Dialectics*. Translated by E. B. Ashton. New York: Continuum, 1992.

Agamben, Giorgio. *Remnants of Auschwitz: The Witness and the Archive*. Translated by Daniel Heller-Roazen. New York: Zone Books, 1999.

Anderson, Benedict. *Imagined Communities: Reflections on the Origin and Spread of Nationalism*. London and New York: Verso, 1991.

Anderson, John. *Essay on the State of Society and Knowledge in the Highlands of Scotland*. Edinburgh: William Tait, 1827.

Anderson, James. *Observations on the Means of Exciting a Spirit of National Industry, Chiefly Intended to Promote the Agriculture, Commerce, Manufactures and Fisheries of Scotland*. New York: Augustus M. Kelly, 1968.

———. *The True Interest of Great Britain Considered: Or a Proposal for Establishing the Northern British Fisheries*. London? Publisher unnamed, 1783.

Anderson, Perry. *The Origins of Postmodernity*. London and New York: Verso, 1998.

Anderson, Terence, and William Twining. *Analysis of Evidence: How To Do Things with Facts Based on Wigmore's Science of Judicial Proof*. Boston: Little, Brown, and Company, 1991.

Andrews, Malcolm. *The Search for the Picturesque*. Stanford: Stanford University Press, 1989.

Arnot, Hugo. *A Collection and Abridgement of Celebrated Criminal Trials in Scotland, from A.D. 1538, to 1784*. Edinburgh: William Smellie, 1785.

Bacon, Francis. *Novum Organum*. Translated by Peter Urbach and John Gibson. Chicago: Open Court, 1994.

Banfield, Ann. "Time Passes: Virginia Woolf, Post-Impressionism, and Cambridge Time." *Poetics Today* 24 (2003): 471–516.

Barrell, John. *English Literature in History, 1730–80: An Equal, Wide Survey*. London: Hutchinson, 1983.

————. "Fire, Famine and Slaughter." *Huntington Library Quarterly* 63 (2000): 276–98.

Barthes, Roland. *Camera Lucida: Reflections on Photography.* Translated by Richard Howard. New York: Hill and Wang, 1981.

Baudrillard, Jean. *The Mirror of Production.* Translated by Mark Poster. St. Louis: Telos, 1975.

Beattie, J. M. *Crime and the Courts in England 1660–1800.* Princeton: Princeton University Press, 1986.

Beiderwell, Bruce. *Power and Punishment in Scott's Novels.* Athens: University of Georgia Press, 1992.

Bender, John. *Imagining the Penitentiary: Fiction and the Architecture of Mind in Eighteenth-Century England.* Chicago: University of Chicago Press, 1987.

————. "Enlightenment Fiction and the Scientific Hypothesis." *Representations* 61 (1998): 6–28.

Benjamin, Walter. "Theses on the Philosophy of History." Translated by Harry Zohn. In *Illuminations,* edited by Hannah Arendt. New York: Schocken, 1968.

————. "The Work of Art in the Age of Mechanical Reproduction." Translated by Harry Zohn. In *Illuminations,* edited by Hannah Arendt. New York: Schocken, 1968.

————. "Experience and Poverty." Translated by Rodney Livingstone. In *Walter Benjamin: Selected Writings,* edited by Marcus Bullock and Michael W. Jennings. 4 vols. Cambridge, Mass.: Belknap Press, 1996.

————. "The Handkerchief." Translated by Rodney Livingstone. In *Walter Benjamin: Selected Writings,* edited by Marcus Bullock and Michael W. Jennings. 4 vols. Cambridge, Mass.: Belknap Press, 1996.

————. "Little Tricks of the Trade." Translated by Rodney Livingstone. In *Walter Benjamin: Selected Writings,* edited by Marcus Bullock and Michael W. Jennings. 4 vols. Cambridge, Mass.: Belknap Press, 1996.

————. "Paris, the Capital of the Nineteenth Century." Translated by Howard Eiland. In *Walter Benjamin: Selected Writings,* edited by Marcus Bullock and Michael W. Jennings. 4 vols. Cambridge, Mass.: Belknap Press, 1996.

————. "The Storyteller: Observations on the Work of Nikolai Leskov." Translated by Harry Zohn. In *Walter Benjamin: Selected Writings,* edited by Marcus Bullock and Michael W. Jennings. 4 vols. Cambridge, Mass.: Belknap Press, 1996.

————. *Charles Baudelaire: A Lyric Poet in the Era of High Capitalism.* Translated by Harry Zohn. London and New York: Verso, 1997.

Bentham, Jeremy. *Rationale of Judicial Evidence, Specially Applied to English Practice.* 5 vols. London: Hunt and Clarke, 1827. Reprint, Littleton, Colo.: F. B. Roshman, 1995.

Berger, John. *Ways of Seeing.* London: Penguin, 1972.

Bernard-Donals, Michael. "Beyond the Question of Authenticity: Witness and Testimony in the *Fragments* Controversy." *PMLA* 116 (2001): 1302–15.

Black, Ronald. "Introduction." In *An Lasair: Anthology of Eighteenth-Century Scottish Gaelic Verse,* edited by Ronald Black. Edinburgh: Birlinn, 2001.

Blair, Hugh. *Lectures on Rhetoric and Belles Lettres.* Delmar, N.Y.: Scholars' Facsimiles and Reprints, 1993. Original edition, 1783.

————. "A Critical Dissertation on the Poems of Ossian." In James Macpherson, *The Poems of Ossian and Related Works.*

Blumenberg, Hans. "Light as a Metaphor for Truth: At the Preliminary Stage of Philosophical Concept Foundation." In *Modernity and the Hegemony of Vision,* edited by David Michael Levin. Berkeley: University of California Press, 1993.

Boswell, James. *Life of Johnson*. Edited by R. W. Chapman. Oxford and New York: Oxford University Press, 1980.

———. *The Journal of a Tour to the Hebrides*. Edited by Peter Levi. London and New York: Penguin, 1984.

Bourdieu, Pierre. "The Field of Cultural Production, or: The Economic World Reversed." *Poetics* 12 (1983): 311–56.

———. "The Market of Symbolic Goods." *Poetics* 14 (1985): 13–44.

Bray, Elizabeth. *Discovery of the Hebrides: Voyages to the Western Isles, 1745–1833*. Edinburgh: Birlinn, 1996.

Brown, Bill. "Thing Theory." In *Things*, edited by Bill Brown. Chicago: University of Chicago Press, 2004.

Brown, Mary Ellen. "Old Singing Women and the Canons of Scottish Balladry and Song." In Gifford and McMillan, eds. *A History of Scottish Women's Writing*.

Buchan, David. *The Ballad and the Folk*. London: Routledge and K. Paul, 1972.

Buchanan, John Lane. *Travels in the Western Hebrides from 1782 to 1790*. Waternish, Isle of Skye: Maclean Press, 1997.

Buck-Morss, Susan. *The Dialectics of Seeing: Walter Benjamin and the Arcades Project*. Cambridge, Mass.: MIT Press, 1989.

Burns, John. *A Celebration of the Light: Zen in the Novels of Neil Gunn*. Totowa, N.J.: Barnes and Noble, 1988.

Buzard, James. "Translation and Tourism: Scott's *Waverly* and the Rendering of Culture." *The Yale Journal of Criticism* 8 (1995): 31–59.

Calder, Jenni, ed. *Stevenson and Victorian Scotland*. Edinburgh: Edinburgh University Press, 1981.

Callinicos, Alex. *Against Postmodernism*. Cambridge: Polity Press, 1989.

Carney, Seamus. *The Appin Murder: The Killing of the Red Fox*. Edinburgh: Birlinn, 1994.

Caygill, Howard. *Art of Judgement*. London and New York: Blackwell, 1989.

———. *Walter Benjamin: The Colour of Experience*. London and New York: Routledge, 1998.

Chakrabarty, Dipesh. *Provincializing Europe: Postcolonial Thought and Historical Difference*. Princeton: Princeton University Press, 2000.

Chandler, James. "Proving a History of Evidence." In Chandler, Davidson, and Harootunian, eds. *Questions of Evidence: Proof, Practice, and Persuasion across the Disciplines*.

———. *England in 1819: The Politics of Literary Culture and the Case of Romantic Historicism*. Chicago: University of Chicago Press, 1998.

Chandler, James, Arnold I. Davidson, and Harry Harootunian, eds. *Questions of Evidence: Proof, Practice, and Persuasion across the Disciplines*. Edited by James Chandler, Arnold I. Davidson and Harry Harootunian. Chicago: University of Chicago Press, 1994.

Charalambides, Ch. A., Markos V. Koutras, and N. Balakrishnan, eds. *Probability and Statistical Models with Applications*. Boca Raton, Fla.: Chapman and Hall, 2001.

Clark, T. J. "Modernism, Postmodernism, and Steam." *October* 100 (2002): 54–74.

Clery, E. J. *The Rise of Supernatural Fiction, 1762–1800*. Cambridge and New York: Cambridge University Press, 1995.

———. *The Feminization Debate in Eighteenth-Century England: Literature, Commerce and Luxury*. Basingstoke, Hampshire and New York: Palgrave, 2004.

Clyde, Robert. *From Rebel to Hero: The Image of the Highlander, 1745–1830*. East Lothian: Tuckwell, 1995.

Collins, William. "Ode to a Friend on His Return, &c." In *The Works of William Collins*, edited by Richard Wendorf and Charles Ryskamp. Oxford: Clarendon, 1979.

Cooke, Sophie. *The Glass House.* London: Arrow, 2005.

Copley, Stephen and Kathryn Sunderland, eds. *Adam Smith's Wealth of Nations: New Interdisciplinary Essays.* Manchester: Manchester University Press, 1998.

Court, Franklin E. *Institutionalizing English Literature: The Culture and Politics of Literary Study, 1750–1900.* Stanford: Stanford University Press, 1992.

Craig, Cairns. *The Modern Scottish Novel: Narrative and the National Imagination.* Edinburgh: Edinburgh University Press, 1999.

Crawford, Robert. *Devolving English Literature.* Oxford: Clarendon, 1992.

———, ed. *The Scottish Invention of English Literature.* Cambridge and New York: Cambridge University Press, 1998.

The Cruel Mother. In *The English and Scottish Popular Ballads*, edited by Francis James Child. Mineola, N.Y.: Dover, 1965.

Cutler, Edward S. *Recovering the New: Transatlantic Roots of Modernism.* Hanover, N.H.: University Press of New England, 2003.

Daiches, David. "Stevenson and Scotland." In *Stevenson and Victorian Scotland*, edited by Jenni Calder. Edinburgh: University of Edinburgh Press, 1981.

Daston, Lorraine. *Classical Probability in the Enlightenment.* Princeton: Princeton University Press, 1988.

———. "Baconian Facts, Academic Civility, and the Prehistory of Objectivity." *Annals of Scholarship* 8 (1991): 337–64.

———. "Marvelous Facts and Miraculous Evidence in Early Modern Europe." In Chandler, Davidson, and Harootunian, eds. *Questions of Evidence: Proof, Practice, and Persuasion across the Disciplines.*

Davie, Donald. "*Rob Roy.*" In *Walter Scott*, edited by D. D. Devlin. London: Macmillan, 1968.

Davis, Leith. *Acts of Union: Scotland and the Literary Negotiation of the British Nation, 1707–1830.* Stanford: Stanford University Press, 1998.

de Man, Paul. *Allegories of Reading: Figural Language in Rousseau, Nietzsche, Rilke, and Proust.* New Haven: Yale University Press, 1979.

Dear, Peter. *Discipline and Experience: The Mathematical Way in the Scientific Revolution.* Chicago: University of Chicago Press, 1995.

del Caro, Adrian. *Nietzsche Contra Nietzsche: Creativity and the Anti-Romantic.* Baton Rouge: Louisiana State University Press, 1989.

Derrida, Jacques. *Of Grammatology.* Translated by Gayatri Spivak. Baltimore: Johns Hopkins University Press, 1976.

———. *Mémoires for Paul de Man.* Translated by Jonathan Culler. New York: Columbia University Press, 1986.

———. *Acts of Literature.* Edited by Derek Attridge. New York: Routledge, 1992.

———. "Force of Law: The 'Mystical Foundations of Authority.'" Translated by Mary Quaintance. In *Deconstruction and the Possibility of Justice*, edited by Druscilla Cornell, Michel Rosenfield and David Gray Carlson. New York: Routledge, 1992.

———. *Specters of Marx: The State of the Debt, the Work of Mourning, and the New International.* Translated by Peggy Kamuf. New York: Routledge, 1994.

———. "Faith and Knowledge: The Two Sources of 'Religion' at the Limits of Reason Alone." Translated by Samuel Weber. In *Religion*, edited by Jacques Derrida and Gianni Vattimo. Stanford: Stanford University Press, 1996.

———. *Le Toucher: Jean-Luc Nancy.* Paris: Galilée, 2000.

Deutsch, Helen. *Loving Dr. Johnson*. Chicago: University of Chicago Press, 2005.

Devine, T. M. *Scottish Emigration and Scottish Society*. Edinburgh: John Donald, 1992.

———. *Clanship to Crofters' War: The Social Transformation of the Scottish Highlands*. Manchester: Manchester University Press, 1994.

Dodgshon, R.A. *Chiefs to Landlords: Social and Economic Change in the Western Highlands and Islands, c. 1493–1820*. Edinburgh: Edinburgh University Press, 1998.

Dreghorn, John Maclaurin, Lord. *Arguments and Decisions, in Remarkable Cases, before the High Court of Justiciary, and Other Supreme Courts, in Scotland*. Edinburgh: J. Bell, 1774.

Duncan, Ian. *Modern Romance and Transformations of the Novel: The Gothic, Scott, Dickens*. Cambridge and New York: Cambridge University Press, 1992.

———. "Adam Smith, Samuel Johnson, and the Institutions of English." In Crawford, ed. *The Scottish Invention of English Literature*.

———. "Introduction." In *Rob Roy*, edited by Ian Duncan. Oxford and New York: Oxford University Press, 1998. Original edition, 1817.

———. "The Pathos of Abstraction: Adam Smith, Ossian, and Samuel Johnson." In *Scotland and the Borders of Romanticism*, edited by Leith Davis, Ian Duncan, and Janet Sorenson. Cambridge and New York: Cambridge University Press, 2004.

Dwyer, John. "The Melancholy Savage: Text and Context in the Poems of Ossian." In Gaskill, ed. *Ossian Revisited*.

———. *The Age of Passions: An Interpretation of Adam Smith and Scottish Enlightenment Culture*. Phantassie, East Lothian: Tuckwell, 1998.

Eagleton, Terry. *Illusions of Postmodernism*. Cambridge, Mass.: Blackwell, 1996.

Ehrilch, J. W., ed. *Ehrilch's Blackstone*. San Carlos, Calif.: Nourse, 1959.

Elam, Diane. *Romancing the Postmodern*. London and New York: Routledge, 1992.

Ermarth, Michael. *Wilhelm Dilthey: The Critique of Historical Reason*. Chicago: University of Chicago Press, 1978.

Felman, Shoshana, and Dori Laub. *Testimony: Crises of Witnessing in Literature, Psychoanalysis, and History*. New York: Routledge, 1992.

Ferguson, William. *The Identity of the Scottish Nation: An Historic Quest*. Edinburgh: Edinburgh University Press, 1998.

Ferris, Ina. *The Achievement of Literary Authority: Gender, History, and the Waverley Novels*. Ithaca, N.Y.: Cornell University Press, 1991.

Fleischacker, Samuel. *On Adam Smith's Wealth of Nations*. Princeton: Princeton University Press, 2004.

Flint, Christopher. "Speaking Objects: The Circulation of Stories in Eighteenth-Century Prose Fiction." *PMLA* 113 (1998): 212–26.

Foucault, Michel. *The Order of Things: An Archaeology of the Human Sciences*. Translator unnamed. New York: Vintage, 1970.

———. "Truth and Power." In *The Foucault Reader*, edited by Paul Rabinow. New York: Pantheon, 1984.

Freud, Sigmund. "Mourning and Melancholia." Translation supervised by Joan Riviere. In *Collected Papers*. London: Hogarth Press, 1950.

———. *Moses and Monotheism*. Translated by Katherine Jones. New York: Vintage, 1955.

———. "The Uncanny." Translated by Alix Strachey. In *Studies in Parapsychology*, edited by Philip Rieff. New York: Macmillan, 1963.

Frye, Northrup. *Anatomy of Criticism: Four Essays*. Princeton: Princeton University Press, 1957.

Gadamer, Hans-Georg. *Truth and Method*. Translated by Joel Weinsheimer and Donald G. Marshall. New York: Continuum, 1998.

Gallagher, Catherine, and Stephen Greenblatt. *Practicing New Historicism*. Chicago: University of Chicago Press, 2000.

Gaskill, Howard, ed. *Ossian Revisited*. Edinburgh: Edinburgh University Press, 1991.

Giddens, Anthony. *Consequences of Modernity*. Stanford: Stanford University Press, 1989.

———. *Runaway World*. New York: Routledge, 2000.

Gifford, Douglas. "Stevenson and Scottish Fiction: The Importance of *The Master of Ballantrae*." In Calder, ed. *Stevenson and Victorian Scotland*.

———. *Neil M. Gunn and Lewis Grassic Gibbon*. Edinburgh: Oliver and Boyd, 1983.

———. "Contemporary Fiction I: Tradition and Continuity." In Gifford and McMillan, eds. *A History of Scottish Women's Writing*.

Gifford, Douglas and Dorothy McMillan, eds. *A History of Scottish Women's Writing*. Edinburgh: Edinburgh University Press, 1997.

Gilbert, Geoffrey. *The Law of Evidence: By a Late Learned Judge*. 2nd ed. London: Printed by Catherine Lintot, 1760.

Ginzburg, Carlo. *No Island Is an Island: Four Glances at English Literature in a World Perspective*. New York: Columbia University Press, 2000.

Girard, Rene. *Violence and the Sacred*. Translated by Patrick Gregory. Baltimore: Johns Hopkins University Press, 1977.

Golan, Tal. *Laws of Men and Laws of Nature: The History of Scientific Expert Testimony in England and America*. Cambridge, Mass.: Harvard University Press, 2004.

Gordon, Avery F. *Ghostly Matters: Haunting and the Sociological Imagination*. Minneapolis: University of Minnesota Press, 1997.

Gourevitch, Philip. "The Memory Thief." *The New Yorker*, June 14, 1999.

Gray, William. *Robert Louis Stevenson: A Literary Life*. Houndsmills, Basingstoke: Palgrave, 2004.

Greig, J. Y. T., ed. *The Letters of David Hume*. 2 vols. Oxford: Clarendon, 1932.

Guillory, John. *Cultural Capital: The Problem of Literary Canon Formation*. Chicago: University of Chicago Press, 1993.

Gunn, Neil Miller. *Morning Tide*. London: Souvenir Press, 1975.

———. *The Atom of Delight*. Edinburgh: Polygon, 1986.

———. *Highland River*. Edinburgh: Canongate, 1991.

Hacking, Ian. *The Emergence of Probability: A Philosophical Study of Early Ideas about Probability, Induction and Statistical Inference*. London and New York: Cambridge University Press, 1975.

Hamilton, Paul. *Metaromanticism: Aesthetics, Literature, Theory*. Chicago: University of Chicago Press, 2003.

Hammond, J. R. *A Robert Louis Stevenson Companion: A Guide to the Novels, Essays, and Short Stories*. London: Macmillan, 1984.

Hansen, Mark. "The Time of Affect, or Bearing Witness to Life." *Critical Inquiry* 30 (2004): 584–626.

Hanway, Mary Ann. *A Journey to the Highlands of Scotland*. London: Fielding and Walker, 1776.

Hart, Francis Russell. "Neil Gunn's Drama of the Light." In *The History of Scottish Literature*, edited by Cairns Craig. 4 vols. Aberdeen: Aberdeen University Press, 1987.

Hart, Francis Russell, and J. B. Pick. *Neil M. Gunn: A Highland Life*. London: John Murray, 1981.

Harvey, David. *Condition of Postmodernity.* Oxford and New York: Blackwell, 1989.

Harvie, Christopher. *Scotland and Nationalism: Scottish Society and Politics 1707 to the Present.* 3rd ed. London and New York: Routledge, 1998.

Hawkins, William. *A Summary of the Crown-Law, by way of Abidgment of Serjeant Hawkins's Pleas of the Crown.* London: E. and R. Nutt, and R. Gosling, 1728.

Hawles, Sir John. *The English-Man's Right; a Dialogue between a Barrister at Law, and a Jury-Man.* London: Printed for L. Curtis, 1680.

Hechter, Michael. *Internal Colonialism: The Celtic Fringe in British National Development, 1536–1966.* Berkeley: University of California Press, 1975.

Heidegger, Martin. "The Question Concerning Technology." Translated by William Lovitt. In *Basic Writings,* edited by David Farrell Krell. San Francisco: Harper, 1977.

Henson, Eithne. "Johnson's Quest for 'The Fictions of Romantic Chivalry' in Scotland." *Prose Studies* 7 (1984): 97–128.

Herder, Gottfried von. *"Auszug aus einem Briefwechsel uber Ossian und die Lieder alter Bolter."* In *Von Deutscher Art und Kunst,* edited by Heinz Kindermann. Darmstadt: Wissenschaftliche Buchgesellschaft, 1968.

Home, Henry, Lord Kames. *Sketches of the History of Man.* 2nd ed. 4 vols. Edinburgh: W. Creech, 1778.

Hont, Istvan, and Michael Ignatieff. "Needs and Justice in *The Wealth of Nations*: An Introductory Essay." In *Wealth and Virtue: The Shaping of the Political Economy in the Scottish Enlightenment,* edited by Istvan Hont and Michael Ignatieff. Cambridge and New York: Cambridge University Press, 1983.

Horkheimer, Max, and Theodor Adorno. *Dialectic of Enlightenment.* Translated by John Cumming. New York: Continuum, 1994.

Howard, William. "The Symbolic Structure of *Rob Roy.*" *Studies in Scottish Literature* 14 (1979): 72–89.

Hume, David. *A Treatise of Human Nature.* Edited by E. C. Mossner. London and New York: Penguin, 1984.

———. *Dialogues Concerning Natural Religion.* Edited by Richard H. Popkin. Indianapolis: Hackett, 1998.

Hume, David. *Commentaries on the Laws of Scotland Respecting Crimes.* 2 vols. Edinburgh: The Law Society of Scotland, 1986.

Innes, Thomas. *A Critical Essay on the Ancient Inhabitants of Britain, or Scotland.* London: Printed for W. Innes, 1729.

Jacobus, Mary. *Psychoanalysis and the Scene of Reading.* New York: Oxford University Press, 1999.

Jameson, Frederic. *The Prison-House of Language: A Critical Account of Structuralism and Russian Formalism.* Princeton, N.J.: Princeton University Press, 1972.

——— . *The Political Unconscious: Narrative as a Socially Symbolic Act.* Ithaca, N.Y.: Cornell University Press, 1981.

———. *Postmodernism, or, The Cultural Logic of Late Capitalism.* Durham: Duke University Press, 1991.

Jay, Martin. *Cultural Semantics: Keywords of Our Time.* Amherst: University of Massachusetts Press, 1998.

———. "Is Experience Still in Crisis? Reflections on a Frankfurt School Lament." *Kriterion* 100 (1999): 9–25.

———. "Roland Barthes and the Tricks of Experience." *The Yale Journal of Criticism* 14 (2001): 469–76.

———. *Songs of Experience: Modern American and European Variations on a Universal Theme.* Berkeley: University of California Press, 2005.

Jemielity, Thomas. "Samuel Johnson, the Second Sight, and His Sources." *SEL: Studies in English Literature, 1500–1900* 14 (1974): 403–20.

Johnson, Samuel. "Sermon 25." In *Samuel Johnson: Sermons*, edited by Jean Hagstrum and James Gray. *The Yale Edition of the Works of Samuel Johnson*. 15 vols. New Haven: Yale University Press, 1978.

———. *A Journey to the Western Islands of Scotland.* Edited by Peter Levi. London and New York: Penguin, 1984.

Jones, Carole. "The 'Becoming-Woman'—Femininity and the Rave Generation in Alan Warner's *Morvern Callar*." *Scottish Studies Review* 5 (2004): 56–68.

Keynes, J. M. *Treatise on Probability.* London: Macmillan, 1921.

Kidd, Colin. *British Identities Before Nationalism: Ethnicity and Nationhood in the Atlantic World, 1600–1800.* Cambridge and New York: Cambridge University Press, 1999.

Kiely, Robert. *Robert Louis Stevenson and the Fiction of Adventure.* Cambridge, Mass.: Harvard University Press, 1964.

King, P. J. R. "'Illiterate Plebeians, Easily Misled': Jury Composition, Experience, and Behavior in Essex, 1735–1815." In *Twelve Good Men and True: The Criminal Trial Jury in England, 1200–1800*, edited by J. S. Cockburn and Thomas A. Green. Princeton: Princeton University Press, 1988.

Knox, John. *A View of the British Empire, More Especially Scotland; with Some Proposals for the Improvement of that Country, the Extension of its Fisheries, and the Relief of the People.* London: Printed for J. Walter, J. Sewell, and W. Gordon, 1784.

Koselleck, Reinhart. *Futures Past: On the Semantics of Historical Time.* Translated by Keith Tribe. Cambridge, Mass.: MIT Press, 1985.

Kristeva, Julia. "About Chinese Women." Translated by Séan Hand. In *The Kristeva Reader*, edited by Toril Moi. New York: Columbia University Press, 1986.

———. "Revolution in Poetic Language." Translated by Margaret Waller. In *The Kristeva Reader*, edited by Toril Moi. New York: Columbia University Press, 1986.

LaCapra, Dominick. *Writing History, Writing Trauma.* Baltimore: Johns Hopkins University Press, 2001.

Lacoue-Labarthe, Philippe. *Poetry as Experience.* Translated by Andrea Tarnowski. Stanford: Stanford University Press, 1999.

Laing, Malcolm. *The History of Scotland from the Union of the Crowns on the Accession of James VI to the Throne of England, to the Union of the Kingdoms in the Reign of Queen Anne.* 2 vols. Edinburgh: Manners and Miller, 1800.

Landsman, Stephan. "From Gilbert to Bentham: The Reconceptualization of Evidence Theory." *The Wayne Law Review* 36 (1990): 1149–86.

———. "The Rise of the Contentious Spirit: Adversary Procedure in Eighteenth-Century England." *Cornell Law Review* 75 (1990): 497–609.

Lang, Berel. *Act and Idea in the Nazi Genocide.* Chicago: University of Chicago Press, 1990.

Langbein, John H. "The Criminal Trial before the Lawyers." *University of Chicago Law Review* 45 (1978): 263–316.

———. "Shaping the Eighteenth-Century Criminal Trial: A View from the Ryder Sources." *University of Chicago Law Review* 50: (1983): 1–136.

———. "Historical Foundations of the Law of Evidence: A View from the Ryder Sources." *Columbia Law Review* 96 (1996): 1168–202.

LeBlanc, John. "Return of the Goddess: Contemporary Music and Celtic Mythology in Alan Warner's *Morvern Callar*." *Revista Canaria de Estudios Ingleses* 41 (2000): 145–54.

Leishman, David. "Breaking Up the Language? Signs and Names in Alan Warner's Scotland." *Études Écossaises* 8 (2002): 113–29.

Lenman, Bruce. *Integration, Enlightenment and Industrialization: Scotland 1746–1832.* London: Edward Arnold, 1981.

Levin, David Michael. *Modernity and the Hegemony of Vision.* Berkeley: University of California Press, 1993.

Leys, Ruth. *Trauma: A Genealogy.* Baltimore: Johns Hopkins University Press, 2000.

Lincoln, Andrew. "Scott and Empire: The Case of *Rob Roy.*" *Studies in the Novel* 34 (2002): 43–59.

Liu, Alan. *The Laws of Cool: Knowledge Work and the Culture of Information.* Chicago: University of Chicago Press, 2004.

Locke, John. *An Essay Concerning Human Understanding.* Edited by Peter H. Nidditch. Oxford: Clarendon, 1975.

Lonitz, Henri, ed. *Theodor Adorno and Walter Benjamin: The Complete Correspondence, 1928–1940.* Cambridge, Mass.: Harvard University Press, 1999.

Lukàcs, Georg. "Scott and the Classical Form of the Historical Novel." Translated by H. Mitchell and S. Mitchell. In *Scott's Mind and Art,* edited by A. Norman Jeffares. New York: Barnes and Noble, 1970.

Lyotard, Jean Francois. *The Differend: Phrases in Dispute.* Translated by Georges Van Den Abbeele. Minneapolis: University of Minnesota Press, 1988.

MacDiarmid, Hugh. "The Caledonian Antisyzygy and the Gaelic Idea." In *Selected Essays of Hugh MacDiarmid,* edited by Duncan Glen. Berkeley: University of California Press, 1970.

MacInnes, John. "The Panegyric Code in Gaelic Poetry and its Historical Background." *Transactions of the Gaelic Society of Inverness* 50 (1976–78): 435–98.

Mackay, David N., ed. *Trial of James Stewart (The Appin Murder).* London: Sweet and Maxwell, 1907.

Mackenzie, Alexander. *The History of the Highland Clearances.* Edinburgh: Mercat, 1991.

Mackenzie, Sir George. *The Laws and Customs of Scotland in Matters Criminal.* Edinburgh: George Swintoun., 1678.

MacLeod, Angus, ed. *The Songs of Duncan Bàn Macintyre.* Translated by Angus MacLeod. Edinburgh: Scottish Gaelic Texts Society, 1952.

Macpherson, John. *Critical Dissertations on the Origin, Antiquities, Language, Government, Manners, and Religion, of the Ancient Caledonians, their Posterity the Picts, and the British and Irish Scots.* London: T. Beckett, 1768.

Macpherson, James. "A Dissertation Concerning the Aera of Ossian." In *The Poems of Ossian.* Boston: Phillips, Sampson, and Co, 1851.

———. *The Poems of Ossian and Related Works.* Edited by Howard Gaskill. Edinburgh: Edinburgh University Press, 1996.

Macrae, Norman, ed. *Highland Second Sight, with Prophecies of Coinneach Odhar and the Seer of Petty, and Numerous Other Examples from the Writings of Aubrey, Martin, Theophilus Insulanus, the Rev. John Fraser, Dean of Argyle and the Isles, Rev. Dr. Kennedy of Dingwall, and Others.* Dingwall, UK: Souter, 1909.

Maechler, Stefan. *The Wilkomirski Affair: A Study in Biographical Truth.* Translated by John E. Woods. New York: Schocken, 2001.

Makdisi, Saree. *Romantic Imperialism: Universal Empire and the Culture of Modernity.* Cambridge and New York: Cambridge University Press, 1998.

Maley, Willy, ed. *One Hundred Best Scottish Books of All Time.* Edinburgh: The List, 2005.

March, Cristie L. *Rewriting Scotland: Welsh, McLean, Warner, Banks, Galloway, and Kennedy.* Manchester: Manchester University Press, 2002.

Martin, Martin. *A Description of the Western Islands of Scotland, Circa 1695.* Edited by Donald J. Macleod. Edinburgh: Birlinn, 1994.

Marx, Karl. *Capital: A Critique of Political Economy, Volume One.* Translated by Ben Fowkes. 3 vols. London and New York: Penguin, 1990.

Marx, Karl, and Friedrich Engels. *The German Ideology: Part One.* New York: International Publishers, 1993.

McCarthy, William Bernard. *The Ballad Matrix: Personality, Milieu, and the Oral Tradition.* Bloomington: Indiana University Press, 1990.

McCrone, David. *Understanding Scotland: The Sociology of a Stateless Nation.* London and New York: Routledge, 1992.

McGann, Jerome. "Walter Scott's Romantic Postmodernity." In *Scotland and the Borders of Romanticism,* edited by Leith Davis, Ian Duncan, and Janet Sorenson. Cambridge and New York: Cambridge University Press, 2004.

McKay, Margaret M., ed. *The Rev. Dr. John Walker's Report on the Hebrides of 1764 and 1771.* Edinburgh: John Donald, 1980.

McKeon, Michael. *The Origins of the English Novel, 1600–1740.* Baltimore: Johns Hopkins University Press, 1987.

McLynn, Frank. *Robert Louis Stevenson: A Biography.* New York: Random House, 1993.

Meek, Donald E. "The Gaelic Ballads of Scotland: Creativity and Adaptation." In Gaskill, ed. *Ossian Revisited.*

Meek, Ronald L. "Adam Smith and the Classical Concept of Profit." In Meek, *Economics and Ideology and Other Essays: Studies in the Development of Economic Thought.* London: Chapman and Hall, 1967.

———. "The Rehabilitation of Sir James Steuart." In Meek, *Economics and Ideology and Other Essays: Studies in the Development of Economic Thought.* London: Chapman and Hall, 1967.

Meisel, Perry. *The Myth of the Modern: A Study in British Literature and Criticism after 1850.* New Haven: Yale University Press, 1987.

Mellard, James M. *Using Lacan, Reading Fiction.* Urbana: University of Illinois Press, 1991.

Millgate, Jane. "*Rob Roy* and the Limits of Frankness." *Nineteenth-Century Fiction* 34 (1980): 379–96.

———. *Walter Scott: The Making of the Novelist.* Toronto: University of Toronto Press, 1984.

Mitchell, Dugald, ed. *The Book of Highland Verse.* New York: AMS, 1976.

Morano, Anthony A. "A Re-examination of the Development of the Reasonable Doubt Rule." *Boston University Law Review* 55 (1975): 507–28.

Moretti, Franco. *Modern Epic: The World System from Goethe to Garcia Marquez.* London and New York: Verso, 1996.

Mufti, Aamir R. "Critical Secularism: A Reintroduction for Perilous Times." *boundary 2* 31 (2004): 1–9.

Nairn, Tom. *Faces of Nationalism: Janus Revisited.* London and New York: Verso, 1997.

Nelson, William. *The Law of Evidence: Wherein All the Cases that have yet been printed in any of our Law Books or Tryals, and that in any wise relate to Points of Evidence, are collected and methodically digested under their proper Heads.* London: Printed by Eliz. Nutt, and R. Gosling, 1717.

Newsom, Robert. *A Likely Story: Probability and Play in Fiction.* New Brunswick: Rutgers University Press, 1988.

Newton, Isaac. "The Method of Natural Philosophy." In *Newton's Philosophy of Nature*, edited by H. S. Thayer. New York: Hafner, 1974.

Newton, Michael. *A Handbook of the Scottish Gaelic World*. Portland: Four Courts Press, 2000.

Nietzsche, Friedrich. *On the Genealogy of Morals*. Translated by Walter Kaufmann. New York: Vintage, 1969.

Nussbaum, Felicity A. *Torrid Zones: Maternity, Sexuality, and Empire in Eighteenth-Century Englsh Narratives*. Baltimore: Johns Hopkins University Press, 1995.

———. *The Limits of the Human: Fictions of Anomaly, Race, and Gender in the Long Eighteenth Century*. Cambridge and New York: Cambridge University Press, 2003.

O'Brien, Karen. "Johnson's View of the Scottish Enlightenment in *A Journey to the Western Islands of Scotland*." *The Age of Johnson* 4 (1991): 59–82.

Ogden, C. K., ed. *Bentham's Theory of Fictions*. London: Kegan Paul, Trench, Trubner, 1932.

Oliver, Kelly. *Witnessing: Beyond Recognition*. Minneapolis: University of Minnesota Press, 2001.

O'Neal, John C. *The Authority of Experience: Sensationist Theory in the Enlightenment*. University Park: The Pennsylvania State University Press, 1996.

Parker, Noel. "Look No Hidden Hands: How Smith Understands Historical Progress and Societal Values." In Copley and Sunderland, eds. *Adam Smith's Wealth of Nations: New Interdisciplinary Essays*.

Patey, Douglas Lane. *Probability and Literary Form: Philosophic Theory and Literary Practice in the Augustan Age*. Cambridge and New York: Cambridge University Press, 1984.

Pecora, Vincent P. *Self and Form in Modern Narrative*. Baltimore: Johns Hopkins University Press, 1989.

Pennant, Thomas. *A Tour in Scotland and Voyage to the Hebrides, 1772*. Edited by Andrew Simmons. Edinburgh: Birlinn, 1998.

Philip, Neil, ed. *The Penguin Book of Scottish Folktales*. London and New York: Penguin, 1995.

Pittock, Murray G. H. *The Invention of Scotland: The Stuart Myth and the Scottish Identity, 1638 to the Present*. London and New York: Routledge, 1991.

———. *The Myth of the Jacobite Clans*. Edinburgh: Edinburgh University Press, 1995.

———. *Celtic Identity and the British Image*. Manchester: Manchester University Press, 1999.

Poovey, Mary. *A History of Modern Fact: Problems of Knowledge in the Sciences of Wealth and Society*. Chicago: University of Chicago Press, 1998.

Popper, Karl. *The Logic of Scientific Discovery*. Translation assisted by Julius Freed and Lan Freed. New York: Routledge, 1959.

Potkay, Adam. *The Passion for Happiness: Samuel Johnson and David Hume*. Ithaca, N.Y.: Cornell University Press, 2000.

Price, Richard. "Whose History, Which Novel? Neil M. Gunn and the Gaelic Idea." *Scottish Literary Journal* 24 (1997): 85–102.

Radcliffe, David Hill. "Ossian and the Genres of Culture." *Studies in Romanticism* 31 (1992): 213–32.

Rajan, Tilottama. *Deconstruction and the Remainders of Phenomenology: Sartre, Derrida, Foucault, Baudrillard*. Stanford: Stanford University Press, 2002.

Raynor, David. "Ossian and Hume." In Gaskill, ed. *Ossian Revisited*.

Raysor, Thomas Middleton, ed. *Coleridge's Miscellaneous Criticism*. Folcroft, Pa.: Folcroft Press, 1936.

Riach, Alan. *Clearances.* Christchurch, New Zealand: Hazard Press, 2001.

Richards, Eric. *A History of the Highland Clearances: Agrarian Transformation and the Evictions 1746-1886.* 2 vols. London and Canberra: Croon Helm, 1982–85.

———. *The Highland Clearances: People, Landlords, and Rural Turmoil.* Edinburgh: Birlinn, 2000.

Roughead, William, ed. *The Trial of Mary Blandy.* Edinburgh and London: William Hodge, 1914.

Sandison, Alan. *Realpolitik. Robert Louis Stevenson and the Appearance of Modernism: A Future Feeling.* London: Macmillan, 2004.

Schaffer, Simon. "Self Evidence." In Chandler, Davidson, and Harootunian, eds. *Questions of Evidence: Proof, Practice, and Persuasion across the Disciplines.*

Scott, Joan. "The Evidence of Experience." In Chandler, Davidson, and Harootunian, eds. *Questions of Evidence: Proof, Practice, and Persuasion across the Disciplines.*

Scott, Walter. "Romance." In *Miscellaneous Prose Works of Sir Walter Scott.* Edinburgh: Robert Caddell, 1850.

———. *Waverley; or, 'Tis Sixty Years Since.* Edited by Claire Lamont. Oxford and New York: Oxford University Press, 1986.

———. *Rob Roy.* Edited by Ian Duncan. Oxford and New York: Oxford University Press, 1998.

Seltzer, Mark. "Wound Culture: Trauma in the Pathological Public Sphere." *October* 80 (1997): 3–26.

Shapin, Steven. *A Social History of Truth: Civility and Science in Seventeenth-Century England.* Chicago: University of Chicago Press, 1995.

Shapin, Steven, and Simon Schaffer. *Leviathan and the Air-Pump: Hobbes, Boyle, and the Experimental Life.* Princeton: Princeton University Press, 1985.

Shapiro, Barbara J. *Probability and Certainty in Seventeenth-Century England: A Study of the Relationships between Natural Science, Religion, History, Law, and Literature.* Princeton: Princeton University Press, 1983.

———. *"Beyond Reasonable Doubt" and "Probable Cause": Historical Perspectives on the Anglo-American Law of Evidence.* Berkeley: University of California Press, 1991.

———. *A Culture of Fact: England, 1550–1720.* Ithaca, N.Y.: Cornell University Press, 2000.

———. "Classical Rhetoric and the English Law of Evidence." In *Rhetoric and Law in Early Modern Europe,* edited by Victoria Kahn and Lorna Hutson. New Haven: Yale University Press, 2001.

Shaw, William. *An Enquiry into the Authenticity of the Poems Ascribed to Ossian.* 2nd ed. London: Printed for J. Murray, 1782.

Sherman, Stuart. *Telling Time: Clocks, Diaries, and English Diurnal Form, 1660-1785.* Chicago: University of Chicago Press, 1996.

Shusterman, Richard. "The End of Aesthetic Experience." *The Journal of Aesthetics and Art Criticism* 55 (1997): 29–41.

Simmons, Andrew, ed. *Burt's Letters from the North of Scotland.* Edinburgh: Birlinn, 1998.

Simpson, David. *The Academic Postmodern and the Rule of Literature: A Report on Half-Knowledge.* Chicago: University of Chicago Press, 1995.

Sinclair, John. *General View of the Agriculture of the Northern Counties and Islands of Scotland.* London: Printed by Colin Macrae, 1795.

Siskin, Clifford. *The Work of Writing: Literature and Social Change in Britain, 1700-1830.* Baltimore: Johns Hopkins University Press, 1998.

Skinner, Andrew S. "Sir James Stewart: 'Economic Theory and Policy.'" In *Philosophy and Science in the Scottish Enlightenment*, edited by Peter Jones. Edinburgh: John Donald, 1988.

Smith, Adam. "The Principles which Lead and Direct Philosophical Enquiries; Illustrated by the History of Astronomy." In *Adam Smith: Essays on Philosophical Subjects*, edited by W. P. D. Wightman and J. C. Bryce. Oxford: Clarendon, 1980.

———. *The Theory of Moral Sentiments.* Edited by D. D. Raphael and A. L. Macfie. Indianapolis: Liberty Classics, 1982. Original edition, Oxford University Press, 1976.

———. *Lectures on Rhetoric and Belles Lettres.* Edited by J. C. Bryce. Indianapolis: Liberty Fund, 1985. Original edition, Oxford University Press, 1983.

———. *Inquiry into the Causes of the Wealth of Nations.* Amherst, N.Y.: Prometheus, 1991.

Smith, Iain Crichton. *The Black and the Red and Other Stories.* London: Victor Gollancz, 1973.

———. *The Notebooks of Robinson Crusoe and Other Poems.* London: Victor Gollancz, 1975.

———. *Towards the Human: Selected Essays.* Edinburgh: Macdonald Publishers, 1986.

———, ed. *Ben Dorain: Translated from the Gaelic of Duncan Ban Macintyre.* Newcastle, UK: Northern House, 1988.

———. "The Double Man." In *The Literature of Region and Nation*, edited by Ronald P. Draper. New York: St. Martin's, 1989.

Smith, John. *Gaelic Antiquities: Consisting of a History of the Druids, particularly those of Caledonia; A Dissertation on the Authenticity of the Poems of Ossian; and a Collection of Ancient Poems, Translated from the Galic of Ullin, Ossian, Orran, &c.* Edinburgh: Printed for T. Cadell, 1780.

Smollett, Tobias. *The Expedition of Humphry Clinker.* Edited by Angus Ross. London and New York: Penguin, 1985.

Sorensen, Janet. *The Grammar of Empire in Eighteenth-Century British Writing.* Cambridge: Cambridge University Press, 2000.

Sorensen, Janet, Matthew Wickman, Ian Duncan, and Charlotte Sussman. "Internal Colonialism and the Novel." *Eighteenth-Century Fiction* 15 (2002): 51–126.

Sprat, Thomas. *The History of the Royal Society.* London: Printed by T. R. for J. Martyn, 1667. Stafford, Fiona. *The Sublime Savage: A Study of James Macpherson and the Poems of Ossian.* Edinburgh: Edinburgh University Press, 1988.

Steuart, James. *Principles of Political Oeconomy.* London: A. Millar and T. Cadell, 1767.

Stevenson, Robert Louis. *Familiar Studies of Men and Books.* Edited by Robert Louis Stevenson. New York: Scribner, 1925.

———. *"Virginibus Puerisque" and Other Papers: Memories and Portraits.* New York: Standard Book Company, 1930.

———. *Kidnapped and Catriona.* Edited by Emma Letley. Oxford and New York: Oxford University Press, 1986.

Strickland, Stuart Walker. "The Ideology of Self-Knowledge and the Practice of Self-Experimentation." *Eighteenth-Century Studies* 31 (1998): 453–71.

Sunderland, Kathryn. "Adam Smith's Master Narrative: Women and *The Wealth of Nations.*" In Copley and Sunderland, eds. *Adam Smith's Wealth of Nations: New Interdisciplinary Essays.*

————. "Writings on Education and Conduct: Arguments for Female Improvement." In *Women and Literature in Britain, 1700–1800,* edited by Vivien Jones. Cambridge and New York: Cambridge University Press, 2000.

Swearingen, Roger G. *The Prose Writings of Robert Louis Stevenson: A Guide.* Hamden, Conn.: Archon Books, 1980.

Symonds, Deborah A. *Weep Not for Me: Women, Ballads, and Infanticide in Early Modern Scotland.* University Park: The Pennsylvania State University Press, 1997.

Thompson, E. P. *The Making of the English Working Class.* New York: Vintage, 1966.

Thomson, Catherine Claire. "'Slainte, I goes, and He Says His Word': Morvern Callar Undergoes the Trial of the Foreign." *Language and Literature* 13 (2004): 55–71.

Thomson, Derick. *The Gaelic Sources of Macpherson's "Ossian."* Folcroft, Pa.: Folcroft Press, 1969.

Tonkin, Elizabeth. *Narrating Our Pasts: The Social Construction of Oral History.* Cambridge and New York: Cambridge University Press, 1992.

Toynbee, Paget, and Leonard Whitley, eds. *Correspondence of Thomas Gray.* Oxford: Clarendon, 1935.

Trevor-Roper, Hugh. "The Invention of Tradition: The Highland Tradition of Scotland." In *The Invention of Tradition,* edited by Eric Hobsbawm and Terence Ranger. Cambridge and New York: Cambridge University Press, 1983.

Trezise, Thomas. "Unspeakable." *The Yale Journal of Criticism* 14 (2001): 39–66.

Trumpener, Katie. *Bardic Nationalism: The Romantic Novel and the British Empire.* Princeton: Princeton University Press, 1997.

Twining, William. "The Rationalist Tradition of Evidence Scholarship." In *Rethinking Evidence: Exploratory Essays,* edited by William Twining. Oxford and New York: Blackwell, 1990.

————. *Theories of Evidence: Bentham and Wigmore.* London: Weidenfeld and Nicolson, c1985.

Underwood, Ted. "Romantic Historicism and the Afterlife." *PMLA* 117 (2002): 237–51.

Virilio, Paul. *The Aesthetics of Disappearance.* Translated by Philip Beitchman. New York: Semiotext(e), 1991.

————. *The Vision Machine.* Translated by Julie Rose. Bloomington: Indiana University Press, 1994.

Warner, Alan. *Morvern Callar.* New York: Anchor, 1995.

————. "Existential Ecstasy." Spike Magazine, www.spikemagazine.com/0300alanwarner.php (2001).

Warner, William Beatty. *Chance and the Text of Experience: Freud, Nietzsche, and Shakespeare's Hamlet.* Ithaca, N.Y.: Cornell University Press, 1986.

Watson, Roderick. *The Literature of Scotland.* Houndmills, Basingstoke, Hampshire: Macmillan, 1984.

Watt, Ian. *The Rise of the Novel: Studies in Defoe, Richardson, and Fielding.* Berkeley: University of California Press, 1957.

Weinbrot, Howard D. *Britannia's Issue: The Rise of British Literature from Dryden to Ossian.* Cambridge and New York: Cambridge University Press, 1993.

————. "Celts, Greeks, and Germans: Macpherson's Ossian and the Celtic Epic." *1650-1850: Ideas, Aesthetics, and Inquiries in the Early Modern Period* 1 (1994): 3–22.

Welsh, Alexander. *The Hero of the Waverley Novels: With New Essays on Scott.* Princeton: Princeton University Press, 1992.

———. *Strong Representations: Narrative and Circumstantial Evidence in England.* Baltimore: Johns Hopkins University Press, 1992.

Wheeler, Roxann. *The Complexion of Race: Categories of Difference in Eighteenth-Century British Culture.* Philadelphia: University of Pennsylvania Press, 2000.

White, Hayden. *Metahistory.* Baltimore: Johns Hopkins University Press, 1973.

Whyte, Christopher. "Fishy Masculinities: Neil Gunn's *The Silver Darlings.*" In *Gendering the Nation: Studies in Modern Scottish Literature,* edited by Christopher Whyte. Edinburgh: Edinburgh University Press, 1995.

Wickman, Matthew. "Of Probability, Romance, and the Spatial Dimensions of Eighteenth-Century Narrative." *Eighteenth-Century Fiction* 15 (2002): 59–80.

———. "Terror's Abduction of Experience: A Gothic History." *The Yale Journal of Criticism* 18 (2005): 179–206.

Wigmore, John H. *The Principles of Judicial Proof as Given by Logic, Psychology, and General Experience, and Illustrated in Judicial Trials.* Boston: Little, Brown, and Company, 1913.

Wilkomirski, Binjamin. *Fragments: Memories of a Wartime Childhood.* Translated by Carol Brown Janeway. New York: Schocken, 1996.

Williams, Ioan, ed. *Novel and Romance, 1700–1800.* New York: Barnes and Noble, 1970.

Williams, Raymond. *The Long Revolution.* New York: Columbia University Press, 1961.

———. *The Country and the City.* Oxford and New York: Oxford University Press, 1973.

———. *Keywords: A Vocabulary of Culture and Society.* London: Croom Helm, 1976.

———. *Marxism and Literature.* Oxford and New York: Oxford University Press, 1977.

———. *Politics and Letters: Interviews with New Left Review.* London: NLB, 1979.

Williamson, George S. *The Longing for Myth in Germany: Religion and Aesthetic Culture from Romanticism to Nietzsche.* Chicago: University of Chicago Press, 2004.

Wilt, Judith. *Secret Leaves: The Novels of Walter Scott.* Chicago: University of Chicago Press, 1985.

Withers, Charles W. J. *Urban Highlanders: Highland-Lowland Migration and Urban Gaelic Culture, 1700–1900.* East Linton: Tuckwell, 1998.

Wittig, Kurt. *The Scottish Tradition in Literature.* Westport, Conn.: Greenwood, 1972.

Womack, Peter. *Improvement and Romance: Constructing the Myth of the Highlands.* Houndmills, Basingstoke, Hampshire: Macmillan, 1989.

Woolf, Virginia. *To the Lighthouse.* San Diego: Harcourt Brace Jovanovich, 1927.

———. "Modern Fiction." In *Collected Essays.* 3 vols. London: Hogarth, 1966.

Wordsworth, William. "Preface of 1800." In *Lyrical Ballads,* edited by W. J. B. Owen. London: Oxford University Press, 1969.

Youngson, A. J. *After the Forty-Five: The Economic Impact on the Scottish Highlands.* Edinburgh: Edinburgh University Press, 1973.

Žižek, Slavoj. "Introduction." In *Mapping Ideology,* edited by Elizabeth Wright and Edmond Wright. London and New York: Verso, 1994.

Index

abjection, appeal of, 136–37

accessories to crime, under Scottish law, 25, 203 n.44

Adorno, Theodor: and epic naïveté, 131; and fascism, 182–84; and Holocaust, 132–33; and intersections of experience and race, 127–28; on Nazi view of Jews, 136–39; and poetry, 129; on work of Walter Benjamin, 207 n.2, 210 n.55, 215 n.29, 217 n.34

adversary trial procedure, 26

aesthetics, modernist, 174–75, 184

Aesthetics of Disappearance, The (Virilio), 167

aleatory contracts, 29

alienation: and collective experience in "Praise of Ben Dobhrain," 162; and desire, in the novel, 142; in Gunn's fiction, 180; industrialization and, 64, 142; modernist sensibility of, 175; and solidarity, 142

Althusser, Louis, 10–11

"An American Sky" (Crichton Smith), 164–65

Anderson, James: disagreement with Smith's theory, 82–85, 213 n.39; and Highland improvement, 75; on industry and activity, 212 n.28; and judicial equivalence ideology, 79–80

Annexing Act of 1752, and Highland improvement, 73–74

anti-Highland satire, 10

antiromance, and romance, 141

anti-Semitism, 137

Appin Murder: and Highland improvement, 23; in *Rob Roy*, 51; in Scott's novels, 46; in Stevenson's David Balfour novels, 46, 57–58; Alan Breck Stewart and, 25. *See also* Stewart Trial

Arcades Project, The (Benjamin), 44–45

Argyle, Earl of, 51

Argyll, Duke of, 34, 208 n.22

Aristotelian experience, 32

Aristotle, and concept of probability, 27

Arnold, Matthew, 178

Atom of Delight, The (Gunn), 178–79, 185

Auschwitz, as metaphor of decay of experience, 137

authentic experience *(Erfahrung)*, 136–37

Balfour, David (character in Stevenson's novels), 46, 55–57, 60–62

balladry, in eighteenth century, 94

Banfield, Ann, 175–77

Barrell, John, 122–23

Beiderwell, Bruce, 48–49, 52

Bender, John, 58

Benjamin, Walter: and decay of experience, 64–65; and double logic of the novel, 59; and Stevenson's work, 62–63; and storytelling, 43–46, 67, 172; and witness experience, 64

Bentham, Jeremy, 30

Bergson, Henry, 176

Bernard-Donals, Michael, 135

Beyond the Pleasure Principle (Freud), 112

Blackstone, William, 31

Blackwell, Thomas, 116

Blair, Hugh, 77, 93, 116–18, 122–24

Blandy, Mary, 30–31

Boswell, James, 117, 143, 147, 219 n.8

Bourdieu, Pierre, 77

Breck, Alan. *See* Stewart, Alan Breck

Acknowledgments

If I imagine this book as Blake did a grain of sand, I cannot but discern in it the traces of marvelous teachers and friends like Stephen Barker, David Paxman, Philip Snyder, Perry Meisel, Anselm Haverkamp, Jayne Lewis, Christopher Grose, Vince Pecora, Robert Maniquis, and Max Novak.

But some influences are even more direct. This book is most deeply indebted to the tremendous support, insight, and patience of Felicity Nussbaum and Helen Deutsch. Less directly, though no less crucially, Robert Crawford and Ian Duncan expressed interest in my work from seemingly faraway places in ways which galvanized my project and opened my eyes to the riches of Scottish studies. A fellowship at the Clark Library acquainted me with a fabulous staff and exposed me to archival resources which eventually anchored my argument. Two trips to the National Library of Scotland weighted this anchor more heavily. Eric d'Evegnée's fortuitous discoveries as my research assistant in 2001 changed the entire course of the project, and Andrew Schultz's selfless labor as my research assistant late in 2005 helped me meet my deadlines when the manuscript was nearing its completion.

Though nurtured at the University of California at Los Angeles, this project may never have taken its current form outside of Brigham Young University. In particular, my colleagues Ed Cutler, Nick Mason, and Jill Rudy have been godsends as readers, cherished friends, and allies. Robert Means fought and won the good fight in securing costly but vital resources for the library. The English Department and College of Humanities have been unstintingly generous in funding my requests for travel, research assistance, and materials. And, more esoterically but no less significantly, BYU's peculiar blend of utopian vision and existential solitude has fostered in me a critical and professional consciousness more inclined toward intellectual risks. This would have been a different and a duller book—and, perhaps, not a book at all—had circumstances sent me elsewhere.

It literally would not be a book without the University of Pennsylvania Press. I express my deep gratitude to my editor, Jerome Singerman, for his faith in the project, his skill in navigating its perils, and the wit with which each was articulated. The press's two anonymous readers provided invaluable criticism and support, due in part to their dialectically different but insightful points of view. The intelligence and generosity of "anonymous" figures in this profession always amaze me.

We all know the convention whereby the author thanks those who contributed to the book and then assumes responsibility for its errors. I wish I had the gumption, tongue in cheek, to attribute the shortcomings here to the friends I list above. Alas, I do not.

Earlier versions of the project appeared elsewhere: a section of Chapter 5 in *PMLA* 115, no. 2 (2000): 181–94, a portion of the Introduction and Chapter 7 in *The Yale Journal of Criticism* 18, no. 1 (2005): 179–206, and part of Chapter 6 in *Scottish Studies Review* 6, no. 2 (2005): 99–112. I am grateful to the editors and readers of these essays for their help in shaping these sections of the book, and to the presses at MLA, Johns Hopkins, and the Association for Scottish Literary Studies for their permission to republish them.

I owe my profoundest expressions of gratitude to my family—especially to my parents, Lance and Patricia, who have been so supportive of my education; to my wife, Kerry, whose élan of spirit enables her to live with an academic; and to my children, Hadley and Elena, who kindly and repeatedly forgive their father for being one.